D1143507

501 217 124

my
word

Also by Terry Christian:

Reds in the Hood
Brothers: From Childhood to Oasis, with Paul Gallagher

my word

terry christian

First published in hardback in Great Britain in 2007 by
Orion Books
an imprint of the Orion Publishing Group Ltd
Orion House, 5 Upper St Martin's Lane,
London WC2H 9EA
An Hachette Livre UK Company

1 3 5 7 9 10 8 6 4 2

A CIP catalogue record for this book is available from the British Library.

ISBN 978 0 7528 7437 1

Printed in Great Britain by
Mackays of Chatham plc, Chatham, Kent

www.orionbooks.co.uk

To Daniel and James, the old Trafford girls and boys,
and everyone I've met that's made my life so interesting

introduction

"I never thought I'd call the Channel 4 duty office, but* The Word *is a total disgrace. I'm disgusted by the sheer downmarket nature of this programme. I'm lost for words..."

So you want to work in television. You want a book that's going to be honest about it, that's going to tell you how it works, how talent will always out and that the best will always come through. Then I suggest you go to the biography section of your local bookshop and pick up a copy of Bob Monkhouse's autobiography. If, however, you want to read the truth about an industry rife with nepotism, people running around like headless chickens, cocaine snorting and general drug abuse, sexual excess with threesomes and foursomes, back-biting, power struggles, plagiarism and venomous egos venting their spleen, then read on. Because that was us lot on *The Word*.

As a show, *The Word* influenced just about every light entertainment programme format, from *Richard and Judy*, Chris Evans's *TFI Friday* and Jonathan Ross, to whole channels like Sky One, and the condescension that masqueraded as humour on *The Word* has affected the whole of entertainment, from comedy and quiz shows to the current craze for pushing the boundaries on reality TV. It was us who were responsible for introducing all the wannabees who would happily screw Quasimodo and eat a shit butty if it meant they'd get on the box. The horrible realization was dawning that human dignity wasn't so much for sale as being thrown away like cheap confetti at a wedding – we were the direct descendant of The Circus Maximus and Victorian freak shows.

What did I gain personally from my involvement with the show? I was disliked by my bosses and most of the Channel 4 executives, hated by the press and a proportion of my peers, my radio career was more or less in tatters, my television career didn't exist, I had a bad case of piles, an anal fissure, alopecia and an even more twisted attitude. But do you know what? I'd do it all again tomorrow.

Anyone who knows me will tell you that I've never tried to court popularity. I was trained by the best and spent eight years with complete artistic freedom, doing what the hell I liked on local BBC and independent radio. I had a different vision then, an off-kilter way of working and an endless passion and enthusiasm. Whether it had any effect or not, you can judge for yourself as you read this book. It's now twelve years since *The Word* finished on Channel 4. It was a show that changed the face of TV, and not necessarily for the better, but like a lot of my work before and after, it did make a difference to people's lives, which had a ripple effect throughout broadcasting.

For over five years *The Word* took over my life; I was pursued by people who regaled me with questions about my fellow presenters and those golden TV moments on the show: 'Who was that bloke who ate the maggots? Urgh!' 'Did you give that Amanda De Cadanet one?' 'Did you shag Dani Behr?' 'Are you a queer or something?' 'Did you and Mark Lamarr have a fight?' 'What happened with that Olly Reed? Was he really pissed?' 'Was Shaun Ryder of the Happy Mondays on heroin when he came on the show with Zippy and Bungle from *Rainbow*?' 'Why did that girl out of rock band L7 show her chuff?' 'Did you give her one, too?' 'Did you really show Margi Clarke your plums?'

Every Friday was a surreal symphony of drugs, egotism, ritual humiliation, arguments and the constant nagging pressure that this week's show had to be just as talked about as the last week's. Even now, twelve years on, I'm still pestered with the same questions. Perhaps it's because, for all it's downmarket nature, *The Word* wasn't as fake as other television. For the first two series it wasn't contrived and didn't rely too heavily gimmicks – even series three was fairly spontaneous. Yet despite this, there were more talking points after the twenty-two shows that made up the average *Word* series than have been generated from the hundreds of hours of reality TV to have assailed our screens ever since. In addition, *The Word* introduced new bands, such as Oasis and Nirvana, to British TV screens for the first time. *The Word* pre-dated the tabloids' obsession with TV and it's so-called stars, yet for the duration of it's five-year run it was the most written-about, talked-about show on television. OK, the press absolutely hated it, but then we didn't employ spin doctor's and PR companies to control and manipulate them.

As far as we were concerned, we were anti-establishment, even if that meant behaving like the annoying, most disruptive kids in school. Everyone hated us. There was jealousy from those who longed to work in TV and from established stars who wouldn't dare do a show like ours, as well as jealousy from tabloid journalists who hated being beaten to all the good gossip by a TV show they despised and didn't understand.

The Word is the most influential, ground-breaking show to have been on British TV in over twenty years, and all the annoying young TV types who worked on it suddenly found their condescension interpreted as humour and adopted by mainstream TV. They've tried to copy elements of *The Word* for the past ten years, but without quite grasping what made the programme special, what made people leave the pub twenty minutes early on a Friday night so they could get home in time to watch it. It made other TV shows look dull and staid and gave the industry a long overdue kick up the backside.

The problem is that although the programme's imitators copied elements of the show, they all lacked *The Word*'s maverick quality – it's street-level knowledge of music and popular culture, spontaneity, inclusiveness, bravery, rawness, sensitivity, vulnerability and fuck-you attitude, which came, in part, from the award winning radio shows I'd presented.

Before *The Word* you hardly ever heard a northern accent on mainstream TV or Radio, whereas now you've got Mark Radcliffe and Marc Riley, Chris Evans, Sara Cox, Stuart Maconie, Melanie

Sykes, Caroline Ahern, Vernon Kaye, Tess Daly, Peter Kay and plenty of others. It wasn't so long ago that hearing a northern accent on the Radio One breakfast show would have seemed like pure fantasy. Finally northerners are getting a look in, gaining some ownership and going mainstream – too bloody mainstream if you ask me – and it all started with *The Word*.

The Word is a piece of television history that's still talked about in pubs and living rooms across the UK. It was a huge success in Ireland and had quite a fan base in Holland, where Channel 4 is beamed into many Dutch homes. Even America's A&E channel were keen on showing it, but felt it was too left field and current to be broadcast six months later, plus it would probably have needed subtitles for Americans to understand it! I was even singled out by one American TV executive as the 'wild card' that made the whole thing tick, a recognition I never received from TV executives in Britain, although Jeremy Isaacs, former Channel 4 controller, was extremely flattering about my presentation style.

It was a show that refused to be ignored, yet all these years later it's still reviled in some quarters by those who were offended by its accessibility, originality and lack of respect, as they saw it.

'*The Word* is the worst television show of all time and you shouldn't watch it,', the press cried in outrage. 'And Terry Christian is the worst presenter on television ever.' These proclamations were repeated ad nauseam over *The Word*'s five-year run, even though we continued to attract 49 per cent of the audience share in our Friday night slot. The truth was that nobody who watched *The Word* cared what the press and trendy glossies said about the show, which left our middle-class, middle-brow detractors feeling powerless.

The actor and playwrite Stephen Berkoff was far more measured and accurate when, in an interview, he aired his thoughts on how the class system affects creativity and ideas in the Arts in Britain: 'If you have a class system, it tends to act like a contraceptive. The middle classes are like a big Durex, preventing any kind of dissemination from taking place.'

The media does act like a condom in this country, suppressing any views that don't match their own, and in my opinion, *The Word* at its best was a televisual undermining of middle-class hegemony and that strange student-like cooler-than-thou culture that dominates.

Saying that there's a thick layer of snobbery in television and the media in general branded me, according to various commentators, 'loudmouthed', 'whinging' and 'negative'as well as having a 'chip on my shoulder'. When we made *The Word*, for some on the team it was just an attempt to make something hip, glossy and fun, while for others it was about getting up certain people's noses and exposing the snobbery, tyranny of aspiration and fashionability in the industry. Interestingly, though, a lot of the people I set out to annoy also happened to work on *The Word*, which meant the programme had an almost schizophrenic edge to it.

The production team on the first series of *The Word* was 99 per cent public-school educated, and how second-rate it all was. The amateurism, lack of conviction, sycophancy, preciousness, inefficiency, manipulativeness and raw ambition they showed were staggering. And that wasn't just *The Word*'s production team, as they were a template reproduced throughout TV and the majority of the national press and radio at the time. Very few of the original *Word* production team had much media experience; it was like a Youth Training Scheme for posh kids who were being fast-tracked into telly. They thought they knew all about urban youth culture, but in reality they were about as 'urban' as a second home in Tuscany.

The majority of them had neither met nor spoken with a Black or Asian person until they were eighteen (although, to be fair, I suspect one or two of the younger ones may have had an Eastern European nanny). Some had been on round-the-world gap years, courtesy of their fathers credit cards, but had never ventured beyond the south east of England. They'd effectively lived in a bubble, so I suppose it was Karma that they ended up working with a prick like me who went out of his way to burst their bubbles. That isn't to say that they were stupid and useless just because they happened to be from well-to-do backgrounds. It was clear to me, though, that they'd learned to talk confidently and convincingly without having much actual knowledge, an accomplishment which appears to be useful in education, journalism and television. It's strange that I'd worked for eight years in radio, yet it was only when I worked on *The Word* that I learned the great truth, that we live in an age of almost inconceivable credulity, where anyone will believe literally anything.

It's amazing that as we begin the 21st century the same questions of class, geography and power still dominate in much the same way as they always have, and the media in the early nineties was definitely one of the last bastions of power for the upper middle classes. It's ironic that in an industry obsessed with audience demographics, the demographics of the people in charge are rarely questioned. When Greg Dyke was Director General of the BBC, his pronouncement that the BBC was, 'disgustingly white' caused a minor outcry, probably because it was difficult to ignore his point, given the lack of brown faces on TV. However, when he added that the BBC was 'too southern and too middle class', his pronouncement was more or less ignored. Why? And if it's true, why do so few people ever comment on the fact. Is it because all those in the top jobs – most of whom I think you'll find are from the south of England, public school and Oxbridge educated – are confident that nobody will ever state the fact too loudly, certainly not if they want to get on in life.

This book isn't meant to be read like a class war pamphlet, it's just that as a northerner from a working class background with an identifiable northern accent, I stood out from 99 per cent of my fellow broadcasters in 1990, and the sad thing is that, give or take the odd comedian, those features would still make me stand out today, some fifteen years down the line. The positive for me was that, in radio and television, being distinctive is what marks you out and makes people remember you. That's something nowadays that people will sell their souls for, hence all those presenters who have boob jobs or dress up like refugees from a different decade. They spend fortunes on PR to get them in the press for any spurious reason, all so that some well-spoken half-wit will think they're 'a bit of a character'. It doesn't seem to matter that they might be devoid of ideas, integrity, sensitivity, passion or conviction – profile is everything today.

So, here is the story of a well-read, outspoken, northern, working-class lad, who wanted to make a difference, had a passion for change, was mad on music and football, who worked for years with blonde Home Counties girls and a collection of what Britain's finest public schools had thrown up – 'thrown up' being quite an apposite phrase – as well as hanging out with some of the biggest stars in Hollywood and pop music, only to realize later on that he was almost as deluded as the people he was kicking out against.

As one disgruntled *Word* viewer put it in one of the thousands of complaints phoned into Channel 4 concerning *The Word* and myself: 'Your presenter is a heap of shit. You've got a raving fucking poofter on there – this isn't entertainment. I'd love to talk to that twat. He wants whacking. Ring me back tomorrow and I'll discuss it with you.'

So there you have it. Fights, walkouts, drug-taking, pornography. . . and that was just show two of series one. And you wonder why people wanted to watch. . .

'That Terry Anderson is an unintelligent and rude lout. He's vile and quite awful, with a most unattractive voice.' **Channel 4 duty log**

The question or thought in many people's minds, and probably a fair one during *The Word*'s run, was Who the f*** does Terry Christian think he is? So perhaps I should fill you in on my background, just to explain why so many of my contemporaries regarded me with thinly veiled dislike.

I grew up in a large Irish family where my dad's wage as a labourer for Esso on the docks of the Manchester Ship Canal was our only income. My dad was a shop steward in the Transport and General Workers Union, solidly labour and suspicious of the bosses. He despised what he called 'suck-holes' – crawlers to you and me – and would speak of them as if they were the lowest lifeform on the planet, although, like most of his opinions, he would dress it up with a dark humour.

He was brought up with his brothers and sisters in one room in a tenement on Augustine Street in Dublin's famous Liberties area. As a seven-year-old he'd seen his father die of a mixture of alcohol and poverty, and as a child he'd suffered TB, followed by a serious TB abscess on his spine as a young adult. He grew up in an Ireland still suffering the Colonial hangover. The 1916 Easter Rising and subsequent war against the Black and Tans in 1920–21 as well as the civil war that followed the Free State, didn't exactly turn Ireland into a beacon of light and opportunity for it's population. Having no father meant my dad and his two brothers were constantly in danger of being sent away to the prison-like conditions of Artane and the random beatings and cruelties of the Christian Brothers. The Irish Republic wasn't exactly liberty, equality and brotherhood for people of my father's background, who were just looking for a job, food and somewhere decent to live. If that had been difficult under British Dominion, it was almost impossible in the new Free State and then for a time in the Irish Republic.

My mother's background was similar to my father's. Born just off Corporation Street in the centre of Dublin, she was the second youngest of eight children. To escape unemployment, her father, Lawrence Cullen, joined the Connaught Rangers in 1904, aged eighteen. Known as the Devil's Own, the Rangers was one of the most notorious and glamorous regiments in the British Army. In 1914 he was posted to the Western Front, where he was wounded in 1916, but remained as part of the Royal Army Medical Corps, disposing of corpses and carrying the wounded out on stretchers. In March 1918 he was a victim of mustard gas and was taken prisoner by the Germans, finally being repatriated to the UK in December 1918, too ill to work again. He had served a total of fourteen years in the British Army, as a regular soldier in the mud, blood and trenches of the Western Front, and in India before that, climbing all the way up the greasy pole to private.

Early in 1919 he was pensioned out of the army but was unable to work because of ill health. Branded a West Briton by the Irish, because of his service in the British army, he moved his whole family over to Hulme in Manchester in 1930 but died in 1938, when my mother was just eleven, as a result of complications caused by the mustard gas poisoning. Upon his death a panel of doctors wouldn't allow his widow and mother of his eight children to have his army pension as they said they couldn't be sure his early demise was due directly to mustard gas poisoning. At the hearing my grandmother was awarded only ten shillings a week to keep her family. Such utter penury meant that my mother and several of her brothers, despite passing their eleven plus, were unable to go to grammar schools as they couldn't afford the uniforms. Instead they had to leave school and work from the age of fourteen. Unsurprisingly, my mother grew up a dyed-in-the-wool socialist who, like my father, never saw the world as a place of equal opportunities.

Having worked on and off as a bicycle messenger for various butchers in Dublin, my father moved to Manchester in 1945 at the age of eighteen. It was just after victory against Japan had been declared, and though the war had only just finished, there were a lot of reconstruction jobs to be found in Britain.

On arriving in England he found that the only jobs available were just as poorly paid and arduous as his butcher's rounds and he had to stay with a lot of Irish immigrant workers at the Salvation Army Hostel in Manchester City Centre. He was so miserable he longed to return to Dublin, and the only reason he didn't was because he couldn't face the ribbing he'd get off his friends and neighbours. As he used to tell us, he was afraid they'd say 'Did you only go over there to see the time, Danny?'

He used to go for jobs around Trafford Park, where he was told he could have the job, but to be aware that they didn't like the Irish. In the end he stuck it out and met my mother at one of the Irish clubs, and they married in 1947. Within a year of getting married he suddenly had difficulty walking and was unable to work. Some six months later he was paralysed from the waist down, all due to a TB abscess on his spine. He returned to Dublin and spent the next two years in a sanatorium, where a priest gave him a chord to wear around his waist, a relic of St Martin (I couldn't tell you which one). My father then had a controversial operation in which doctors in Dublin drained the fluid from the abscess – the odds of it working were thousands to one, but, a minor miracle, it worked and he was able to walk again.

All this time my mother had remained in Manchester, saving what money she earned as a seamstress to visit him while he was in hospital in Dublin, where she'd stay with various aunts and uncles. By the time my father started working again, two years later, my mother was pregnant with my oldest sister Janet and the rest of us followed with varying age gaps. First was our Tony, then Mary, then myself, my youngest brother Kevin and finally the baby of the family, Sheila.

Tragedy struck when my oldest sister Janet died aged eleven of a burst appendix – my mother had taken her to the doctor on several occasions after Janet had complained of stomach pains, but each time the doctor said it was gastroenteritis and sent her home. It was a tragedy that had a deep effect on our family. Immediately after Janet's death my father would walk all the way to Stretford Cemetery every night, straight from his twelve-hour shift in Trafford Park, just to stand by her then unmarked grave for a couple of hours. My parents never mentioned Janet again to any of us, and nor were my siblings Tony and Mary allowed to mention her until twelve years after her death. I forgot about her myself, except for a feeling of sadness as a very young boy, and a recurring dream about an older sister who had gone up to heaven to be a nun.

With a big family to support and one wage coming in, it's fair to say we weren't exactly privileged. I can remember the day we got our first fridge, the day we moved into a new council house with an indoor toilet and the day we finally had a phone installed. They were all luxury items I never experienced until my teens. In the household in which I grew up the bountifully shining light of consumerism was permanently eclipsed by the bitter moon of necessity – needing a new pair of shoes or new school blazer or winter coat meant two things: you'd receive the cheapest garment on the market – which invariably meant the market stall – and it would take you at least two years to grow into it. This wasn't such a big deal when I was at primary school, as the area of Manchester I grew up in was pretty poor with predominantly big families, some so big they were almost states in themselves.

As a youngster I lived with my two brothers and two sisters on Duke Street, in an area of Old Trafford called Brookes Bar, which is about half a mile from Manchester City Centre and just across a busy main road from Moss Side and Hulme. Old Trafford was mainly Irish and West Indian. It was a fairly rough and tumble place where you learned to fight from the age of four. I remember an eight-year-old holding a penknife to my throat when I was only five as I walked back from the paper shop with a lucky bag. I recall being upset about him stealing the lucky bag, but not particularly traumatised by the knife; I was just determined to furnish myself with a similar weapon in case it ever happened again. Growing up there we formed our gangs street by street, having fun throwing stones at kids from adjacent Clifton street and Oxford Street, who thought they could just walk down our street at will. We thought this was the ultimate cheek. Once we'd sorted out the borders we spent several weeks patrolling the back entries that separated our row of terraces from theirs; as far as we were concerned those back entries were the only thing we had in common with them.

Back then you saw very few cars on our street, only the local doctor's or priest's when they came visiting, or the odd West Indian man who'd done loads of overtime and managed to buy himself a Zodiac on HP. On a Sunday our street was full of West Indian blokes washing their Zodiacs, surrounded by their friends and Catholic Irish kids being shouted at by fierce-looking mothers to change out of their going-to-Mass-clothes before they started playing football or messing about lighting fires on the crofts.

The crofts were bare patches of earth that were really just dumping grounds for any unwanted household rubbish, from old sofas to beds and chests of drawers, and as you can imagine they made a marvellous scenic view from the back bedroom windows of the terraces that hemmed them in on all four sides.

The sixties were ending and the seventies were beginning, and apparently we'd never had it so good. But our world was as narrow as the streets we lived in, hemmed in and closed off from aspiration and expectation. To speak out of turn, voice an opinion when not called for, or answer back to an adult was to invite a variety of corporal punishments: the ruler across hands and legs at school, or our fathers belts at home. Authority figures always intimidated us. Even when we went to the library, which we used to do every Saturday morning, the librarian would insist we showed her that our hands weren't dirty before we touched the books.

As Catholic boys, at church and in school, we were told we'd been born with the stain of sin on our souls and that God would punish the wicked, so as six-year-olds we had to confess our sins to the priest and pray to God for absolution. Surrounded by a concoction of poverty and physical and spiritual oppression, we were natural rebels and hard-faced little tykes. Good catholic boys who went on the annual Wit walks, made our first communions, first confessions and confirmations, and dreamed about how much money relatives would cough up on our communion day, while our parents tormented themselves about how they'd afford to dress us up in the required new outfits.

As eight-year-olds we pestered the local priests at St Alphonsus – Father Carter, Father Lohan and Canon O'Donnel – to make us altars boys, because it was traditional that altar boys got tipped at weddings and funerals. Stephen Flynn once bragged that he'd been given almost three quid for kneeling next to a coffin in his cassock at the vigil the night before a well-known Irish builder was buried. The whole neighbourhood made its way down to St Alphonsus church to shake the hands of the grieving family and say, following Irish tradition, 'Sorry for your troubles.'

The building trade employed a lot of my school friend's fathers, especially those from the west of Ireland, who my dad referred to as Culchies. The were mountainous men with hands like shovels, from Connemara, Mayo, Donegal, Sligo and Roscommon. A breed apart, they were stoic and hard as nails. The worked fifteen-hour days and were treated like shit by the authorities, their employers and especially by the country that had forced them to emigrate to make a living.

They came from the farms, boreens and bogs of the old country to Manchester, following in the footsteps of 150 years of Irish immigrants before them. There they queued at the bars in the pubs, asking for the 'sub' and hoping the contractor hadn't done a runner with his wages and would pay up as promised. Having to buy the foreman drinks all night – bribery for the next job – they'd only see their children for perhaps an hour on a Sunday morning. These were men who sacrificed their own lives to provide something better for the children they hardly saw grow up. Like their forefathers and kin folk across the globe, who dug the canals, built the railways and laid the roads, they were the miners and sappers of capitalism, the people who built Manchester.

My childhood was spent owning those streets. Amongst the kids were a sizeable proportion who were black or mixed race – the mixed-race kids invariably having Irish mothers and West Indian fathers. Our next-door neighbours, the Reids, were a young Jamaican couple, and Mrs Reid, who was pregnant with her first child, was always in our front room as my mam taught her how to knit a shawl and booties for the baby. She called the baby Courtenay and my older brother and sister and myself were invited next door for his first birthday party. Loud ska and blue beat blasting out, so names like Desmond Dekker and Jimmy Cliff tripped off my tongue as easily as those of the Beatles by the time I was six. The centrepiece of a well stocked table at the party was a gigantic bowl of rum punch, which they let us have a small taste of, surrounded by masses of food. We were the only white people there, and besides Courtenay we were also the only kids. I remember my four-year-old self crawling under the table with Courtenay, so we were hidden by the tablecloth, and eating big pieces of cake. No adults told us off or ordered us about. We were free to plough between the forest of legs of people packed like sardines throughout the Reids' house. It was the first party I'd ever been to, and it was full of noise, life and laughter.

Half the kids on the street my age and younger were black or mixed race, and they were all Duke Street kids first and foremost. There was Victor and Horace, who was also called Junior; Tony Henry; Danny Kelly; Richard and Rennie Simpson, who became best friends with my younger brother Kevin and myself, and Carl and Raymond, both sometimes called Junior. There was also a multitude of Irish kids: the Markys, Colleens, Sheridans, Finns, Slatterys, Fletchers, Mitchells, and a couple of families like the Ogdens and the Pyes who were, as far as we knew, English. Then there was Roman down the street, who was Ukrainian.

Older teenage kids would try and bully the younger black kids and tell us not to hang out with nig nogs and coons. They got away with the bullying because the kids' parents were reluctant to step in and cause problems with their neighbours and there were very few black or mixed race kids on our streets over the age of eight who could sort the bullies out. It was a brutal lesson in tribalism, but we didn't care and would often throw a sly stone at the older lads, or stick nails in their bicycle tyres when they weren't looking.

I suppose the black kids, or coloureds as our parents called them, were different to us, but to me it made them interesting and we enjoyed the fact that we knew more about them than our parents did. The difference that my younger brother Kevin and I appreciated the most was the food they ate. While our parents would moan about the smell of curry wafting around, we loved it. Richard and Rennie lived with their grandma and she had West Indian lodgers in the house, which meant they ate later than us. We'd have our tea around five o'clock, then come six thirty we'd wait in the street for Richard and Rennie to come out after their tea, always making a point of asking them to bring a bit for us to try. Their grandma would put some of the leftovers in old ice-cream tubs for us. 'What's that?' we'd ask, desperate for anything that wasn't stew or scrag end of meat, potatoes and cabbage, which was the only vegetable we ever seemed to have. We'd get rice and peas, or a dumpling in some gravy, or if we were lucky, the remnants of a jerk chicken leg or a smashed-up bone from some curried goat – I wasn't too keen on the saltfish though. For some reason this used to annoy my mam, I think she was worried that Richard and Rennie's granny would think she hadn't fed us, but we just liked the adventure of new tastes and new smells.

Fighting was second nature to us, and I grew up fighting other people's battles as much as my own. Perhaps it was my dad's fault for taking me to see so many films like *The Magnificent Seven*. The only time any of us ever spent with my dad was when he took us to the Imperial Cinema on Chorlton Road, just around the corner. That was where we learned to be men, watching John Wayne and macho larger-than-life Western heroes on the big screen. The hero would always stand his ground and slug it out; he'd rather take a bullet or fight against impossible odds than surrender.

As a young lad, I'd strut around the neighbourhood or local park with my friends and watch certain boys showing off, picking on other kids, almost imploring them to try it on with me or my mates. To this day I don't know where that in-built aggression came from. I wasn't a psycho who saw a red mist descend, although I did have a temper. It was like a controlled explosion that could be switched on at will, and it gave me the illusion of power.

Once the family went over to Dublin for a week's holiday at my Aunty Mag's. She lived in Belle View buildings, which was basically a tenement in the Liberties, the roughest inner-city area in Dublin. It was a mish-mash of rundown tenements bordered by tall red iron railings, and the Guinness brewery was a stones throw away which, together with the nearby bakery, exuded the strong smell of yeast and hops.

The Liberties was dirt poor, but most of the local kids were really friendly and looked out for each other. However, while we were playing football with the locals in the street once, I took great umbrage with a boy who kept insisting that every time he was tackled it was a free kick. The rest of the gang went along with it, cowed by the kid's big gob and bossy nature, but I got annoyed. I remember pushing him and he called me 'a feckin' inglish bowsie,' I didn't understand what it meant, but I was insulted nonetheless and proceeded to punch his lights out, then I did the same to his brother and his cousin. For the next few days, whenever I went out to play with my Irish cousins, some of the local kids would tell me to 'Feck off back t'ingland yer bowsie bastard,' led, of course, by their bloodied gang leader and his brother and cousin. I noticed, though, that the cajoling came from a distance, and I realize now that at the age of eleven I became a victim of that oldest of Irish weapons against English ascendancy, the boycott.

My cousins found it all fairly amusing, but I was fuming, especially as they wouldn't tell me what a bowsie was. I finally found out in the bar of a Limerick hotel some ten years ago, when a friend of my cousin John Christian said that he'd described me to him as 'a bit of a bowsie'.

'What's a bowsie?' I asked.

'An argumentative thug,' he replied.

In the area I grew up in, there were only two kinds of kids: those who would fight and those who never went out, so fighting was far from an expression of personal courage. Over the years, like many kids from my background, I channelled my physical aggression into verbal sarcasm, which seemed to have a far more devastating effect on my enemies and dissenters within my peer group than violence. The fact is that some kids behave like borderline psychos when they're not, while others don't act tough despite having the ability to beat the living shit out of you. The only way to tell the fake from the genuine is to gently shift them out of their comfort zone with a remark that's pointed but not too direct, winding them up a bit without them being able to identify you as the source of annoyance, just to see how they react. It helps you avoid confrontation while at the same time enabling you to keep some respect – not everything needs to be resolved with fisticuffs. As a well-known Yiddish saying goes, 'Experience is a very good school, but the fees are high.'

As a family we were respectable and polite, but we were never close – I don't think large Irish families ever are. The last thing I'd consider, once I was past the age of ten, was confiding in my mother, and my younger brother Kevin was the same – perhaps we felt we were incarnations of her own unfulfilled ambitions. As for my dad, those types of conversations just never ever took place as his attitude was just to grudgingly do as your told and keep your lip buttoned. It was a struggle in our family to be an individual. The age gap between myself and my older brother meant we were a generation apart and I didn't want anything to do with my sisters as they were always pinching or annoying me. My younger brother Kevin, on the other hand, was often forced on me so I could act as mentor/babysitter – not that I was an ideal candidate for either role with the things we got up to: 'No, Kevin, set fire to the stuffing inside that old chair first and don't waste those matches.' 'Go on, Kevin, go and ask that man at the bus stop for a penny for the guy.'

We spent most of our free time lighting fires on the crofts, trying to break into condemned houses or scrounging things for nothing. When the ice-cream van came around, we'd loiter behind the kids who queued and then walk up to the hatch and say to the ice-cream man, 'Excuse me, mister, have you got any broken lollies, wafers or cornets?' Why we did this I've no idea, because as far as I can remember it was as pointless as asking our parents for money to buy ice cream.

We used to do the same in the local chip shops, asking for any scrapings. Again, we had a 100 per cent failure record. Later, when we used to walk the mile or so to Longford Park to play football, past the posh semi-detached houses with front and back gardens, we'd knock on the doors of the poshest-looking houses on the way home and ask for a drink of water in the forlorn hope that they'd give us lemonade. It always makes me laugh when I hear people say, 'If you don't ask, you don't get,' as by our teens we'd learned that if you don't ask at least you save your breath and your dignity.

My big brother Tony was a fanatical Manchester United fan who'd been to every home game since the '58/59 season. In our area United were the be-all and end-all. To local kids the Manchester United footballer George Best was the most glamorous person on the planet. He drove a Jag, all the girls loved him and every lad wanted to be him; he was the greatest footballer the world had ever seen or will ever see. As far as we knew, George was just like us, from the same terraced houses with outside loos and grimy backyards on the streets of Belfast. He had a genuine God-given talent and he was our hero. In our dreams we all lived in a Georgie Best world.

If we had a talent for anything it was clinging to stories, whether they were about George Best, Dennis Law or just a relative coming for tea. We'd hear how Brian's big brother had seen George Best score a goal so fantastic even the opposing fans applauded, or about the uncle who came round and gave someone a ten bob note, or the priest who drank half a bottle of whiskey and started singing rebel songs when he came to visit, so that the mother had to wait until seven o'clock to give the kids their tea, 'because there wasn't enough to offer the good Father, who, God bless him, we thought was after wanting to move in.'

Once a small gang of us bumped into Manchester City manager Joe Mercer and the legendary United manager Matt Busby, strolling together in Longford Park, and we asked them for their autographs. Realizing we had no pen or paper, we asked if they'd wait while we ran home to get some, saying we only lived around the corner. In fact, the nearest of our houses was over a quarter of a mile away, but we ran as fast as we could, bursting through the door of my friend's house on King's Road, grabbing his mam's writing pad and a tiny bookies biro, as well as a couple of old football cards and bickering over who would have the George Best, Dennis Law or Tony Colemans.

We must have been gone nearly half an hour, but there were Busby and Mercer, two of the greatest managers of all time, managing what were then the two biggest teams in Britain, waiting exactly where we'd left them, minding our football on the grass, smiling and joking as they signed some scraps of paper and scuffed football cards. That day really made a difference to our motley crew of sweaty, scruffy Irish and mixed-race kids, with our filthy hands and snotty noses. Kids who loved football but had never even been to see a match. It made us feel special that they talked to us in an encouraging way, giving us a story we still tell people to this day. Family legends grew out of stories like those, memorial scraps of shared fun that gave our streets and lives a certain glamour in our eyes.

In reality, though, our environment was grey and grainy, like an old black and white photograph. Our houses were tatty, freezing and over run with mice, inside and out. There was oil cloth in the hallway for some, bare floorboards for others. Thecoal fires in the front rooms and back kitchens were the only form of heat. Our dads were always working or down the pub and our mothers were always worrying about money while doing endless piles of washing and ironing or going down the launderette.

Pocket money was a scarce commodity, and although my big brother Tony had a paper round and went to see United every week, I didn't get to see them play until I was seven years old. The wait felt endless, and when I finally got to go it was one of the few childhood dreams I had fulfilled. Perhaps that's where my reservoir of aggressive dissatisfaction comes from, from the fact that as a child I never got what I wanted – not for Christmas, not for my birthday and certainly never just as a treat. I was aware that my parents couldn't afford it, whatever 'it' happened to be at the time. I'll never forget my brother Kevin asking my mum why Father Christmas brought better presents for kids who already had loads of toys and were rich.

When I wanted my first pair of football boots at the age of nine, I was given a second-hand pair from my cousin Christopher, who was four years older than me. They were cheap and nasty with moulded rubber studs and they were two sizes too big for me, so they were constantly falling off despite having laces long enough to scale Everest. I wore them for two years, including a short stint playing for the primary school team when we won the Stretford East league. We were undefeated with no draws, but were ever so slightly sartorially challenged in the footwear department.

All kids pester their parents for the things they want, but I gave up when I was ten. I desperately wanted a bike at the time, and it finally arrived just before my fourteenth birthday. My dad bought it from my older cousin Phillip in Dublin for a fiver and wheeled it back on the ferry and boat train from Dublin via Holyhead to Manchester. It was a metallic green slightly rusty girl's shopping bike with a pair of chopper bike handles attached. It took a brave kid to face the ridicule of his peers riding that around the streets of Manchester aged sixteen. There wasn't a time throughout my childhood, except perhaps when I passed my eleven plus, that I was ever an object of envy.

Our economic circumstances really hit home when I passed my eleven plus and went to grammar school. St Bede's was very traditional with a veneer of snobbery, and over half of the pupils came from relatively well-off backgrounds – we thought that if you lived in a semi-detached house you were dead posh! On our first day, the headmaster gave a speech about knuckling down and working to better ourselves. We were told we shouldn't end up as labourers and failures, and that the only way to do this was to work. The inference to my young mind was that only lazy, stupid people became labourers and that they were failures, therefore I was the son of a failure, so step one for me to better myself was to deny the worth of my parents.

Consequently, when kids at school asked me what my dad did I told them he was an engineer. I made out we lived in one of the posher semi-detached houses up the Firswood end of Old Trafford, sometimes saying I was from Chorlton instead of Old Trafford. The same used to happen at Christmas time, when I'd exaggerate about how many presents I'd received, adding a non-existent annual here or pricey gift there. It was comical really. Why I felt ashamed is still hard to fathom – perhaps it was the way some other boy whose dad was a doctor or architect would ask in front of others, 'Oy, Tez, what does your dad do?' Probing for weaknesses, as they saw it, and trying to goad kids from ordinary backgrounds. From what I saw middle-class kids only seemed to like people who liked them or were like them. It was a world of weird hierarchies that I struggled to understand so I guess it's inevitable that authority figures continue to wear me down.

It was in art class that I first felt authority's big stick.

Our art teacher was an ex-army boxer from Wythenshawe in Manchester who looked a lot like ex-British heavyweight champion Brian London. He was from the between-the-wars generation of better-off working-class kids who'd benefited from the old-style grammar schools and their elocution lessons. To hear him speak you'd have thought he'd walked straight out of *Tom Brown's Schooldays*.

I was eleven and had been at my new school for three weeks.

'Sir, when we've finished our drawing can we do some painting?'

'When you've finished your what?'

'Drawing.'

'Droor-ring, Drooring. What on earth are you trying to say?'

'Drawing, sir . . . sorry.'

'What you are trying to say,' he said, tapping his finger so hard against my temple it hurt, 'is "drawing". What you *are* saying is "droor-ring", so say it properly, boy.'

'Droring.'

'Right, out here.'

He dragged me away from my easel and out to the front of the nervously giggling class. He introduced my fellow pupils and myself to George and Alexander, which were basically two sticks of differing thickness, then he bent me over the desk and struck me three times on the backside with one of the terrible twins.

The following week he crept up behind me as I sat at my easel attempting to draw a tiger based on the William Blake poem 'The Tiger'.

'Ah, Christian, what's that supposed to be?'

'A dror. . . er sketch of a tiger, sir.'

I hated the humiliation and the way he drew attention to what he saw as my faults, and as a result I became quite defiant to the teachers at school.

My defiance wasn't physical, it just manifested itself in a bad attitude, which festered and became the germinating seed of my inverted snobbery. By the time I was in the fifth year, I no longer cared about the detentions or the three on each hand with a leather strap. I wasn't the only one in the school from a council estate. Soon, other kids came out of the closet, too, the lorry driver's son, the warehouse worker, road digger and joiner's sons. We weren't posh, but we had each other and a rebellious streak. We were outsiders. If we ever got out of the narrow streets we came from, there was no way we'd become stuck up or think we were better than anyone else just because we had more money.

Every day we inhabited two different worlds. One of alma mater, Latin and academia, and one on the estates of Moston, Moss Side, Collyhurst, Ancoats, Hulme, Ardwick and Stretford. Looking back, what we shared most was the feeling of never fitting in. In the morning we were like black South African workers leaving the township and crossing the line to work in the white district of Cape Town, where people frowned on us, then in the evening we'd return to the township, where what we'd experienced on the other side marked us out from our old friends. We spoke a language they couldn't understand, we had hope for the future and we were too afraid to sink back into the narrow world we were born into, too afraid of our parents who put all their hopes on us.

'Hey, Tezzer, Anita and her mate Laura are in on their own tonight as Anita's mam's at the bingo. They've asked me and you to pop round.' All this said with a conspiratorial glint in the eye, but it's Thursday night and I've got a shed load of homework to do.

'I'd love to,' I say, and I really meant it, 'but I've got to do that homework.'

Friends just didn't understand; it was as if we were speaking different languages, I was morphing into an alien and, spoiling his chance of adding to the local folklore. But I was also spoiling my own chances – I wanted to be part of that folklore, but at the same time I was beginning to see a bigger picture, a new version of what tomorrow could be. I would have loved to take some of those old friends with me, and it seems macabre now that already, at such a young age, we were subtly encouraged to use our educational background to judge others.

In truth we had nothing. Cubs and Scouts were too dear for us, as were play centres and day trips. My teenage years were a constant ache full of feelings that were impossible to rationalize. At home I struggled to find a space or place in the house that wasn't freezing, away from our one black and white telly, to do my homework. I fought for table space with my two sisters and younger brother, sitting in the back kitchen and turning on the gas rings on the cooker for ten minutes at a time to give out some heat.

'Stop clicking your tongue', 'Move that text book', 'Will you stop humming under your breath'. That was the home life of a scholar for me. Come my O levels, I passed seven and failed three, and although

I got my best grades in my favourite subjects – German, history and English – I didn't choose to study any of them for A Level.

In working class families back then, if you got a good education you were pushed to pick subjects that promised a job later, subjects like physics, maths, chemistry or any other science. I wasn't that interested in science at the time, but with that fear of unemployment or labouring in the future, I picked physics with maths, biology, chemistry, and general studies as my A Level subjects, then spent the next three years reading Camus, Robert Tressell and everything by George Orwell, Alan Sillitoe, Aldous Huxley, and Brendan Behan, mainly so I could chat up sixth-form girls from other schools doing arty subjects.

I would do my homework listening to Piccadilly radio and Mike Shaft from 7 to 10 p.m., with a different specialist music show every night. One night it would be soul and jazz funk, including 'Taking Care of Business', with ex-Wigan Casino DJ Dave Evison spinning the biggest northern soul dance tunes, while another night would be rock, and another would have all the new releases and album charts. On Sunday nights I'd tune into Alexis Korner's blues show on Radio 2 – his infectious enthusiasm and knowledge brought me the raw sounds of J.B. Lenoir, Lazy Lester, Sonny Boy Williamson and even old soul stuff like Otis Redding. Then late into the night it was James Stannage on Piccadilly again. I remember every kid at school getting tiny transistor radios so they could stay up all night listening to James Stannage, who was Britain's first shock jock, making a name for himself by insulting people, calling them toerags and herberts and tearing up the rule book. Only in Manchester could a broadcasting maverick like that exist thirty years ago.

Outside of school, the top priority on my personal agenda was chatting up girls and drinking in pubs and clubs. One of the lads who'd followed me from our old primary school to St Bede's was John Maher, a tall broad-shouldered lad with a great sense of humour. There were only a few of us who passed our eleven plus to get into what was a fairly elitist Catholic Grammar school: Paul Henry, John Maher and myself. We were like the three musketeers, walking to school and back every day from Old Trafford, hanging around together during break times and joking and laughing constantly.

One evening, walking home from school, we were approached by four older black youths in Whalley Range. 'Give us your money,' they said. As we never had so much as two pence between us, that was out of the question. One of the black lads singled out John Maher, probably because he was much bigger than Paul or myself, and proceeded to give him a rather vicious beating. I was thirteen and it was the first time in my life that I'd failed to physically stick up for a friend – the shame I felt inside was corrosive.

A week later John no longer walked to school with Paul and myself, having been bought a bicycle by his parents. I suspect it was just jealousy on my part, but I used the fact that John used to ride to school instead of walking with Paul and myself as an excuse to fall out with him, as if this excused my not sticking up for him. Nothing was ever said between us, but the shame I felt about letting it destroy our friendship still haunts me to this day.

When John was sixteen he joined the first punk band in Manchester, called The Buzzcocks, leaving school in the Christmas of 1976 to go on tour with The Clash and various other bands. He told us how snotty The Clash and their stuck-up following were about them when they played the famous Screen on the Green in London. Because of all the emotions I had tied up with John Maher, a childhood friend who I'd betrayed and hurt in the most profound way, I found the Buzzcocks touched me in a way no other band had to that date. The Buzzcocks were romantic and idiosyncratic in comparison to The Clash, Eater and Chelsea, with their dot-to-dot formulaic punk, but Johnny Rotten loved them. Change was happening. 'Do anything you wanna do' sang the OKish Eddie and the Hotrods. We would.

The whole Punk movement exploded in Manchester. The Sex Pistols were one of a host of punk, new wave, and reggae bands featured late on Sunday nights on the ground-breaking Granada TV show *So It Goes*, hosted by former Catholic Grammar school lad and Cambridge graduate Tony Wilson, who went on to set up Factory Records. After some dodgy folk rock on series one of *So It Goes*, the second series featured The Jam, Iggy Pop, Ian Dury, The Clash, Steel Pulse, and Siouxsie and the Banshees. Everyone buzzed about it at school. There had never been anything like it on telly, only BBC2's *Old Grey Whistle Test* which, while we were buying copies of The Buzzcocks first EP, *Spiral Scratch*, was still featuring dull plodding rock bands like Poco, Rush and Blue Oyster Cult.

Older lads at school frequented the legendary Electric Circus, the first bona fide punk club outside London, which was situated in the grim surrounds of north Manchester's Collyhurst. Later on, deciding we were punks too, we made excursions to Rafters, a punk club on Oxford Road in Manchester City Centre. We weren't really punks as such, and we had no decent clothes to wear, but the punk clubs would let anyone in and didn't ask your age at the bar. Our favourite live band in 1978, which cost £1.20 to get in see, were a band from Liverpool called Deaf School, but we'd go to see any old rubbish, like The Radio Stars, Spizzenergi, The Skids, Radiators from Space, and, for the steeper price of £1.50, Elvis Costello and Sham 69. For an extortionate £1.75 we saw Jamaican reggae artist Dillinger, who's famous 'Cocaine In My Brain' was de rigueur at every punk gig.

Three quid's worth of paper-round money was enough to get in, sort our bus fare and pay for a round of drinks at 35 pence a pint. We were also fascinated by The Fall, for their sheer cheek, nylon shirts, dedicating songs to Elvis Presley and celebrating their extra-ordinaryness. 'We Are Northern White Crap And We Keep Talking Back', Mark E. Smith became the inspiration for our attitude when dealing with the outside world in our everyday lives.

With my friends from Old Trafford I'd go to the local Irish Club, St Brendan's, where they'd serve you a pint even if you were thirteen as long as they thought you were there with your parents. Or we'd go to the local Polish club on Shrewsbury Street, which also had a PG certificate drinking policy for teenagers. If we wanted a youth club we'd go to The Hideaway in Moss Side, where sound systems blasted out reggae from the likes of Trinity, Lee 'Scratch' Perry, Niney

Holness, Yabby You, and Burning Spear all night long, or we'd go to St Alphonsus School hall for the Friday night disco, where two twenty-three-year-old blokes force-fed us northern soul, even though we wanted Roxy Music, Bowie, punk rock and other chart stuff.

Going to an all-boys Catholic school meant we were obsessed with girls. Some of us more than others. My problem was that I rarely had enough money to take girls out, so although I had several girlfriends around Old Trafford – not at the same time, mind – they were mainly girls I'd see for a night out at the pictures or local youth club once every three weeks or so. Although I was self-conscious and initially shy, I was quite successful with the girls and fairly cheeky. I remember being at a sixth-form disco at school where we'd invited all the girls from the local secondary schools along. A rather fetching punky-looking brunette caught my eye as I chatted with my mates. She was deep in conversation with another lad from our year, and I just casually walked over, gently took her hand, turned around to the lad and said, 'Excuse me, mate, she's with me.' It worked a treat.

My forward nature with women wasn't because I was a budding lothario, but because when we went out in Manchester there were always more lads than girls, so if you wanted to get the one you fancied, you couldn't hang about shuffling your feet. What you needed were ice-breakers rather than chat-up lines: 'Hey, you've got the same name as my aunty.'

'Why what's your aunty's name.'

'Well what's your name.'

It was a rather annoying time for me when I did my A levels as most of my friends who hadn't gone to grammar school had, despite the high unemployment, got themselves jobs, so they were out boozing and clubbing every night except Sunday. Going out meant everything to us, even my dad thought that if you didn't go out every night you were a bit of an odd ball.

When we did go out for a big night we'd usually meet up at a pub called Tommy Ducks in Manchester City centre. It was a very traditional pub, apart from having a ceiling decorated with knickers, and, more importantly, they didn't bother asking you to prove you were eighteen. The ceiling decoration came about as any woman who removed her underwear on the premises and handed them over at the bar while they were still warm had them displayed on the ceiling and, in exchange, received a tin can containing a special pair of Tommy Ducks knickers inside. If you were too shy to take your underwear off at the bar, you were allowed to remove them in the toilets. We thought Tommy Ducks was a top pub, and it also claimed to hold a wider range of spirits than any other pub in Britain. It certainly lived up to its reputation when about fifteen of us went out for my eighteenth birthday and I drank seventeen different shorts, including ouzo, bourbon and grappa, on top of five pints of Greenhall Whitley's – Greenhall shitleys as we called it – bitter, then proceeded to vomit my way in a semi-conscious haze through Manchester town centre to our all-night drinking den, the New Continental Club.

The Conti, as we called it, was a favourite amongst sixth-formers, student nurses, villains and hookers. After staggering out of the Conti we'd head for an infamous down-market curry house called Charlie's in the piazza. Charlie was an African geezer who's all-night curry place was a must for most Mancunians. Curries came in degrees of heat and were named accordingly: Half Suicide, Suicide, and the never attempted Charlie's Special. In fact, anyone finishing a Suicide was refunded on the spot, and anyone finishing a special was given a T-shirt. I have to say that in dozens of visits I never saw anyone refunded or swanning about in a Charlie's T-shirt, although I witnessed several students turning green and rushing to the toilets after a few mouthfuls of a Suicide.

We knew all the pubs and clubs in Manchester City centre that didn't question your age, and we rampaged through them all. We'd go to the three best-known gay pubs, The Thompson's Arms, The Rembrandt, and Napoleons, although depending on the night they'd turn us away from The Rembrandt and Napoleons for being too young, but The Thompson's Arms relied on its reputation among the gay community of being jail-bait central, so there were never any problems getting a drink there. As for all the so-called macho thing about drinking in 'puff pubs', we were never bothered, and some of our mates eventually screamed out of the closet a year or two later. Even the roughest, toughest, most unreconstructed Manchester lads, who'd beat you to a pulp for even suggesting they were gay, have enjoyed a few under-age pints down the Thompson's.

Another favourite haunt was Pips, behind the Cathedral on Fennel Street, with it's famous punk nights and its Roxy Room, where they'd play Roxy Music, David Bowie, Sparks, Velvet Underground, and especially Iggy pop all night. The legend about Pips was that, after Roxy Music had played a concert in Manchester, Bryan Ferry and some of his entourage turned up at Pips and asked to go into the room named after him, but the doormen refused because he was wearing jeans. What Bryan Ferry would have made of a room full of drunken fifteen- and sixteen-year-old scallies dancing to 'Love Is The Drug' in a warren-like club of different rooms, all playing different music we'll never know, but I should think he'd have been a bit scared, if only of ending up on the same sex offenders list as Gary Glitter, given the underage clientele.

Pips was representative of Manchester: slightly downmarket, but young, vibrant, lively and a bit rough and ready, with a looseness about it that made our city such a fabulous place to be young. The roughest club we ever went to was Kloisters, which everyone called Harry O's for some reason, on Oxford Road. They did special offers of 22 pence a pint, with shorts for 16 pence a shot, and it was always full of large groups of moody lads and girls from the north Manchester estates with the filthiest reputations. As we used to say, 'If you can't pull in Kloisters, you want to start pulling your plonker, because there's no hope for you.' We used to joke that it was the only disco that served plasma on draught and that if you went to the bar and ordered a pint, the bar maid would ask you what your blood group was. One particular night, one of our mates was asked round the back of the club to the car park by an extremely foul-mouthed, tartily dressed girl from Wythenshawe. We later heard that he was followed outside by three lads who were the girl's accomplices, who beat him up and stole all his money, which was about £2. He ended up spending the night in the MRI having his head x-rayed.

We didn't really cane loads of drugs, we were mainly into beer. Our equivalent of ecstacy at the time were the old northern soul mod pills called 'blues' or 'blueys', which cost £1 for two or £2 for five. They were basically amphetamine pills cut with barbiturates, so they made you feel nice and relaxed while at the same time giving you lots of energy to dance, chat up girls and feel a buzz. The downside was that they could also cause you to suffer acute insomnia, talk broken biscuits all night, and they were very addictive. We used to think that by popping a couple of 'blueys' we attained the gift of the gab, making it easier to chat up girls, and nine times out of ten we would end up sucking the face off some girl in the club. In retrospect the girls probably snogged us because they were fed up of dancing and listening to us talk shit, so thought the only way to shut us up and have a breather was to clamp their lips to ours. I remember once being invited to a student nurse's birthday night at Fagan's on Oxford road. You had to dress up smart to get in, so we all turned up in suits, only for two of our mates, who just happened to be black, to be refused entry. They were really miffed as they were wearing very flash suits and had spent ages getting their Afros looking just right.

'Why can't we come in?' they asked 'You're letting them in. Is it because we're black?'

The doormen replied unsmilingly, 'No. Those hairstyles are a fire hazard, and your mates aren't coming in, either, so fuck off.'

We were all mad on music and luckily one of our friends had a great connection: a gay lad who'd been five years above us at school really fancied him. Despite being of Irish Catholic origin, this lad was openly gay from the age of fifteen, and he ended up as the social secretary at a local college, booking bands and sorting out their nights. He used to get us loads of free tickets for all the concerts at the poly and university, and because he knew all the promoters, we even got tickets for the Free Trade Hall and Apollo. We went to see everyone: U2, Dexy's Midnight Runners, Steel Pulse, Roxy Music, Bob Marley, Gregory Isaacs, Dennis Brown, Marvin Gaye, The Lurkers, Squeeze. . . the list was endless.

I fell in love with Manchester in those two years, between the ages of sixteen and eighteen. Maybe it was the sudden feeling of freedom, as if I was about to escape a childhood that, although not unhappy, was stressful. The constant front I had to put up outside of home was exhausting and wearing, as was the lack of money, space or any outlet other than going to the match on a Saturday or the odd night at a youth club. Nights where you'd hang around wearing a watch strap on each wrist, studded with drawing pins, trying to look hard with your mates, putting on a 'show me' face that left no room for an easy smile, while eying up the girls and the local rivals, who may or may not want to cap the night off with something more violent than a snog outside the chippy. Suddenly it began to feel like that was disappearing.

It never occurred to me that my childhood or early adolescence had been particularly unhappy, but I guess the brain heals the pain like an injury, so things always seem better than they are now. Memory's great gift seems to be romanticizing reality, and what a reality it was. Gorse Hill versus Old Trafford versus Moss Side. Old Trafford versus Stretford. Which tribe would dare come down just to show they could, who thought they could parade around and feel like they ran the place. The mouthy black kid acting the hardman from Moss Side, left bruised and beaten outside the local chippy, two knitting needles sticking out of his stomach – a reminder from the Riordan brothers that you shouldn't gob off on someone else's patch. And all the time you're rooted to the spot, wishing you were somewhere else with someone else, living a different life.

But now we were growing up and discovering Manchester City centre and it's freedom and ownership. We were young, daft and had very little money, but we had contacts and felt we belonged in the city centre, comfortable and part of everything. When we went out, we pooled our money and looked after our mates. Indeed, in all my time on the dole, I never stayed in one night, my old friends who were working just paid for my beer every night without issue. It was an unwritten mutually understood code that you stood your round – having a reputation for being tight-fisted would follow you around for a lifetime.

Manchester was its people, full of moody lads with knowing smiles and a dry sense of humour that could parch an ocean, and girls who oozed sexiness, with throaty laughs and accents that sounded like warm treacle. Years on I can't remember the incidents and the jokes, just the laughter and a line from a song by the punk band the Salford Jets: 'We're heading for the club, that's the Twisted Wheel to you, Cos we're the Manchester Boys and we don't stand in the queue, we don't stand in the queue.'

We were Manchester boys, with a friendship forged on an anvil of hard times and fun. We're all myth-making creatures by nature, but for us there was no city on the planet better than Manchester.

I just had to knuckle down and get my A levels, then I could go to university the following year with a full grant, my own room, a gob full of ice-breakers and be out every night enjoying the big City, bright lights, women and sheer freedom.

I got three A levels, thanks to that grade B in general studies, and went to Thames Polytechnic in London to study for a degree in applied biology.

I'd applied to several universities through UCCA, with my top choice being Bangor University in Wales to study Marine Biology, mainly because I loved all the Jacques Cousteau documentaries on the telly. Unfortunately, I didn't get the grades, so I went abroad, for the first time, to the south of France with a mate of mine, trying to get as tanned and drunk as possible. By the time I returned to Manchester it was almost November, I hadn't got the grades to go to university, and I hadn't bothered applying for polytechnics. After a week I realized there were absolutely no jobs around, so I went to the careers office in town, where the careers officer said it wasn't too late to get into polytechnic. I was feeling a bit down at the time, having had a great time in France, then coming back home to find that half my mates were at work and going out with steady girlfriends at the weekend while the other half had gone off to university or polytechnic, leaving me feeling a bit stranded. I told the careers officer that I fancied doing biology and was informed there were places available at Thames Polytechnic in London. A good mate of mine from school called John Lardner, who used to go to Rafters and all the punk gigs in town, was already at Thames Poly doing a degree in applied biology, so I plumped for that one. After all, London meant the legacy of punk, the Nashville, the Music Machine, the Rainbow, the Marquee, the Sex Pistols, The Clash, and Wardour Street – that's exactly why John had gone down there, so I thought I'd have some of that, too.

London was a strange place to me then, especially that cut-off south-eastern area known as Woolwich, where Thames Polytechnic was based. I could have moved to somewhere like Grantham and had more excitement and night life. All Woolwich had was right wing skinheads and one ramshackle night club called The Tram Shed, which seemed to have ska reggae Artist Desmond Dekker appearing every other week. It was enough to drive an ambitious lively young man to drink and drugs. . .

I had first tried Marijuana when I was sixteen. Although there was a fair amount of it around where I grew up, only some of the black guys and the trendier Bowie/Roxy Music types from the posher end of Old Trafford really bothered with it. At school, though, it was different. Some of the kids had money, and at sixth form parties there was always a spliff going round.

I can remember at one particular party chatting up this gorgeous girl and getting all the right signals back, when suddenly this lad from the year above slouched over with a big spliff and a daft Billy Idol haircut. She went off with him like a shot, and to my young mind, steeped in scientific equations, the message I got from that was marijuana = sex. Once I got to polytechnic I tried the lot: marijuana, speed, LSD, you name it, I had it, though I drew the line at a Billy Idol haircut.

While I was at polytechnic I met the lad who was to be my best mate for the next couple of years. Neville was a half Indian lad from Wallington in Surrey, who for some odd reason had gone to school in Peckham. He was so laid back he was almost horizontal, mainly due to the fact that he smoked dope all day, every day. As far as Neville was concerned I couldn't smoke enough dope. Neville had all the creature comforts at polytechnic, even down to carpet in his room, and he also played a mean rock guitar. He wasn't averse to putting his crappy little record player through his guitar amp and a huge home-made speaker that looked like something ACDC would have on stage with them, then he'd blast out the halls of residence with his awful records. We'd regularly stay up all night smoking spliffs and exploring his strange record collection, which consisted mainly of a mixture of weird hippy music like Mountain, Budgie, Sensational Alex Harvey Band, Van Morrisson and real head stuff like Doctors of Madness, Annette Peacock and *Gandharva* by Beaver & Krause. In fact, his record collection was only made bearable by the huge amounts of marijuana we smoked.

Neville had me sussed as far as my feelings of inadequacy went, with all my aggressive posturing and twisted take on the world, and he used to say, 'Anything to cause a bit of trouble to fit in with your image.' Although I did like causing a bit of trouble and imagined myself as an unreconstructed macho type, I was fairly responsible about my course work and the like – well, for one term anyway. Neville was my guru – and with his long hair and kaftan he looked like one, too – and told me to take it easy. He rarely turned up to college himself, saying 'What's the point, it ain't that hard or that important – skin one up, Terry.' The irony is, I ended up getting booted out with a numb head, whereas Neville got a degree in applied biology and even looked after the marijuana plant at the Botanical Gardens in Kew for a time.

Neville and myself took particular delight in winding up the other Thames Polytechnic students, especially the business studies students. They were all young Tory bores who liked shit music like Meatloaf, Genesis, and Supertramp, and they played rugby. They were a calamitous selection of bland types, and they all had cars bought for them by mummy and daddy, although they never seemed to have any money to buy a drink in the bar and were always trying to scrounge our dope and get Neville to put their shitty records on his system.

I remember feeling a bit sorry for some of them at first and buying them pints in the student bar (this was in the halcyon days of the full grant). But then it was the end of term and I had the Christmas holidays to look forward to, working for a pound an hour at Telemon Tyres in Trafford Park. You can imagine how narked I felt when, having pleaded poverty and scrounged off me all term, most of them said they were off skiing or to the Caribbean with their families for Christmas.

Since then I've noticed that it's always people who've got money who moan about lacking funds. When you're genuinely broke you feel too ashamed to tell anybody.

Because I started late at Thames Polytechnic, there was no accommodation available in the student halls in Woolwich, so I had to stay at a teacher training college out in Eltham called Avery Hill. I offered my services as DJ at their rubbishy Friday night discos and for Thursday nights down in the underground bar called The Dive. There I DJ'd with another lad who was a mate of mine from Thames Poly, called John Hilton. He was a Mod from Reading and had all the clothes, records and a sneaking disdain for the rugger bores on his course. We'd play a mixture of old soul, Motown, Stax, a bit of northern, ska, reggae, Iggy Pop, The Only Ones, Buzzcocks, Joy Division, The Fall, Dexy's Midnight Runners, Two Tone bands like The Specials and The Beat and The Jam.

A lot of students moaned: 'Too loud.' Have you got any Police or Blondie? How about Fleetwood Mac?'

'Fuck off, you tosser,' we'd reply. Well, we weren't studying diplomacy.

There were some girls staying at Avery Hill doing the International Baccalaureate, a kind of A level for posh kids, and they were all attractive punk types who were into Iggy Pop, Velvet Underground and Lou Reed. They liked my accent and, thanks to their obsession with bands like The Fall and Joy Division, they thought Manchester was cool. One night, a rather bold girl with Kate Bush-style hair who was wearing a minidress and fishnet stockings, asked if I'd sleep with her. She was my introduction to half a dozen girls on the IB course, and over the next eight months I slept with four of them on a rotation basis. I had a decent record collection and an endless supply of dope; I was nineteen and had fulfilled all my ambitions in life. I had sex every single night with a variety of partners and in a variety of combinations, I had my own room and a crappy little record player I'd bought off Neville for the grand sum of £10.

I also became known around the Woolwich campus and at Avery Hill for selling a variety of far left papers. First I sold the *Socialist Worker*. I'd been a member of the Socialist Workers Party (SWP) since I was sixteen, when I'd been seduced by thoughts of revolution and changing the system at a huge three-day outdoor Rock Against Racism gig in the Summer of 1978 at Alexander Park in Moss Side. There was Graham Parker and The Rumour on the Thursday night, and The Buzzcocks and Britain's finest ever reggae band, Steel Pulse, on the gloriously hot and sunny Saturday afternoon. During the encore, the Buzzcocks jammed on stage with Steel Pulse, doing a song called 'Jah Pickney': 'We gonna hunt the National Front, cos they believe in apartheid, for that we gonna whup their hide.'

I bought a four-colour screen-print poster saying, 'Zimbabwe', and signed up to the SWP, then forgot all about it until I went to polytechnic, though I was always a dyed-in-the-wool socialist.

I noticed at polytechnic that people seemed reluctant to buy the SWP paper and that all the other members of this revolutionary tear-it-down party were actually rather posh. I also noticed another bunch of lefties around who seemed outwardly more working class – they wore donkey jackets rather than the SWP's combat jackets – and kind of sneered at the SWP. They were members of the WRP or Workers Revolutionary Party, and they were Trotskyists, who had the added allure of being semi-led by the actress Vannessa Redgrave, who often appeared topless in arty films shown late on Sunday nights on BBC2. I remember liking them – the WRP not the films, although the ones with Susan George in were pretty good – and I also noticed that their paper was daily and contained a TV listings page, which made it a far more saleable commodity on campus than the SWP paper, as a lot of the girls in particular had portable tellies in their rooms. I immediately scrapped my Che Guevara combats for jeans,

Dr. Martens boots and a donkey jacket, and became a full-time comrade in the WRP.

I parted ways with the WRP when I forgot to hand my takings in for several weeks and found myself pursued by my ex-comrades for owing roughly £15. I was a bit broke as it was the end of term and felt that keeping the money was kind of Socialism in action; besides, Vanessa Redgrave could afford it.

Next up I joined the Labour Militants, who also favoured the donkey jacket and jeans look, and I sold their paper for a while just to wind up my old WRP comrades, who used to accuse me of being a revisionist. Rather than get all agitated about it, I just used the same argument I use against all my political opponents, whether they're left or right wing: 'Wind your neck in Trotsky/Lenin/Adolph /Mussolini, you won't fuckin' do anything about it.'

All told, I'm probably in debt to a variety of left-wing organizations to the sum of almost £40 – no wonder the revolution never happened.

Unfortunately, all my activities – political, sexual and social – were extra curricular, and after a year I was kicked off the biology course. To be honest, polytechnic in London, even with all the drugs and sex, was boring compared to Manchester. Perhaps my ambitions with regard to higher education were limited. After all, what I'd really wanted from polytechnic was just an excuse to leave home and have my own room, somewhere to take girls back. Oh and of course, as my mate Neville would say, 'cause a bit of trouble.'

chapter two

'I'm surprised to see Terry Christian working anywhere outside of a burger van.'
Daily Mirror, 1999

After my brief stay at polytechnic I ended up, in the summer of 1981, back at my mam's house in Manchester, signing on. My mother was fairly disgusted at the way I'd messed up and been kicked out of poly and was obviously worried that I didn't seem overly motivated about finding a job. In fact, there weren't any jobs around in Manchester. My dad tried to see if he could get me something at Esso in Trafford Park, but there was nothing. 1981 was the worst year in living memory in Manchester for unemployment among the young.

Luckily, I had a mate who ran a couple of market stalls selling Castaway clothing – a poor man's Lois or Lee Cooper – and at the time two-tone baggy jeans, Fred Perry polo shirts, Ben Sherman-style button-down-collar shirts and canvas funk belts were all the rage. I ran one of his stalls on the covered market in Moss Side Precinct three days a week. He rented the stall for £8 a week, and the takings were so meagre that in all the months of working there I never got anywhere near being mugged, probably because the big supermarket in the precinct had shut down because of repeated robberies, so the area wasn't very busy.

I remember trying to get in on the bootleg T-shirts game. The bloke with the stall beside mine was an Ancoats lad who'd occasionally flog bits of stolen sportswear he'd received from his United supporting mates who'd been on the rob in Europe. It was mainly Lacoste polo shirts, Gabicci crew-necks and stuff like that, but he also had a good earner selling bootleg T-shirts of bands like The Specials, Selector, and The Beat, which he'd sell outside concerts they played in Manchester or Liverpool. He asked me if I'd be interested in chipping in £100 to print up 400 T-shirts when Annie Lennox and Dave Stewart's band The Tourists played at the Manchester Apollo, saying he'd try and flog them for a fiver each, undercutting the official T-shirts by a couple of quid.

I borrowed the money off my mate who rented the stall, and one very wet night we hung around for five hours with a pile of T-shirts outside the Apollo in the pouring rain and looked on despairingly as less than 400 people turned up for the concert, none of whom wanted to buy our soggy merchandise. To add insult to injury, the following day the press announced that The Tourists were going to call it a day, and when Annie Lennox and Dave Stewart re-emerged a year or so later with the Eurythmics, I was still loathe to like them, even though I thought their music was good.

Moss Side precinct was a funny place, full of young lads aged between nine and thirteen wagging off school, wandering around the covered market, nicking anything that wasn't nailed down. One young lad who looked eight but was in fact twelve, had the proportions of a Dickensian urchin and the skills of David Blaine. He used to stroll past my stall each day wearing a different pair of two -tone baggy jeans, about five sizes too big and held up on his skinny waist by a variety of different-coloured funk belts.

'Oy, Mister, I nicked these off your stall yesterday,' he'd say. I couldn't believe it. He wasn't much taller than 4 foot 6, and the funk belts I sold for £1 each were looped through a series of wire coat hangers, hanging at least ten feet off the ground at the front of the stall. I had to use a long pole to put them there, yet somehow he'd managed to nick one. I even bought him a 7 pence curried patty to find out how he'd done it, but he scoffed it without revealing the secret and strolled off with a 'see you sucker' swagger.

One of the highlights of our day on the stall was when a bunch of young black teenage lads with dyed blonde hair dressed in strange dark clothes came lurching through the market like a parade. They'd stare straight ahead, looking like extras from a zombie splatter movie. 'It's the Hulme Numan boys,' people would mutter. We never looked them in the face, because if you did they'd seriously kick the shit out of you. Gary Numan, for fuck's sake! As well as loving Gary Numan, they also used to follow one of the local reggae sound systems around. Having said that, less than two years later, when hip hop turned into electro and breakdance, I'd often think about the Hulme Numan Boys from 1981 and their strangely eclectic tastes – they were well ahead of their time.

Another thing I loved about the people of Moss Side was that even though a lot of them knew I was signing on, nobody grassed me to the DHSS, not even when I appeared on national TV for nine weeks as an unemployed youth on the dole. That was my big break into the marvellous world of the media.

It was September 1981 and Manchester was in the throes of a recession that felt like the great depression. Four and a half million people in Britain were unemployed. Thatcherite policies were biting hard, manufacturing firms were shutting down, jobs were scarce and people's frustration at the lack of opportunity and oppressive policing fuelled a summer of riots in Britain's inner cities. It was then that bridges were broken between local communities and the police, and today's gun crime problem proves those bridges have never been rebuilt. Riots happened all over the country: Toxteth in Liverpool, St Paul's in Bristol, Handsworth in Birmingham, Brixton in London and, less than a quarter of a mile from where I lived, Moss Side in Manchester. The police had been harassing a lot of the youths around Moss Side, so when it kicked off it happened in a big way – a policeman was shot through the leg with a crossbow and the local police station was besieged by rioters. On the third night of rioting, the dibble, as we called them, after Officer Dibble in the cartoon *Top Cat*, went in really heavy handed. There were no traditional Bobby's helmets on view, as in Britain's other rioting inner city areas, instead James Anderton's Greater Manchester Force donned white Ulster-type riot helmets and full Robocop regalia.

I remember that third night of rioting clearly. It was a warm summer evening and we were sitting drinking outside the Throstle's Nest pub off Seymour Grove in Old Trafford a quarter of a mile from Moss Side, looking on as one police van after another full of white-helmeted riot police screamed past from the main police headquarters around the corner in Trafford Bar. We could smell Moss Side burning even from there. Miles of shops and buildings were in flames – Princess Road, Clarendon Road, Great Western Street, and Rabies Street. The police went in very heavily and rioters and anyone else within range got a leathering. We heard the screams from alleged rioters in the back of the police vans as we escorted one of our friends, Terry Ryan, back to his parents' house off Moss Lane, all the time being threatened by police to 'fuck off home quickly or else'. After that there was no chance of trust between the local community and the police which enabled criminal gangs to gain a stranglehold on the area.

The Scarman report on that summer's riots declared that the youth of Britain were dissatisfied and needed a voice, so Granada TV gathered together 100 youngsters from the dole queues of Manchester's inner city areas and put them in a TV studio for an ITV show called *Devil's Advocate*, hosted by ex-*World in Action* editor Gus MacDonald, who later became head of Scottish Television, a Labour party bigwig and a Lord. The idea was that Gus would play devil's advocate, encouraging us to be angry and misunderstood, then making us justify ourselves.

I ended up on the show because my mother did school dinners at my old primary school with one of our neighbours, Mrs Flanagan, and Mrs Flanagan's eldest son Kevin ran a youth group for unemployed youngsters at St Anthony's Catholic church in Trafford Park. He'd been asked by the programme's makers to supply some articulate youngsters to appear on the show. Kevin was a big trades union man and knew I was a staunch socialist, so he suggested I might want to go on the show. One of my oldest friends, Pete Burgess, had just been made redundant by Manchester Liners, so I said I'd go along to the meeting at Granada TV with the producer

Maxine Baker if my mate Pete could come, too.

We met up in the pub for a couple of swifties at lunch time, then got the 94 bus to Deansgate. Maxine was really nice and not in the slightest bit patronizing – ah the golden days of TV – asking us about our opinions on sexism, racism, the riots, nuclear weapons, socialism, the class system, everything. After she'd noted down our answers and chatted to us about ourselves, she gave us each £5 for expenses, which amounted to a 20 pence bus ride, and told us if we turned up for filming at eleven o'clock on Sunday we'd get £15 each. We thanked her and thought, this TV lark isn't bad.

On the Sunday we gathered with all the other kids from Old Trafford, Hulme and Moss Side, who we knew either by sight or through acquaintances. They sat us in a studio with loads of bright lights, and then Gus MacDonald terrified me by coming over and saying, 'Terry I'm going to come to you first and ask you, do you think it's your right to work.' I gulped hard and thought, shit! All the other kids were looking over at me, but then I noticed some tasty-looking girls in the audience and thought, hey why not, what we're discussing is only the sort of stuff my friends and I argue about in the pub every night. When I replied, I was surprised at how well it came out. When I watched the show go out the following Sunday I couldn't believe how Mancunian I sounded and how weird it felt to see myself speaking. Remember that there were no video cameras back in 1981, and very few video recorders unless you were fairly well off, so the first time I saw myself on a monitor was on national television.

Among the 100 youngsters who appeared during the show's run was a seventeen-year-old by the name of Johnny Marr, later to become a world-famous guitarist with The Smiths. As a lad he dressed a bit like Ian McCullough from Echo and the Bunnymen, and we used to talk about music, especially the local Manchester bands we were into. Although Johnny was a socialist, he was strictly focused on being in a band.

As a signed up member of every left-wing group that had ever existed, I saw being on national telly as my opportunity to put a dent in the capitalist system. Fired up with dogma, I was pretty outspoken about how I thought Tory policies were forcing the youth to riot on the streets, and I sounded like a comical Wolfie Smith character. As it turned out the show was a great success, and I even got fan mail from viewers, mainly young girls my age asking for photos and stuff. I used all the usual catchphrases: 'Nationalisation without compensation', 'All property is theft', even quoting Orwell's famous comment, 'The Church of England is just the Tory party at prayer.' In fact, I tried to make sure that whatever I said caused the audience to gasp. I was trying to wind people up and shift them out of their comfort zone: it felt just like flogging papers outside Woolwich Arsenal train station, only without the element of danger. There I was, spouting on national TV every Sunday evening for two months about my right to work, the indignity of being unemployed and freedom for Tooting, when three days a week I was flogging jeans and signing autographs on Moss Side market, whilst signing on once a fortnight!

They were my first tentative steps on the road to becoming a genuine media fake. I decided after a couple of weeks to jack in working on the stall as it was getting a bit obvious and some of the local girls had started to jokingly threaten to grass me up if I didn't give them a free pair of jeans. I also started studying how I looked and reacted on camera, as well as taking note of the kind of snipey little sound bite they would include on the show. I scored a fair few points off the great Gus Macdonald, and the producer Maxine Baker commented that she'd rarely seen a politicians manage to do that. I also started getting recognized in the street, and though I had a girlfriend at the time, I got a bit carried away with the huge amount of female attention I received whenever I went out with my mates. I was a star!

For the final show of *Devil's Advocate*, they picked just six of us to appear with the new SDLP founder Shirley Williams, Labour MP Barry Jones, and Tory MP Marcus Fox. We were each paid £100 for this one-off show, even though out of the other five youngsters, one lad did five years for armed robbery and ABH while his younger brother was later shot dead in broad daylight, one of the first victims of Moss Side's gang wars.

In 1983, ITV made a *World in Action* special on the 100 kids from the show *Devil's Advocate*. Johnny Marr, who was then in The Smiths, and my good self, who worked at BBC Radio Derby for God's sake, were held up as the successes, but over a third of the girls had become single-parent mothers, and a quarter of the lads had been in trouble with the police, while over a dozen were in prison, including one for murder.

As the series went on, Gus Macdonald, the producer Maxine Baker and the head researcher Helen McMurray were very encouraging about me working in telly. They even suggested I apply for a job as a TV researcher at Granada. I did send a letter to Granada and was interviewed by a guy called Rod Caird, some young high-flyer within the organization, who basically spent twenty minutes telling me I was wasting my time. Fuck him, I thought. I'd had over fifty fan letters and loads of girls chatting me up – I knew all about telly.

After *Devil's Advocate* finished, I was still on the dole and feeling deflated: I'd gone from hero to zero in the space of two months. Then out of the blue about three weeks later, I had a call from a couple of producers at BBC Radio Derby, who asked me if I'd be interested in moving down to present a one-hour show aimed at young people, going out each weekday evening from 6–7 p.m. It seemed incredible, I mean I liked listening to the radio, but never had I closed my eyes and allowed myself to imagine for a second that it was something I could do. However, I needed a job and this was the only one on the horizon.

I went down to Derby for an interview and got on really well with the producers Jon Barton and Simon Shaw, who then sold the idea to a dubious management. I was employed by the BBC from 17 December 1981 as a freelance radio presenter for the princely sum of £100 per week – I felt like I'd won the Pools. All the national papers immediately got on to the story, and I became the subject of a few small feel-good articles in the tabloids and broadsheets, with headlines like, UNEMPLOYED TERRY'S RADIO SWITCH and UNEMPLOYED TERRY LANDS DREAM JOB. Some of the bosses at Granada were furious: why hadn't their local programmes people found this young lad something? Of course they weren't admonishing their employees out of concern for my career prospects, but because I'd been networked on ITV on a Granada-made show and then the BBC had crept in and stolen all the publicity!

Working for the BBC turned out to be brilliant, and in Jon Barton and Simon Shaw I had two of the cleverest people in the business training me up and flattering me by saying I had an innate ability to think on my feet. Jon Barton was the Education Producer and he was directly in charge of the show, which was called *Barbed Wireless* – a name thought up by journalist and one-time *TVAM* presenter Kathy Rochford. His energy and idealism were inspirational. He'd been an English teacher and I used to love talking to him about books, writing, anything in fact. We used to have a daily political debate, which he nicknamed the 'lunchtime argument', where I was the loony leftist to his intellectual liberal. I think the number of people from a variety of ordinary backgrounds who graduated from *Barbed Wireless* to full-time jobs in the media is a legacy Jon Barton and his successor Jan Rogers should be genuinely proud of.

I went out and found local Derby lads and girls who were into different types of music and gave them regular slots on the show. One of them was Devon Daley, who until recently was the producer of Trevor Nelson's show on Radio 1. I bumped into Devon in a record shop in Derby, buying American import jazz funk records, and he gave me a right hard time about what I should and shouldn't be playing in that genre. Had I been some overly precious media arsehole, I'd have walked off in a huff and spent the rest of my life hating him. Instead I admired his passion, didn't take his comments personally – besides, I *was* a bit of a twat – and asked him to do a slot.

Meanwhile, Jon Barton brought Ivan Gaskell, who now works as a football reporter on *BBC Grandstand*, onto the show. He first broke his teeth as a fanatical fourteen-year-old Derby County fan on

Barbed Wireless, interviewing the county's youth team and doing pieces on local basketball. The *Barbed Wireless* team took him out for his fifteenth birthday and got him drunk in the Blessington pub across the road. His nickname after that vomit-filled night was Five Pints. Jon Barton wasn't amused when he heard about it.

My first taste of celebrity limelight happened in my second week at Radio Derby. I'd arranged to interview Jim Brown, the drummer from UB40, at his flat in Birmingham, together with the group's lead singer, Ali Campbell. UB40 were huge and very hip at the time, and I loved reggae and the political content of their lyrics. I arrived at Jim Brown's Flat in Mosely in Birmingham at around midday on 27 December 1981. I rang the bell and the door was opened by a stunningly beautiful mixed-race girl, who was so pretty I couldn't bare to look at her and felt like some hideously ugly creature that had turned up on her doorstep.

'Er, I'm here to, er, um... is Jim... ? Er, UB40, interview radio Brown.'

I felt completely overwhelmed. Only three weeks earlier I'd been signing on, living in a council house with my parents and youngest sister, aimlessly smoking dope during the day at various mates' houses and listening to UB40's *Signing Off* album. Now I was on the drummer's doorstep, feeling like an absolute nothing.

She looked at me, smiled and, in a friendly, warm Birmingham accent, said, 'You're that lad off the telly. I can't believe it, we loved watching you. Come in. Jim's still in bed, he won't believe this.' I walked into the flat and she shouted excitedly, 'Jim, get up, it's that lad off the telly. He's come to interview ya.'

Suddenly Jim walked in without his shirt on, obviously straight out of bed, beamed a smile at me and said in disbelief, 'You're that lad off the telly.'

I was offered a drink, then Ali Campbell came round with his girlfriend, who was the equally attractive sister of Jim Brown's girlfriend and they seemed just as surprised to see me.

I stayed at Jim's flat for about three hours, they gave me sensimilla to smoke, offered me various other goodies – beer, whiskey, vodka, rum and food – and generally made me feel like a star. There I was, interviewing one of my favourite bands, and they were treating me like I was Bob Marley popped round for a cuppa and a spliff. Before I left they gave me a copy of their latest album *Present Arms* and *Present Arms in Dub* on cassette, and I've still got them both. Then instead of getting the bus to New Street Station, Ali Campbell's girlfriend took pity on me and gave me a lift, which was very generous of her as by that time I'd smoked several joints of very strong wacky baccy, could barely focus and looked obviously wasted. I was so wrecked that on the train back to Derby from Birmingham I accidentally got off at Burton on Trent and had to wait an hour in the freezing cold before another train arrived. I was completely overcome with excitement – my very first radio interview and I'd had a fantastic day out. I felt like I must be famous, too, because UB40 knew who I was.

Barbed Wireless was a pioneering show that set out to make a difference and bring new talent from a variety of backgrounds to the BBC. All we had to do was whatever we had a passion for, and on our show, passion, conviction and a sense of righteous fun were everything. Despite the fact that I was absolutely dreadful in those early days – and fully aware of it, too – I interviewed and conducted debates with everyone from Neil Kinnock and Edwina Currie to UB40 and U2. The show was mayhem at times, though. On the very first show, which went out at six o'clock on 4 January 1982, I had Everett Moreton and David Steele of The Beat live in the studio, and I asked them to say what they thought of the show so far. David Steel said, 'I think it's good, it's different. Usually youth shows like this are full of middle-class twats.' Jon Barton had a job explaining that one to the management.

After that, punk band The Anti-Nowhere League rioted in the studio, 23 Skidoo walked out in a huff after I jibed them about walking around in shorts and sunglasses on a February afternoon and about how posh and pseudo they were, Mark E. Smith Of The Fall threw up outside the studio and Boy George and Jon Moss of Culture Club crawled around on all fours while giving a live commentary. Like *The Word*, it wasn't a show that catered for the pretentious or precious, it was raw, real and seriously edgy, and we had the complaints to prove it. On *Barbed Wireless* I found a raison d'être and an opportunity to do something I loved. I also got my own room when I moved there, got free entry to nightclubs and gigs in Derby and Nottingham because I was on the radio and found that there was no shortage of women, either. Even at that tender age I exuded the sweet aphrodisiac of fame.

I stayed at the BBC in Derby for six years, travelling up to Manchester regularly at weekends to go clubbing with my old mates and watch United's home games. It was great going out in Manchester as I'd still get recognized in clubs by women who remembered me off the TV or thought they'd met me before. It felt great to tell girls, 'Well actually I work on the radio.' BBC radio Derby didn't sound particularly cool, but it was better than saying I was a student or a civil servant! My mates used to love approaching girls I'd been chatting up just so they could stick a spanner in the works: 'Hey, he's not giving you all that bullshit about working on the radio is he? Last week he told a girl he was in the SAS!' I soon sussed this out, though, and started telling girls I was just a student, then when my mates went over while I was at the bar or in the loo, the girl would say, 'No, he's not, he said he as a student.' That way I looked like I was too modest to mention my big, impressive job.

To counteract this my mates decided to up the stakes and went up to the DJ in the club to get him to play a record and mention me on the microphone: 'OK, this one's for Terry Christian, who'd like you all to know that he's a DJ on Radio Derby.' My mates would then all point at me and let out a loud, ironic cheer while I went completely red. Working at BBC Radio Derby didn't sound so cool over the PA system of a sweaty Manchester club on a Saturday night.

As *Barbed Wireless* developed, it became a specialist music show with regular features and interviews with up-and-coming bands from various music genres, including reggae, jazz funk, hip hop, electro, and rare or northern soul. Alongside my Producer, Jan Rogers, and the other people on the team, we developed a style of music show which, fifteen years later, Radio 2 stumbled across with it's *Beginners Guide to Reggae* and *Beginners Guide to Northern Soul* shows, with guest DJs. As I mentioned earlier, the lad who did the jazz funk/modern soul slot on our show from 1983, Devon Daley, was until recently Trevor Nelson's producer on Radio 1, and when he first landed the Radio 1 job he said to me, 'Not bad, is it, Terry. It's only taken me twenty years.' Quite a meteoric rise for a working-class black kid from Derby – he was so shocked they took him on.

We also had Wings Levi from the Culture Sound System in every week, playing the latest reggae tunes and bringing in local MCs from Derby and Nottingham to toast live on air over the dub sides of records, plus any reggae artists who happened to be visiting the area, like Smiley Culture, Asher Senator and Papa Levi, who all did impromptu sets. The show had a mish-mash magazine format and was incredibly cheeky, lively, informative and inclusive, so the listener always had the feeling it was just about to fall apart.

The first time *Barbed Wireless* won the Sony Award in the best specialist music category was back in May 1985, and the award was presented during a black-tie evening event at the Grosvenor House Hotel in London. I was surprised the show had even been nominated, but there was my name in black and white, next to a variety of national radio music documentaries. I didn't expect to win, though, so I carried on drinking steadily while Terry Wogan got on with hosting the ceremony. The event was full of famous people off the television and I even had a pee in the toilets next to ex-Prime Minister Harold Wilson. Finally it got to our category, and the legendary jazz singer from Harlem's Cotton Club, Adelaide Hall, came on stage, opened the envelope and announced my name.

In my speech I said I was absolutely gob-smacked and I meant it. Afterwards I staggered over to the bar and bumped into UB40's Ali Campbell and his brother Robin. It was the first time I'd seen Ali since that December day in 1981 at Jim Brown's flat. He recognized me and congratulated me on the win, then proceeded to introduce me to the Zombie cocktail. The members of UB40 had been introduced to this lethal brew a year earlier by Elvis Costello, who they'd met while recording in Jamaica, and it consists of four different shots of rum, brandy and grenadine, topped off with either orange or pineapple juice. They bought me four and I was, as the cocktail's name implies, a zombie. One day I'll manage to spend more than half an hour with those lads without being wrecked by the end! The next day our manager Bryan Harris paraded me around the radio station with my hangover and trophy but not one of my colleagues, apart from some journalists in the newsroom, said well done.

Barbed Wireless was nominated for the Sony Award again in 1986, and, since the winners are usually notified beforehand, I insisted that Jan Rogers tell me if I'd won. 'Honestly, Terry, we've not heard anything this year.' I was a bit disappointed but not all together surprised, but I decided to enjoy the trip down and a good few drinks into the bargain anyway. That year the awards were a lunch-time event hosted by Noel Edmunds. I relaxed and got steadily drunk, not expecting to win as we hadn't been informed beforehand. Once again we were mainly up against network shows, and once again it was me and *Barbed Wireless* that were the winners. I thought there must have been some mistake as I walked up to collect the trophy, and, the next day there was the usual unenthusiastic response to my double victory from my colleagues at the radio station. We did get showered with praise, though, by all the big BBC bosses, and I quote:

> 'I was delighted to see today news of your prize-winning effort in the Sony Radio Awards. The specialist music category is one of the most hotly contested of all. To have carried off the prize with *Barbed Wireless* for a second consecutive year is no mean feat. If the producers have heard of regionalisation, do please pass on my congratulations.' *David Waine, Head of Broadcasting, Midlands.*

> 'This is really becoming a habit! Congratulations to the Barbed Wireless team on it's second Sony Award.' *Roger Protheroe, Special Assistant to the Assistant Director General.*

And the verdict of the Sony judges: 'The presentation was sharp and witty, and it offered an excellent showcase for local music and musicians.'

I had become the first person ever to win two Sony Awards, and I was only twenty-four years old. Within a year Radio Derby had cut my air time in half and reduced my money by £50 a week; within two years they'd made me redundant. They say that what doesn't kill you makes you stronger, although I suspect not everyone makes it into that second group.

I had half expected the talent spotters from network radio to be on to me in a flash. Within a year of my winning a second Sony Award, Simon Mayo from neighbouring station BBC Radio Nottingham was taken on at Radio 1. He's more their type, I thought bitterly: mainstream and a bit posh. I was ready to leave Derby and it saddened and frustrated me that I wasn't given an opportunity to do so. Commercial radio was, in the main, too bland, and national radio, as far as I could see, was filled with posh southerners. I remember thinking spitefully that even my fellow northerner Andy Kershaw had gone to private school.

I was the youngest person ever to win a Sony Award and the first person to win two; the world should have been my oyster. There was just one big problem: I had an accent. I did consider – for about a second – having elocution lessons, but why should I deny my roots. I'd done well so far, nobody could criticize my track record, so why should I change just to fit in with how everyone else sounded. Radio 1 was the obvious choice for me and I contributed fairly regularly to Richard Skinner's *Saturday Live* show where I was able to get Junior C Reaction a session. I also did several interviews with Mark E Smith of The Fall for *Saturday Live*, a couple of pieces on *Northern Soul* and interviewed The Ramones just before they played at the Birmingham Odeon.

Part of our remit at *Barbed Wireless* was to encourage the local music scene, but Derby had only ever produced two artists of any note. One was the late Kevin Coyne, who'd been signed to John Peel's long defunct Dandelion Records and who became the first artist Richard Branson signed to Virgin, and the other was a punk band who came along as part of the Oi movement, called Anti-Pasti. I got heavily involved in the local music scene, putting on band nights, encouraging local bands, playing demos on the show, sending tapes off to record companies on their behalf and even bringing A&R men up to Derby.

One night I was down the local Afro-Caribbean club on Osmaston Road when I saw this superb ten-piece reggae band called Junior C Reaction. The lead singer and two guitarists had been in a well-known reggae band in the seventies called the Pressure Shocks, one of those fantastic live bands who seemed to just disappear after about five years on the circuit. Errol Cowell was the lead singer and he had a really special voice, as well as being a songwriter of some note. I told him I thought the band were easily the best live British reggae band I'd seen since Steel Pulse in 1979, and after speaking to him about his frustrations and experiences, I decided that, if he was in agreement, I'd manage them and try to steer them to a record deal. Within three months the band had expanded to a twelve-piece, including a four-piece horn section, and they regularly played in the colleges and Afro-Caribbean clubs across the country – everywhere, in fact, apart from London, where they were desperate to play.

The Band released a single, 'Cry Jahoviah', on a label called Centurion Records, which Errol set up himself in 1985. The single was played on both Janice Long's and John Peel's Radio 1 shows, and there was some interest from record companies, but they were reluctant to travel outside of London to see the band play. The group sounded red hot live and had a fantastic version of an old Delroy Wilson number called 'Better Must Come', which they finished their live shows with.

The Junior C Reaction version took the original song and added an a capella gospel-style call and response introduction, and a bass line that was similar to Wayne Smith's reggae hit 'Under Me Sleng Teng'. They added the horns from Marcia Griffiths 1968 Studio One hit 'Feel Like Jumping', and later broke into a dub-style drum and bass with occasional horns and the twenty-year-old bass player,

Melvin Fox doing a kind of sing-jay style version of 'Working In A Coalmine'. Given that the miners' strike was in full swing at the time, the song was both politically and socially relevant, as well as being a defiant blast.

> *'I've been trying a long time, still I can't make it*
> *Everything I do just seems to go wrong*
> *Seems like I've done something wrong*
> *That's why they're trying to keep me down, Lord*
> *Who Jah bless no man can curse*
> *Thank God I'm not the worse*
> *Better must come one day, better must come.'*

The response at live gigs was electric, and at some of them they'd have to play the song three times as an encore. I started to pour all my energies and personal frustration into getting Junior C Reaction a record deal. The only problem was that we didn't have enough money to go into a decent 16-track studio to record the song.

One night I had a young lad – we'll call him Mike – as a guest on *Barbed Wireless*, who was working for The Prince's Trust. He was plugging the fact that in the East Midlands area the organization wasn't able to spend the interest on the money they had to give out as grants, and that the only people who knew how to claim the money and fill in the forms were the local Boy Scouts, who had claimed money for minibuses and the like, which strictly speaking wasn't even allowed. He was coming onto the show to inform people how they could apply to get their projects funded by the Jubilee Trust fund.

After the show Mike and I were down the pub joking about the allocation of Prince Charles's charity money when an idea struck me: how, in theory, could I blag a thousand quid from the trust for Junior C Reaction. At the time, all the band members lived in the Normanton area of Derby, which was full of Afro-Caribbeans and Asians. There were twelve band members, as well as four or five people involved with the engineering side or guesting for live shows.

Could I pretend the band were in fact a musicians' collective? And would it be possible to fill in a form and get a grant for a rehearsal room to be sound-proofed and buy equipment like amps etc., then spend the money on making a demo tape instead.'

Mike was on a Manpower services scheme after spending twelve months on the dole, and he only had another two or three months left in his post as fund allocator for the trust, so he got quite keen on the idea. He agreed to help us fill in the bogus application and then sign it on to his bosses, who would automatically approve the money as long as we weren't trying to claim more than £1,500. In all likelihood, we'd probably receive just over half the money, and in addition, because it was a relatively small amount, they were unlikely to check up on us in a year's time. God bless Mike, who didn't even ask for a cut of the money, he just wanted to stop the Scouts getting fat off Prince Charles's charity dough.

Prince's Trust money can change people's lives, and for a short time in this case it did – or at least it left them with some memories. They recorded two tracks and sent them out, and on the strength of the demo, Junior C Reaction were signed to Cooltempo, a subsidiary of Chrysalis Records, for the grand sum of £8,500 for two singles, with an option on an album. The first single was a reworking of 'Better Must Come' and it came out in September 1986 and went straight onto the Radio 1 C list, thanks to my direct involvement, sorting the band out with a live session on *Saturday Live*.

It didn't see much action in the charts, peaking at 92, and we soon discovered that our A&R man was the young apprentice at Chrysalis and Junior C Reaction were seen as a small band for him to cut his teeth on. Only 3,000 twelve-inches and 2,000 seven-inches were ever pressed, and the £10,000 needed to buy the band on as support act on UB40's sellout UK tour never materialized. By the time the second Single, 'I Am/If It Don't Fit', was released, despite some backing from Radio 1, the band were completely disillusioned with the record company's lack of interest and ground to a halt.

Being the white manager of a reggae band was always an interesting proposition. I once met up with a man who was responsible for hiring out the Nottingham Palais, which held about 1,000 people, to put on Junior C Reaction. He asked if I wanted an all-night license, but I said, 'No thanks, just until two in the morning, it's a concert we're promoting, not a sound system dance.'

I was told in no uncertain terms that this was a mistake: 'I mean, you know what these coons are like, they dunna want to leave their haarses (houses) until midnight and they always come late.'

I'm not sure how I was supposed to react to this conspiratorial comment on the nature of coons and their nocturnal habits, but I was shocked and disgusted at how blatant it was.

Junior C stuttered along for few more years, playing the Oxford and Cambridge May Balls and other universities and colleges as well as the Afro-Caribbean circuit, but I'd lost my appetite for the job as it felt like I was banging my head against a brick wall. With all the ego clashes, fallings out and lack of money, just keeping the band together was a full-time job.

We used to have huge problems hiring minibuses and vans in the early days as they'd all been hired out to the police, who were bringing thousands of coppers up to man the picket lines on the coalfields of Staffordshire, Nottinghamshire and South Yorkshire, all of which were within a forty-mile radius of Derby, and in protest we used to play at miners' benefit gigs. When we did manage to get hold of a couple of vans, we were constantly stopped by the police because they thought we were flying pickets. They were delighted to find two vans full of musical equipment and black people, some of whom had dreadlocks, as it was a great excuse to search and unload the van, while asking stupid questions and searching for drugs.

We also played the 1987 Notting Hill Carnival and Red Wedge gigs for Neil Kinnock's Labour Party, including headlining one at Dingwalls in London, alongside Paul Weller and Paolo Hewitt DJing. But the problems – Errol prophesied exactly what happened with the record contract and was quite reluctant to sign the deal; I regret now that I talked him into it – and paranoia all got too much. The story of Junior C Reaction would fill a book on its own, and every time I watch the Alan Parker film *The Commitments*, about a working-class white soul band from Dublin's Northside, I think their manager Jimmy Rabbit had an easy time of it.

Messed about by the record company and cut loose after two singles, without any support from the record label, Junior C Reaction eventually split, and seven years later Errol died of Hodgkinson's disease, though I still think it was of a broken heart. Music was a passion that burned inside of Errol, but those passionless, convictionless, career-minded, middle-class record company clones didn't give a shit about that. At least for a short time Junior C Reaction proved that you could be black and come from a place like Derby and still achieve recognition.

Another musical fascination of mine was Mark E. Smith. My friends and I had seen The Fall in their early days, and they were the only group we ever went to see regularly, though we could never grasp what it was that attracted us to them. They weren't hip as such – in fact they looked all wrong – and there were times when you thought, who are these dickheads and what's that horrible noise? And yet they hypnotized you.

In the mid-eighties I went to see this fairly un-listenable band who were getting a lot of play on the John Peel show. The lead vocalist was trying desperately to be Mark E. Smith, and though the band could produce some power, the guy looked like a bit of a prat and just couldn't carry it off. (It made me realize that it was the way Mark E. Smith came to life during each performance that made the band what they were.)

Every eight months or so I'd arrange a Saturday lunch-time drink with Mark E. Smith and travel up to meet him in a Manchester city centre pub with a BBC Radio Derby tape recorder. For two hours, over endless pints, Mark would both amuse and horrify me with anecdotes, opinions and stories. He was respected because he never kissed arse, and though he was damning of his peers, he never actually wished them ill. Nearly all The Fall band members were of

Irish Catholic origin – Mark said it was accidental and that they were just the sort of people he got on with. Perhaps it was the idea of Mark E. Smith sacrificing himself for a higher ideal that fascinated me, or the fact that Catholic boys have a great party spirit and like their drink and every other excess, but because of all that early 'mea culpa' confessional stuff they always seemed to fall short of being hedonists. Mark was very opinionated and came out with some really memorable lines which I found hilarious, including one where he dismissed Morrissey of The Smiths as 'Boy George with short hair'.

If John Barton, Simon Shaw and Jan Rogers were my teachers at the BBC, then Mark E. Smith was my personal tutor, helping me understand everything from a particular perspective. It was mad in a way, but it was hard to deny the often painful truths that Mark came out with on our half dozen or so drinking and interview sessions over those years. Mark's a hard person to be around and not question how fake and fraudulent your life and beliefs are.

When Richard Skinner left Radio 1 to go join Capital, the producer of *Saturday Live* on Radio 1, Phil Ross, approached his boss Johnny Beerling with a tape of one of my *Barbed Wireless* shows. Mr Beerling gave it a cursory listen and dismissed it saying, 'He sounds like Andy Kershaw,' They obviously felt that with Andy presenting two shows a week on Radio 1 and *The Old Grey Whistle Test* on BBC2, together with Dave Lee Travis, they had their full quota of northern accents.

Bizarrely, an education programme on Radio 4 called Wavelength Plus FM (*W.P.F.M*) offered me a job after hearing me present a two-minute round-up of summer holiday events for young people in the east Midlands. I presented two series of *Wavelength Plus FM* – great name! – before making way for Jo Whiley and Gary Crowley. I think I was a shock to Radio 4 listeners as one old lady once rang in during a show and asked the producer whether or not she could do something about 'that chap with the awful left-wing accent'. Although the show's producer found it funny, she must have taken it seriously, because she proceeded to send me off every week to some rather posh old major type for voice training. I was assured that they weren't elocution lessons, but they certainly felt like it.

'No, try and say it less northern.'

He was like my old art teacher. I think I drove him round the twist and I half expected to walk in one day and find a good glass of Port on the table, a loaded revolver and a curt note suggesting I do the decent thing.

It was during those days in London presenting on Radio 4 that I encountered the sickeningly patronizing view that wasn't uncommon in broadcasting back then: if you had a defined northern accent, you must be thick. I recall being lost once in the strange Kafkaesque underground bunkers of Broadcasting House, and stopping a badly dressed, bearded and balding thirtysomething chap – you know the type: corduroy trousers hush puppies, plaid shirt and tie – to enquire if he knew the whereabouts of a particular studio. He gazed at me in wonder and then, fighting against his cut-glass upper-class vowels, he attempted to imitate my accent.

'Well 'appen you just walk down t' corridor and turn t'right.'

I looked at him as if he were something that had gone green in the bottom of a milk bottle and he obviously realized I thought he was a complete numpty by the expression on my face.

'Oh I'm sorry,' he said, 'It's just that you've got such a warm unusual accent.'

I headed off down t'corridor and thought, have I ever met anyone from Manchester who says 'appen or t' instead of the? I'd always been told that northern dialects in Britain have a sound represented phonetically by an inverted m, which served for both the 'u' in sun and the 'o' in mother. They're historically right – Shakespeare himself pronounced 'love' like a Lancastrian – but history cuts no ice when you're looking for media jobs in London.

When I was eighteen I was sitting in a pub in London once with some of my mates from Thames Polytechnic when a girl on an adjacent table leaned over and said, 'You're from up north, aren't you? You say boozz up there instead of bus.'

'No, up there we say patronizing southern cow.'

Sometimes it's tough being a victim of a centralising linguistic culture.

By this time I was a walking encyclopaedia of music. I'd seen over a thousand different bands over the years and had managed a twelve-piece reggae band, getting them a deal with Chrysalis at a time when flogging a reggae band to a major label was harder than organizing a wet burka competition at a Taliban disco. I'd worked as a promotions manager at a nightclub, employing DJs like Chad Jackson and Graeme Parke, and promoted my own club nights and bands from Pop Will Eat Itself and The Fall to Misty In Roots. I really wanted to make a difference to people who had genuine talent, but like many from my background, I didn't have the polished social skills and confidence to cope with lifes weird hierarchies. I didn't misuse my power by swanning around and posing, I just tried to use it to affect change and cause a reaction. Yet there I was, approaching my late twenties, and I'd never earned more than £11,000 a year or owned a car that was worth more than £250. I didn't have a pension, a mortgage or a shirt that had cost more than twenty quid. I'd never stayed in a flash hotel, I still had all the same mates I'd grown up with in Old Trafford, Hulme, and Moss Side, and no matter how hard I worked or successful I was, because of my accent, voice and background, I was always viewed as an outsider and 'acquired taste'.

It was inevitable that after six years at BBC Radio Derby, the show would finally come to a close. There were cuts for freelancers across the board at the BBC, and despite trying for various different jobs my accent was always a stumbling block. However, the most forward looking commercial station in Britain at the time was Piccadilly radio in Manchester. They had always been very cutting edge in terms of introducing genuine personalities on air such as Mike Sweeney, Britain's first 'shock jock' James Stannage and the eighteen year old Chris Evans. Also, unusually for a commercial station, they tried to always have at least one show a week where they covered up-and-coming bands on the local music scene. With both Tony Michaelides and Mark Radcliffe showcasing the best in new talent from the area at various times. Pioneering, and led by maverick Managing Director and owner Colin Walters, Piccadilly Radio was Mancunian in the way it took risks and led the way forward, but not only that, they wouldn't have any problem with my accent on air – it was almost de rigeur thanks to Mike Sweeney's Salfordian twang.

Piccadilly Radio's latest plan was to split frequency and have separate distinctive FM and AM channels, which would be called Key 103FM and Piccadilly Radio on AM. This was a move that other radio stations would follow, but back in September 1988, Piccadilly were the first to launch an adult-orientated FM service, where presenters would only speak once every three records and the play list would include album tracks as well as singles and be just about the music. I sent them a tape with the aim of getting a slot on the new FM service as I desperately wanted to move back to Manchester. My radio career ambitions had always been to work at Piccadilly: they were the cutting edge of broadcasting then, and in my opinion, it was only their least interesting and blandest presenters, like Gary Davies and Andy Peebles, who moved on to national radio, which speaks volumes about the state of national radio back then. When excellent presenters like Mark Radcliffe first moved down to radio 1 in 1983, it wasn't to be a presenter, but a producer of bands and sessions, and likewise with Chris Evans, who moved to Greater London Radio (GLR) to be a producer initially and only later became a presenter. Both had accents, so go figure. It's a damning indictment of that lack of vision and eye for talent at the top.

It was December when I finally got the call from Key 103. I was told that they'd consider me as the presenter of their zoo format breakfast show, teaming me up with Beccy Want, but first I'd be put on from 6–9 p.m. on weekday evenings and 2–5 p.m. on Sundays, when I could play when I could play and interview whoever I wanted. The money was OK and I couldn't wait. The exile returns. It's strange that when I'd last lived in Manchester I was a college dropout and on the dole, now I'd be returning to the radio station that had first inspired me as the winner of two Sony Awards.

I was working six days a week, presenting and producing a three-hour-a-night music magazine show for Key 103. I was still the Crusader and still doing my own thing. I didn't just play and showcase bands like The Inspiral Carpets, The Stone Roses, 808 State, A Guy Called Gerald and the Happy Mondays, I also pushed for them to be included on the day-time playlists. And as well as music I brought in poets like Lemn Sissay and local comedians like Henry Normal, who has since introduced Frank Skinner to national TV, written the *Mrs Merton Show*, *The Royle Family* and *Alan Partridge*, as well as founding TV production company Baby Cow with Steve Coogan. It was very different for a commercial station. Though I worked on the drive-time show, unusually for a presenter on independent local radio, I had 100 per cent control over what records I played, who I interviewed and the general content of the show. For the first hour each evening I'd play a mixture of tracks from the station's playlist as well as all-time classics by artists like The Beatles, Marvin Gaye, The Doors, Bobby Womack, Curtis Mayfield, Bob Marley, Bob Dylan, The Byrds, Al Green, etc. Then I'd slowly bring in more current stuff, mixed in with all the latest and greatest from Manchester's up-and-coming music scene. In 1989 there were some classic albums from Soul II Soul, Inner City, De La Soul, The Pixies, The Cure and New Order, as well as the first sign of those breaking northwest bands who would be at the forefront of what became known nationally as Madchester.

Manchester was incredible for music and bands at the time, without having a cooler-than-thou crowd lording it over everyone. The Hacienda heaved with people from all over Britain, Konspiracy was packed out with people listening to the latest hip hop and house tunes, every band on the planet seemed to play at the Boardwalk, The Hang Out club was mixing house music, The Stone Roses and Happy Mondays with Hendrix, Sly and the Family Stone, Iggy and The Stooges, Love and, of course, The Beatles. The music and nights were different, but the people were the same pop kids and scallies; it was like one big football crowd enthusing over the same team. It was sixties psychedelic garage bands meets rave culture, and riding high on the whole scene were two bands who would change the face of British music for years to come, The Stone Roses and the Happy Mondays.

The Stone Roses were a phenomenon. Unheard of further north than Leeds and further south than Stoke-on-Trent, they regularly pulled in over a thousand people to their gigs in Manchester, and for a time they became the resident band on a Friday night at the thousand-capacity International club, which was run by their manager, Gareth Evans. Here were the band who single-handedly invented the warehouse party, and yet they were getting no national recognition.

Back in 1985, despite a sizeable following, the Stone Roses found themselves blacklisted by The Hacienda, because their manager, Howard Jones, had just left as manager of the Hacienda under a cloud. The only way they could get a decent gig was to put one on themselves. The band's tour manager, Steve Adge, decided he'd utilize the space under the arches near Piccadilly train station and pretend the gig was an all-night video shoot for the band. He hired a camera crew and a PA system, then distributed tickets for the all-night party at £5 each. Every ticket informed the bearer that they were extras in a video shoot and a fee of one penny was taped to each ticket. These warehouse parties became a regular feature until, after half a dozen or so, the police cottoned on and put the blocks on.

That was the legacy of The Stone Roses. In Manchester they were the biggest thing since The Smiths, but the Londoncentric music press weren't interested and the national media were oblivious. The Happy Mondays were being fêted by the music press and those in the know in London, thanks to their association with New Order, The Hacienda and Factory records, while in their hometown Manchester they were a word-of-mouth enigma. Their shows were an amorphous mass of drug-fuelled Mancunians and Salfordians, all twenty-four-hour party people who liked indulging in strange shamanic dancing. Ecstacy, LSD, cocaine and whizz were in abundance and nobody paid the blindest bit of notice when people openly smoked marijuana in the pubs and clubs. The young people of Manchester in the summer's of '88 and '89 indulged in a hedonistic orgy of casual drug-taking, the likes of which hadn't been seen since their parents' generation twenty years earlier. Manchester was the most kicking place on the planet – Ibiza without the beach.

There was a unique and almost unreal period from January 1989 to the spring of that year which you almost wanted to capture and bottle. Everything seemed possible in Manchester and there was an air of excitement and expectancy, a headiness with regard to the future and a re-embracing of the past. Everyone who wanted to be involved in the scene was allowed in, it was all-encompassing and seemed so positive. There was no cynical moaning, just a sense that any and everything would and could happen. It was a pure version of what punk rock had set out to achieve over ten years earlier, but this time it was just for what local journalist Sarah Champion called the 'pop kids' because it wasn't elitist or cool in any way, it was do it yourself. Records were being released left right and centre, and there was huge self-belief and a kind of confidence among young people in Manchester, in the future and their own City, which was like a shared, well-known secret. People felt it truly was the coolest thing on the planet to be a northern scally; it was as if all the pressure was off and we could just be ourselves, Mancunians, and be totally unapologetic about it. We lived the life rather than dreamt about it.

Then in May 1989 The Stone Roses released their debut album on Silvertone records. I had seen them years back in 1985 at a showcase at Dingwalls in London. I remember being very impressed with them and ringing up Tony Michaelides, who'd just taken over doing the Manchester music show from Mark Radcliffe. He sent me a copy of the band's first single on twelve inch, a rather disappointing double A side 'So Young' and 'Tell Me', while a mate of mine scrounged a copy of the band's first demo tape, recorded at Spirit Studios in August 1984. Now at last, five years after being ignored and written off outside their home town, they were in the ascendancy, young prophets of a scene that would have the biggest impact on British music since punk and the biggest influence since Merseybeat in the sixties. The album, *The Stone Roses*, entered the charts at number 32, even though the band were virtual unknowns outside the M60 ring road. Madchester was kicking in big time.

It only started feeling a bit wrong to me when Tony Wilson at The Hacienda started to desperately take possession of what had been a young and spontaneously eclectic scene. He tried to thread it all together with all this indie/dance crossover trendy Hacienda nonsense, as if kids who'd loved New Order in the early eighties hadn't been into jazz funk and electro, or Buzzcocks fans hadn't loved northern soul.

For me the scene was destroyed the day it was marketed to the London media as cool and fashionable. I mean, why should people be surprised that a bunch of so-called indie band musicians like The Happy Mondays also liked house music? In Manchester, as far back as I could remember, black lads had liked Gary Numan, The Buzzcocks and The Smiths, while still going to reggae sound-system clashes. Manchester had a special cohesion about it, and music for the Irish, Jewish, Italians and West Indians was more than just a shared passion, it was an obsession. With the marketing of 'indie-dance crossover Madchester', a certain crabs-in-a-bucket mentality took over and everyone wanted a slice of recognition. The whole scene was summed up best in The Fall record 'Idiot Joy Showland', and a lot of talent, particularly on the black music side of things, was left behind by the blatant self-publicists. The minute Manchester was recognized as trendy in the national press, music press and glossy magazines, it was over. Telling you how you should dress and all that home counties nonsense, as if music = fashion and vice versa. At first the music press tried to scorn the whole thing, and when that didn't work, they sheepishly courted an association with it via Tony Wilson, Factory records and The Hacienda. But whenever trendy music journos or TV and radio people actually came up to Manchester, you could sense their rank hostility to it.

I was nevertheless lucky enough to be working on the local station that was giving airtime to all these Manchester bands, plugging their gigs and giving them live sessions and interviews. I used to have guest

DJs in every night from all the happening clubs, including Mike Pickering – now with M People, and Graeme Park, who I'd once employed to play Saturday's House Nation night at The Twentieth Century Club in Derby for the grand sum of £70 – who were responsible for The Hacienda's flagship 'Nude' night. They used to be live on my show every Friday evening between eight fifteen and nine o'clock, before they disappeared off to The Hacienda for another night spinning discs at what was then the biggest club night on the planet.

Then suddenly everything took off and there was a feeding frenzy for the best part of a year in London as the magazines, papers, radio stations and TV shows fought over all things Mancunian. Manchester was 'hip' – we were much more than just that – and style magazines printed reams on the 'scally culture', baggy hooded tops, flared jeans, drugs and the local vernacular, turning everything that was good and real into fashion titbits. Everything was top, buzzing, sorted, offside and on top, and phrases rarely used by Mancunians like nish, clish and nitto somehow got integrated into the vernacular, too; even posh kids were dressing like working-class scallies in a bid to be hip.

Mike Briscoe, who was then programme controller of Key 103 had said he wanted someone to give the station an edge and get people talking about it. There had been several glowing write-ups about my show in the local press and music magazines like the *NME* – there was even a half page write-up about me in the *Guardian* by radio critic Ken Garner, under the banner headline THE NAKED SOUNDS OF MUSIC CITY:

> *'He's got a gob on him has that Terry Christian (Manchester's Key 103, weekdays 6–9p.m.): "Only about four members of the Pogues are actually of Irish Origin, but every member of The Smiths had Irish descent. So there you go The Smiths are more Irish than the Pogues."*
>
> 'Whatever next? Driving into what Christian quite correctly called "the music capital of the Western World" last Friday night,

it was typically tippling it down. Just another wet bank holiday in Manchester. The car radio threw out the news : there were all-dayers, all-nighters, clubs, gigs the lot.

'Christian, a two-time Sony Award winner when at BBC Radio Derby, returned home to Manchester last Christmas. His show comes alive after a compulsory hour of drive-time music until 7 p.m. Last Friday there was a live interview with Phranc, self proclaimed, "All American Jewish lesbian folk singer", who then performed a tribute song to Martina Navratilova; an amusing discussion about Irish cultural identity with Gavin Friday, formerly of the Virgin Prunes (banned by Channel 4) and a weekly selection of dance floor hits from Mike Pickering, DJ at Manchester's Hacienda club on Friday's Nude Night, currently one of the top house music club nights in the world. Before the show was over, Phranc and Friday were on stage at the Royal Northern College of Music and the usual queue had started outside the Hacienda.

'But it's our Terry that lifts it all out of the ordinary. The cheeky swine is a radio natural. Gavin Friday, infamous Dublin ligger, says, "I don't like hanging out with hip people, just people I know."

'Like Bono? Ex-members of Thin lizzy? The Boomtown Rats? Yeah tell us all about it Gavin.'

Recognition at last? Nah, that wouldn't fit comfortably into the pattern of my life. Things started to go wrong when the multi-millionaire, jailbird-to-be, Owen Oyston made a hostile takeover bid for Piccadilly Radio, breaking Colin Walters and a lot of other people's hearts into the bargain. Alas it would never again be the Mancunian station it once was. Oyston reportedly paid £39 million for a radio station valued at £17 million, and around the same time Michael Knighton failed to buy Manchester United from Martin Edwards for £12 million.

Unfortunately for me, my timing was as acute as Mr Oyston's business acumen. Within a week of Owen Oyston taking over the station, I was off on holiday for a fortnight in Greece. When I returned, one of the station's presenters, Tim Grundy – son of Bill Grundy and a hater of the Happy Mondays who featured heavily in my shows – had been promoted to programme controller, the old controller having been sacked, and a new regime was in place. They decided they didn't like me, my weird music or what they described as my cocky attitude.

I was shown the door for playing what Tim Grundy described in the local press as 'too much obscure music'. My reply in the same article was simply, 'Shakespeare is obscure if you are illiterate.' Local journalists had a field day and Piccadilly were slagged off for axing the one show on the station that truly reflected what was going on in Manchester. The *Manchester Evening News* offered me a full page every Friday, which had previously been written by Manchester's youngest ever music journalist, Sarah Champion, called 'The Word', to cover up-and-coming bands and gigs in the Greater Manchester area. Britain's first official Black Music Station, Sunset Radio, was just starting in Manchester, and offered me a Sunday afternoon show to cash in on all the publicity, while Britain's first official independent music station, KFM, who were around nine years before XFM, but were callously ignored by London's music press, was due on air in January 1990 and offered me four nightly shows a week. I was earning just over half the money I'd been on, but things were looking up, especially when, within a fortnight of Piccadilly sacking me for playing 'obscure music', The Stone Roses, 808 State and the Happy Mondays all appeared for the first time ever on the same edition of *Top of the Pops*.

What could have been, and for a short period was, phenomenal about the whole Manchester scene then was that it had cultural and sociological implications. The sneering almost hostile attitude of the middle-class, London-based music press, who used to dismiss Madchester as 'just a fad' was revealing. There's no fury like that of a control freak losing control – all that hard work and brown-nosing gone to waste. The Manchester music scene was rooted in the urban, mainly white working classes, so it came from the bottom up, so to speak, and didn't need the approval of some sad, severely privileged

Home Counties numpty. Young people from Manchester, judged in the past for the way they talked and what their daddies did for a living, were cooler than the trendy posh kids because they lived the life and made the music.

Manchester, just like London, is an immigrant city built on an Irish, Jewish, Italian triangle. But unlike our capital city, Manchester is short on snobbery; there's no old money around and people are looked up to or admired because of their success at making or selling things, or indeed by excelling in the world of art, sports or entertainment. Each minority had important shared values, and loyalty to your own, and to your family, mattered. For those immigrants, Manchester had a sense of place and gave them a sense of belonging. Indeed the next generation of immigrants, whether West Indian, Asian or African, were all soon wrapped up in the city's comforting cosmopolitan embrace.

Because of it's small city centre, everything in Manchester was within easy reach, and it had a very different feel to places like London, Birmingham or Sheffield. Maybe it was the Catholic thing, but its cohesion was raw, generous and exciting, without being wholly decadent. Painters like L.S. Lowry and Harold Riley would be spotted at the football, as indeed were famous band members like Ian Brown and Mani of The Stone Roses, Bez from the Happy Mondays, Johnny Marr from The Smiths, TV presenters and music mavericks like Anthony H. Wilson and the late New Order/Joy Division manager Rob Gretton, who was a season ticket holder at City, or actors like Chris Eccleston and various *Coronation Street* stars – and for the right reasons. There was none of that Dickie Attenbrough/John Major at Chelsea syndrome. World-famous actors like Albert Finney, Robert Powell and Ben Kingsley might be spotted in a greasy spoon café or a working men's pub in Salford. The gap between art and sport, low life and high life, and people of all classes was narrower in Manchester and gave the city a special sense of itself.

Morally, Manchester has always had a kind of looseness about it, a joie de vivre and a tolerance for outsiders. When the National

Front, the British Movement and other fascist types tried to organize in Manchester in the seventies and eighties, they weren't tolerated, and the local football hooligans from both United and City violently kicked them out of town.

Manchester's rules of behaviour were ingrained, and there was a sense of right and wrong that existed outside the law. The Irish writer and ex-IRA man Brendan Behan was imprisoned during the later days of the Second World War in Manchester's Strangeways prison. While in jail he commented on several of his fellow in-mates, mainly Mancunians and Salfordians, most of whom had been fighting for over two years with the infamous Desert Rats against the Italians and Rommel's Afrika Korps in North Africa and had been imprisoned for shooting their own officers. As Behan said:

> 'And by the looks of them, they could have shot a few more, but a more decent bunch of people I have never met in my life. They were good soldiers who had fought bravely under great duress and terrible conditions for two years, and then when some twenty-year-old public school type officers straight from Sandhurst went out and started ordering them about and using the cane on them, these veterans just turned around and plugged them.'

Behan was most struck by how his fellow prisoners, despite their ill treatment by the warders and justice system, never singled him out, even though, as a known IRA member, he had tried to bomb the shipyards at Liverpool during the early days of the war. They didn't agree with his politics or his stance, but they could respect him and treat him as an individual, and this is what struck a chord with this rebel amongst rebels.

Ideas about respectability aren't as rigid in Manchester as elsewhere, being true to yourself and your tribe is all that's important. I loved my background and wanted to embrace it and show what a positive force it could be if, unlike all the other 'I'm All Right Jacks', you could stay true to your roots. Manchester's riots in 1981 exiled and elevated me to critical success in radio. Now in

1989–90 it had exploded in terms of music and youth culture, and once again I was around at the right time, so that my city could give me a leg up. The world of national television was waiting . . .

chapter three

'The famously inarticulate and cerebrally challenged Terry Christian' Piers Morgan, the Sun, 1991

It was a rather grim November day and I was mulling around at my mam and dad's, feeling a bit lost, like time was grinding me down. I was working one day a week at Sunset Radio, writing 'The Word' page for the *Manchester Evening News* and waiting to hear from KFM in Stockport. I could tell my mam was worried, too: all working-class people fear the spectre of unemployment and debt – they've always been the weapons used to keep them in line – and she constantly told me she'd light a candle for me in church after mass every Sunday. I felt as if I'd had my chance and blown it, and I was angry at myself for the way my life was working out. Was it me, was I too cocky? Too selfishly focused on what I wanted to achieve? Too bogged down by my background?

Then out of the blue I received a phone call from a rather posh-sounding chap called Matthew Bowes, who asked me if I'd like to go down to London and audition for a new television show.

'No, mate, I haven't got the time.'

He was so shocked he started laughing.

'Listen, don't be like that, we've called around several journalists in Manchester and asked them who we should audition from up there and they all mentioned your name.'

I was flattered, but I could just imagine the kind of conversations that had been going on in media land. 'Manchester's trendy, let's go up to Yorkshire and audition some Mancunians.'

My past experience with people from network radio had taught me that they tend to be prejudiced against northern accents, and I was sure that network TV would be the same. I didn't want to raise my hopes about some pie-in-the-sky job on the telly when financially, to coin the official accountancy phrase, I was on my arse.

'Listen, I'd love to come down, but Im busy.' A total lie, of course.

'Don't be like that, you should come down, it's not an audition as such, we'll just put you in front of a video camera and see what you look like, and then we might decide to give you a proper audition.'

'Well, OK, if you pay my train fare,' I countered.

'Erm, we'll pay your train fare if you make it to the proper audition.'

'Cheers, but forget it, it's not worth the hassle.'

As I hung up I thought about the eight years worth of unpaid tax bills lying in some darkened office waiting to find me and wondered if I'd made yet another mistake. I knew I was only bluffing to find out if they were genuinely interested. Still, it was just a daydream. Jobs presenting on national television, as Prince Charles would no doubt agree, weren't for the likes of me.

On the other hand, though, I remembered how it felt to be famous for a while, an unemployed youngster suddenly recognized because he was on national telly. I recalled the day, way back during the run of *Devil's Advocate* in 1981, when I'd bumped into a couple of my old primary school friends who, like me, were unemployed, only they were about to go to court. I was having a mooch around Manchester city centre at lunch time and popped into an Irish pub called Mulligans, which was just across the way from the law courts. Both the guys in question were up on separate aggravated burglary charges and just happened to be having their hearings on the same day. I remember one of them being really quiet, skinny and scruffy at school, the recipient not only of free school dinners but of the shameful ginger biscuits teachers offered during morning milk break to those kids who hadn't had breakfast. Suddenly he was treating me like I was a somebody, rather than just a kid he'd grown up with.

'Here y'are Terry.'

He reached into his pocket, pulled out his wallet and removed a neatly folded tatty piece of paper which had been torn out of an old copy of the *Manchester Evening News*. It was the report of the robbery and his subsequent arrest.

'What do you reckon? Oi, Tommy show him yours.'

Another neatly folded clipping came out. It was tragic, but understandable. If your name was in the paper and your photo was on top of it, you were immortal, raised up miraculously from stifling anonymity. As for me, I was famous in Derby and well-known in Manchester, so being recognized and pointed out by semi-strangers was nothing new. I'd lived with it at a low level for years, so as far as I was concerned, it was very over-rated.

At the time that Matthew Bowes phoned I was broke, with a pile of bad debts, working part time for the grand sum of £180 a week. I wasn't exactly living the dream. All I had were two bags of clothes and books and a mountain of records. I wasn't exactly prowling the streets, begging for loose change off church mice, but what I had materially wasn't much to show for eight years of working on the radio, except, of course, for those two bloody Sony Awards, which seemed more like a curse than anything else.

I was sat in my mam's house for twenty minutes, thinking how nice a trip to London would have been, and that maybe there was a million to one shot that it might have come off and I'd be a TV presenter, but I'd never know because I'd refused to buy a ticket in life's lottery by acting like I wasn't bothered about earning good money and being famous. I was feeling really stupid. Why did I say I'd only go to the audition if they paid my train fare? Who the f*** did I think I was? Then the phone rang, and it was the 24 Hour Productions office on the line.

'OK, we'll pay your train fare,' he said.

Result. I hadn't expected Matthew Bowes to ring me back after I'd acted so nonchalant.

The audition wasn't a big deal, just ad-libbing for a minute in front of a video camera and then interviewing a female boxer. It was a matter of a day or so before they called me back and asked me to come down to Cliveden – the stately home where John Profumo carried on his infamous affair with Christine Keeler in the sixties and which is now a hotel – for a meeting about this new show they were thinking of doing. And they also happened to mention that I would be needed in London in a fortnight for a full day of auditions at Channel 4's studios on Charlotte Street.

I travelled down to London on the train, where I was met by a chauffeured car containing the boss of 24 Hour Productions, Charlie Parsons and Matthew Bowes. We were heading to a TV forum of youth TV's inner sanctum at Cliveden, and I'd been invited to a brainstorming session with various people about what kind of programme this new and as yet unnamed Channel 4 show was going to be. As I made small talk with Charlie and Matthew, all I could think was, am I having some weird drugs flashback from my polytechnic days, because I didn't know what the hell I was doing there. It seemed peculiar, but I'd never understood these posh types, and as long as they paid my expenses it was fine by me. It was all quite exciting and cutting edge. *The Word*'s working title at the time was *Club X Two*. The follow-on to one of the most dreadful Channel 4 programmes of all time, *Club X*, which had been an arts and music programme aimed at the so-called 'yoof', but which was so incomprehensibly pseudo-bollocks awful, it was laughable.

I was introduced to the selected youth panel, which included a lot of faces from *Network 7* and former and current Janet Street Porter TV cronies. I was adamant that if Channel 4 were going to make another show aimed at the youth market, it should avoid the patronizing 'Hey, wow, kids' scenario full of privately educated upper-middle class student types, trying to enlighten the masses on the benefits of the Moscow Knitwear Theatre and PVC kecks. Or even worse, the kind of sixth-form fanzine journalism dressed up in designer gear that had paraded as cutting edge TV, like *Network 7* or BBC2's *Reportage*. I boldly stated that youth TV shouldn't be aimed at grown-up educated upper-middle-class students from the south east, but should be something inclusive for fourteen to eighteen-year-olds – Sarah Champion's pop kids – who actually still had a sense of humour and weren't afraid to admit that their main interests in life were going out, music and sex. Accessibility was the key word, in so far as it shouldn't be too trendy and aspirational, or make the audience feel too distant from the programme.

Even though I'd just been invited to the forum as another voice, I was quite fearless and unabashed about giving my opinions. I've always liked opinionated people, and we see and hear less and less of them nowadays. It's a mixture of fear, laziness and sheer dullness; nobody wants to say anything that might upset someone else. It's George Orwell's 'thought crime syndrome from his novel *1984*; will I be voted out of the *Big Brother* house.' I resented what I saw that day at Cliveden: a bunch of jumped-up graduates, posing as an amateur intelligentsia providing 'the kids' with what they thought was good for them. What had been going on in Manchester proved that today's youngsters weren't bothered about being cooler or trendier than anyone else, they were into enjoying being young and doing their own thing, unselfconsciously being themselves.

There were all kinds of ex-*Network 7* people around the table, and I felt them wince when I said I didn't know anyone in the youth age group who liked the show – people just laughed at how pretentious it was. When asked for my personal opinion of the show, I replied diplomatically, 'Too glib and middle class.' Yes. I know, diplomacy Al Quaeda style – there I was, beating around the bush again. Still, I think Charlie – as always really – found my frankness regarding youth TV and how it didn't reflect young people and had all been shit, quite amusing. I think he admired my sheer gall, even if he didn't wholeheartedly agree.

Don't get me wrong, I had some ambitions to work in TV, but I hated the word 'networking'. Everything about the phrase is slightly sinister: a network of spies, a network of terrorists, a network of paedophiles. It never refers to anything nice like a network of philanthropists or charity workers. Of course, in the media all networking is, is agreeing with whatever seems to be popular at the time, with the onus on the word 'seems', and it's always about what's going on in London, because to the big movers and shakers in media-land, nowhere else exists. Another thing I hated about it was the whole safe, middle-class stodginess of it – everything was for show and there was never any raw honesty about anything.

Charlie Parsons had been the editor of the last series of *Network 7*, taking over from Janet Street Porter. After *Network 7's* run had ended, Charlie and his partner Waheed Alli set up a TV production company called 24 Hour Productions. The first commission they had was for an arts show aimed at the youth market called *Club X*. It was frightening how bizarre and bad this series was, but the Channel 4 editor responsible for commissioning it, Stephen Garret, had nevertheless gone ahead and given Charlie the nod to revamp things fairly drastically before going ahead with another series, under the working title *Club X Two* in an attempt to bring 'appreciation of the arts to the youth'.

Someone brighter than I might have sussed that they had the job in the bag already, but it didn't occur to me as I had no TV experience, apart from being part of an audience of unemployed kids and a couple of screen tests for *The Tube* in 1988 and for an ITV kids' show that was meant to replace *Magpie*, called *Splash* in 1986. The *Splash* audition had gone really well until I had to run through an army assault course at the end. I bumped my testicles climbing up and over one of those netting things and let rip with a series of expletives – mind you, in my defence, I had been told that this part of the screen test was going to be run out over the end titles to music, so no presenter dialogue would be audible. Strangely enough, though, the show's producer Michael Ward wrote the following note to my agent at the time, Paul Vaughan:

> *Dear Paul,*
>
> *As for that talented little git, Terry Christian, after doing what was an excellent audition, he went and spoilt it at the end by swearing like a trooper whenever anything went wrong. As I cannot risk a repeat of this on a live children's show, I am unable to offer Terry the job. However, I'm sure he'll turn up on television one day, perhaps on some late-night show on channel 4 where it's OK to swear.*

The Tube audition was even more bizarre. A bevvy of wannabes, including the late Caron Keating, Ros Holness – member of Toto Coelo and daughter of 'I'll have a P please, Bob' – and myself were herded together in a Newcastle Hotel and primed for our shot at the big time. I remember it being a very nervous occasion as we all wanted the job really badly. As it transpired, none of us got the job – the female presenter role went to London DJ and singer Wendy May, from the famous – well, in Camden Town anyway – band the Boothill Foot Tappers, and the lad's job went to a thirteen-year-old kid – also from London – called Felix. I swore that day that I'd have my revenge by getting the little knob end's paper round.

I knew that TV auditions weren't about how you said your lines to camera, talent, wit or even looks, they were about whether or not you were the sort of person they were looking for at the time. As it turned out, at the final *Word* auditions I was. I knew what I wanted to do on TV: a rather left-field chaotic experience that was must-see telly for the new 'pop kid' generation. A show that had people talking the next day, that had them wanting to punch the set, that had them on the edge of their seats and that made them think, yeah, I could do that, in fact, I should get the chance to do that. I wanted it to be all-embracing, to give the audience a sense of ownership, even if that just meant forcing them to have an opinion about it. We weren't going to be fashionable or trendy, just fun and rather cheeky. I was also aware that I wasn't some performer, like a clown. Being on telly should look like fun, but it shouldn't be a pleasure – there should always be an element of fear involved, a fear that maybe you shouldn't be there. I remembered the mantra Manchester United manager Alex Ferguson allegedly taught his young players. 'Leave nothing to chance. Preparation is paramount for success. Fail to prepare, prepare to fail.' I can honestly say that in over one hundred shows of *The Word*, that fear of failure and not belonging remained because I made it stay. As for the preparation part . . . er, well. . . !

The final auditions for what was then *Club X Two* threw me in with all these young, beautiful, über-trendy youngsters from London, who huddled together, waiting their turn and exuding all the anxiety of an examination room, yet somehow worse. Everyone knew there were only two jobs going: one male presenter and one female presenter.

I found the whole thing fascinating. I couldn't dredge up any fear because I didn't think I had a cat in hell's chance of landing the job. It was just a day out to me and, to be quite frank, for every plus I could think of about presenting a TV show, I could also see a minus, and apart from the crap money and insecurity, I was happy with my newspaper and radio work in Manchester. I just enjoyed the whole experience with varying degrees of amusement.

Amongst the illustrious people screen-tested for the presenting jobs were Rob Newman of *The Mary Whitehouse Experience*, Davina McCall, Dominic Diamonds, Caron Keating, Wendy Lloyd, Simon Cowell's one-time girlfriend Terri Seymour and, from Manchester, my old sparring partner from KFM Jon Ronson, who I had recommended and who was actually a nice Jewish boy from Cardiff whose family were rumoured to be worth millions – and a girl from Peckham called Marian Buckley who worked for Manchester's *City Life* magazine, plus a bevvy of other girls and boys, some recognizable, most not, who claimed to have done some modelling, although by the look of them it was probably of the clay variety at primary school. I remember one girl being a right prima donna. She slagged me off like mad when I nipped out to the loo for a crafty cigarette during her audition with me. I wandered through to the control gallery to get a light, and there she was on the monitors, ranting on about Terry this, Terry that, and how I'd put her off and made her mess up her lines, yet two minutes earlier she'd been all sweetness and light to my face. In fact, her sunny disposition and natural empathy for others is well known in the industry, as was the rumour that she got her first radio job by shagging a middle-aged radio producer when she was only sixteen.

Although I didn't think I was going to be the show's presenter, a look at many of those being auditioned made me wonder who on earth thought these overdressed misfits from London's West End were the best candidates for the job. There was a bald-headed, good-looking mixed-race bloke who was dressed in 1930s gangster chic and was so screamingly lispy he made John Inman sound like Barry White, and a gaggle of strange posh girls and boys who couldn't even read, never mind follow the autocue. I knew at least a dozen people who would have done a far better job at the audition. But then the general consensus in most places outside London is that TV people are out of touch with what ordinary people want to see on the telly.

I was disappointed, but not in the least surprised to find that practically all the people working behind the scenes on the show had all been to public school, as had most of those being auditioned. They all seemed to know each other or have heard of each other. Perhaps the TV world has moved on since then, though I'm afraid I never witnessed it's leap towards a more meritocratic and socially mobile industry.

I've had a lot of experience working with people from well-to-do backgrounds who went to private schools, and it strikes me that they share a few things in common. Before I launch into a tirade against the so-called great and the good, let's remember that these are the same people who invariably vent their prejudices with regard to ordinary people in TV documentaries and the national press. Whether it's single mums, chavs, scallies, unemployed teenagers and scroungers, northerners or Essex girls, we're all depicted as fairly low characters, who are politically incorrect, racist and homophobic, despite having very little evidence to justify the accusations, so I make no apologies for generalizing in the same way. And of course it is a generalization, but like most generalizations it has an element of truth to it.

The most common trait among our public school fraternity is that they invariably cannot take any form of criticism; they're what you would call 'precious'. I think it's because all their lives they've been insulated from other people's opinions by the fat wads of cash surrounding them. They're not used to anyone from the so-called lower classes saying, 'You're an idiot' or 'You are just a bunch of fatuous ex-public schoolboy layabouts.' They can't stand to lose or be wrong about anything, so lying becomes an automatic reflex;

they'd rather die than admit they cocked up. Many also seem to believe that anyone from the working classes will accept their opinions, judgements and old flannel on any given subject.

A snob will never accept that he's a snob any more than a racist will admit to being a racist. The facts are, that everyone in the media who isn't from a middle class and/or home counties background sees the parochialism, hypocrisy and narrow-mindedness within weeks of starting work, and the reason they choose not to mention it is because they're too afraid. After all, if you're an outsider in the business to start with, you have enough on your plate without sticking your head over the parapet and pointing out the obvious flaws in the system, especially if you want to prove yourself and get promoted. Imagine the Emperors New Clothes, and if when the kid says that the emperor isn't wearing any clothes, instead of agreeing with him, the crowd lynched him – that, I'm afraid, is the equivalent of our fair-minded media's response back in 1990 to accusations that it was a south-eastern upper-middle-class hegemony. Of course, I'm sure it's very different nowadays . . . Ahem.

Perhaps things have changed, but even the Nazis, when planning an invasion of Britain in World War Two, were determined to infiltrate the public school system in the UK. Commenting on the strange increase of ex-public schoolboys in Major Attlee's Labour Party in the 1930s, the unknown Nazi compiler of the *Informationsheft* concluded, 'The whole system is calculated to rear men of inflexible will and ruthless energy who regard intellectual problems as a waste of time, but know human nature and how to dominate other men in the most unscrupulous fashion.' Historians have wondered whether the compiler of the guide received this information from Hitler's Foreign Minister Joachim von Ribbentrop, who, when German Ambassador to the Court of St James before the war, tried to get his son Rudolf into Eton, but was told it was 'full'. Instead he sent his son to Westminster, and so that London public school has the doubtful honour of having an old boy who served in the elite 1st SS as well as – let's be cheeky – supplying two editors and a number of producers on *The Word*. In fact, during my time at

Channel 4, Westminster and St Paul's seemed to be the feeder schools for the entire channel and it's various production companies.

These, however, were all minor concerns at the time. By the end of the day I was more or less given the nod that I'd got the job, but I wasn't exactly breathless with anticipation. I was contacted by the production company and told that once I'd signed with 24 Hour Productions I'd be paid a signing-on fee of £1,500, then they'd pay me £250 a week until pre-production started on the show, when my money would go up to £400 a week, and while the show was on I'd be paid £500 a show. Even after hearing that I still felt that presenting a national TV show would be a hassle, and that it had to be worth more than £500 per week, so I asked for £1,000 per show. Eventually I settled for £500 a show plus £100 expenses, but I still felt I should have been paid more, especially when I overheard Russ Lindsay, the late Caron Keating's manager and later her husband, describe the job to a researcher as a £1,000-a-show job. Still, beggars can't be choosers and I was in debt, so I needed some income quickly and I wasn't bothered about how I got it. You also have to understand that at the time I couldn't imagine anyone wanting to pay me £1,000 for anything.

Four months after the first auditions and two months after I'd been taken on as the male presenter, the search for a female co-host was still going on and the show had yet to be given a name. On 26 April 1990, I was in the offices of 24 Hour productions for a meeting with Charlie Parsons and Waheed Alli, now Lord Alli.

Waheed is a smoothie of Bangladeshi descent, who hails from a unsalubrious part of north London, and he's very smartly turned out, thoughtful and well spoken. I liked him a lot, but I think what I liked about him was that, despite his upper-crust veneer, he reminded me of the council-estate kids I grew up, the ones who always had a little scam or graft on the go and whose enthusiasm used to brighten up an otherwise dull day of hanging around. Waheed took his work – or rather making money – very seriously, but he understood that really it was all a game and that you had to have fun with it. He talked way over my head, explaining in his relaxed matter-of-fact fashion how the future of television was all about independent production companies and how if you had a commission for a programme and a TV slot, it was tantamount to a licence to print money.

Later on Charlie came in and we started to discuss a title for the show. I knew that getting the right name for this kind of show was crucial in that it couldn't be naff. Looking back now I can see that I was out of my depth with these frighteningly self-assured people, and yet I was confident that I could deliver a good show and make it very different to anything else on TV, even if it was tucked away on Channel 4 at six o'clock on a Friday evening. My confidence was based on eight years of radio success, where I had a reputation for being talked about, perspicacious and edgy, even though I was a huge bag of inadequacies when it came to everything else in my life, and this, of course, made me ideal material as someone who craves fame and recognition. What qualifies a person to be famous and to want everyone to know who they are? It's not ten O levels and a degree in cybernetics, but more a venomous mixture of a big ego and low self-esteem, which more or less sums me up!

Charlie Parsons was throwing some show titles around, and that's how I know exactly the date of the meeting. I had a diary, which was mainly a list of gig dates, but I noted down in it all the suggested names for the show, so I could laugh at them with my mates in the pub later on. These are the names in varying degrees of Channel 4 youth telly naffness, and I hope you enjoy them as much as me and my mates did. *It's Sorted*, *The Friday Brain Drain*, *Opportunity Knockers*, *Open to Offers*, *Before the Watershed*, *A Tough Break*, *Off the Square*, *On the Square* – there were obviously a couple of Freemasons on the team – *Top of the Wall*, *The Postie Crew* – get it *The Post E* crew – *Don't Lose It*, *The Post E Hangout*, *The E cord*, *Totally Cabbaged*, *The Post E Parochial* – northern presenter = parochial, obviously, plus trendy drugs reference again – *On the Roof*, *Warp Factor E*, *The Scam*, *That's Entertainment*, *The Weekend Starts Here*. Very druggie suggestions, and don't look at me, because none of them were mine.

Charlie and I agreed that as the show was going out live at six o'clock on a Friday evening we wanted it to excite the audience and give them a sense that the weekend had arrived. We wanted the kind of buzz I used to get off shows like *Revolver* and *The Tube*, with the anarchic feel of *Tiswas* – minus the wackiness, of course – the sense of fun and inclusiveness that Pete Waterman's *Hitman and Her* exuded and the fantastic cutting-edge bands of Granada TVs Tony Wilson-fronted *So it Goes*. It had to be risqué and cheeky, irreverent and at times downright rude. I even worried that I may be over-qualified to present it! It all still felt slightly unreal to me when I tentatively threw in my suggestion for the show's name.

'What about calling it *The Word*,' I suggested.

At the time I thought *The Word* was a really crap name, but it was also the name of the page I'd been writing for the *Manchester Evening News*, covering up-and-coming bands from Greater Manchester. The Word had been a regular page on a Friday night in the *Evening News* since 1985, when music journalist and author Mick Middles originally penned it. And if the TV show had the same name, my editor at the *Evening News*, Mike Unger, who'd originally come up with the name, might just give me a pay rise if he thought the show was named after a page in his paper. This turned out to be true, too, as my fee rose from £72 a week to £102 – bless him, even though he is a Scouser.

Charlie immediately clicked with the title and said, 'Yes, I think somebody else at Channel 4 mentioned *The Word* as a possible title.' Now I may have been inadequate, lacking in confidence and all the rest, but I wasn't as green as I looked. I knew right off that nobody at Channel 4 had suggested that title, or if they had, they hid their light under a bushel, and to this day have never come forward to lay claim to it, which isn't very TV-like at all. Let's be frank here, it was a shitty enough name for them to have come up with, but at 24 Hour Productions and Channel 4, as you might gather from the show names we rejected, there were a proportion of people who weren't even as imaginative as plain old shit.

The Word was born, and now the pressure was on to find a female to co-present the show with me. Despite auditioning Davina MaCall,

Caron Keating and a whole train of pouting models, Charlie still hadn't found the girl he was looking for.

'Listen, Charlie,' I said, 'there's a girl I've been working with on the radio in Manchester and she's pretty, very funny and likeable, a real character. She'd be brilliant.' In contrast to me, I thought at the time. 'Erm, yes,' Charlie looked dubious, probably thinking, not another twat. 'We can't really have two presenters from Manchester on the show.'

'Wouldn't you have two presenters from London on the same show? So why not Manchester?

'They wouldn't like it.'

'Who? Channel 4?'

'Yes, and don't forget the audience, it might be a bit much for them.'

'Well, you should give her a screen test anyway, she'd be good on something else.'

Charlie never did bite, and for the next three years, every time we auditioned for a new presenter, whether it was Katie Puckrick, Dani Behr or Hufty, I kept pestering Charlie and the editor of the second series, Sebastian Scott, and Paul Ross, who edited series three and four, about this same girl. None of them ever acted on my suggestion, although she was eventually screen-tested for *The Big Breakfast,* and was so funny she had all the camera crew in stitches, which went down like a rat sandwich with Chris Evans, or so I heard from my old KFM colleague Craig Cash. It's a shame that no matter how hard I pushed, nobody at Channel 4 seemed to want to screen test Caroline Ahern. I always felt sure she'd be a big success on TV, despite the fact that she's from Manchester. Let's face it, compared to the visionary genius of our Channel 4 bosses, what did I know about talent spotting? I suggested Caroline Ahern, but they discovered Caitlin Moran.

'Amanda who?' I had no idea who Amanda De Cadenet was. It's not as if I didn't read the tabloids, but as I would endlessly explain to people like Charlie, if you don't live in London and go out in the West End, every night, gossip pages featuring the latest wild child/it girl phenomenon are quite dull and forgettable. I'll guarantee you that 97 per cent of the population would have walked past Tara Palmer-Tomkinson without having a clue who she was before she appeared on *I'm a Celebrity Get Me Out of Here!* These types are the hobby horse of a very small group of people. And the fact that at least one gossip columnist who used to work on a well-known national tabloid got her job by chatting up the editor at a Polo match says it all. Come to think of it, why was the editor of a supposedly socialist paper at a Polo match? As a brief aside here, if you have a first class honours degree in journalism and are currently slogging your guts out at some small free paper in the north of England, aiming for a job on a national, just remember, work hard and believe in yourself – ha ha ha.

In the media, the journey working-class people make when stepping out of their class is rarely acknowledged, as is the fact that they didn't grow up with the same privileges as their colleagues. The fact is, if you don't come from a privileged background, they don't want to hear about it.

'Terry, have you ever been skiing?'

'No, we couldn't afford things like that. I'm one of six kids from a council estate.'

No matter how nicely or matter-of-factly you say this, or how jokingly you brush it aside, you'll always be described as chippy. One guy I worked with once gushed about Pulp and their song 'Common People', and he turned to me and, in all innocence, asked, 'What's woodchip?' It always seemed to me that there was far more sympathy and understanding given to an Australian from an ordinary background or an American brought up on the wrong side of the tracks, any foreigner, in fact, than to a working class British person.

Whenever famous British actors broach the subject of their humble origins, whether it's Richard Burton, Michael Caine, Albert Finney or Sean Connery, they're always jeered, patronized or accused of being loudmouthed, ungrateful and boring by the press. Michael Caine the professional cockney, Richard Burton the Welsh drunkard,

Albert Finney the lazy northerner, Sean Connery the money-grabbing tax exile. These interesting, artistic role models for the aspiring working classes seemed to consistently have the door of understanding slammed in their faces. Yet if you think about it, what were the odds of an acne-scarred kid from a family of twelve children, born in a tiny mining town, like Richard Burton was, becoming the acting legend he became? All his brothers worked down the pit, his mother died when he was two and yet one day he would spend over a million dollars buying his wife – the world's number one Hollywood idol, Elizabeth Taylor – a diamond.

And how about a former milkman, raised in a Scottish tenement like Sean Connery, becoming the worldwide household name that he is? Or a huge Hollywood superstar like Michael Caine making his journey from Elephant and Castle to Beverly Hills. It's as if the media begrudge that slog from disadvantaged background to hero, or perhaps they're just too wrapped up in trivia to see it.

All I knew about Amanda De Cadenet at that time was what Matthew Bowes, Charlie's first appointment at 24 Hour Productions, had told me.

'She's a wild child. She's really posh and is going out with John Taylor from Duran Duran, and she used to go out with that Nathan bloke from teeny bop band Brother Beyond when she was only fifteen. She used to get up on the tables and take her clothes off in nightclubs with her mate Emma Ridley.'

I'd already heard four things that made me recoil in horror: posh, Duran Duran, Brother Beyond and Emma Ridley. What were these people trying to do to what I felt was my show?

In retrospect, the only surprise choice was me, of course. Let's face it there are two types of presenter loved by TV bosses: posh people pretending to be smart working class, like Johnny Vaughan, Jeremy Clarkson, Jimmy Carr, etc., or posh people acting dim, like Tara PT, Amanda and many, many more.

Amanda was auditioned at Channel 4's studios on Charlotte Street, and I had to do a two-header with her during her audition, where she was very coy and flirty, and I must admit I did find her good fun. She gave the air that she was doing the whole world a favour by just turning up, which I thought made her ideal as a co-presenter on this particular show. She genuinely thought she was a huge star, and the more starry she acted, the more those posh kids who worked on the show ran around for her. In many ways she was my antithesis: there was no way I was ever going to take part in that West End circus, mugging for cameras and pretending I was a star. I was the presenter of a youth show, which I was determined should be undermining, raw and sensitive to it's audience, not something that appealed to people who pretended to be left wing and liberal, but who in real life represented totally fascist, right-wing, narcissistic aspirations. I wasn't going to start thinking I was any better than anyone else, and certainly not our audience. For me, the great thing about having Amanda on board was that she acted as a permanent reminder of how not to behave.

She was very regal in the way she swanned around, often accompanied by Sean Borg – now a big PR type in London – who was both Amanda's friend and, if he'll forgive me for saying it, her lady-in-waiting. When Amanda moved, her small entourage moved with her, carrying her bags and the little plastic bottle of Evian she always had on her person, but never seemed to drink. Amanda was permanently eating crunchy bars and talking on her mobile, which to my mind made her at least as interesting as 75 per cent of the young female presenters around at that time. The reason Charlie signed her up immediately however, was because she was great tabloid fodder – just seventeen years of age, posh, pushy, ambitious, diva like, blonde and with big boobs.

The fact that Charlie had employed Amanda and refused to screen test Caroline Ahern still niggled, though, and once, when I'd had a horrendous vision of what working with Amanda might be like, I blurted out to Charlie, 'You just think she'll be tabloid fodder and good wanking material for all those teenage boys who might watch.'

The gleam in Charlie's eye told me I'd banged the bishop right on the head.

The man responsible for commissioning *The Word* was Stephen Garrett, a tall, ultra-sensitive – about himself, I mean – ex-public schoolboy who was trust-funded up to his eyeballs. The same eyeballs which, in conversation, flicked from the floor to the window to the wall to the ceiling, and only occasionally met my own for the merest instant before flitting off elsewhere. It made him seem a bit shifty, but at the time I put it down to shyness, though I'll admit that my opinion of him lowered to that of a snake's belly over the following years. However, I'll give him credit for having the guts to go ahead with a show like *The Word*, very few people in his job now would have the balls to do it. Mind you, as he'd also commissioned *Club X*, and hadn't lost his job over that televisual abortion, he was presumably bulletproof.

Stephen was mildly amusing, in a Radio 4 sort of way, and quite likeable, too – very serious and superior and he spoke slowly and softly in self-consciously measured tones, a bit like Margaret Thatcher. I couldn't help thinking that the last time he'd probably done anything spontaneous was when he had a dump in his nappy as a baby. One of the first things I noticed about him was how he'd almost physically wince if you disagreed with him during a conversation. Now to me, a meeting is basically an honest exchange of views – you put forward your thoughts and make a case to back up your opinions, then I'll do the same. There's no need to get your knickers in a twist, especially if you're the boss, as you have the final say.

I remember feeling both flattered and insulted when Stephen said that I reminded him of Tony Wilson. I have that odd love-hate thing Mancunians have with Wilson. I guess we always suspected him of being a bit Oxbridge and pretentious – a walking talking agenda – but he could cause trouble and wind people up just for fun, which is always an admirable trait. I hotly denied that I was like Wilson, perhaps a little too fiercely, and posh bosses like Stephen don't like you to be overly passionate. It might frighten the horses and set the servants to murmuring. I can't remember exactly what we talked about, with regard to the show, but I remember coming away from the meeting thinking, well, it won't be that sort of show, mate, so you'd better get used to it. It made me wonder what he thought of me, and it didn't take long before I found out.

chapter four

'Terry Christian. Has this arsehole got sinus trouble? He is tacky, pathetic, has no interviewing style and insults his guests. When are you going to take him off?'
Channel 4 duty log

'You won't see those bags again until San Francisco, mate.'

The baggage handlers reply when I asked about the whereabouts of my luggage from my Manchester to Heathrow flight was a gut-wrenching introduction to the rock-star lifestyle of a TV presenter. It was 2 May 1990 and reality was beginning to bite. At last I was starting my new job working as a TV star – OK, that's enough. I had an interview with American comedian and Oscar-winning actor Robin Williams in his hometown the following day, but all I could think was, would the Pan Am jet I was about to board eventually land after an eleven-hour flight.

I'd never been on a flight that had lasted longer than four hours. In fact, I didn't step onto a plane until I was twenty-four, and prior to that it had never occurred to me that I might not like it, until, thanks to a freebie educational visit to Rhodes courtesy of Portland Holidays, I found myself seated on what looked and felt like a charabanc with wings. I spent the next four hours nervously listening to the changes in engine noise as the Dan Air 737 bumped and lurched its way through turbulence and headwinds. For me, the forthcoming trip to San Francisco was going to be an eleven-hour white-knuckle ride.

The whole experience had been rather turbulent so far anyway. I'd been given a contract at the end of February 1990, but kept the job a secret from all but my very closest friends and family until I actually started working. Far from feeling elated, I felt slightly embarrassed by the whole thing. I sat out this strange period of inactivity being paid £250 a week for doing nothing much. The reality of my job only struck home when I was told I'd better get a full passport as I was going to to the USA, so I had to dash over to Liverpool to sort that out, and then go in to see a doctor for a full medical at Granada TV. This was an experience akin to joining the Army. It was quite surreal and the first medical I'd had since school. The doctor – a consultant no less – efficiently checked my bits and bobs. It's odd how, when a doctor puts a stethoscope to your chest you look down and watch, and when he tests your reflexes you stare intently as he taps on your knee, but the minute he cups your testicles in his hand and asks you to cough, you look at the wall or out the window, when by rights you should be watching him like a hawk.

I hung around Heathrow airport waiting to meet up with my new boss and employer Charlie Parsons. I'd met Charlie a total of four times: once at Cliveden, again at the final auditions at Channel 4 plus a lunch in London when we'd discussed a title for the show, and the last time, when he'd ventured up to Manchester to sit in on my late-night radio show on KFM. I wonder how many people out there have presented a radio show with their prospective employer sitting in the studio, observing the proceedings while the show's guests – that night they were A Certain Ratio, who'd just signed to A&M, and World of Twist, who'd just signed to Circa Records – are casually skinning up joints. Also on my show was my regular co-host Jon Ronson, a climber who now makes these fascinatingly strange TV shows about the weirder side of life. I think you're great, jon, and yes, Louis Theroux did sort of rip you off, but in a better way. I'm ashamed to say that Jon and I joined in with the spirit of things, though we never inhaled, though I suspect that Charlie thought that Jon and I never *ex*haled.

Charlie finally turned up to meet me at Heathrow airport, while I fiddled about with a Game Boy I'd been sent by some PR company.

I was amazed by the little gadget, and as I was so terrified of flying I needed something to take my mind off what seemed an unimaginably long flight for only a two-day visit. The sheer hedonism of it!

Charlie looked at the Game Boy. 'Such a waste of fucking time,' he uttered contemptuously. It was nearing boarding time as we made a quick trip to the airport bookshop. Still slightly embarrassed at being caught playing a Game Boy by my new boss, I scanned the shelves and picked out a 700-page book by R. F. Foster called *Modern Ireland 1600–1972*, so that he'd hopefully realize that beneath my scallyish Game Boy-playing, skunk-smoking exterior, there beat the heart of a bookish intellectual. I noticed him look at it briefly and caught a smile crossing his lips; I suspect he was thinking, 'Daft twat, he'll never read that.'

We boarded the Pan Am flight to San Francisco and took our pre-booked seats. Charlie was rather pleased with himself as he'd decided *The Word*'s budget would be spent not on flying presenters first class and staying in five-star hotels, but on the screen, where the public could see it.

Charlie had got his personal assistant to pre-book seats next to the emergency exit, over the wings. His demeanour belied the fact that he thought this was a piece of strategic planning on a par with Napoleon's battle of Austerlitz, as it meant we had loads of leg room – not that we needed it as neither of us is taller than 5 foot 7. Unfortunately, I knew that the emergency exit is the weakest part of an aeroplane's structure, and I was equally horrified to find that we were in the non-smoking section of the aircraft. To make matters worse, the flight was completely full and there weren't any spare seats at the back, and I felt too self-conscious and nervous to take my seat belt off and wander to the back of the plane to ask if someone in smoking would mind swapping seats for ten minutes, so I could have a fag.

Charlie soon fell asleep, and I tried to take my mind off the fact that I was 33,000 feet up in the air by drinking the equivalent of a bottle of whiskey and a bottle of vodka while watching the two in-flight films, *Driving Miss Daisy* and *Steel Magnolias*, which played on a loop for the entire flight. With fear tearing at the corners of my adrenalin-crazed drunken mind, I couldn't follow the insubstantial plots of either movie. I'd had about an hour's sleep the night before worrying about the flight and there is no way even today, now that I'm more or less over my fear of flying, I could ever sleep on an aeroplane. All the time we were in the air, I kept recalling my younger brother Kevin's words of reassurance: 'What's to be scared of? So you crash and die, what difference does it make? A few less crappy meals, a few less years of drinking and watching the telly and shagging. What's so special about your life?'

Funnily enough, despite it's philosophical, almost existential slant on the human condition, it didn't give me a shred of comfort.

I'll tell you what I do love about flying, though. When the wheels touch the floor again, it feels fantastic!

I was in the US of A; it was like a dream to me. I'd never pictured going there in my life. Nobody in my whole family, including aunts, uncles and cousins, had ever been there, which for a huge extended Irish family is tantamount to treason, and now here I was, on a continent that looks like one big movie set.

The bag I'd checked in some sixteen hours earlier at Manchester Airport turned up on the conveyor belt. It was a cheap £9.99 nylon affair of the type kids use to carry their PE kits to school, and inside I had three shirts, two of which cost me £15 each from the Arndale Centre in Manchester. The other was a black Levi's denim second from a warehouse jeans shop called Nixon's in Derby, and it was to be worn for several big-name interviews and a photo shoot for *Vogue*. In other words, I'd brought my best clothes. Welcome to San Francisco

I got the first stamp in my passport, which I'd collected only a week earlier, while trying not to breathe a freshly forming hangover on to the American customs official. It was the very first ten-year passport I'd owned in my life and I was twenty-eight years old. This show was about to turn me into a celebrity, and I didn't care if it was A, B, C or Z list.

San Francisco was fantastic. We arrived at around two in the afternoon, Pacific time, which meant I'd slept for one hour in the last forty. As Charlie and I travelled by taxi, gazing out at the May California sunshine I wanted to pinch myself. Was this real? Was it really me here in the USA, getting ready to interview Robin Williams and Tim Robbins for a forthcoming national TV show. Charlie, who'd travelled to the States several times but had never visited San Francisco, was excited, too, and chatted about how he'd love to move to San Francisco and work as a taxi driver behind the wheel of a big Cadillac. Then, with a resigned sigh he said, 'Perhaps in another life.'

It's strange that when you travel to America for the first time you feel as if you know it. It's the movies, a familiar dream, a déja vu, and it lifts your spirits because all the fantasies you had as you grew up are somehow tied up with it – the Disney films with their all-American families and picket fences, the Westerns with their big-sky country, the gangster films with their speakeasies and clip joints. I'll never forget the rush I had. I felt, despite my tired, semi-inebriated state and jetlag, that this was the greatest day of my life to date, and I sat back in the taxi, relieved to be off the aeroplane and savouring the feeling. As Charlie spoke of where he'd live and what he'd do in another life, I thought I'd already stepped into one. Did Terry Christian belong here? All the slights both real and imagined, all the bitterness and venom I felt inside, seemed suddenly to evaporate. I felt full of vigour, as if a huge weight had been lifted from me. America, the land of the free – apart from its foreign policy, of course. I felt I should have gone and lived there when I was younger – ah well, as Charlie would say, perhaps in another life. After a thirty-minute journey, which felt like floating on a cloud to me, we pulled up outside the five-star Portman Hotel in San Francisco.

'Do you have reservations?'

'Yes, but we're staying here anyway.'

I thought it was quite funny, but it didn't even raise a smile from the desk clerk and it got an unamused tut from Charlie.

Still expecting the sharpness of reality to prick my fantasy bubble, I took the glass lift up to my room. The bed alone was the size of most of the dingy flats I'd rented, and the bathroom was as big as the council house I'd been brought up in. There were gold taps and even a small colour TV in case you wanted to watch it from the swimming pool-sized bath or the shower that was encased in glass, like a huge crystal monolith.

Showered and changed, Charlie and I were due to meet up with Jo Owen, *The Word's* New York-based celebrity booker, who was to arrange all our big celebrity interviews.

My first impression of Jo was that he was one of the flakiest, poshest and downright strangest people I'd met in my life. My instant reaction was to think, blimey, what planet do you live on? Interestingly enough, as I got to know her over the years – bearing in mind that I'm not always the easiest person to get along with – I came to realize what a truly lovely person she is, even though she's slightly barking. There are no corners to Jo; she isn't two-faced and is always positive, and she isn't averse to putting her foot down when producers or directors try to ride roughshod over her, which I'm afraid I did for the first few months.

Jo had perhaps the most difficult job on *The Word* team. Based in New York, she had to arrange all the big-name Hollywood interviews. She understood the film business and Hollywood agents and PR people perfectly. She knew how ultra-sensitive they were about their clients and was able to navigate a tricky maze of prickly egos with vigour and a large dollop of charm. I feel bad now that I allowed my inverted snobbery to give me a shallow first impression of her; it was undeserved and mean-spirited. I didn't dislike her, I just sort of dismissed her as just another posh bird divorced from reality, who'd landed herself a cushy number swanning around the glamorous people in the States because her family were rich.

We met up in the bar and wandered around San Francisco's Bay Area in the sunshine, drinking in various bars, stopping for something to eat and pointing at seals. We did this for three or four hours until my face was burned bright red on one side. Someone had told me that San Francisco is quite chilly in May, which it was, but the sun was still fierce.

Eventually we returned to our hotel with plans to sleep for a couple of hours and then go out and paint the town red. Five hours later, Charlie rang my room. He was tired, so he wasn't going to bother going out, and though I was excited about being in the States, the flight and alcohol had wiped me out, too, so I wasn't exactly unhappy about the turn of events.

Later on I woke up and wandered down to the bar at some ungodly hour of the morning, only to spot Charlie returning to the hotel. I'll say no more, except that it was Charlie's first time in San Francisco, and as a gay man I'm certain the city held more excitement for him than for a pair of dull heterosexuals like Jo and myself.

The next day I woke up early and went down to breakfast. I was guided by a tuxedo-wearing waiter called Robert to a table so huge it looked as if it had been laid for King Arthur and his knights.

'And what would sir like?' Robert asked.

'Er, egg and bacon.'

'And how would you like your eggs: fried, boiled, poached, raw, scrambled, benedict?' That one must be for travelling Catholics.

'Er, fried.'

'And would you like them sunny side up, sunny side down, over easy, flambe'd, casseroled, speadeagled and poked roughly from behind, à la broiled pomme de terre with a cherry on top?'

'Er, fried with the yolk on top,'

'So that's sunny side up.'

'And could I have some toast?'

After being offered ciabatta, rye, Bavarian black bread, soda bread, bagels, white, brown, wholemeal and Mothers fuckin' Pride, I decided not to ask for sausages or tomatoes, as I hoped at some point to eventually leave the hotel. In the end I get white bread, and when my bacon and egg arrives it's covered in cocktail sticks with bits of paper on and purple leaves that taste like ear wax, as well as an Amazonian forest's worth of lettuce and various pickles and chips – OK, fries if you want to be arsey. I briefly flirt with the idea of asking the waiter to mince over and grab us a bottle of HP sauce, but

I don't hold out much hope of success. Shit I need a cup of coffee. Here we go, I think, time for an A–Z of the world's coffee-producing countries and their different roasts, but no I'm merely offered black or with milk or cream. Call that choice?

When I've finished my breakfast he brings me the bill, which he calls a cheque, for twenty dollars. I haven't got any dollars on me, so I sign the room number on the bottom and escape towards the lobby. Suddenly a high-pitched voice shouts after me, 'Yoohoo, the gratuity is fifteen per cent you only put ten on.' I can't believe the cheeky bastard's calling me back because he hasn't had 15 per cent tip. Welcome to the USA.

After meeting up with Charlie and Jo, we ride the trolley cars up the steep streets of San Francisco, tour the university campus and go around the famous hippy district Haight Ashbury, the birthplace of flower power, enjoying the love-generation ambience, which consists mainly of stalls selling cheap jewellery, second-hand jeans and atrocious T-shirts made from tie-dyed cheesecloth and other offensive fabrics. Afterwards we loll around in Golden Gate park to see the bridge. The following day is my first-ever piece of filming for TV, and I'm due to interview Robin Williams about a movie called *Cadillac Man*, which we have to attend a screening of that night.

Cadillac Man is a comedy in which Robin Williams plays a car salesman, and it is, as we say in Manchester, about as funny as woodworm in a cripple's crutch. Fighting back hysterical laughter at how bad it was, I noticed the audience of TV people and journalists chuckling at the supposed funny moments, a mirthless ripple crossing their faces, manifesting obsequiousness rather than amusement – the laugh of the office creep. It was all part and parcel, I was to discover, of the Hollywood junket. Don't let the PR people know you think the product stinks or they won't invite you back, and let's face it, it's a right cushy number being one of the chosen few.

Robin Williams' co-star in the film was the up-and-coming Hollywood actor Tim Robbins, who I'd only seen in the awful Terry Jones pythonesque historical knockabout *Eric the Viking*. He seemed like a really genuine, nice guy, if a little on the earnest side, and Jo had pointed out to me that he was seen very much as an up-and-coming star, thanks to a new movie he'd just completed about a Vietnam veteran suffering from post-traumatic stress, called *Jacob's Ladder*. Robbins told me he preferred New York to LA and found much of the movie business quite shallow and dorkish, but that was about as interesting as he got unfortunately.

Robin Williams had always been a favourite of mine, especially as my friends and I had grown up watching him on the sometimes hilarious *Mork & Mindy*. He didn't disappoint. Our access on *The Word* to big Hollywood names was obtained entirely through false pretences. We pretended to be really interested in their latest movie, but really we wanted to find out about their personal lives and opinions. Were they still going out with Ivana Trump on the quiet? Did they still use the services of Heidi Fleiss and her call girls? And what's the most excessive Hollywood party they'd ever attended? To do this we'd pretend to be part of the junket covering the new movie. All junket interviews take place in the same room, with two cameras set up and a plastic plant perched behind the star. You then join a queue of other journalists outside and wait your turn to interview the star, just like Hugh Grant and Julia Roberts in *Notting Hill*.

Like the setting, the questions are always the same:

1. Are there any similarities between your character, the misanthropic, flesh-eating, paedophile necrophiliac psychopath and the real Robin Williams/Arnold Schwarzenegger /Tom Hanks.
2. What's the basic plot of the film – yawn.
3. What appealed to you about the role (apart from sixty million dollars and a share of the gross).

Then, having got these three questions out of the way, causing the film PR's expression to glaze over, you have five or ten minutes to ask the questions you really want to ask and are likely to actually broadcast.

Over the years of interviewing Hollywood stars, I became adept at relaxing their PRs with a couple of dull questions early on and a sickeningly gushing schmooze beforehand, so that I could normally blag a decent fifteen to twenty minutes with the star instead of the allotted five or ten. But Robin Williams was something else. Wearing my best, black Levi's denim shirt, I kicked off the interview. After the usual questions, I asked him about his wealthy up-bringing in San Francisco, and whether he'd ever been a hippy and then whether there had ever been a generation as un-colour coordinated as his. This last question set him off on a whole routine where he played a camp hippy called Rainbow Light and was about to do a makeover on me.

'Well, first of all we'll have to do something about that Black & Decker haircut, and then we'll have to get you out of that San Quentin prison shirt.'

That was it, once he started his improvised routine, I dissolved into uncontrollable fits of giggles, as did the cameramen. He was giving a performance and I never even got a chance to ask another question. Charlie wasn't so pleased when I, exhilarated at having met Robin Williams up close and personal, explained how the interview had gone.

'Yes, but we have to edit it, Terry. You just don't understand television.'

It was funny, but could they edit it? I started to have nightmares in which I saw myself as a grinning, inane nervous wreck, laughing at any old shite Robin Williams said and then using the lame 'you had to be there' excuse. A week later I watched it again, and guess what? I was right, even down to the excuse!

Charlie had this effect on just about everyone who worked for him. He has a good instinct for television, a vision of what he likes and the guts to try something new – as long as he understands it, which at times could be limiting. But as many a director and producer left with a crushed ego would comment later: whenever Charlie wanted something doing it would always be delegated in a manner that left them thinking he was saying, 'I'd do it myself, but I haven't got the time.' Which isn't exactly confidence-boosting.

Charlie obviously liked me and saw something in me, but although he didn't set out to, he couldn't help chipping away at what little confidence I had. Although I wouldn't say I'm soft, I am fairly sensitive.

A few weeks after returning to London, Amanda De Cadenet and I met up with a Channel 4 press man at their studios on Charlotte Street. He was in his late twenties, campish, posh and another one whose eyes, which mainly gazed at Amanda's cleavage, never seemed to look directly at you. I thought he was an oleaginous creep as, urged on by his liquid lunch, he drooled over Amanda, asking about all her rich and famous London chums. I suppose I felt a bit left out.

For one and a half hours Amanda and I helped this semi-inebriated man compile our biographies. I went through my career history, the Sony Awards I'd won, the bands I'd managed, Radio 1, Radio 4 and Piccadilly Radio – a life in the trenches on the frontline of rock and roll etc. Then he asked me if I'd ever done anything outside the media as a job. Other than summer jobs at Esso and Butlins, I hadn't really. I'd sold doughnuts on the beach in Cavalaire in the South of France and two years earlier, during a two-month period of unemployment, and with a big gas bill to pay, my older brother had taken me on for two weeks packing sheets, curtains and duvet covers in a Warehouse in Salford for Dorma. Satisfied with this, he gave Amanda a showbiz kiss and me a limp wet hand, then went off to do some work or phone up his mates, which in that sort of job invariably amounts to the same thing.

What a good job he did. When we saw our official Channel 4 biographies, which in my case went out to the press for the next five years, they went like this:

Amanda De Cadenet, beautiful teenage temptress, racing-car driver father Alain De Cadenet, wild child, John Taylor Duran Duran etc. Me. . . I scanned the half page looking for mention of my Sony Awards, that I'd been the youngest person to win one and the first person to win two, Radio 4, Radio 1, Madchester scene, nightclubs, Newspaper columnist band manager. But no, it was, and I quote, 'Mancunian ex-DJ and former sheet metal worker Terry Christian.'

Sheet metal worker?

He spent ninety minutes taking notes for that! And to think that some people worry that the press make stuff up.

I had a seventeen-year-old posh blonde bimbo with big tits for a co-presenter, and what I reckoned to be a control freak for an editor, a complete nutcase covering the show's press and a commissioning editor whose views on how he saw *The Word* and youth television in general made him seem as balanced as a room full of drama students. So far so good in my TV career.

chapter five

***J.J. Hunseker: 'What does this mean...integrity?' Sydney Falco: 'A pocket full of fire crackers...waiting for a match. You know it's a new wrinkle. To tell you the truth, I never thought I'd make a killing out of some guy's integrity.' J.J. Hunseker: 'I'd hate to take a bite out of you, you're a cookie full of arsenic.' An exchange between Burt Lancaster and Tony Curtis in* Sweet Smell of Success**

I wasn't overly impressed at being told I'd have to move to London. It meant looking for a place to stay and finding money for deposits, all of which I found a complete bind, because I lacked the proverbial pot to urinate in. In fact, I had a total of £94 in my building society and bank account. I thought I'd find somewhere decent for about eighty quid a week. Yes, I know, I was daft. The last time I'd rented a one-bedroom flat was in Derby in 1987. It was an unfurnished flat above a building society with a separate bathroom, kitchen, living room and bedroom, and the rent was twenty-four pounds a week. I knew London was more expensive, so I though I might need at least eighty quid for the same thing down there. What a shock I had. The minimum rent for a one-bedroom flat was around £150 a week.

I'd had visions of myself presenting a national TV show earning £600 a week and wandering around my penthouse New York-style Loft conversion in Chelsea. Hello. Then I visited some estate agents and, to quote Marlon Brando as Colonel Kurtz in *Apocalypse Now*, 'Oh the horror, the horror!'

Of all the miserable experiences that await you as a newcomer in London, the search for a decent place to live is probably the most soul destroying. The landlords and estate agents are without exception the most avaricious, unpleasant, bloodsucking lowlifes ever to wash up on the shore of a capital city. I did the rounds, wandering around flats glassy-eyed as I listened to estate agents taking the art of euphemism and hyperbole to such extravagant heights that it crossed the boundary into sheer invention.

Portered block: Some bloke who can't speak English and is getting paid less than the minimum wage will be slumped over a desk asleep. This added 'security' would of course deter all but the bravest and most single-minded terrorist group.

Pied à terre: French for 'small hovel close to the city'. Believe me, it won't be big enough to swing a kitten, let alone a cat – at least not without dashing its brains out on the wall.

Studio flat: A small cell with four walls, a bed, a chair and a single low-wattage lightbulb. If ever Britain becomes a police state, the studio flats of London will make marvellously efficient interrogation rooms.

Swimming pool and gym: If you fail to kill the kitten by dashing its brains out on the wall, the swimming pool might just be big enough to drown it.

Close to local amenities: Next to a brothel and above a kebab shop.

With thoughts of wading through *Loot* and trudging the streets from N5 to N20 and back to SE18 to no avail, Matthew Bowes took pity on me and kindly allowed me to stay at his flat in Kensington. Matthew was great company and very knowledgeable about all kinds of subjects, but as Charlie Parsons' right-hand man, he was also unappreciated and often bafflingly overlooked when better posts popped up at 24 Hour Productions. Then eventually a mate of mine from Derby, Gavin Claxton, who was presenting a show for BBC World Service and wanted to live in London, found a two-bedroom flat for us to share.

All Gavin's legwork eventually paid off and he found a lovely housing-association/care-in-the-community-type flat in Colindale.

I know, I know, in fact we both know now. Absolutely nothing prepares you for the full horror of living in Colindale and the delights of the Northern Line. Any further north and it might as well be in Stockport.

Our flat was newly furnished and there was a chip shop nearby which charged £1.85 for fish and chips when they cost exactly one pound less up north – the price of living in such an up-market area, I guess. We were also near two of the most horrible pubs I've ever visited in my life, where the people look like they'd stepped out of the bar in *Star Wars* and the first question in the pub quiz was, 'Who are you looking at?' Oh and an absolutely huge supermarket. That was Colindale, now visit and have fun.

Having moved lock, stock and barrel to my new penthouse apartment at the centre of all grooviness, I found I had to fag all the way across to the 24 Hour Productions office in the Isle of Dogs. How can this possibly be fair, I thought. I'm a youngish dude about to be earning 600 quid a show on national TV, living in the capital of Cool Britannia and all I see all day is Mile End, the Isle of Dogs, the insides of various tunnels and the unabashed glamour of Colindale.

Getting the tube and then two buses into the office everyday was driving me mad. In fact, the main topic for whinging at 24 Hour Productions was how far from civilization – i.e., the West End – the offices were and the horrific journeys people undertook every day. Now you'd imagine that a nice young East End lad from Woolwich, Bethnal Green or even a nice girl from Thamesmead or Bermondsey wouldn't mind working in the Isle of Dogs for a TV company, but then, daahling, media folk live in places like Maida Vale, Notting Hill, Ladbroke Grove, Kensington, and Knightsbridge, they aren't council estate riff-raff who are happy to eat cockney delicacies like jellied eels and 'do lunch' at the Dog and Murderer pub in Bow. As the words to that famous nursery rhyme 'Oranges and Lemons' should go: 'When I grow rich, I won't live in Shoreditch.'

At the 24 Hour Productions offices, we had meetings about what to put on the new show. I thought this was going to be our weekly expression of the touching belief that the collective wisdom of idiots would bring forth gold. I imagined that we'd all come up with ideas, Charlie would go through them and we'd discuss what might and might not work on the show. Instead, we briefly mentioned a couple of ideas, Charlie looked down and said: 'Erm, I don't think that will work,' then gathered up all the papers and fucked off into his office.

Matthew Bowes and myself were massive Smiths fans and suggested doing a piece on an eighteen-year-old lad called Elliot Marks, who had organized a huge Smiths convention at Manchester University, which attracted young Smiths devotees from America, Japan and all over the world, and included a coach tour to well-known Smiths sights in Manchester like Rusholme, The Iron Bridge next to Kings Road in Stretford, where Morrissey had lived, and Salford Lads Club. Charlie kept turning us down flat, even though it was a great idea for a piece. Then two weeks later, a tall, blond, rugger-playing twenty-one-year-old researcher and ex-Rugby school kid who's dad had written all those *Confessions of a Window Cleaner* books in the seventies mentions the same idea and Charlie immediately gives him the nod to go ahead with it.

Matthew and I were really angry and deflated. It just didn't make sense to either of us, especially as I wasn't just a huge Smiths fan, I'd grown up in the same area as Morrissey, had the same Irish Catholic background as The Smiths and even had friends who'd gone to school with Morrissey, who we could have spoken to. I also knew Elliot Marks well and had covered the very first convention he'd organized a year earlier for the *Manchester Evening News* and my radio show, and as I'd been brought up within a mile or so of every location his tours visited, I'd easily be able to direct the crew to them. But that all makes far too much sense for the television world.

To be fair, when the piece was aired, it was one of the best we ever did, but it was a great subject matter and very raw, in so far as it dealt with people's enthusiasms, emotions and stories, so it would have been hard to screw up.

I went into the office all day every day and finally came to the conclusion that it was a complete waste of time as my input didn't seem to be wanted, though that didn't stop me sticking my oar in. Eventually my attitude at these meetings is best summed up by the H.L. Mencken quote: 'Every normal man must be tempted at times to spit on his hands, hoist the black flag and begin slitting throats.' Not entirely constructive, to be sure, but I was aware that in radio or TV it's always the presenter who gets it in the neck if a show goes wrong, and that's exactly what happened.

***'Three puffs, two lesbians and that twat Terry Muslim, why should anyone watch this crap...? What time is the repeat on?'* Channel 4 duty line**

I was told I would spend at least two months in Los Angeles before the live series started. The first programme of *The Word* was to be broadcast live at 6 p.m. on Friday, 17 August 1990, and an unaired pilot for the show would be filmed live the week before, on 10 August. By this time I was grateful to be out of the office; as far as I was concerned the show bore all the hallmarks of a disaster waiting to happen.

I was on the flight to LA with Steve Braun, the director for our forthcoming shoot, more than happy to be away from the sixth-form study room that was the 24 Hour Productions office. We were interviewing Arnold Schwarzenegger, Sharon Stone and everyone else involved in the film *Total Recall*. We stayed at the four-star La Maison Hotel, opposite the Beverly Center, the local mall for residents of the hills. It's expensive – not at all the way we'd be doing things in future – there's a Hard Rock Café opposite and then nothing but wide roads and buildings that don't look like offices or apartments. It's so dull it shouldn't even be on the map. Considering its size, I thought, LA is certainly not a city for the ravers.

We know the hotel is posh when we bump into Patsy Kensit coming out of the lift. She's fresh from being in *Lethal Weapon* and Jo Owen knows her, so stops her for a five-minute mutual gush.

Initially I hated the so-called City of Angels because it didn't seem to have a centre or scene, as such, but within three days I loved it for those exact reasons: it's a distillation of the pretences of every in-crowd in every city. Boil the recipe down to its pure essence and it's completely shallow, fake and desperate – to my mind it was London's West End, but viewed without the rose-tinted spectacles. Even the air seemed hung with a kind of sexual damp: the wannabeness, the silicon breasts, the waiters and waitresses who memorized menus as if they were were a film script. I'd amuse myself by stopping them halfway through their speed recall of starters and main courses to ask, what was that seventh one you mentioned?

Outside, I'd walk the boulevards and drive around in the sunshine – once the sun had burned through the cloudy orange smog by eleven in the morning. The palm trees, smell of dry-cleaning fluid, raw petrol, perfume and swimming-pool chlorine all added to the oppressive perfection and end-of-the-road materiality of the place. Every Tudor mansion and Spanish hacienda with their motorway-width drives stank of achievement. Hollywood, Beverly Hills and Malibu all seemd frozen in a timeless self-approval.

At about eleven o'clock in the morning on a balcony in a suite at the Four Seasons Hotel in Beverly Hills, we interviewed Arnold Schwarzenegger. I was dressed in my best orange – yuk – fifteen-quid long-sleeved Fred Perry-style polo shirt and a scruffy pair of jeans. Arnie came in, gave me a vice-like handshake and I proceeded with the interview. Arnold embodies the spirit of Los Angeles. This Austrian muscleman and muscle-head of limited acting ability had used sheer drive and will power to carve out a place as the highest paid actor in the world at that time. Once you're loaded and successful, you are to be admired.

There was a Kitty Kelly-style kiss-and-tell book about Arnie and his early days in Graz in Austria doing the rounds at the time. I hadn't read it, but somehow I kept touching accidentally on contentious stories from the book. We'd been told beforehand that we mustn't mention it or the interview would be pulled. I asked Arnie about his early relationship with the cinema and he told me how he and his friends loved John Wayne and Clint Eastwood and would sneak into the cinema by walking in backwards as the crowd from the previous show was leaving. He smiles a showbusiness smile and obviously thinks this anecdote should have us rolling in the aisles when that kind of tale wouldn't even get you an open-mic spot down your local. I asked him if he'd ever taken steroids and his eyes harden and narrow as he talks of his disdain for, and campaigns against drugs. He controls the interview but seems uncomfortable, so I ask him about his large gay following, which he brushes aside. I decide not ask him whether he's ever left his towel on a sunbed to the fury of British holiday-makers. Well he isn't German, after all, he's Austrian. . . just like Hitler. When the interview is over I thank him and hold out my hand, but he merely pats my shoulder with some force and lurches off. He's got the hump, we can tell, and none of us are wondering why.

The next day Jo Owen has his PR on the phone, screaming at her about references to stories from the infamous book that none of us has read or even seen for sale anywhere. Jo patiently explains that she'd understood that there should be no reference to the book, and that not only had we not read it, we hadn't even heard of it. Honestly these Americans really needed to understand our total commitment on *The Word* to zero research. Still if it's full of dodgy stories on the body-building circuit it might be worth a gander on the flight home. After all, the guy may one day run for president. Ridiculous, of course, and about as likely as having an ex-member of the Hitler Youth as Pope.

We escape with a slap on the wrist, or perhaps it should be shoulder. We're twenty minutes into our first Hollywood interview and the whole show, which is still two months off going to air, is on the verge of a Tinseltown blacklisting.

We return to LA a fortnight later with Jo Owen, Steve Braun and Sam Anthony, who is our producer. Sam has been working on Tony Slattery's *Movie Watch* and amuses me with tales of his shoots on BBC2's *Rough Guide*. This time we're on a budget and are staying at a motel apartment complex just behind Grauman's Chinese Theatre, off Hollywood Boulevard. No more posh hotels for us. The area is full of tourists by day and crawling with Hispanic crack gangs by night. The odd single gunshots in the night don't frighten us that much, but when the automatic fire starts it is a bit hairy. Jo is so frightened that Charlie allows her to move out and stay in the four-star Roosevelt Hotel down the road.

The World Cup is on in Italy and I'm concerned about whether or not it's being covered on American Television. I'm relieved to discover, via our Bolivian concierge, that on the TVs in our apartment we have a Mexican channel called KMEX, which will be showing the matches live, although the commentary will be in Spanish.

As far as I'm concerned, the weather's 115 degrees Fahrenheit, the hottest since records started in LA, beautiful girls surround us, even though, with all that silicon, they look like a photo finish in a Zeppelin race, we have forty dollars a day per diems to spend and a nice big apartment each with all mod cons and a swimming pool... and the World Cup's on and England, Scotland and the Republic of Ireland are all in it. In my head, I'm on my holidays.

I look down the fixture list pullout I've brought with me from the *Daily Mirror* and work out that with the time differences the 4 p.m. kick-offs in Italy will be on at 8 a.m. in LA and the 8 p.m. kick-offs will be at midday our time. Luckily I notice that we won't miss any of England or the Republic of Ireland's early-round games, but according to our schedule, should they both go through to the knock-out stages it could get close.

I decide to have some fun with Steve and Sam. Every time they discuss the following day's filming with me, whether it's interviewing Liam Neeson, Mimi Rogers, Will Smith or whoever, I look really obstinate and aggressive and say: 'There's no way I'm leaving here at 8.30 a.m. in the morning to talk to that lemon Emilio Estevez. It's Bulgaria versus Morocco, I'm not missing that!' At the time they didn't know me, and I suppose I can seem a bit in your face and abrasive, so they thought I was being serious. As a wind-up it had worked really well, until at about 4 a.m. my phone rang. Half asleep

I said hello into the speaker, only to find it was Charlie Parsons, the fuehrer, on the other end.

'Terry, what's all this nonsense about you not going on the shoot tomorrow because you want to watch Cameroon versus Argentina.'

'Charlie, I'm winding them up. What are you ringing me at this time for; they knew I was winding them up, didn't they?

Apparently they hadn't.

The situation worsened the day England had to play Belgium, as a place in the World Cup quarterfinal beckoned for the winner. We had to drive to Irvine Beach to interview Sean Stussy the Surf-wear clothing magnate. The interview was scheduled for 1.30 p.m. and Irvine was a forty-five-minute drive away, so we needed to leave by twelve to give us time to set up when we arrived. The England match kicked off at 11 a.m. LA time, so at least I'd get to see most of it.

There was ten minutes of the match left and the score was still 0–0 when they started banging on my door. 'Terry, come on we've got to go.'

'Fuck off, I'm just getting dressed. I'll be two minutes.'

It's Waddle and Barnes and Gascoigne and Pearce and Platt and Beardsley and Lineker. I hang on, blocking off the door to my room, flushing the loo and turning on the taps as if I really am getting ready, all the while cursing under my breath, Who gives a toss about some ropey T-shirt and shorts seller – that's not interesting telly, it's bollocks. It's full time and the score's 0–0, so it's going to extra time. Right, I'll have to go.

I scowled my way into the van with Rupert and Dave, our American crew, and desperately started to search the dial for match commentary. I find one medium-wave station that's carrying live commentary, but it's in Spanish. I followed the game through an aural maze of miss-pronunciation that would put Trevor Brooking to shame. Barnes was pronounced BarnNEZ, Waddle was simply Wod and the effervescent Gazza was Gas-KOG-NEY. I listened attentively as we drove, while the other four were driven crazy by the poor reception blasting out of the speakers but didn't dare suggest I turn it off.

When we stopped for lunch, extra time was entering injury time and I decide to sit in the van alone to listen to the dying embers of the game and the subsequent penalty shoot-out.

Suddenly Sam Anthony came running up. 'Terry, it's on in the diner, quick.'

Sure enough, there are a dozen TV screens scattered around the diner showing England versus Belgium, and apart from the odd cursory glance from the Hispanic serving staff nobody is paying the blindest bit of notice. I look up at the screen; it's a free kick to England. Gascoigne chips it over the Flemish wall, Platt has broken free of his marker, he volleys. . . 'YES! WHAT A F****ing GOAL.'

I'm jumping around like a lunatic, as are Sam and Steve, and the whole restaurant stares at us like we're on drugs. They could never hope to comprehend.

After this high excitement, Sean Stussy let's us interview him about how he sells T-shirts and shorts for a living. We try to blag some free gear – well, I do: 'This is cool, Sean. Wow, I've never seen anything like this, I could wear this for that shoot at the Mayan tonight, couldn't I, Sam. . . well, if I had some shorts or trousers like those to go with it.'

All the time I'm screaming inside, just say help yourself, you dippy tight-arsed Yank. He gives us one T-shirt each. Big deal. And mine is purple (yuck). As far as I'm concerned, his gear's over-rated and over priced and he's a big-headed, boring fuckwit. As I'd initially thought, the whole piece is never even used on the programme.

We also went to Emilio Estevez's pad on Malibu beach. It was surprisingly small considering he was a fuck-off rich Hollywood actor at the time, but then again, it's location, location, location, and this little detached pile directly on the beach would have set him back a couple of million. He'd split acrimoniously from Demi Moore some time back and she was now his next door neighbour, but of course we weren't allowed to mention that.

We've been working in LA during some of the hottest days on record and we've sweated through every item of clothing we brought with us, so we're dressed for comfort rather than style in a collection of spongy, damp vests and shorts. I'm wearing my horrible purple Stussy T-shirt and a pair of nasty cheap patterned Bermuda shorts, circa 1988 England football hooligan, which cost me £8.99 for my holiday in Kos two years earlier, and I notice that I niff a bit.

Emilio is tiny and dressed in a light pastel blue linen suit with no socks and yachting shoes. He greets us and says, referring to our beach wear, 'Oh, I didn't realize it was for that sort of show.'

What sort of show did he think it was, I wonder, surely not *Miami Vice*. My internal dialogue leaves a lot to be desired sometimes.

'It's kind of casual and young,' I explained.

'Hey, are you Australian?'

One thing that's guaranteed to wind me up about our American cousins is the supposition that if you don't have a clipped Hugh Grant/Roger Moore/David Niven accent, you must be Australian. I bite my lip, though – well, it doesn't do to confront a pint-sized Hollywood star with his misconceptions. I mean, how would poor Emilio feel if I said, 'What's the population of Australia? Say ten or eleven million? What's the population of Great Britain? Sixty million? So if somebody speaks fluent English with an accent that isn't American, then aren't they more likely to be British than Australian? I suggest that instead of spending your dates at the movies wearing bad eighties linen suits, watching crap like *Crocodile Dundee*, you take in some Ken Loach or Mike Leigh films.'

Alas, what I said instead was, 'Oh, it's very similar.' You fucking ignorant, pampered rich kid, film star daddy midget with your shitty eighties Brat Pack suit.

'You really sound Australian – that's cool.'

It was probably the shorts I was wearing rather than the accent.

'Anyway, what happened with you and that Demi Moore? Did she dump you or did you dump her?'

Emilio coughs and splutters, then raises his eyes and looks askance at his PR lady, who frowns at Jo Owen, who glares at me and Steve Braun. The American film crew stifle giggles. No American TV interviewer would ask an A-list Hollywood actor such a question and, as we were to find out in time, with good reason.

I back-track, talking about his new *Young Guns* film. Emilio is back in his role as the Western psychotic gunslinger and regulator Billy the Kid, and I'm back in junket-interviewing mode.

'Are there any similarities between you, the real Emilio Estevez, and your part as the bushwhacking, back-shooting, semi-literate, pseudo-intellectual, psychopathic, murdering young cowboy Billy the Kid?'

Emilio has done all his research on William Bonney aka Billy the Kid. His bookshelves are full of biographies of the famous regulator, and as a fan of Westerns myself, I find this fascinating and am impressed. But we're under pressure from Charlie Parsons to deliver something different, not staid or dull and certainly not informative.

As Rupert, the cameraman, changes his film, still trying to fight back the giggles – who says Yanks have no sense of irony – Steve Braun points at the mounds of white powder scattered all over the carpets and rugs and says, 'Hey, Emilio, it looks like you had a good party here last night.'

Emilio smiles and informs us that it's flea powder for his dogs.

I scratch my thigh through the faded Bermudas. A two-million-dollar pad on Malibu beach and it's got fleas, maybe Colindale isn't so bad after all.

We finish off talking about *Young Guns II*, the Hollywood brat pack, his famous father Martin Sheen and his first big movie break in British film director Alex Cox's cult classic *Repo Man*.

Steve's worrying that it's not different enough.

'Hey, Emilio, is it OK if we film the contents of your fridge?'

Emilio says no, it's just a fridge, dismissing the suggestion in a friendly manner, but Steve's pushy and insistent. Emilio, who's quite shy and eager to please, finally relents. There's hardly anything in it other than a few bottles of beer, but to Steve it's a triumph of British Television; he's filmed five bottles of beer in an otherwise empty fridge the size of a barn and it's Emilio Estevez's fridge.

I'm cringing. Emilio Estevez, in contrast to some of his brat-pack peers, is fairly down to earth, friendly and helpful. But we've crashed his vibes and Jo Owen is going to get grief from his PR about the intrusive nature of our filming and line of questioning.

Afterwards, as we head towards Liam Neeson's agency and then on to Jeff Goldblum's house, Jo starts having a go at Steve.

We all bully her, saying, 'You're working for us, not for those Hollywood ponces.'

We didn't appreciate the amount of effort and brown-nosing she'd put in to get us inside the homes of Hollywood's biggest up-and-coming stars. She rightly told us we didn't have a clue. What a cheek, I thought. Here she was, a daughter of the British upper middle classes, brought up with servants, personal tutors and colonial boarding schools in Malaysia, telling *us* we didn't have a clue how the business worked. Eventually, of course, we realized just how right she was, though unfortunately not before we'd sniped about her to Charlie, so not only was she getting grief off her hard-won Hollywood film contacts, she was also getting grief off her boss in London. All because some jealous producer, frustrated director and naive jumped-up inverted snob decided it would be great to film the meagre contents of a brat-pack actor's fridge and mock his broken relationship.

Television. It's all about teamwork and laying the blame at someone else's door.

Orders come through from London to take me shopping, so Steve and Jo accompany me to the Beverly centre. Give or take the odd scally lurking about, it doesn't look that different to Manchester's Arndale centre, just smaller and pricier. After wandering around for two hours, turning my nose up at various pastel-coloured linen suits – so this was where Emilio got his *Miami Vice* threads – I buy two Quicksilver surfer-type T-shirts and a dark green/turquoise shirt. Now at least I had something to wear for tonight's shoot.

Limousines are pulling up outside the red roped-off entrance to down-town LA's Mayan Theatre, which is now a night club. Inside it's huge and spectacular, decorated like the 1920s Hollywood movie set of an ancient Mayan temple. The men who get out of their limousines are bronzed, square-jawed, tall and dressed in black tie, the women have toned Californian hard bodies with silicon breasts, like statuesque goddesses in skimpy little black dresses and six-inch stilletoes. I, on the other hand, am wearing a pair of faded Levi's and a luminous orange Quiksilver T-shirt. The cameras are rolling and I commence my piece to camera.

'I'm outside the legendary Mayan theatre in downtown Los Angeles, where, for one night only, the nightclub voted the world's number one by American *Billboard* magazine and featured on the cover of *Time* magazine comes to entertain the Beverly Hills glitterati. Yes, tonight the spiritual home of Manchester and Salford's assorted scallies, the Hacienda club, brings it's famous Nude night, with DJs Mike Pickering and Graeme Park, to Los Angeles. But will it be a quid for a pint of Stella and three pound fifty to get in?'

I'm standing there, watching limo after limo pull up outside the club, amazed to see that Manchester is so big in LA. LA's largest rock station, KROQ, plays wall-to-wall Stone Roses, Charlatans, Happy Mondays, Inspiral Carpets, New Order, The Smiths and Morrissey, plus plenty of those Basildon boys Depeche Mode. The Manchester vibe is in the area and suits it. The Stone Roses were due to play a gig at the 3,000-capacity Hollywood High School in ten days' time and tickets had sold out in twenty minutes, while their debut album had already sold 350,000 copies in the States. Unfortunately, though, I'd heard that the band had just cancelled their trip Stateside.

Steve Braun is chatting to two pretty young LA girls, who are dressed a bit more casually and trendily than the rest, and he brings them over to me.

'Hey, Terry, these two girls are massive Stone Rose fans and they've got tickets for their gig here the week after next.' Steve knew that it was cancelled, but I think he wanted the girls to meet a genuine Mancunian – one who knew the Stone Roses and who would tell them bluntly that the gig was cancelled.

The girls are really excited about the Stone Roses coming to town. They love them and think they're the best thing ever. They are the band's biggest fans in LA AND that's why they've come tonight, to meet some like-minded people.

I bathe in my fame by association with the Roses, and revel in their interest, brushing aside their comments that I sound Australian (argh), then I drop the big one on them.

'Oh, the Hollywood High School gig. It's been cancelled.'

Both girls are twenty-two years of age and they burst into tears, absolutely heart-broken.

I'm mortified that two girls are crying because of me.

'Er, I'm sure they'll reschedule, but apparently they hadn't agreed to do it in the first place and it was booked without their knowledge.' Hey, though, the Hacienda night will be great. . . Er, do you want a tissue.'

We see the girls when we're filming in the club and they look as miserable as sin; I've ruined their night. One of them speaks to me. 'Hey, you're from Manchester and you go to cool places like the Hacienda and know the Stone Roses. . .'

'Yeah, that's true,' I say, feeling important.

'We can't believe you're wearing Quiksilver,' they say, both laughing mockingly.

I'm red faced and wonder what's so funny. All around me the black-tie-clad thirtysomething men and their equally overdressed girlfriends/escorts shuffle uncomfortably to Black Box and the New York garage sounds of Kariya, Tawanna Curry and house favourites like Voodoo Ray, Mr Fingers, Pacific State, 'Move Your Body' and all the other tunes that had Madchester's hard-core raving. There are a fair few British scallies in the club, too, all with beautiful young Valley and Orange County girls in tow. They enjoy the buzz but are bemused by the overdressed LA glitterati surrounding them, treating them as if they're just a part of the club's strange decorations. Cinderella-style, as the clock hits midnight, the decorations make for the exits, as if their limousines might turn into pumpkins. We finish filming by vox-popping the punters in the club and chatting to Mike Pickering and Graeme Parke about their world tour with Hacienda. At a quarter to one the bar shuts, but the music stays on until about

2.30 a.m., by which time there's less than 200 people in the club and they're almost all British lads and their Valley-girl molls. This is nightlife LA style, an organic, decaffeinated dance followed by a quick excuse-me before midnight.

We've finished filming and are drinking after hours. Steve has met up with an American friend of his who's a scriptwriter on the hit American TV drama series *Thirtysomething*. He found the evening interesting. I yawn. I could do with a decent night out, in fact, I could do with a big fat spliff.

In all, we spent two weeks in LA. We filmed at the radio station KROQ in Burbank, and their top competition prize on air was an all-expenses-paid trip to see the Stone Roses at Spike Island. I had to laugh, imagining some big-haired Californian girls giving up waterskiing, brunch and the beach for a weekend gig in Widnes that ended up one of the biggest cock-ups ever as they built the stage facing in the wrong direction. We'd also filmed The Inspiral Carpets and their now famous roadie Noel Gallagher at their hotel and gig at the Roxy on Sunset Boulevard, as well as the Hacienda club at the Mayan. They were three very happening, interesting pieces, yet by the time they went to air they'd been rolled up into one gutless, inane four-minute feature about Manchester coming to LA.

As well as this quality stuff, we spent three days filming some shit about how Hollywood films represent America's armed forces, in particular the Navy, who have a special department to advise Hollywood on authenticity, with particular reference to the straight-to-video dog's dinner *Navy Seals*, starring Charlie Sheen, and all those other 'authentic' films where Chuck Norris/Sly Stallone/Dolph Lundgren defeat the German/Russian/Japanese/Chinese/Arab terrorist armies single-handed.

I also spent a whole day with some tart whose boobs made Jordan's breasts look like they should be in a trainer bra, and who dressed in pink and stuck huge billboards of herself and her inflated udders all over Hollywood. They called her Angelina and she was a sad nobody who'd had loads of plastic surgery and was supposedly famous because of one article in a free LA newspaper. Just looking at her made me feel ill. We spent a day making a piece about how she'd become famous for doing nothing, when in fact no one in California knew who the fuck she was and I was ashamed to be seen in the same vicinity as her.

'That was a complete waste of a day,' I moaned, 'and we missed Ireland versus Romania. Angelina my arse, she's some faded old brass who's had an overhaul and a filler article in the pink press.'

Steve and Sam were bickering again. On every shoot I went on there was always a power struggle between the producer and the director about who's the boss. It's a microcosm of the sixth-form public school common room – 'I say, Browne, I'm the prefect here.' – so I ignored them and sat chatting to Rupert, our American cameraman, and Dave our American sound man. We always hired local crews and these were two of the best and so we used them on just about every subsequent LA shoot. Rupert was a double-barrelled W.A.S.P from Boston and a complete anglophile who had a voracious appetite for the latest bands and the British music scene; he was also a big fan of The Clash. He took a peek out of the car window to make sure Steve and Sam were out of sight before lighting up a Tampax-sized joint of Californian sticky bud.

'Are those guys gone?'

'I'm sure they smoke marijuana, Rupert, it's no big deal. Anyway, what makes you think they wouldn't but I would?'

Dave laughed. 'Yesterday Rupert said, "Do you reckon Steve smokes," and I said, "Nah." "How about Sam?" "Maybe." "Terry?" and we both said, "You bet."'

'Well, so as not to disappoint you. . .'

I found I was more relaxed with the Yanks than I was with posh Brits because I was less prejudiced against them, or maybe it was because they were nothing but the direct result of Britain's rapacious imperial past or it could just have been that they always smoked pure grass and were only too pleased to have a fellow conspirator on board. It never failed to amaze me that young Californians would steer clear of coffee, tea, alcoholic spirits, red meat, and live off healthy grilled salads, yet they'd smoke half an ounce of grass in a joint the thickness and length of the Alaskan oil pipeline, breathe the LA air that smelt like pure rocket fuel and risk their lives driving us for two hours on the freeway while stoned out of their minds to film yet another non-story that would never make it to air.

It was a regular part of *The Word*, these non-existent stories put together by some office half-wit, based on a lot of ill-thought-out assumptions and invariably involving a three-day shoot for something that would make three minutes of dull television. I could tell just by looking at the script that it wouldn't work, usually because it was based on a false assumption that some bake in the office 6,000 miles away in London was super intelligent and that all Americans were stupid.

'There's no story here,' I'd say. 'It's a waste of time, we'll never use this.'

'Terry, don't be so negative.'

I'm proud to say that my journalistic instincts were 100 per cent right, though, about what made it to air on *The Word*, and what didn't.

The problem with a lot of the stories thought up in London and faxed over to us in LA was that the mindset of many of the researchers and producers was too narrow and unchallenging. Cocaine-fuelled paranoia was rife in youth TV, and TV in general, which paralysed any genuine communication. This, combined with corporate competition, encouraged producers and researchers to fit into Charlie Parson's off-kilter West End mindset rather than develop something original and find out what was really going on in the day's youth culture. What really used to annoy me was Charlie's fixation with the idea of glamour, which wasn't going to give the show the depth and edge it needed to succeed. Glamour, as Arthur Miller once said, is a youth's form of blindness that lets in light, incoherent colour but nothing defined, and like the rainbow is a once-uplifting vision that moves away the closer you get to it. In my unkind opinion, loads of the ideas they came up with were shallow and shit, just like the toffs who came up with them.

It's time for another annoying production meeting at 24 Hour Productions, and we're discussing ideas for *The Word* again. It really is a pain in the arse. Loads of the ideas are completely wank and the whole system of filtering ideas and discussing them defies logic, while Charlie hides in his office after each meeting. I'm beginning to get rather aggressive with Charlie – this show is a fantastic opportunity to do something genuinely great and worthwhile, but he's acting like a complete plum.

The production crew and researchers are ex-public school London media babes, all except one girl, Marian Buckley, who I knew in Manchester when she was the lifestyle editor of *City Life* magazine. Marian is from a council estate in Peckham and has a first class honours degree from Oxford. She's my ally, along with Matthew Bowes, against what I see as 'the aliens'.

'Ibiza. We should go and film in Ibiza. That's where it's all happening, that's the well of all the current youth culture in Britain.'

The Peckham girl has her hobnailed boot right on the G-spot, but alas it wasn't for the south-east's upper middle classes at the time. It would take them another five or six years to catch on, by which time Ibiza had become too mainstream and lost it's hedonistic fun-filled cheap and cheerfulness.

Charlie looks askance and I chip in, 'She's right, Charlie, there's no point in spending all our time fannying about in America when all those lads from the Hacienda and all the bands and people involved in the rave scene disappear to Ibiza for the summer.'

Charlie took up the challenge: 'So what's the story? The beginning middle and end of it.'

'Well, we've been on three trips to the States, filming fifteen bleedin' hours a day on nothing stories, desperately trying to get them to have a beginning middle and end, and none of them have any relevance or interest to a youth audience. Why not just go and have a look at what's going on in Ibiza, film it in all it's glory, report on it and show people having a good time. That's what I'd like to have seen when I was fifteen or sixteen years old. Something I could aspire to that was actually attainable, not some made-up story that seems glamorous because it's in LA and there are a few palm trees in it.'

If anyone was a genuine mentor to me in the TV world, and understood the way it worked and fought quietly against the tide of mediocrity, it was Matthew Bowes. I remember questioning him at length about Charlie's ridiculous beginning, middle and end nonsense. He said it was an LWT news style which was adopted by Janet Street Porter, then Charlie and everyone on *Network 7* and later the whole of Youth TV. A pre-shoot script was written, let's say about a man who had trained his Alsation dog to attack black people. On the phone the man says he thinks his black neighbours are all dangerous drug dealers, so to stop them coming near the house he's trained his dogs to attack because of the colour of their skin. This then goes into a pre-shoot script, but when you arrive to speak to the man, he says the dog's just a regular guard dog and will attack anyone breaking in, regardless of their skin colour, but that in his neighbourhood there are a few black gangs who are quite dangerous. This, of course, provokes a producer to ask him to use the exact words in the pre-shoot script, 'No, say your black neighbours are all dangerous drug dealers, like you told our producer on the phone.'

'Well, yes, I did say that, but thinking about it since, it's not true.'

The producer and director of the shoot are now screaming, 'But that's what you said.'

The pre-shoot script is the bible. The most famous story of this LWT way of working was when John Birt was in charge of news at LWT and a news crew was sent out to Iran to cover the fall of the Shah. They were convinced at LWT that because of the Americans' interest in oil, they would never allow the Shah to be overthrown. So the LWT crew arrived with their script in Tehran and called the office in London in turmoil: 'The Shah has packed up and is flying out, some Ayatollah bloke is flying in to take over, the streets are full of people and the Americans aren't coming.' Back at LWT they told the crew to stick with the script and that that was the angle they were taking.

Ibiza and other genuine examinations of what was going on in youth culture would come up at every meeting, but it seemed that several of our sloane wannabe producers were in agreement with Charlie's hatred of all things Balearic. For all it's reputation for being cutting edge, 24 Hour Productions and later Planet 24 were always quite staid, posh and out of touch, and the level of journalistic thinking when it came to stories was almost non-existent, which was probably true of all youth TV at the time.

'Oh, it's just a phase – X, Y or Z in London is more important.' In other words, ignore everywhere else as nothing will ever happen there because we'll make sure it won't, by not covering it.

Ibiza Uncovered finally came to Sky One in 1998, which means *The Word* could have been there and done it eight years earlier. Meanwhile, Ibiza had been the continental nightclub Mecca since the seventies and early eighties, while we were bogged down by an overtly camp London view of LA and New York as the home of glamour – and an unattainable glamour at that.

Glamour was apparently the magnet that would draw a young audience, but endless days making our subjects stick to answers on a pre-shoot script, feeding them lines like actors, coupled with the frustration of those production meetings completely disillusioned me about TV. I had nightmares that *The Word* would be as crap as *Network 7* and all those other self-important, dull youth shows. I guess the middle-class media weren't interested in working class culture like the rave scene, which came directly from the jazz funk all-dayer scene, which in turn came from the old northern soul all-nighter scene. None of these would have been familiar to those brought up in the quiet, suburban home counties, and we simply didn't have any researchers or producers from the estates of south-east and east London or Essex working on the team, because they weren't posh enough for TV in those days.

I remember thinking that I'd never met such a large number of people with their heads up each other's arses. It was all very camp and arty, which I found a complete turn-off. The irony is that, had *The Word* gone down the path they wanted, it would probably have got better reviews, but I doubt it would have attracted the same number of viewers. I've always found Britain's media and arts scene pretty uninteresting. The only parallel I can draw is that I'd never dream of paying to see a British film at the cinema. The good ones, which are few and far between, might be worth hiring out on video, but like much of our theatre it draws practically all it's themes and material from a narrow middle-class view of the world. As I once saw it described by an American writer, it was good taste constantly looking over its shoulder.

What did I expect from working on TV? Fun, passion, conviction, imagination, creativity, an opportunity to excite people with the facts. What did I find? Well, to begin with it was like being the new kid at a school with lots of rules and regulations that let you know you weren't the right caste or class to be there in the first place.

I remember being in a bar cum theatre pub, it might have been in Soho, and there were loads of us media lovey types sitting around a huge table when a very attractive extremely posh young woman started up a conversation with me.

'I'm an artist. you know.'

'Oh aye.'

'Yes, I draw and paint, look.' She took a copy of Plutarch's *Lives* out of her satchel – it's a must-read for students studying Ancient History A level. 'I've just been commissioned to do a portrait of Alexander the Great, and in Plutarch there's a description of Alexander's character that I'm using to create the portrait.'

'Very good,' I said, wondering whether she was chatting me up.

'The only problem is, I have to do the portrait of Alexander on his horse and I'm not that good at horses – or at least the type of horse Alexander would have ridden.'

'Oh. . . isn't there a description of Bucephalus in Plutarch?' I ask.

The young lady has her jaw on the floor, gazing at the ashtray in front of her as if it has acquired the gift of speech.

Finally she gathers her thoughts, looks at me in astonishment and says, 'How did you know that?'

'How does anyone know anything?' was my enigmatic reply.

A strange look swept across her blank but beautiful features. I felt like Captain Kirk in one of those old Star Trek episodes, when he asks a computer a question of such profound paradoxical significance that it starts blowing smoke out of it's terminals. Of course, what I should have said was that when I was nine my Uncle Peter bought me a *Look and Learn* book for Christmas, and that I always remembered Bucephalus because when the beloved horse died, Alexander the Great named a city in Asia Minor after it – no sane person could fail to be impressed by that. In fact, at that tender age my ambitions knew no bounds, and I swore that by the time I was thirty I too would conquer the world, build a city and name it after our cat, a golden city of wonder that would be a source of great awe and inspiration to all who visited it. . . called Tiddles. However, like a good journalist that never reveals his sources, I refused to reveal the source of my impressive piece of knowledge.

Despite the deluded, self-confident poshness of that first *Word* production crew, they were far too arty for a show that was aiming for a slightly off-kilter mainstream, however, that artiness did result in some very innovative things visually. *The Word* set, for example, was absolutely fantastic. It was Arthur Lee on Acid; it was bright, exciting, welcoming, fun and suited the show's flash yet cheeky nature.

At the time, the use of a blank screen to project or superimpose video images behind the bands while they were performing was sheer genius. The idea came from a very arty, almost anarchic producer/director called Tim Burke, who was one of the great characters and individualists from that first series. He was obsessed by visuals and it was at the meeting at Cliveden that he first pushed this idea of superimposing video images and using chroma key. It was one of the most important, and for me striking, things about *The Word*, and something the show stuck with – along with the Liquorice Allsorts-style set – for the length of its run. So take a bow, Tim Burke, for doing something truly innovative, and Cath Pater-Lancucki for designing a superb set.

As for music, I was obsessed with it, and more importantly I wanted it to be credible, i.e., not watered down. It could be rock, soul, funk, house, hip hop, reggae, anything as long as it was the real deal. I grew up without a record player in the house until I was eleven, when an auntie of ours gave us an old Dansette, and each new album and single that turned up in our house after that became an object of wonder and delight, from Frank Sinatra and Irish rebel songs to our Tony's Led Zep and Yes albums.

Our music booker and producer was an overweight Leeds lad called Tim Byrne, who was very showbiz in some ways, but also a hard-nosed Yorkshire lad of Irish descent who knew what he wanted and wasn't overly precious – except about record company freebies and protecting his patch. From day one we argued and fought like mad. I got on his nerves because I constantly criticized him and his choice of music and features and also his way of dealing with the record companies. The truth, however, is that he was operating in the real world. When you're booking artists for a television show you've got to play ball with the big record companies. You won't get Whitney Houston on your show without taking a couple of new priority acts from the Arista record label. I saw this as a betrayal of humanity; he saw me as a naive prick.

We first clashed on a shoot with The Charlatans in their home town of Northwich in Cheshire. As soon as we got there he started slagging off Chris Evans, who I'd never met, but had heard several years earlier on Piccadilly Radio when, as an eighteen-year-old, he was very funny and edgy, to the extent that even my hard-to-please cynical mates used to talk about his Saturday-morning show. Chris had been given the push by Piccadilly and had just done his first TV show on satellite TV. Tim Byrne had worked with him and hated him, saying he was the worst TV presenter ever. I didn't believe this could be the case. After all, there was no way Chris Evans would have been bland, and that to me has always been crime number one. I suspect that what Tim didn't like about him was that Chris left him in no doubt about whose show it was, and that Tim's job was just to book the bands and not be in charge. Tim had already tried telling me that there was no need for me to be involved in the shoot, and that my face and my questions wouldn't appear in the piece: 'To be honest with you, Terry, look at *The Chart Show*, people don't want or need presenters on youth shows.'

I happened to be the first journalist ever to give the Charlatans a write-up, on 'The Word' page in the *Manchester Evening News*, and I subsequently played their debut single 'Indian Rope' and the demo tape of their first big hit 'The Only One I Know' on my radio show a good nine months before it was released. So there was no way I wasn't going to be at this, the shoot for their first such piece on television. This was very much my territory. I knew all about the band as well as knowing them on a personal level, which Tim didn't, but Tim kept pushing me to ask all these *Smash Hits!*-style inane questions: 'How did the band get together?' 'What are your influences?' He was doing my head in.

I hate the world he lives in, I know it's called the music business, but with Tim it's all business and not enough music. Tim is quite funny, but he's got his agenda and he sticks to it, although often his arguments are weak. Previously, he'd been a music producer on a Saturday morning kids' show on ITV, booking the likes of Bros, Brother Beyond and various other aural atrocities. To be fair to him, *The Word* was going out at 6 p.m. on a Friday evening, so he obviously felt that musically we needed to tap into some of that same Saturday-morning-kids-TV audience. I, on the other hand, thought we should be more edgy musically, without being elitist.

In the end, we kept up our war of words and got on each other's nerves all the way through the first series, culminating in our biggest barney on a return trip from the States at Christmas. He kept mentioning the name of the forgettable Saturday morning kids show he'd worked on, in terms of it's pioneering music content – they were the first to have Bros on or something like that – when I flipped and said, 'Yes, Tim, in all the years of pop music on TV – forget *Ready Steady Go*, *Thank Your Lucky Stars*, *Top of the Pops*, *The Old Grey*

Whistle Test and *So It Goes*, for the real cutting-edge history of pop, the most important show was the one your boyfriend presented with a sore arse and a glove puppet.'

All these years later, I'm presenting radio shows covering the latest batch of up-and-coming cutting-edge bands from the Northwest, while Tim Byrne counts out the millions he made as manager of Steps – and not a glove puppet in sight.

chapter seven

'A coloured is a very frightened to death Afro-American. A Negro is one that makes it in the system and he wants to be white. A nigger, he's loud and boisterous, wants to be seen. Nobody likes a nigger. A black man has pride. He wants to build, he wants to make his race mean something. Wants to have a culture and art forms. And he's not prejudiced. I am a black American man. Now you go ahead and print it.'
James Brown, the Godfather of Soul

I'm beginning to fall in love with the USA. Already our next trip to the States is being planned. We'll spend almost three weeks in Los Angeles, where we'll interview Jeff Goldblum, Christian Slater, Sharon Stone, Will Smith, Patrick Swayze, Whoopi Goldberg, Demi Moore, Steve Martin and a whole raft of stars. We're also going to catch up with the Happy Mondays, who are in LA recording their *Pills 'n' Thrills and Bellyaches* album and – the biggest buzz for me – we're going to Aiken, South Carolina, to interview the Godfather of Soul himself, in prison, Mr James Brown.

It's Tim Burke, the director responsible for using the chroma key special effects on the set who has sorted everything out. At first Charlie wasn't sure who James Brown was – typical – but after a lot of prompting he agreed that we could go ahead with it. It's been a labour of love for Tim and he's fought tooth and nail to get this through. He's had to liaise with James Brown's high-powered attorney-types in Washington DC, who run James Brown's On the Potomac production company. Luckily for Tim, the company are in the process of putting together a James Brown Documentary, which they're shooting on film. The deal is simple, they'll get us access to James Brown in Aiken if we pay for their crew to shoot the whole interview on film. They'll get to keep all the footage, but we'll be allowed to broadcast our four-minute interview first on British TV. It's a snip at $10,000, and an exclusive, as well as being James Brown's first TV interview outside the USA for four years.

I talk to Tim – are we really going to interview James Brown? I can't quite get my head round it.

We fly to Charlotte, North Carolina, which is a pleasant enough eight-hour journey if you don't suffer from the kind of over-active imagination I do and you aren't sitting next to someone with terminal BO. Within five minutes of sitting on the plane I have to mention it to Tim. 'Listen, Tim, have you had a shower?' He says yes, but I notice he doesn't say how many months ago. 'You fucking stink. Have you got any deodorant with you?'

At Charlotte airport we meet up with Larry Freyday; the senior attorney, Vince, who works for James Brown; the producer, who's a rather jovial middle-aged black woman called Joyce, and Dan Paisley, who is the cameraman/director on the shoot – they've all just flown in from Washington DC. They all notice that Tim stinks, too, but are too polite to mention it to him. I try and keep my distance from him, so they don't think the whiff is coming from me.

Larry is about thirty years of age and is actually from Aiken. There are only two famous people who've ever come from Aiken South, Carolina, one is James Brown and the other is the top American football star at the time, William Perry, known as 'The Fridge'. Larry works for both of them, and his first job on graduating in Law from university was to negotiate William Perry's first professional contract – ker-ching. Apparently, William Perry's mother had heard that Larry had just graduated in Law, so called to ask if Larry would do it. 'Yes please,' was the reply.

We board a twenty-seater propeller plane to Augusta Georgia, which sways around in the air for a bumpy palm-wetting ninety minutes. A half-hour drive over the state line and we're in Aiken. It looks like the town from the film of Harper Lee's famous novel *To Kill A Mocking Bird*. There's a town square with a courthouse, manicured lawns and willow trees, and lots of grizzle-faced, the south-will-rise-again Ku Klux Klan types driving around in pick-up trucks with rifle racks on the back. This is the deep south – racially the town is now a fifty–fifty mix, but only ten years earlier the hotel we are staying in, The Holly Inn, was a whites-only affair. I half expect to see Gregory Peck in a white suit and panama hat walking down the street, mopping his forehead with a monogrammed handkerchief.

The On the Potomac production people, with the exception of Aiken-raised Larry Freyday, marvel at the inn, the way a first-time visitor to Egypt might marvel at the Sphinx. For the USA, this 1890 Hotel is ancient. As Tim and myself check in, we lay on the British manners, with lots of pleases and thank yous. We're taking the piss a bit, but the middle-aged white woman on reception is almost having an orgasm.

'No, thank you very much, it's my pleasure,' etc. As we get in the lift, I comment that here in the deep south, to be British and Caucasian makes us double white in the eyes of the locals – there's no way they're going to be chasing us through the night with a lynching rope and a pack of hounds. As the teetotal attorneys and producers head for their rooms, we freshen up at the bar with a couple of beers with Scotch chasers. If there's one thing we Brits do better than the Americans, it's drink. We get a couple of suspicious looks off the old boys in the bar and are grilled by the bar maid as to why we've arrived in town with a couple of sharp-suited negro lawyers. We tell her and she nods, then we pile on the compliments, saying how friendly, delightful and polite everyone is down south, and she buckles at the knees and starts thanking us. We in turn say, no thank you, you are most kind even kinder than us. She gives us a free beer, then a free Scotch. We get slowly drunk while telling her how kind she is for the next hour until we're joined by the production people and head off for something to eat.

I ask Larry about growing up in Aiken – I guess there are, or were, shades of *Mississippi Burning* about the place. He says the younger generation are changing and racism among people is pretty unheard of nowadays. I ask him if, when he was growing up here, it would have been OK for a white guy to go out with a black girl and he says that would have been fine. I then ask, what if you were a black guy and you wanted to go out with a white girl. Larry's eyes say it all. 'No way, it just wouldn't happen.' I enquire as to whether this is because you might get beaten up, but Larry assures me, 'No, man, they'd have lynched you.' I can see how that would have squashed your desire somewhat, still they seem a polite enough bunch, and from what I'd seen of the white women of Aiken, when God was handing out good looks, they were lost at the back of the queue somewhere, in fact hanging would have been less shameful than going out with most of the ones I saw.

I'm tired and desperately need some sleep – the jet lag, the travelling, Tim's BO, the worrying about travelling and the free whiskeys have all taken their toll. This is the deep south; the temperature is 100 degrees in the shade and the humidity is sub-tropical. Our rooms in the hotel are fairly basic, but they do have air-conditioning. I turn it on and it sounds like I've got my ear pressed up against the propellers of the aeroplane that flew us here.

I'm in the bathroom, about to take a long delayed dump, when I spot something very long and whiskery coming out of the overflow hole in the sink. I freeze. That's not a rat's whisker, surely. I summon up the courage to look, only to find that a cockroach the size of my hand is trying to squeeze it's way through. I quickly put the plug in the sink and turn the hot water tap on full, watching as the scalding hot water reaches the overflow pipe and washes the giant roach away. Cockroaches don't like the light, so I try to sleep with the light on, as well as the noisiest and most inefficient air-conditioning unit in the world. This is what you get when you go for quaintness and character: giant insects, a waste disposal unit right next to your ear, a hot room and a bed that feels as if it was slept in by Robert E. Lee and half the Confederate army with their boots on. Well, what do you expect for $29 a night – it's location, location, location.

The following day it's down to business, we are going to interview James Brown. I'm coached by Larry and Vince.

'Address him as Mr Brown and what are you wearing, Terry?'

'No, no jeans. A shirt with buttons, and as long as it's smart you don't have to wear a tie.' I knew all this anyway, but I couldn't help thinking, hang on, I'm not the one in nick. As it turns out, on this particular day every week, James Brown is allowed out of prison on day release to work at a community centre with alcoholics and homeless people. Larry and Vince slip the warder looking after James Brown $1,800 to go and take an hour-long walk around the block while we take Mr James Brown to a doctor's house to conduct the interview.

Forget the NHS if you qualify as a doctor, go to the states. This house looked like South Fork, and the swimming pool was Olympic-sized with diving boards and slides. Tim and myself joke that this is probably James's bag man who supplies his prescriptions. James Brown is currently in prison for leaving the scene of a crime where it was alleged he tried to murder his wife – she dropped the charges – he then resisted arrest by firing shots at the police and driving towards the state line. A police chase ensued, which only ended when they shot all four tyres on his four-wheel drive vehicle. When he was arrested, he was found to be high on the animal tranquillizer PCP, or Angel Dust, which makes you violent and feel as strong as the Incredible Hulk. Of course, we've been briefed that none of this is the kind of thing that should be brought up in the interview, and as a long-standing soul fan granted a private audience with the man himself, I am happy to oblige.

We film the interview in what is a large sitting room with a huge grand piano in the middle. James Brown will be seated at the piano during the interview. I am at my forelock-tugging, obsequious best – it's not me, but knowing the history of James Brown I am actually in awe of him. Because the interview is being shot on film, it seems to take an eternity to light the interview, and while Tim Burke and the production crew faff about with screens, lights and angles, I have James Brown to myself. I talk to him about the legendary male soul singers, the all-time greats. For soul purists, the vocal giants among the soul men are the late Sam Cooke; Little Willie John, who wrote the song 'Fever' and recorded the quintessential version – forget Peggy Lee – Clyde McPhatter of the original Drifters and the late, great Jackie Wilson. They also all happen to be dead – and in case you're wondering, even though he's dead, Otis Redding is one of several subs, along with James Carr, who were warming the bench. James Brown agrees.

James is a huge fan of Gospel and proceeds to play the piano and, in a sweet, clean voice, he sings a line of Sam Cooke's 'Change Is Gonna Come'; it sounds exactly like Cooke. Then he tinkles on the piano some more and starts to sing Little Willie John's hit 'All Around The World', 'Grits ain't groceries and eggs ain't poultries and Mona Lisa never smiles.' I'm blown away by his sheer talent and how closely he can imitate his fellow R&B singers; it's like Sammy Davis Jr doing Frank Sinatra and Dean Martin at the Sands. He then does an old Jackie Wilson number with that soaring flyaway vocal style and I'm praying they get the cameras set up in time to catch some of this – I've got James Brown in full flight now. He's telling me stories about the old days and the artists he's worked with: 'They call it funk, but what it really is, is James Brown music. There's only four kinds of music out there: your Mozart, your Beethoven, your Brahms and your Brown.' He grins. 'I got some great musicians in the past – Maceo Parker – he thinks he blowing his horn for fun; I tell him what to play and those crowds are jumpin' for him every night, then he thinks he's ready to play his thing, so I replace him and had even bigger records without him.'

This is what I'd heard about James Brown, every virtuoso musician who ever played with him was told exactly what to play, and it had better be exactly how that record sounded. 'Kids go to see you play music, they want to hear it the way it sounds on the record.' I put Bootsy [Collins] out front, and when he thought he had somethin' goin', I took young musicians and cut *Hot Pants* and bigger records. I wanted them to know it wasn't them doin' it.' He then contends, 'Of all those guys, none of them ever did make it.'

I start wondering whether to disagree, but we're not filming yet and I don't want to crash the legend's vibes before the cameras are even on. I've got him on a roll and I also realize the truth in what he's saying. Yes Bootsy Collins had success for a time with Parliament/Funkadelic, and Fred Wesley, Brown's trombone and keyboard player, had some underground dance tunes with Fred & the New JBs, and Maceo Parker had some recording success, but most of that was with George Clinton's Parliament. James Brown's band always worked best as a churning funk engine, and maybe life as a back-up man to Mr Brown was tough, given the lengths their boss went to to remind them just how dispensable they were. This guy's not the Godfather of Soul, he's The Alex Ferguson of Funk. I ask him about his dancing and, given his age, if he's still able to do it.

He tells me he'll be doing his utmost until the day he dies. He hikes up one trouser leg to reveal his right knee. It's a gruesome sight, scarred, furrowed and slightly discoloured; he looks like he's been playing professional football for twenty years. 'I can still drop down on my knees when I sing "Please Please Please", but now I need help getting back up'. I'm having one of those weird feelings: I'm locked in a dream and James Brown is talking to me. The Godfather of Soul, Soul Brother number one, Mr Dynamite, Mr Sex Machine, The hardest working man in showbusiness, James 'Butane' Brown. The James Brown who played to over three million concert goers in 1967 alone, selling more than 50 million records that year. The Mr Brown who racked up seventeen Billboard hits in a row in two years, and sixty-six weeks on the album charts with *Live at the Apollo Vol. 1*, an album the record company didn't want him to make, so he paid its $5,000 costs himself. The man has 500 suits, 300 pairs of shoes, his own jet, diamonds, cars and a funky place cum castle in Queens, New York, with black santas on the lawn at Christmas. During the race riots in Boston and Washington DC in 1968 they put him on TV to cool down the rioters, where this funky lyricist turned sloganeer, chanted, 'Don't terrorise, organize! Don't Burn, Learn.' James Brown – truly a living legend.

'Is it true that only Elvis Presley has had more chart hits than you?'

'Now Elvis Presley, there was a boy died because he came out of the country life and ways. Night he died I chartered a jet to Memphis and stood over his casket. Tears in my eyes, I said, "Elvis, how you let this happen? How you let it go?"'

'Like me, Elvis was country. If you're country, you stay country, or you'll die a little bit every day. To a country boy, the city, well, it's like prison. I first went to jail when I was a boy, sentenced to as many years as I'd lived for breakin' into automobiles. First thing that gets you in there is the noise, then the smell. Like a zoo.'

I'm fumbling with my dictaphone, thinking, Hurry up you dozy arseholes, you're missing the interview.

I ask him about the deep south and why he's so attached to it when it's always had this racist reputation. James Brown knows this question. 'Now my daddy always said when we live in New York or Philadelphia that some white man been nice to you at the store counter, maybe when you lay your head on the pillow that night he gonna come along and blow it off. The Northern white man is sneaky. Southern white man, least he let you know where you stand. He tell you to go round to the back door to get your sandwich, you gonna find a sandwich.'

James plays the piano for me again. I end up having a private twenty-five to thirty-minute concert from him, meanwhile the clock's ticking and the crew are still fannying about with the lights. Vince, Mr Brown's attorney, has words with Tim Burke. James Brown's prison warder escort is at the door and we've not filmed a thing yet – our hour is nearly up. There are whispered negotiations in the background, and eventually Vince goes outside. Later I hear that the warder gets slipped $500 to take another hour-long stroll, the negotiation was to make sure that 24 Hour Productions would stump up for the extra payment. When I hear I'm not surprised; it was only three months earlier that James Brown was caught in his prison cell with $40,000 in cash stuffed under the mattress.

At last we're set up and ready to go.

Tim Burke starts to be what I see as a pain in the arse; it's his vision for *his* James Brown piece not *mine*. 'We haven't got time for all this specialist stuff about the great soul singers and James Brown the King of Soul, Terry.'

Tim feeds me a load of what I consider to be ultra bland questions. James Brown churns out the answers, but every question is so stock and banal I feel embarrassed asking them.

'What's special about the James Brown sound?' I ask and he gives me the old Brahms, Beethoven and Brown line.

Tim is insistent on the final question: 'Mr Brown, have you got a message for your fans in Britain.'

'Yes, I'll be over soon, God Bless you and thank you. Oh, and keep hold of the fish and chips.'

James Brown is lead away and I kind of know I'll never see him again; it's been very special for me, and I clutch my little dictaphone and curse the fact that all the best stuff wasn't on camera. But as I found out, in TV light entertainment on, they don't actually want anything good, and if we had filmed it all, it would never have been used, especially on *The Word*.

As soon as the interview is over, Tim Burke, wearing the same clothes he's had on for the past two days, jumps in a cab to Augusta. He has a flight to Charlotte, then a connection to New York, where he will spend all night developing the film and taking a copy for *The Word* before catching a flight to London and jumping straight in a cab to the offices of Planet 24 in the Isle of Dogs. No rest for the wicked, I say. When he gets back to the offices he falls asleep on one of the couches and the following day he turns up at the office at 10 a.m. instead of 9.30. Charlie chews his ear off; he has a go back. Charlie says he sacked Tim, Tim says he resigned. I suspect he's gone so no one will ever know that he's the person who came up with the idea for the chroma key behind the live bands on the show.

For me, it's a Friday night out in Aiken, South Carolina, with Larry Freyday. Larry's great company and a celebrity of sorts in

Aiken. He's a tall, well-built, good-looking ex-college boy with a law degree, and he represents the two most famous people ever to come out of Aiken.

The town has two nightclubs, a black one and a white one; we're going to hit both. The black club is a smart modern place with a well-dressed fashionably chic-looking crowd. It also has a fantastic sound system and a few too many mirrors for my liking. Larry is greeted at the door as if he's the latest Hollywood A-lister. Everyone knows him.

I spent eighteen years growing up in an area where almost a third of my neighbours were black, as well as managing a reggae band with whom I toured Britain's Afro-Caribbean clubs. I was used to being one of maybe four or five white people in a club full of Black people, but I'd never been the only one. . . until now. I couldn't understand it – the music was good, the decor was nice, the town's quiet and friendly but you aren't exactly spoilt for choice when it comes to nightlife, and yet none of the white people in the area seemed to want to come here. Larry joked that I was probably the first white person ever to spend more than twenty minutes in the place; I felt like Eddie Murphy's negative in the movie *48 Hours*. We spent about an hour in the club and then Larry asked if I fancied going down the road to the white club.

'What's it like?' I asked him.

'I don't know, I've never been inside.'

We strolled a couple of blocks to a café bar that sold beer and food and was packed to the rafters with white college kids, dancing on the tables to Jon Bon Jovi being played about forty decibels too loud. The heat and humidity inside was unbearable, the young people badly dressed and, skipping any euphemisms here, ugly. Larry was the only black person in the club and he's dressed in a suit and tie. The man behind the bar puts our beers in polystyrene cups so we can drink them outside on the street, along with the other thirty or so revellers who can't be bothered to squeeze inside the confines of this glorified sweatbox. There are two doormen outside, both of whom are dressed in long-sleeved white-buttoned dress shirts. They approach me. 'Where are you from?'

'London, England,' I reply and they nod.

Then they turn to Larry, who I've already sussed is the person they're really concerned about: 'Where are you from?'

'Washington DC,' he says. They nod and say we should enjoy ourselves. I know the answer, but I ask Larry anyway.

'If you're from Aiken, why did you say Washington?'

'If those guys think I'm from Washington, they'll treat me with a lot more respect than if they thought I was from Aiken – then they'd think I was just trying to prove a point by coming here.'

I couldn't believe a place so small could stay segregated through choice, as if by unspoken agreement. I suggest we finish our drinks and head back to the hotel. 'This place is shit, the music's crap and the people are ugly – it'll never catch on. They probably thought you were some detective, like Sydney Poitier in that film In t*he Heat of the Night*.'

Larry smiles and says, 'call me Mr Tibbs,' and we head back to the cockroach-infested hotel.

We're on Zuma Beach, just outside Los Angeles, with the Happy Mondays. The atmosphere is tense as our music booker, the fat lad from Leeds Tim Byrne, has been giving them the needle. They'd been in LA recording their eagerly anticipated third album, *Pills 'n' Thrills and Bellyaches*, for the past month and had managed to wreck over half a dozen hire cars between them. The band's drummer, Gaz Whelan, refuses to cadge a lift if Bez is driving as he's on Ecstacy constantly.

'It's all right in the day time,' he says, 'except he doesn't look at the road, he's always gazing around at the scenery, but at night he's like a maniac, driving for the on-coming headlights.'

Tim wanted to interview the band in the recording studios, but they wanted to get out for a couple of hours and were insistent they be interviewed at Zuma Beach, an hour's drive down the freeway. Tim is moaning, How dare a mere group not drop to their knees in obedience when the great God television speaks. I remember hanging around for almost an hour while Tim bent the ear of Happy Mondays manager Nathan McGough: 'Listen, you need us more than we need you. I'm doing you a favour.'

The whole scenario was doing my head in. I knew the Happy Mondays and there was no way Bez or Shaun would do something just because Nathan said so. That wasn't what their relationship was about.

Nathan was the son of Thelma Pickles, one-time girlfriend of John Lennon, and the adopted son of the great Liverpool poet Roger McGough. He was a good-looking lad, but he was rather middle class and naive, and he definitely couldn't control a bunch of Scallies like the Happy Mondays. Obviously Nathan wasn't going to agree with Tim when he knew there was no way the band were going to do as he suggested, as it would just undermine him in front of us, so it turned into an endless argument, Tim talking shit.

Eventually we agreed to head for Zuma Beach, and on the way I tell Tim he's an arse for thinking we're doing the Happy Mondays a favour. In youth culture terms, together with the Stone Roses, the Happy Mondays were the be-all and end-all of British pop music at the time. Tim doesn't like their attitude, but I remind him that they're not some over-hyped bunch of teeny-bopper pretty boys he can boss around and that the album they're recording will not only go straight to number one in the album charts when it's released, but any singles from it will also go top ten and get the band on *Top of the Pops*, so how on earth could we, a show that hadn't even been aired yet, be doing them a favour!

On the beach, Tim keeps interrupting the interview, demanding I use his predictable line of questioning. How did you meet? What are your influences? What's your favourite colour? I ignore him and then chew his head off. He hates it; he has to feel like the boss. The Mondays are chilled out, except for Bez and Shaun, who are completely battered on a cocktail of class-A drugs. Shaun tells us how cheap drugs are in America compared to Britain and describes LA as 'a top place for a mess-about.' I then ask Bez about the

Mondays forthcoming world tour, and he tells me that he's most looking forward to going to Japan. I ask him why?

'I've heard it's really wild. . . it's er. . . it's full of fucking Chinese.'

Everybody falls about and it's a TV moment that will be talked about for years – at least until we get the Happy Mondays live in *The Word* studio. Then the audience get to witness one-fifth of an iceberg with the other fantastic four-fifths backstage remaining a secret until this book.

Tim Byrne's 'They need us more than we need them,' was never true when it came to the Mondays, they were pure gold on *The Word* and summed up the raw, anarchic spirit of the show.

Depeche Mode were headlining at the Dodger Stadium, and their special guests were Manchester's Electronic, featuring Johnny Marr, ex-Smiths guitarist, Bernard Sumner, vocalist and guitarist from New Order, and ex-A Certain Ratio drummer Donald Johnson. The guest spot with Depeche Mode will be Electronic's first ever gig and they've drafted in Neil Tennant of the Pet Shop Boys, who produced New Order's recent album *Technique*, to help out on keyboards. We interviewed them in the roof bar of LA's famous Mondrian hotel. Bernard's very dry and fields the questions I'm fed by Tim Byrne with the disdain they deserve. Tim says the office want us to ask all our music interviewees what they think of James Brown, so they can do a montage before they show the rather bland interview they've got. I ask Bernard about James Brown, and in his own inimitable laconic fashion he replies, 'I think his best film was *Giant*.'

The assembled musicians fall about laughing. Tim and our director, a nice Home Counties girl called Liza Brown don't get it, so it will never be used on the programme.

After the interview I sit at the bar with Johnny Marr for a long chat. Iraq have invaded Kuwait that very day, so that was the main topic of conversation. It was a pinch-myself moment again. Since *Devil's Advocate* nine years earlier, when both Johnny and myself were unemployed teenagers on a show in Manchester, I'd only met up with him once, and that was when I interviewed The Smiths on Radio Derby before they played a concert for BBC2's *Old Grey Whistle Test.* I had been an absolutely huge Smiths fan, and now here Johnny and myself were, two council-estate kids of Irish descent from Manchester, supping cocktails in the roof bar of the Mondrian in Los Angeles. I was going to be on National TV with my own programme, but it still hadn't sunk in. For Johnny, fame and fortune were like water off a duck's back. He was no different to how he'd been back then, still honest and straightforward, though perhaps a bit more wary. He told me about The Smiths split and how he'd been more heartbroken than any Smiths fan; he said he felt like the group had started to act like arseholes, so he'd split the band.

'Look, Terry, it was a band that I formed when I was eighteen and I split them up when I was twenty-three. I had no choice because we were becoming the opposite of what we'd set out to be.' He sounded like a man who'd sacrificed his first-born son for a greater ideal. That's what was always unique and special about The Smiths. I hoped one day that I could be recognized for having that kind of integrity. So far, with eight years of radio, so good. But hey, there was no real chance of that happening with *The Word*'s circus.

That evening there was an after-show party for both Depeche Mode and Electronic at Bar One on Sunset Boulevard. Via Tim Byrne, we'd been put on the Pet Shop Boys' LA PR Susan Blonde's guest list. I was hanging out with our driver, who was Liza Brown's American cousin Dan. Dan was a fantastic guy, recently graduated from Harvard and with all the outward trappings of your typical WASP jock-type, except that he was Jewish, so he had this fantastically cynical sense of humour – Americans having no irony is a blatant generalization. Dan and I arrived at Bar One early as Tim Byrne and Liza were doing some filming with Depeche Mode. The queue was round the block, but in true Mancunian style I stepped right up to the front and announced, 'Terry Christian and Daniel Brown from Channel 4 Television, England. We're on Susan Blonde's guest list.'

It was like Ali Baba uttering 'Open Sesame'. The burly doormen parted and an attractive smartly dress woman smiled and asked us to follow her. She led us over to a table in the very smart club, where we found ourselves surrounded by a howling mob of Happy Mondays members and their Scally hangers-on.

The day before I'd interviewed Hollywood young gun Christian Slater. He'd seemed like a fairly down-to-earth young guy, but he became rather agitated when I talked about the contrast between the good films he'd made, like *The Name of the Rose* and *Heathers*, with the truly woeful, such as the one where he's a skateboarding pirate radio DJ. He didn't say much at the time, but *The Word* had been barred from doing any future interviews with him, for which I'll hold my hands up and take the blame.

That night in Bar One, while Dan and I were lurching drunkenly around the club, we bumped into Christian Slater playing pool in a back room. He didn't look altogether pleased to see me again and I'd just found out that he'd thrown a precious strop about the questions he was asked during the interview. I recalled that I'd asked about the sex scene in *The Name of the Rose*, where, as a novice monk – he was supposed to be the same age he was in real life: fifteen – he loses his virginity to a young serving wench and whether or not he had an erection during the scene. After all, I'd been fifteen myself, and knew that at that age you have an erection virtually all day, never mind when you're in close proximity to some fetching female flesh. He went along with it rather good-humouredly at the time, and said it had been very cold that day. I then asked him if he'd been a virgin in real life at the time, and he'd ummed and ahhed and finally said no. What I didn't know was that there had been stories in the press when the film came out, saying that he had been having carnal relations with the young Italian actress who played the serving wench. Big deal. Well, in Hollyweird it is. So when I saw Christian Slater in Bar One, I thought I'd better explain that I hadn't known about all that, and who gives a shit anyway, and why not say something to me at the time, instead of acting like a head-up-his-arse type and moaning about it later. Yes, I know, drunk and rather stupid. It came back to haunt me a year later, when I pretended to be astounded by the fact that Christian Slater, who I'd bonded with so well, wouldn't do an interview with us.

Actors like Patrick Swayze and Whoopi Goldberg were the complete opposite the young brat-pack Hollywood types, who are always the most precious. When I interviewed Patrick Swayze, I couldn't get over how much my girlfriend and every other girl I've ever known had loved the film *Dirty Dancing*. The junket we interviewed him on was for the film *Ghost*, and I went through the usual 'Is there any similarity between the part you play and the real Patrick Swayze' questions and then moved on to lots of stuff about his upbringing in Texas.

Patrick was a really warm, modest and down-to-earth guy, with a genuinely sensitive side to him. I remember a waiter coming up to the room in the Four Seasons in Beverly Hills, where the junket was taking place, to deliver a small packet of indigestion tablets Patrick had ordered, kind of thing that would have cost about thirty pence at the time in England. He came in just as I was sitting down to start the interview and handed the packet to Patrick, who told the waiter to hold on while he got his wallet out to tip the guy. I could see the contents of Patrick's wallet from where I was sitting, a couple of fifty-dollar bills, a twenty and two one-dollar bills. The standard tip for something like that is a dollar, and a really generous tip would be two dollars. I could see the dilemma Patrick faced. If he gave a the waiter a two-dollar tip, blimey he's a multi-millionaire film star, it's only a little more than a bog standard tip. But fifty dollars was a bit flash and Hollywood and even twenty dollars was a bit excessive. He looked really uncomfortable and self-conscious, but that just made him seem more human. He eventually bit the bullet and handed the grateful waiter a twenty-dollar bill.

As we filmed the interview, I couldn't help noticing that Patrick had dyed blonde hair. In fact, Sam Anthony had noticed it and joked that he must be doing a surfing movie or something. I liked the line, so at the end of the interview I brought it up: 'Patrick, what's with the blond hairstyle?'

He smiled. 'Oh, that's for my next movie.'

'It's not about surfing, is it?'

He laughed 'Yes it is, man, it's called *Point Break* and I play the real Cahuna dude.'

In all our trips to Los Angeles before the first series of *The Word*, we interviewed a lot of up-and-coming actors: Sharon Stone, Rachel Ticotin, Steve Guttenberg, Jeff Goldblum, Liam Neeson and Will Smith, as well as musicians like Bobby Brown, Johnny Gill and Bell Biv DeVoe. We visited Danny Sugarman one-time manager of The Doors and author of the Books *Wonderland Avenue* and *No One Here gets Out Alive* – the book Oliver Stone based his movie *The Doors* on – his autobiographical accounts of the rise of The Doors and his subsequent struggles with heroin addiction.

We had enough material to put together a fascinating series of intelligent five- and six-minute stories for the forthcoming series, plus we'd spent loads of time in all the English pubs in LA, talking to illegal Brits from London, Manchester, Liverpool and Bournemouth, who'd taken up residence there and earned a crust doing everything from casual building work to organizing illegal raves in South Central LA.

The idea was to make a piece contrasting these working class young Brits living it up in the sunshine with their sloaney rich Eurotrash counterparts who, through Papa's connections, had sorted themselves out jobs in the film industry. Some slightly older English guys told us off the record that some of the British lads out there were villains, and that they were moving in on the drugs trade on Venice beach and coming into conflict with the Black and Hispanic gangs in the area.

Some of the stories we heard were amazing – a lad who'd spent two weeks there and ended up doing Sylvester Stallone's plumbing, and some other lads who imported container loads of junk from second-hand shops in Lancashire and sold it to the Yanks as antiques – even seventies Formica tables and old armchairs that smelled a bit fusty. They didn't even bother doing the stuff up as they were selling it as fast as it came in and making good money. 'The Yanks will buy anything that's old,' we were told. We filmed enough to make a decent hour-long documentary about these contrasting lifestyles, as well as lots of interesting individual stories, but disappointingly, none of it was ever used on *The Word.*

The excellent Doors feature with Danny Sugarman was also never shown. Danny was a genuine walking rock and roll casualty. He'd been The Doors number one fan, then their teenage tour manager, but it was a life that drew him into a world of drugs and rock and roll. Addicted to heroin, he took over management of the band and their affairs, and he spoke of how he still lived with his addictions and that his life was something of a mess, still defined, even today, by a band whose music mesmerized him as a youngster, until they and his drugs became something of an obsession. With the aid of methadrine he'd overcome his heroin addiction, but he couldn't give up The Doors. His best-selling books about his time with The Doors, *Wonderland Avenue* and *No One Here Gets Out Alive*, were his way of weaning himself off an obsession.

Everything about the piece was powerful. We went to all the places in LA associated with The Doors and back to his house in Beverly Hills, which though expensive was neglected, even down to the slime of green algae on the bottom of his swimming pool. Danny Sugarman talked about how, of all the artists from the sixties and seventies who'd become more popular after their death, such as Hendrix, Otis Redding and The Velvet Underground, it was The Doors who sold the best worldwide by quite a large margin, then he apologized again for his obsession of The Doors, as if he was still battling every day with that particular addition.

Burnished by the California sun and full of optimism about the great material we'd filmed, I headed back to London, arriving just three days before the pilot of the *Word* was due to be filmed and less than a fortnight before the first show was to be aired.

For the pilot show, we had a band from Nottingham called Whycliffe, who were mates of one of the show's producers, Dele Oniya; Bill Dean, who played Harry Cross on *Brookside* and ex-*EastEnder* and Michelle Collins as our guests. There was a really shitty item about celebrity sandwiches, something on new-age healing, a couple of video items and a portion of the show where I sat with the guests and reviewed new film and video releases.

I went into the office to look at some of the items we'd filmed and was absolutely disgusted at how the guts seemed to have been edited out of every piece. Instead of being edgy and different, they could have slotted into any rather dull teenage *Blue Peter*-type show. I was quite despondent. In radio you'd never sacrifice your best material just to fit in with a pre-shoot script.

I sat down to write a script for the pilot and handed it over; it came back with loads of crossings-out, so I rewrote it, then it came back again. Every single aside or throw-away remark had been expunged.

'I didn't really get it,' Charlie said when I questioned him about it.

When we shot the pilot no press were supposed to be allowed in, but Marian Buckley had fought for Jon Ronson to be the only journalist present during filming. I'd employed Jon for five months on my radio show, giving him his first break in that medium and Marian had kick-started his journalism career by giving him various commissions to write for *City Life* magazine in Manchester, when he'd been sacked as the manager of popular Manchester Band The Man From Delmonte. Now he'd been offered his first national press writing gig for the newly launched *Independent on Sunday*, and Marian was doing him a massive favour by granting him exclusive press access.

Channel 4 had been hyping *The Word* as their biggest show since *The Tube*, so all Jon had to do was not slag off the pilot. Marian had really laid her neck on the line, but though I know and like Jon, I knew he had no loyalty like that. Jon Ronson is out for Jon Ronson, period.

In the end the pilot was a calamitous mess. Everything was too rushed. Charlie kept changing my script on autocue all the way through and screaming overly fussy instructions down my earpiece. Before the show I'd looked at the running order and commented that it looked like they were trying to squeeze two hours' worth of material into fifty minutes of air time, but this was, of course, completely ignored.

'If you feel uncomfortable about anything, Terry, let us know,' Charlie said all the way up to the opening titles. It was just a question of knowing where to start. My chair was uncomfortable; the position of the monitor on set wasn't right; I was too far away from my guests, so they had to strain to hear me and vice versa, and the autocue was only readable with powerful binoculars 70 per cent of the time. The audience of trendy dancer-types shuffled around disinterestedly until a camera pointed in their direction, and commissioning editor Stephen Garrett just floated around, pulling an important and not very happy face.

On Sunday, Jon Ronson's article appeared in the *Independent*. It wasn't too unkind about me, but didn't give any details about my background – even though he had worked on a radio show with me – and wasn't in the slightest bit enthusiastic or positive either. Jon also quoted Marian Buckley, slagging off the lawyers and Charlie for trying to tell me what I could and couldn't say.

Marian was ready to get a shotgun and go after Jon, and although I had other concerns on my mind, I felt very disappointed in him. It was, after all, just a pilot, to see how it could run, not a rehearsal for the real thing. We weren't even on air and already the Manchester connection had shot itself in the foot. I knew I'd tried my best, but eight years of complicated live radio shows didn't stop me feeling exposed, uncomfortable, and unable to think and control a beast that was far too frenetic and bitty. There was no room for the show to breathe, and every single thing from the practicality of the seating arrangements, to the camera positions, made it a struggle.

Stephen Garrett was having kittens and sending tetchy memos around and I felt totally out of my depth. I'd never actually done any TV presenting before, and I now had one week before I was due to be live on air on a very complicated, overly busy, far too pacy programme on national TV – and I knew that they hadn't taken on board one thing I'd said. I was dreading that first programme and the series was scheduled to last for eighteen weeks. There was no way I could deal with the stress and strain of trying to get these people to see my vision for the show; they weren't wired into that and I was going to be nothing more than a northern muppet.

chapter eight

***'Terry Christian, won't someone somewhere smash his smug irritating little face in.'* Channel 4 duty log**

I watched the pilot in a room with Charlie. It was sheer torture, with few redeeming features except that the set looked good and the chroma key behind the bands worked well. If Charlie had any doubts about my ability to present the show, he wasn't hiding them. They all seemed to stem from my not following his instructions to the T, but at the same time he stressed that I had to take control, feel confident and be myself, and that if I felt uncomfortable with anything I should just say so. But I had said so, in a very direct way that couldn't be misunderstood, and yet nothing had been done about any of my comments.

We talked in circles. What Charlie was saying was to be myself, but not be myself, to control the show, but do as I was told. The criticism was quite clear and concise, and as for the confidence bit, after that, how on earth could I be myself and feel the self-belief a show like *The Word* demanded from it's presenter.

'Another thing, Terry,' Charlie said, 'in a couple of weeks' time, when the show's been on and people are talking about it and telling you you're great, remember this conversation and take no notice. Also, don't be too close to the researchers and associate producers. They'll all be moaning at you about different things. It's better that you stay out of it and keep a distance, and don't get big headed.'

Everyone telling me I'm great – I was looking forward to that bit.

That week I found it difficult to sleep. Every night I went to the crap local pub with Gavin and tried to feel normal. Gavin was lit up with enthusiasm and full of good advice, but I was grumpy and felt like I'd been hauled over the coals. All my self-belief was dissipating and I was still feeling aggrieved about the production meetings at the office.

About a dozen of us – researchers, producers, directors and Charlie – would sit round a huge oval table. Charlie sat at the head of the table, while I sat between him and Dele Oniya, a producer. I felt like Jesus about to be crucified between the two thieves. It was the final meeting before the first show. A script of sorts had been cobbled together by me, with finishing touches by Dele Oniya and Charlie. Needless to say it bore little resemblance to the one I'd originally worked on.

The first show was being discussed and Charlie had come up with a strand he thought of as comedy called Les Misérables, but pronounced in a bad northern accent as Lez Miserable, like a bloke's name, geddit. These were various pieces of shit, which included a girl imitating Kylie Minogue's 'I Should Be So Lucky' dance routine – wow! How radical and irreverent. Let's take the mickey out of Kylie; she's really uncool y'know. However, there was one film clip from the collected bits on the strand of two burlesque variety act-type northern comics called Ratman and Robin, who were sitting on the top deck of a Blackpool tram, and one of them was eating giant centipedes and African cockroaches on the hoof, so to speak. It was a bit off-the-wall, but I thought it would get us talked about, so I suggested we went with that piece.

Other than that, the bands were Adamski doing 'All Shook Up' – we'd pushed Tim Byrne for Deee-Lite's 'Groove Is In The Heart', but dear pudgy Tim wasn't having any of it, saying, 'If that even makes the top forty I'll eat my shades.' Two weeks later it went straight in at joint number one, ho hum. We also had Liverpool band The Farm on performing their new single, 'Groovy Train'. Our studio guests were actor and former stand-up comedian Bill Dean who'd also appeared in The Farm's video and Bond girl Maryam D'Abo, who was a really pleasant, pretty, intelligent woman, though I'd never heard of her.

We'd been working on the show for weeks and that's all we had. On local radio, when you're looking for guests these are the criteria:

1. Is the guest well known?
2. Are they happening now?
3. Have they got something to say?

Three not unreasonable demands. The most important two for TV are being well known, and having something to say. Oh how we'd struggle on this show.

I know I'm not an easy person for my colleagues to work with. I'd had six years at the BBC in Derby, less than a year working on Piccadilly Radio and six months on a few newly licensed local radio stations in Manchester, but to me it had been a lifetime. Inside, I wasn't ready for this kind of attention, for having people decide what I had to wear, what I had to say, when to jump, how to be. I'm not a control freak, but I knew where my comfort zone lay and it wasn't in the colourful, wacky, zany, exhibitionist world of television. How on earth had I ended up in this situation? There was no career mapped out in my tormented mind, so this didn't feel like a step in any particular direction. When it came to television, I'd watched plenty but knew nothing, and in truth I didn't have a particular interest in or passion for the medium. This was just a decent job that had popped up out of the blue and guaranteed my wages for at least six months. It also seemed to garner a twisted reaction from people, who were either impressed, annoyed or jealous I had a gig like this. It's only appeal to me was that I could have a certain amount of fun with other people's reactions to my beckoning superstardom. Shit, people were jealous of me! The novelty of it all.

In reality, I was so frightened by the idea of presenting a live national TV show that I refused to even think about it. There were only four channels in the UK back then and my girlfriend, my family and friends would be watching, maybe even ex-girlfriends and old enemies, all of them waiting and, depending on their mood or feeling at the time, willing me to succeed or fall flat on my backside. And let's say I did fake this TV presentation lark properly and some people thought I was cool and funny, perspicacious and witty, *I'd* still know that it wasn't true, and the prospect of having to go through this mental torture for the next five months didn't exactly fill me with glee. I remember ringing my mum up and feeling as if I'd stepped into someone else's dream; in truth I was embarrassed about the fact that I was going to be on the telly.

I felt like an automaton that Friday when I was wheeled into the LWT studios at around 9.30 a.m. for rehearsals. I was nervous in front of the cameras and embarrassed saying my lines in front of the crew and studio people. They all think I'm shit and a wanker, I'd think and disappear off, my stomach all twisted up as I tried on varying degrees of naff outfits, had make-up slapped on me and people refer to me in the third person.

'Do you think Terry needs a bit more gel on his hair.'

'No, that's as good as you'll be able to get it, it's a bit fine and lank. Darken his eyebrows a bit, though, he's looking a bit washed out under the key light.'

It was my first day experiencing life as a commodity, like a tin of beans, but with eyebrows that were too light and lank, untidy hair. I was a tin of supermarket own-brand beans that you buy for a penny but nobody really likes the taste of them. Where was the fun in this? And where had the fun in me disappeared to?

'Good luck, Terry. Remember, just be yourself and try and enjoy it.'

What sort of pervert did they think I was. As for 'be yourself' it seemed a strangely ironic mantra – in a world where artifice and fakery are the main currency.

The show went by in a flurry of lights, cameras and noise. I've never been as involved and yet so detached from anything in my life. Throughout the show my stomach was knotted with fear. The sheer pace of everything left me behind; there wasn't an instant to breathe. I speak at the beginning, and throw the odd joke and one-liner out, but without any real conviction or belief. The audience are forty or fifty hand-picked trendy London clubbers and dancers and they just look bored – they're scattered about the studio, trying to out trendy and out cool each other. I look at them enviously, at least they belong on a show like this; I don't.

I go to a live satellite link with Amanda De Cadenet in Memphis Tennessee with Billy Zane, Harry Connick Jr and the young cast of the film *Memphis Belle* which Connick stars in. The satellite keeps going fuzzy and cutting out. Three times we go over, and as soon as Amanda starts talking the line goes down. Finally, we get about forty seconds of Amanda talking to Billy Zane and Harry Connick Jr. Bang, it's gone and I'm left floundering on the couch with Maryam D'Abo and Bill Dean.

My confidence is at an all-time low, my self belief shredded. I felt as if I was being set up. I was just someone with an identifiable comedy Mancunian accent who looked young and vulnerable. That must be all they wanted. Most TV presenters start off on local low-profile shows that are pre-recorded, where they're groomed and learn their craft steadily. I'd been thrown in, not just at the deep end, but during a hurricane with a nasty undertow and no life guards. It was as if I'd been dragged through the mire. At last I introduced The Farm and they performed 'Groovy Train'. Thank fuck for that. No wonder so many people in the media have dabbled in Class As. I felt and looked a prick. Despondency crushed me, but I still had to face the crew for drinks afterwards.

'Well done, Terry, good show.' Typical telly clichés, they'd probably pre-scripted those, too.

'At the beginning we feel it's all going to go wrong, during the show it's dodgy, at the end we say it's great – OK, that's a wrap.'

As I drank beer after beer in the Green Room afterwards I was just relieved to have got through it, and part of me wanted to go back and do it properly – now. Gavin, as ever, was doing his best to gee me along. He was only twenty-three, but he understood the nature of performing as he'd been acting since he was a teenager in Derby. 'Keep smiling and basically try and enjoy it.' It was good advice, but I'd had too much of that. The more good advice you get, the more you realize that everyone else has noticed you're pretty shit. There had been a few glimmers of good stuff, though, and as a whole the show was certainly different from what had gone before. At least I was still alive, and next week, we'd be back to do it all again.

There was a parade of people wanting to speak to me, young attractive women eager to talk, as if I was some sort of film star. Bollocks! I couldn't even stop shaking, never mind focus on a conversation. Jesus, if this is the reception a TV presenter gets when he's crap, what's it like when you're good.

I had to watch the show back with Charlie the following Monday and I just wanted the ground to open up and swallow me, or at least the husk of what I thought I was. Charlie said it wasn't excruciatingly bad, and that if I did exactly as I was told, it would get better. The show's initial viewing figures of around 600,000 were as good as *The Tube* got in a similar slot, too, which was encouraging.

I was more excited about the next show, the guests looked a bit better, with Hollywood actress Joanne Whalley lined up and The Pixies performing 'Dig For Fire' and The Charlatans performing 'Then', plus they were airing my James Brown interview. There was nothing else on TV at that particular time that would have given you content that good.

'I think you should wear the silk shirt with the sunflower print on it next week.'

I'm out shopping with our stylist, Helen Thorne, in London's West End. She's a nice girl, but she knows how to boss me about subtly using a mixture of flattery and disappointment. What do I know about clothes on the telly anyway.

'Er, don't you think it makes me look a bit gay, I mean, big yellow and blue flowers on a cream silk shirt.'

'No, it looks cool.'

It's the same scenario as week one – nerves shredded, hair gelled, de-gelled, re-gelled again, and still not right; eyebrows darkened so my eyes don't look like two piss holes in the snow; they even mascara my eyelashes. I'm dressed in a pair of blue Levi's, some trainers and the pièce de résistance, that bloody sunflower shirt.

Helen Thorne smiles like an approving mother: 'You look great.'

I look in the mirror and nearly jump three feet in the air with shock. I decide that I couldn't look gayer if I walked out in front of those cameras with Quentin Crisp's knob hanging out of my behind. To compensate, I walk with a manly swagger and trip over twice making my way to *The Word*'s couch for the dress rehearsal. I catch the eye of some of the lads from The Charlatans on stage and just the presence of a few familiar faces is a comfort. They smile and John Brookes does a limp-wrist sign at me and laughs. I knew that shirt made me look a right one.

The show itself felt a lot better, I had more confidence in the content, sort of understood it and tried to match the frenetic pace. Joanne Whalley had just starred in a film alongside Liam Neeson called *The Big Man*, based on the brilliant book of the same name by one of Britain's best writers – OK, he's Scottish – William McIlvenny. The film lacked the muscularity of the book, but it was great to have Joanne on the show as I felt very short of northern company. I knew a few people who'd known her in Manchester when she was a regular at the Roxy Room at Pips as a youngster.

Joanne was incredibly pretty and fielded all my questions about the film and her career very well. Then I got on to the fact that her dad was a plumber and she was from Stockport and juxtaposed that with her Hollywood golden couple tag as Mrs Val Kilmer – after all, Mr Kilmer's family were in America's Forbes Rich List. I asked her if she'd ever taken Val to her parent's house in Stockport, and she replied that she hadn't and, in fact, she hadn't been to Stockport herself for four and a half years. I found this strange as my roots are really important to me. She started to become a bit tetchy with all my questions about her background and she was bright enough to pick up on the fact that I was inferring she'd become a bit of a snob. I asked if all this meant that Val had never met her parents, but she said her parents either went out to see them in Hollywood, or came down to London to see them. I then rather crassly said. 'Is that because you're worried about what people in Stockport might say about you being married to a bloke called Val?'

It wasn't uproariously funny, but it got a loudish titter from the audience. Joanne, meanwhile, stood up, pulled the microphone off her low-cut blouse and stormed off the set. The camera came back to me, flushed beetroot with embarrassment, and I just said, 'Oops, she's gone.'

It was the first genuine magic *Word* moment. I'm still faintly embarrassed about the whole incident, as I wasn't being malicious or nasty. It was only my second show and the biggest name live guest we'd had on so far had walked off two-thirds of the way through her allotted time. In the Green Room afterwards everyone seemed quite perky. I renewed my acquaintance with Frank Black from the Pixies, who was really excited about my meeting with James Brown, and chatted to various members of The Charlatans. It was a decent show, certainly better than the first one. I even overheard Tim Byrne taking to someone: 'Everybody said how crap the first show was, Terry was dreadful, but it wasn't too bad tonight, was it?' He was a bit of a git, but he'd hit the nail on the head as all I'd had off everybody else who worked in the show that week was how fantastic the first show had been and how well I'd done. Believe me, it wasn't and I hadn't.

The following week I went out filming around Notting Hill and Ladbroke Grove. We were doing a short piece to commemorate the twentieth anniversary of Jimi Hendrix's death, interviewing people who knew him, like Lulu and new rock and pop stars who were fans of his music. It culminates in the director pre-recording a mock-up of me interviewing Jimi Hendrix in heaven, dressed again like a right nonce and with the director insisting in, OK yah style, that I start each question with the phrase 'Hey, Jimi,' so that he can cut in with actual footage of Hendrix talking. It's bit crap, but by now I'm used to it – this is TV.

On the night of the show, once again fighting back nerves and the studio audience's blatant disinterest, I sat on the *Word* sofa and meant to say, 'Today is the twentieth anniversary of Jimi Hendrix's death.' Instead I said, 'Today is the twentieth anniversary of Jimi Hendrix's desk.' It was funny, but not quite as hilarious when it appeared in every publication going and you realize you're going to get it in the ear off all your old mates in Manchester down the pub that weekend. Blimey that must have made their week. Having a few drinks after the show that night – we always had really good after-show parties on *The Word* – I was talking to Graeme Smith, who was the producer of Jools Holland's *Jukebox Jury* on BBC1. He said he was a fan of *The Word* and I chose for that instance not to disbelieve him, athough given the reaction from the press and everyone else in the media, it was hard to. Despite my obvious discomfort, it was very different and was covering more or less the right subjects for its audience. I was delighted and extremely flattered when Graeme asked if I fancied being a guest on the panel of *Jukebox Jury*, they'd even pay me £400. At last an area where I could display my musical knowledge, show my critical faculties while getting paid, and it was filmed in Manchester. It felt like some kind of affirmation. I was now a player in proper TV. I awaited Graeme's call, only to discover that I'd been culled from the show by Janet Street-Porter, who was the show's executive producer. She had told Graeme she didn't want to publicize a Channel 4 show on the BBC by giving it's presenter a showcase. When Graeme pointed out that Channel 4's Jonathan Ross had been a guest, she then said, 'Terry is an awful presenter and has got a really horrible voice'; talk about pots and kettles.

I was really fed up, but suspected it was more to do with the fact that *The Word* was getting a million viewers and the figures were increasing. More importantly, whether it was good or bad, people were talking about us. Janet would have felt a lot of rivalry with Charlie Parsons, going back to their days working together on *London Tonight*, and at the time, if you compared *The Word* to BBC shows like *Dance Energy* and *Reportage*, we were winning hands down.

With Amanda De Cadenet swanning round the United States for live satellite links on the show, I was their man on the ground, and, given my fear of flying, that suited me perfectly. I'd just spent over two months in the States on five separate trips when myself and Steve Braun were sent to Minneapolis for the opening night of Prince's

Glam Slam Nightclub. We'd been given permission to film at Paisley Park and cover the club's opening night and they were hopeful that we'd also get an interview with Prince himself. I'm not too pleased to find out that we'll be flying out on the Monday via New York – it was $200 cheaper than flying direct from London to Minneapolis – filming all day Tuesday and Wednesday, then flying back to Britain via New York so we arrived in London late Thursday afternoon.

The flight was horrendous and we had to wait around for almost four hours at La Guardia airport in New York for our connecting flight to Minneapolis. I felt completely knackered and stressed out. I hadn't been sleeping well or eating properly, and I'd been smoking forty fags a day as opposed to my usual five or ten.

We arrived in our hotel in Minneapolis at around 11 p.m. on the Monday night, and I'm in urgent need of a dump, but can't go. It feels like shitting a brick sideways on; I can feel a painful tear in my sphincter and the toilet bowl is covered in blood. I try to sleep but I feel as if someone's twisting a broken bottle up my arse for the next eight hours. I'm in agony.

All through the shoot the next day I'm tetchy. I'm worried about the excruciating pain up my back passage, about the shoot and about getting myself sorted out in time for Friday's show. Prince doesn't show for his own club opening, but we do get to witness Rosie Gaines in concert and interview her afterwards, then the next day it's off to Paisley Park. Again there's no sign of Prince, but we do get to talk to the very pretty but weirded out Rachel Inez, Paisley Park recording artist and Prince's current squeeze. Meanwhile, half my arse feels as if it's hanging out of my anus and I'm in a lot of pain – it puts me in mind of Voltaire: 'Sometimes the bottom falls out of your world,' only with a twist. I know it's haemorrhoids, but surely they can't be this agonizing. I'm popping Paracetemol like a human Pac-Man, but they aren't helping. I can't eat, sleep or shit, and even taking a piss seems to exacerbate the pain.

When we arrive back in London I go straight to Boots to buy some haemorrhoid ointment, but it makes no difference to the agony further up my anus. I'm distraught. On that Friday's show the live band are Liverpool's The La's, performing 'There She Goes'. They'd been live on my radio show a year earlier and I loved them and thought they were going to be deservedly huge. Also on the show is my old Radio Derby colleague and shock jock turned TV star James Whale. On paper it should be a lively show, and I've got a good feeling about it, the trouble is I'm so exhausted and in so much pain I'm almost hallucinating. One hour before the show, I go into The La's dressing room for a bit of Mancunian versus Scouser banter. Lee Mavers proffers me the spliff he's smoking and, horrified at what I'm doing, I accept and take two tokes – now my exhaustion is exacerbated, I can't think straight, my eyes are like piss holes in the snow and I'm a wreck.

The show is true car crash TV, I've no excuses. James Whale runs rings around me and I can hardly get a sentence out. I blame the whole travesty on jet lag. No way am I going to say that I suspect I've got prolapsed piles, that I haven't slept more than three hours in the past four days and had just smoked a portion of what felt like the strongest spliff I've ever had in my life just to show the La's I'm as nonchalant a scally as they are.

Stephen Garrett is fuming about my piss-poor performances, Charlie blames himself for sending me to the USA and throwing me in at the deep end, but I know it was the joint that did the real damage. I feel as if I've conned my way onto national television, fraudulently projecting an image that isn't me in the auditions, and now I'm stranded without the tools or confidence to carry it through. There were absolutely no excuses – I'm far from a TV natural, and when you need your wits about you, Marijuana isn't exactly performance-enhancing. That night I went back to Colindale feeling very down and slept like a baby – i.e., woke up screaming every three hours and nearly wet the bed.

That weekend I went back to Manchester to stay at my mam and dad's. I met up with some old school friends and they were quite sympathetic, in between taking the piss out of the horrendous outfits I'd been wearing on the show. I also met up with my girlfriend, who was beginning to get completely fed up with me whinging about the job. On the Monday morning I checked in with my GP, Doctor Baral, who stuck a rubber-gloved finger up my arse.

'Aaargh!'

'Yes, well, you've got piles, but you've also got an anal fissure.'

'What should I take for it?'

'Well, nothing. You have to have an operation; it's a tear in your sphincter, so every time you have a bowel movement you're tearing it again, that's why it's so painful. You'll need to go into hospital for an anal stretch, then the scar tissue can heal properly.'

An anal what?

But when? On the NHS the waiting list was at least four months, which meant I would have to do at least another fourteen weeks of the show – more if the viewing figures were good and the run was extended – without missing any live shows despite the excruciating pain I was in.

Doctor Baral prescribed me some powerful equagesics. I would save my bowel movement until just before bedtime, then pop two equagesics immediately after and try to get to sleep before the broken-bottle feeling returned.

My whole life felt a mess: I was irritated at everyone all the time and felt completely down. I was spending the majority of my time in London, yet still had the pressure of writing 2,000 words a week on Manchester's up-and-coming music scene for the *Manchester Evening News*, as well as doing a radio show for Signal Cheshire on a Sunday night.

My girlfriend hated me being on TV, mainly because she could see what it was doing to me. I may seem quite sarcastic and abrasive, but the truth is I was far too sensitive and lacking in confidence to be the sort of television presenter they wanted me to be. As a child, and even as an adult, I never liked being the centre of attention on my birthday and crumbled inside whenever people sang me 'Happy Birthday' – by the time they reached the line 'Dear Terry', I'd almost be hyperventilating.

Every week I'd watch my performances back, noticing how I hesitated as instructions were screamed down my earpiece. I managed to get Charlie to agree not to give me instructions as I was actually speaking, but during the show Charlie would get so excited, he couldn't help himself and occasionally I'd flounder. Sitting on *The Word* couch every Friday evening on the verge of what could only be described as an adrenaline overdose, I felt completely alone. I knew I wasn't able to carry the show as I didn't have the big personality or ability to engage with the studio audience – I was struggling just to hold it all together. There were often times when an interview was going well, then I'd spoil it by saying something of unbelievable naffness and quickly start to crumble. An often used line of mine was that as a presenter on *The Word*, I'd died more times than Captain Scarlet.

With Amanda out and about every week, it was left to me to hold the show together in the studio and drive it on. I knew I wasn't doing a good enough job of it, but like everything else, presenting is a skill that has to be learned, and I was having to do it in front of the public and the critics. Charlie tried to keep my spirits up, but he wasn't great at helping me focus, as I usually came away from our meetings more confused and even less confident than when I walked in. Our executive producer was an ex-Granada woman called Trish Kinane, who had worked alongside her husband on *The Tube*. Trish was fantastically supportive and understood that I wasn't this super confident and focused individual. She could see that I felt like a fish out of water, but I still didn't feel as if I could confide in her or anyone else on the show about my anal fissure and the agony I was enduring.

It was all too easy for the viewers to see the vulnerability and discomfort I felt while presenting the show. Stephen Garrett invited me for a meeting in his office. He's an odd character for me to describe, because he was a good listener and did seem genuinely concerned about me, although always maintaining a rather superior air, which seemed to belong in a bygone era. He tried his best to make me feel at ease, but I still thought he didn't rate, or like me.

I couldn't quite work out what was wrong with my presentation, but he more or less nailed it in one meeting, when he pointed out that although I was very nervous, so were my guests, and sometimes because I was nervous I came across as too abrasive and aggressive towards them. Someone like Jonathan Ross, on the other hand, got away with asking tough or cheeky questions by using plenty of charm. I tried to explain that where I grew up, if someone made you nervous, aggression, not charm, was the way to sort it out. Perhaps I should have said, 'Stephen, the remarks I make aren't really me, they're just the camouflage I wear.' I'd always been an instinctive presenter, but I was grateful for Garrett's good advice and tried to put it into effect in my future TV work.

The recorded items and pieces on *The Word* looked good, but I still wasn't satisfied with the way they were edited. Week in, week out I saw all the best pre-recorded material end up on the editing floor.

Charlie told me I'd be going to Toronto in Canada for two days and that I'd have to direct the Canadian camera crew for the junket we were filming as there would be no director involved. Jo Owen would meet me at the hotel, having flown to Toronto from New York.

Orion pictures were picking up the tab, so I was flown out first class on Air Canada and stayed in a hotel suite – yes, a suite. However, in case of any mishaps I was given a float of $1,800 Canadian, and there was a hire car to pick up at the airport.

It was exciting going over to Canada and being the one in charge. We had to do two onset junkets. On the first day we'd be on location in an area of downtown Toronto that looked like New York – the late Peter Ustinov once described Toronto as what New York would be like if it were run by the Swiss – where they were filming the Movie *Car 54, Where Are You?* which starred ex-New York Dolls band member David Johansen and Al Lewis from the original sixties TV series.

At 8 a.m. in the morning I met up with Pat Pigeon and our other camera and sound people for the next two days and we drove down to the set and hung around while an icy wind howled in from the lakes waiting to grab an actor in between takes. After five hours we'd only managed a quick and rather dull five-minute interview with Al Lewis and were told we'd have no chance of seeing David Johansen until the following day. Unfortunately, on the following day we had another onset junket at a huge studio complex in Toronto, where we'd be interviewing Cybill Sheperd, Beau Bridges, Stockard Channing and Mary Stuart Masterson for a new romantic comedy called *Married To It* that was in production. The problem was we'd be in a queue of about sixty sets of journalists, all hoping for ten minutes with the stars. After hanging around in the freezing cold for half a day, I didn't fancy doing it again, so I decided to try a little white lie to bump us up the queue. Meantime, Jo Owen, Pat Pigeon and the rest of the crew went to a restaurant to start eating and drinking some of that $1,800 float. That was at about 3 p.m. in the afternoon and I joined them soon after. It was at 1 a.m. as I staggered drunkenly into my hotel suite, that I realized I hadn't got a receipt for our hours of revelry, but fuck it, I was a telly star, not a bleeding accountant.

The next morning I was at the studio set bright and early, ready to wait our turn for the stars. This was going to be a long day unless I could schmooze the film's PR company. Luckily, through a stroke of good fortune, the American lady in charge had the same surname as my mother's maiden name: Cullen. 'That's amazing,' I said, 'you've got the same surname as my mother. They're a really old Irish family. They were chieftains around the Wicklow area [or it might have been Carlow] and descended from Heber, who along with his brother Heremon, were the first two kings of Irish Legend, the original Milesians or Gaelic Celts who invaded Ireland from Spain around 2000 BC.'

She was fascinated and very sympathetic when I told her how ill my mother had been and how I was hoping to get an early flight back to the UK to see her, as I was so worried.

Us Irish and our grey-haired mammies, it's a wonder the tears weren't flowing, but it worked a treat and we were soon bumped up to the top of the list. Cybill Shepherd, Stockard Channing, Mary Stuart Masterson and Beau Bridges were all paraded out one after the other. As Cybill sat down she told me how concerned she was about my mother and I just looked down at my notes as if stoically trying to fight back the tears, when in fact I was hiding my embarrassment and looking at my first question.

Cybill was brilliant as an interviewee, very grounded, funny, yet opinionated and enthusiastically giving a serious answer to my question about how difficult it was to get good roles in Hollywood for females in contrast to the golden days of the old studio system, where actresses like Bette Davis, Joan Crawford and Elizabeth Taylor all had these fantastic strong lead roles written for them. She went on to talk about her poor upbringing in Memphis and how her family were chicken farmers, the lowest of the low, laughing at my suggestion that farmers aren't poor. She was very amusing, even saying that nowadays, with all her fame and success, she's still considered nouveau riche in Memphis because her money didn't come from cotton.

I then asked her about being Elvis Presley's girlfriend, and she spoke about what a lovely shy and generous person he was and how their backgrounds had been quite similar. She went on to talk about his fame being of the most choking level imaginable and how no human being could be expected to cope with that amount of attention. In fact, she said how much it frightened her, and how, ever since John Lennon had died, she kept a .38 Smith&Wesson revolver in the glove compartment of her car.

I loved her interview. However, to save on time and as we were shooting with only one camera, we had to do reversals, where I said all my questions to camera so we could cut and edit my questions with her answers. After experiencing several of my better interviews being butchered in the editing suite, I only did reversals for the questions I liked the answers to, and in that fashion more or less pre-edited the interview. Let Charlie mess that one up, I thought, chuckling to myself.

Thanks to my mother's fabled illness, by 11 a.m. we were all done and dusted and decided to go out and get well and truly trashed again. With an early flight the following morning and the best part of $1,000 Canadian burning a hole in my pocket, I decided to go shopping. I bought some ear-rings for my mum, an expensive bracelet for my girlfriend, some CDs for our Kevin, a few for me, some books, a furry trapper's hat, some T-shirts and a couple of Zippo lighters. Before long most of that $1,800 float had disappeared. Besides, it was TV and they had loads of money.

Despite my stumbling and bumbling, *The Word* was going from strength to strength, and Stephen Garrett decided to extend the show's run from eighteen to twenty-seven weeks. I had mixed feelings about the news. It meant I would get paid more, if I was still in the job, that is, and at least it was a vote of confidence for the show, but on the other hand, I would have to wait until April to get my arse sorted out, and it was only October and I was in absolute agony. Stephen Garrett had decided to move *The Word* from it's 6 p.m. Friday-night slot to 11 p.m. on the same night. In many ways we had had a little too much adult content on at 6 p.m. and I thought 11 p.m. would be better. If anyone had needed convincing about moving to a later slot, what happened on the last *Word* show aired at 6 pm would have made up their minds.

Our guests on that final six o'clock show were the eccentric Australian owner of Little Nell's celebrity nightclub in New York, Nell; Australian tennis star Pat Cash, and American white soul singing sensation and Prince collaborator Elisa Fiorillo.

Throughout the show Nell kept pulling her top down to reveal her naked boobs to both the audience and myself, though luckily for us – as it was before the watershed – none of it was caught on camera. She continued to do the same thing when Pat Cash came on, much to his amusement. Like the previous week, when we'd had Jimmy Somerville and Margi Clarke on, the whole show had a good feel to it and I was slowly but surely starting to get to grips with things.

The week before I'd been on a nationwide radio promotions tour, going on radio and talking to local and national press about *The Word* moving to 11 p.m. Driving from Scotland to Southampton, stopping in Glasgow, Leicester, London and Cardiff, was absolutely exhausting and I wasn't even being paid a daily rate – I got paid a straight £500 plus £100 expenses a week for doing *The Word*, whether I worked three days or seven. I was extremely tired and worn out but somewhat uplifted by the nature of the radio interviews, especially when the public called in. It seemed that some people out there really loved *The Word* and were genuinely excited about the show. It was the first time I'd really got a handle on how people outside of London and Manchester felt about the show and it gave my confidence a bit of a boost: 'Oi, Terry, loved it when you introduced that Bee Gees track at the end and then turned to Pat Cash and said, "Now you can say, 'New balls please.'" Cracked me up no end.'

So the viewers at home had found the odd line I said funny, and the overall tone of the show made it very different. There was still plenty of work to be done, but maybe in its new 11 p.m. slot, it would find it's feet.

On our first ever late show on 11 November 1990, we had Boy George and his band Jesus Loves You performing live, an exclusive live interview with Whitney Houston and the outside broadcast with Amanda De Cadenet where she'd be touring the antique clock shops of London with Flavor Flav of Public Enemy. I'd first met Boy George back in 1982, when he'd been a guest on my radio show *Barbed Wireless* just before an up-and-coming Culture Club had played to a lukewarm reception of 150 people at The Blue Note club in Derby. George is one of the true great characters of British pop – a good talker, with a self-deprecating, impudent humour.

I have to confess I was extremely nervous about interviewing Whitney Houston, though, as Americans seem to take offence at any number of things and she was very much a huge star at the time. I'd had it drummed into me all week how special it was to have landed Princess Whitney, so by the time I met her, it felt like an audience with the Pope. We were filming the show at LWT, and the reigning queen of TV, Cilla Black's dressing room was donated to Whitney Houston, who arrived looking absolutely immaculate half an hour before the show was to go on air. I nervously went to greet her and her basketball-playing personal assistant and friend. Whitney was much warmer and friendlier than I'd expected and I had to remind myself that she was younger than me and why shouldn't she be like anybody else; it wasn't like fame was alien to her, growing up with aunts like Thelma and Cissy Houston, and it became obvious as the show went on that she loved our young vibe.

I stuttered and stumbled slightly through Whitney's introduction, but managed what became an excellent interview. As ever on *The Word*, we got our guests to comment on different film pieces and gossip stories, ambushing Whitney with a clip of Eddie Murphy from a compilation video of his appearances on *Saturday Night Live*. After the Eddie Murphy clip, Whitney smiled and said, 'Oh I geddit, I geddit,' then I asked her if she felt she'd been stitched up, as she was now forced to talk about her relationship with Eddie Murphy. I asked her if Eddie had rung her up while she'd been in Britain, and she attempted to imitate my accent: 'Yes, Eddie's roong me oop and I've roong him oop,' much to the amusement of the studio audience.

What was interesting to see was how well she engaged the audience, who were really young and talkative. During the advertising breaks they were all chatting away to her, getting her to sign autographs and telling her when they'd seen her live or memories of buying her albums. I winced when one young black lad with short dreads cheekily shouted out, 'Whitney, can I have your phone number?' When she smiled and said no, he replied, 'It's all right, I've heard you're a lesbian anyway.' This had been on my list of questions that I was expected to ask and had been dreading throughout the interview, so I was relieved that he had taken the burden off me and by how amused Whitney was, joining in the laughter as she replied, 'Not that old one again – typical.'

During the show we ran my Cybill Shepherd interview, which finished with her telling me how she kept a gun in the glove compartment of her car. I asked Whitney if she too had a gun. She denied it most vehemently, saying she was protected by the light of God, then just to fill in time I asked her if she had ever thought of appearing in a movie. She came out with the exclusive that she'd been approached to be in *The Bodyguard* with Kevin Costner and was considering it. Ten out of ten, I'd done my job. At last I was finding my feet and the talents I'd nurtured for so long would begin to bloom on national telly – what a dick I was.

In the meantime the press continued to slag me off for my ineptitude as a presenter, making stuff up about how thick I was. They were also forever stating how inane and banal my interviews were, which even if I watch them back now they certainly aren't. When we'd had Margi Clarke on she was electrifyingly animated about how few dramas dealt with working-class subjects, while soul singer Alexander O'Neal talked about racism as a boy in Mississippi and we even had a discussion with Edwina Currie, then still a Tory MP, about how power and stupidity were so often one and the same that there was something unremarkable about it. As an observation, the latter wasn't exactly an exploding illumination, but perhaps that was what the critics meant by inane and banal.

I still wrote 'The Word' page for the *Manchester Evening News*, which I'd normally type up in the *Evening News* office on a Monday or Tuesday morning, if I was around. While I was there, Andy Spinoza, who wrote the *Evening News*'s Diary page, strolled over and pronounced in his best estuary English, 'Hey up, Terry, I've just had Piers Morgan from the *Sun* on the phone to me, asking me if I had anything on Terry Christian and saying he wants to get you.'

I wasn't sure what that was about. All the press had slagged me off, and they were entitled to their opinion; it wasn't as if I was proud of my presentation skills at the time, and I knew that presenters of youth shows always got a hard time. It was definitely a case of a threatened sledgehammer to crack what in my case was a very vulnerable and soft nut. I kept telling myself to brazen it out. I'd never been a natural on radio either, but I'd persevered and learned by my mistakes; the problem was the sheer petrifying nature of presenting – for a beginner, doing live telly is extremely difficult.

As for Piers Morgan and his threats of digging around, I was hardly Billy Big Bollocks, swanning around town, acting like I was anybody special; I was so ordinary in my everyday life and tastes as to be totally dull. I was earning £500 a show, renting a shitty flat in Colindale and spending the rest of the time at my mam and dad's council house in Old Trafford; I hadn't even been invited to a single showbusiness party. I wasn't exactly Mr High Profile who Joe Public would enjoy being taken down a peg or two, even by someone like Mr Piers Morgan.

A week later an interview appeared in the *Sun* under the headline: TERRY CHRISTIAN: TWENTY OF MY FAVOURITE THINGS.

'So, Terry, what's your favourite food?'

'Pizza.'

'What Music are you into at the moment?'

'Well, I've been getting into the new Jason Donovan album recently.'

I was horrified, not only had I never spoken to or had any contact with anybody from the *Sun*, but the answers to the questions in the piece weren't related in any way and were almost all diametrically opposed to what were my favourite things. Here was an interview that had never taken place being printed in a national paper, and I was horrified to learn that it wasn't even against the law.

I've got an extremely sore ring piece and things aren't looking good. Charlie tells me that our commissioning editor Stephen Garrett is very unhappy about me and doesn't think I'm right for the show. It seems I'm sowing discontent, and in every article and interview I do, he feels I disrespect the people I work with and for. By now I don't know what to believe with Charlie, and yet I like him for some reason. This means that when he (probably unintentionally) fucks me about, I feel more hurt than aggrieved, and the major struggle with my presentation style is just to be more relaxed and enjoy it, but to do that I need to feel I have some support behind me.

In contrast, Stephen Garrett always seemed to have something sensible and constructive to say to me, and seemed much more aware of which parts of the show I felt comfortable with and even the types of personalities I gelled best with on air, although he had issues with my honesty and openness in interviews with the press, who used to twist what I said out of all proportion. I decided to brazen it out and pretend I wasn't bothered about Garrett, instead I focused on what Matthew Bowes had told me about Charlie and decided not to believe what he said and just carry on trying to get a handle on my presenting skills.

As presenters on *The Word* we were all contractually obliged to undertake a certain amount of press to publicize each series. Amanda loved her name being mentioned and seeing her photo in the papers, but for me it was the worst part of working on the show. It involved confronting a faceless parade of agendas from a variety of publications that would take you to lunch or to the pub, interview you for anything from fifteen minutes to an hour, then head off and write something that most of the time bore little resemblance to the conversation you'd had.

At first I was as honest, forthright and charming as possible and even quite enjoyed the process, but I noticed that if a journalist did write a portion of what you'd said verbatim, it was was always taken completely out of context or ended up as part of a diatribe denouncing you as the devil's disciple. Most of you reading this will be thinking, Oh yes, the *Sun*, the *Mirror*, the *Star*, but in fact, when I was doing interviews with any of the red tops – or tabloids, though that gives too much credence to the so-called broadsheets, whose journalists are just as likely to make things up – depending on my mood, I started to be fairly dismissive of the journalist and allow for the fact that they'd probably make the whole thing up anyway, in which case I might as well have some fun and be really horrible.

The biggest culprits for having made up their mind about you before they met you were the so-called style and music magazines like *The Face*, *NME*, *Melody Maker* and *Q*. Much as daily papers have a pre-determined line on politics, these magazines used to take a similar line on individuals, who are given a pigeon hole into which all stories and interviews must fit, and if they don't, they'll be made to. It's very much a case of give a dog a bad name, and as far as I was concerned, not since a certain hound used to scare the shit out of the Baskerville family has a canine been subject to such bad press. I guess it makes life easy for a journalist; it's the hack's equivalent of a ready meal – add water and stir well – but like all ready meals, it's pretty unhealthy and tasteless.

There was also what might be called 'The Attack of the Middle Brow' – a dreadfully insecure bunch who are desperate to be thought of as high brow, but lack the talent and gravitas required, so try and get there by stamping down hard on anything they can label low brow. It's like the famous *The David Frost Show* sketch, with the upper-class, middle-class and working-class men. The upper-class man looks down on the middle-class man, who in turn looks down on the working-class man. The punchline has the working-class man stating, 'I know my place.' I hope I never know my place, and in my opinion *The Word* as a show should have been judged on it's own terms: was it fun? Was it young and lively? Did people enjoy watching it? And on the whole the answer to all those questions was a resounding yes.

There seemed to be a particular breed of cringing middle-brow types. I remember one broadsheet TV and radio critic, whose expression was stuck between a sneer and an arse lick. Reading any of his oleaginous interviews with 'proper' writers or auteur directors and you feared rescue parties might have to be sent to recover him, so deep had he crawled up their backsides. By contrast he had an obvious contempt for anything with a taint of working-class popularism. There's a very irritating trend nowadays in which both hacks and comedians feel they are at liberty to go down the 'ay oop'/'by eck' route with regard to northern working-class people – it's lazy and racist and written by the sorts of journalists who, if they'd been reporting the civil rights marches in the sixties, would probably have had Martin Luther King reprising clichéd lines like

'Dem watermelons sure is good eatin' massa.' You can see it in the chav comments, the *Little Britain* sketches and the constant digs at footballers as overpaid lowlife scum. And what's the common denominator in those who hold these views? Public schoolboys – the off-spring of the severely comfortably off.

Consequently, in interviews, I used to get fed up and enjoy winding them up.

'So, Terry, why do you hate London?'

'It's a bit dull really.'

They would look at me like I'm mad and say, 'Dull! How can you say that? Blah, blah. World capital, restaurants, blah, blah. Nothing up north, blah, blah.'

'Well, not so much dull as just a bit far from anywhere.'

'What do you mean?'

'Well, if you want a night out in Liverpool it's 200 miles away, and it's the same if you want a night out in Leeds, whereas if you live in Manchester, you just have to jump in a car or on a train and you're there having a great night in forty-five minutes.'

Of course, you need to keep a straight face while you say all this. Then you can slate the journalist off, especially if he's from one of the glossies like *The Face*, *Q* or *Select* for never having heard of this or that club in Leeds or Liverpool, or this or that band.

This, of course, gives the journalist in question the right fucking hump, so instead of a modest 400 words saying *The Word*'s crap and really uncool and that you're a bit of a tosser, you get 1,000 words saying you're the Antichrist and *The Word* is the most awful show of all time.

I thought pissing off all these journalists was great fun, but unfortunately it doesn't always read the way you meant it to in print. Basically, your bad press follows you: if Piers Morgan writes in the *Sun* that I'm cerebrally challenged and a moron, other journalists say I'm thick. When the next journalist comes to interview me, he's read all these interviews about how thick I am and is almost creaming himself at the thought of stitching me up and taking the piss out of me into the bargain.

'So, Terry, why is *The Word* so awful?'

'Is that a question or a statement?'

'Why do you hate London?'

'I don't hate London, I just live in Manchester and don't really think about London.'

'What's so good about Manchester? It's always raining, isn't it?'

'Statistically, Manchester gets one inch of rain a year more than Brighton.'

'Are you a professional northerner?'

'What's that? What's a professional southerner? Is there such a thing?'

'Well, you're always going on about Manchester and how much you hate London.'

'No, you and other journalists are always bringing it up, not me.'

'What's your favourite part of London?'

'I like that big clock.'

'Erm, you mean Big Ben?' they say, all superior.

'No, that big clock attached to the Houses of Parliament.'

'What's the most northern thing you've ever done?'

'Kill my brother's kestrel.'

I wasn't that bothered about all the sniping, I just thought it showed how fascinated they were by *The Word* and myself, although after a couple of years it got pretty tedious. What really bothered me at the time was the aching loneliness and isolation I felt. I just didn't fit in anywhere in my life and seemed to be surrounded by people who wished me ill.

The irony was that the show was becoming a big success. I interviewed Jean-Claude Van Damme via satellite link live and it went nice and smoothly, but we were struggling to get big-name guests on, especially as Terry Wogan aired several times a week and seemed to hoover them all up. Charlie was also a stumbling block, because if the stars on offer didn't float his boat, they were out of the equation, no matter how much everyone disagreed with him. We got offered George Best once and I was besides myself with excitement – the all-time true great of football, my personal hero, an absolute icon, with loads of stories to tell about models, actresses and Miss World's as well as some great goal-scoring clips. The only problem was, Charlie thought George Best was too old and our audience wouldn't have heard of him.

'Charlie, George Best is someone that, even if you're not aware of who he is, you'll have heard of him, and at least you can explain to an audience who he is and why he's on the show, unlike Thea Vidale or Maryam d'Abo. I mean it's George Best, he's a living legend and I love him.' Yes, I know, it's pathetic.

I begged and pleaded, as did that week's producer, Richard Godfrey, but to no avail. Bestie was given the golden boot and ended up on Terry Wogan instead, drunk as a skunk and making the front pages of every tabloid newspaper the next day with a television moment that has become as legendary as the man himself. Charlie was gutted. To cheer him up, I put a comforting arm around him and said, 'I told you we should have had Bestie on. Honestly, you're a right fucking balloon sometimes, Charlie.'

Even when we were on at six o'clock, it never crossed my mind to act like a children's presenter. The show was so gay and camp that everyone in the office had started calling it *Out On Friday*. It was very reflective of what was going on on the gay scene, so we had pieces from the USA on *The Rocky Horror Picture Show*, featuring some genuine saddos who'd been to see the show 1,219 times, or Village People live on stage at some working men's club in Batley, Yorkshire. Every week on the couch we'd have guests like Julian Clary, Holly Johnson, Boy George, Jimi Somerville and Margi Clarke. You can see the pattern emerging here. Yet it helped the show work, as these guests were in many ways outsiders, and *The Word* was an outsider's show. It was very effective at reaching out to teenagers in that fourteen-plus bracket who were aware that they were gay. I have to say that a couple of our researchers didn't exactly cover themselves in glory at the time, though.

When Holly Johnson came onto the couch, I welcomed him and said, 'Holly, when you were a kid, you went to the same Liverpool school as John Lennon, didn't you?'

'No, I didn't. John Lennon went to Quarry Bank and I went to. . .' It was all there in my notes, which a particular researcher had spent all week putting together.

There was another occasion when I was interviewing female white rapper Tairrie B.

'You were born and raised in the Bronx in New York, yet you now base yourself in LA.'

'No, I was born and raised in LA, it's my home town. I've never even been to the Bronx.' That's posh researchers for you.

One thing Charlie and I were great believers in was the idea of juxtapositioning – putting unlikely people together or taking people out of their comfort zone to see what happens. In one of the first shows, Amanda came back from America to broadcast live by satellite from Prestatyn Pontins on the first night of a soul weekender. Amanda had never heard of Pontins, so the researcher had to explain to her that it was a holiday camp by the seaside where a lot of ordinary people went for their holidays. Amanda asked where people stayed, and was told they stayed in a chalet, where indeed all of them would be staying that night. Amanda was quite happy about this, but 'chalet' to Amanda meant a large wooden three-storey house in the Swiss Alps with a sauna in the basement.

When she arrived and saw where she'd be staying, she exclaimed rather loudly, 'People actually stay here? Where's the phone? I'm going to call Charlie.' When it was explained to Amanda that chalets in Pontins don't come with phones, she was aghast and proceeded to phone Charlie on her mobile and give him an earful about the horrendously common people staying all around her, how shabby and horrible her chalet was, how the bed's mattress was made of foam rubber and – horror of horrors – there wasn't even a phone in the room. Charlie reassured her she'd be fine and told her to have a great time. It was sublime casting and saw Amanda, who's not one to hide her feelings, disgusted yet fascinated by the wild excesses and lowlife fun had by the soul boys and girls at Pontins. It was all rather misogynistic having loads of naked blokes shaving their chest hair and standing right next to Amanda with only a handful of shaving foam covering their meat and two veg, but Amanda was able to bat them off and shout at the mob, and it made hilarious viewing.

I have to admit that Amanda was looking a lot better on *The Word* than I was. When I had a guest I didn't gel with I really struggled, and I still hadn't got to grips with listening to Charlie shout down my earpiece during filming. Because it was a live show with pre-recorded video inserts, it had to be timed correctly, but the running order could change drastically during the show and I needed to get used to listening to talkback in my ear.

One week they used open talkback for the first fifteen minutes of the show. As the intro music finished and I was told cue in my earpiece and by the floor manager, I froze mid word and stumbled through a tortuous scripted introduction and show menu, all the time hearing dozens of people in the gallery blabbing away to each other. I was wearing this horrible Austin Powers-style paisley shirt, tucked into some very tight white Levi's that really aggravated my behind and made it hard to concentrate. I looked and felt like a right nana. Our guests that night were Jimmy Somerville and Margi Clarke, who saved my life because they're such great talkers and storytellers.

I have to say I lived in a permanent state of physical pain and acute embarrassment. I remember going back on the train up to Manchester one Saturday morning, my face caked in make-up as I'd been so drunk the night before at the after-show party I hadn't got round to washing it off. As usual I was sat in the normal carriage, with loads of young people around talking about me.

'Awroight, Tel.'

Four young lads engaged me in conversation. Real East End boys who were on their way up to Manchester to watch Arsenal play Manchester City. I wasn't a big fan of Arsenal – to me they'd always had a tradition of scrapping and scraping jammy one–nil wins whenever they played United and the games were invariably dull affairs with lots of nasty tackles and no flowing football. They certainly weren't a team I could imagine paying to watch every week. Yet these lads, all aged between nineteen and twenty-two spent every single penny they had travelling to watch George Graham's Arsenal all over the country.

One of the lads was unemployed and, unlike a lot of football fans his age in Manchester, he wasn't supplementing his travels with a bit of crime. He explained at length how expensive it was to follow his team and how he could hardly afford to eat, but that it was important to him. Unlike life, football was fair, justice could be seen to be done most Saturdays, and nine times out of ten the team who played best on the day won. It was something that struck you as being clean in a dirty world. I understood that feeling and it made me realize what a prick I was turning into.

I had a decent job, got free clothes, didn't get my hands dirty, had cars to drive me around, met famous and interesting people and got well paid for it – I certainly didn't struggle financially for my Man United season ticket and, to a degree, I was temporarily insulated from the icy blast of poverty. Manchester United were no longer the be-all and end-all to me, because there was so much more in my life besides how my team were doing. But still I wondered how I'd forgotten that feeling so quickly? There's an old saying that a full belly has a short memory, and it had taken some fanatical young Arsenal supporters to remind me of that fact. I'd bump into them several times over the next few years, travelling up to watch Arsenal play United, City and Oldham Athletic. I even bought them a few drinks, though, I'm sorry to say I can't remember their names; they were top lads, though.

It seems strange that these lads and other strangers often used to say, 'You're so down to earth.' I tried my best, but I couldn't help feeling a bit of self-loathing every time someone said it. I suppose the biggest illusion of fame is that you think that it's not you who's changed but the people around you. It's said often, but in my experience it was a complete fallacy. I'd been a little bit famous since I was nineteen and could feel the imprint of its arrogance on my psyche even just as a local radio DJ. It's a kind of power, and the more fame you get, the more powerful you feel, as if you can make all your dreams come true; it's a crude yearning for self-gratification.

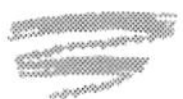

Suddenly *The Word* office was a brighter place, the viewing figures were good and everyone was talking about the show, even though a fair proportion of what was said wasn't particularly flattering. It was decided that for our last but one show before Christmas we would do the whole show live from Universal Studios in Los Angeles. Charlie was excited at the thought of big-name A-list Hollywood guests and the like. It was exciting to fly over to LA with the whole team: the producer Richard Godfrey, the director Stephen Stewart, the set designer Cath Lancucki, the budget man Miles Bullough and, of course, Charlie, Amanda, Matthew Bowes and my old mate, our music booker Tim Byrne.

We travelled en masse to LA on the Saturday after the Friday's show, so we'd have the best part of a week to put together our Christmas special. To add to my haemorrhoids and anal fissure, I developed a raging temperature and bad bout of the flu. I'd felt it coming on, but as a rule I was rarely ill, so I just thought it was a bad cold. By the time we landed in Los Angeles, though, I had the shivers, no appetite and felt as weak as a kitten. However, there was a really busy schedule ahead.

I'd already spotted an advert on American TV about a huge nativity play with real camels, sheep, donkeys and flying angels suspended by wires from the gigantic roof of what was called the Crystal Cathedral in Anaheim, a huge church made completely out of glass. Every day I'd drag my aching-all-over body out of bed to film inserts for the show and spent a collection of exhausting fifteen-hour days travelling and hanging around endlessly on location shoots or, as it became known, 'Hurry up and wait'. What the fuck am I doing watching a bloody nativity play in a big glass church, I thought. Why did I suggest this?'

When I bumped into Charlie I'd tell him how terrible I felt. 'Yes, you look it, Terry, just get something to eat and go to sleep,' he'd say. Notice he never said, 'Well take a day off and I'll get Amanda to present that shoot.'

We'd been followed to LA by Andy Coulson from the *Sun*, who despite the dubious nature of his profession, was a good laugh to have a pint with. He'd come over with a photographer to follow Amanda De Cadenet around, as she was engaged to John Taylor of Duran Duran. Amanda claimed to be annoyed about the harassment, but she still enjoyed herself, spending most of her time ordering bottles of champagne off room service and putting them on her room bill when we were supposed to pay for everything out of our $40 a day per diems. I had brunch with her once on the roof of the hotel on our one half day off. Matthew Bowes had joined us briefly and was filling us in on how tough it was proving to get good guests after all the cheeky questions and naughty send-ups we'd done on Hollywood stars. He said he'd hardly left the hotel room that was doubling as a temporary office. When he headed back to his room, Amanda flirtatiously asked him his room number. Matthew laughed and answered her in as joking a manner as she'd posed the question.

As he walked off, she asked me what Matthew's surname was. Amazed that she'd been working on the show for four months and didn't already know, I told her.'

'Anyway, Terry, do you want some champagne.'

'Only if you're paying.'

'I'll just put it on my room.'

The waiter came over, the champagne arrived in its bucket of ice and Amanda signed the bill with Matthew's room number and the signature M. Bowes.

I found it funny, but I told her off and made her change it to her own room number. I knew Matthew wasn't exactly rolling in it and it was a rotten thing to do to one of the crew.

Amanda was a strange one really. She was a girl I suppose only lads would like. Yes she was flirty and coy, but she had a great sense of humour, too. By nature she was quite down to earth, but she could put on this snotty, horrible, sloany front at times and do that London media thing of gushing like a broken toilet pipe, with just as edifying results, when she wanted to charm someone or get her own way. If she ever started coming the snooty Sloane around me, I'd just ask her to turn it in and she would do immediately, as it was just part of an act. Although I'm not a great believer in horoscope nonsense, we are both Taureans, and I think we found each other amusing company, even when we were shouting at each other, which happened from time to time.

Our music booker Tim Byrne was enamoured of Amanda, and the whole time we were in LA, he stuck to her like shit to a blanket. He was into hanging out with pop stars and name dropping Kylie Minogue and the like, he even told me once that Kylie liked me – imagine me and Kylie, the woman whose arse kept tabloid sales afloat throughout the early Noughties. Anyway, on the night before our live show, Amanda was off cavorting around the Roxborough Club in Beverly Hills for some VIP party, while I was feeling as rough as the proverbial bear's arse. In fact. . . well, let's not go there.

Amanda and Tim were going out, but Amanda was insistent I go with them. Tim Byrne gets on my nerves and that would go doubly for how he feels about me. I've been in LA all week and haven't been out once, so I'm feeling like all I've done is work, eat and – very carefully and painfully – shit. I've written my script and am looking forward to presenting the show in the sunshine the following day with guests Johnny Rotten and Ricki Lake, so finally, after much badgering, I agree to accompany them to their A-list night out. Tim makes an effort to be OK with me, and I don't feel particularly uncomfortable around him as there's nothing devious about him, I'm just not his cup of tea. When we get to the Roxborough, I wonder how we'll get in as they're very keen on identity cards in LA and Amanda's only eighteen, but before I know it we're in the club. I go to the bar and order a drink and am just conversing with a very attractive would-be actress from Kentucky when my arm is almost yanked out of its socket.

'Come on, Terry, we're going into that roped-off section, it's a party for George Michael.'

I'm pulled very firmly and forcefully by Amanda into a crowded room where everyone is packed like sardines and there's a small school dinners-type serving hatch, which I assume is the bar, twenty deep with people crushed around it.

'Come and meet Ridley Scott's son.'

I'm dragged through a seething press of people to meet a smart-looking, short, dark-haired young English guy who seems somewhat taken aback as Amanda paws him and starts gushing like that broken toilet pipe. I'm a decoy for Amanda. Ridley Scott's son is with his beautiful American girlfriend, I get introduced to her and she seems a really nice girl. After five or so minutes, Amanda is deep in conversation with the famous director's son's girlfriend, and ten minutes later we head for the door to go somewhere else. Amanda is working the scene in LA. She'd never met Ridley Scott's son before, but she's like a whirlwind in action, spotting people left, right and centre.

Before we do *The Word* live from Universal Studios, a film crew from the popular US TV show *Entertainment Tonight* arrives to interview Amanda about her forthcoming nuptials with John Taylor. In the short time we'd spent in the Roxborough, Ridley Scott's girlfriend has been persuaded to loan Amanda her Porsche 911. This way, *Entertainment Tonight* can do a shot of Amanda arriving to present her British TV show in style, before being interviewed in her trailer about her celebrity life in London, England and her heart-throb rock-star husband-to-be. I have to go to Universal in a minicab with our producer Richard Godfrey, driven by an Uzbekistani driver who speaks little or no English.

'You know, Richard, she blagged that Porsche within ten minutes of meeting a complete stranger.'

Richard, who always reminded me of James Mason, drily commented, 'Yes, she hasn't even passed her driving test in Britain and she's not insured, either.'

The journey to Universal takes about forty-five minutes on the freeway. I arrive and make my way to my trailer, keeping an eye out for Princess Amanda and her borrowed Porsche. Two hours later she still hasn't arrived, then suddenly she turns up in a minicab, distraught as she wants to get dolled up properly for the *Entertainment Tonight* crew who've been awaiting her arrival for the past two hours.

'Fucking bitch!' she mutters.

Yes indeed, the young lady who allowed Amanda to borrow her Porsche had the cheek not to fill the tank with petrol beforehand. So when our Amanda was screaming down the freeway in the fast lane, the Porsche came to a juddering halt because it had run out of petrol. So what does Amanda do? She takes the keys, dodges through the traffic and flags down a passing cab, leaving the Porsche abandoned on the freeway without bothering to tell anybody until way after the show some six hours later.

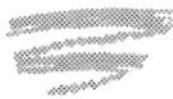

On the show itself, things are almost as disastrous. We are positioned in the Old Wild West street. The main camera, with the autocue on it, had the sun directly behind it, so it shone straight into my eyes, which were already puffed up with flu and sleepless nights because of my arse trouble. The sunlight is also reflecting back onto the camera's autocue from the window of the mocked-up general store behind us, so I can hardly read a thing, plus I'm stuffed up and aching all over with that weird, fuzzy influenza headache. There are five minutes to go and I'm surrounded by a few dozen tourists and an all-American camera, sound and lighting crew. The talkback in my ear piece isn't working, and for some reason it keeps on picking up what sounds like taxi calls. My first guest, Johnny Rotten, warns me that if somebody doesn't get him a beer he's walking off. I look around and there isn't one member of *The Word*'s production crew in sight. There's a bar about 100 metres away, but I haven't got any dollars on me and neither has Johnny. Two young English lads are looking on. 'Hey, mate, you couldn't do us a favour and buy Johnny a bottle of beer?' I ask.

'No chance, I've only got five dollars on me.'

'It'll only be two dollars and I'll give you ten after the show – plus you'll get an anecdote out of it.'

Thankfully he provided the waiter service, and with 30 seconds to go before the opening titles of our live-from-LA show, Johnny is brought back from the brink of walking away.

The show was all over the place: I couldn't hear any talkback, Johnny slandered people, especially Malcolm McLaren his old Sex Pistols manager, left, right and centre, and all Rikki Lake and myself could do was giggle. Our music guests were Dwight Yoakam and Def Jef, and at the end Amanda gave Richard Carpenter an award from the British music industry for his late sister Karen. The whole show had been a bit flat. The guests were OK, but no better than we would have had in England and it lacked the atmosphere of a live studio audience.

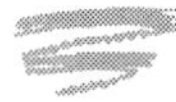

The following week, back in the studio for our official Christmas show, we at last have Steve Coogan on as a guest. In Manchester, people had been raving about Steve as an impressionist since he was a teenager. The only comparison I can think of is the way, as a football fan, you hear about some amazing fourteen-year-old whiz kid in the youth team, like Ryan Giggs when he was at Man City or Wayne Rooney at Everton, then you watch them bloom into the greatness they were destined for – and I don't mean playing for Man United, though then and again. . .

Steve Coogan was definitely going to be a big name and he was an ideal guest for us. I'd pushed to get him on the show from day one, only to have that 'Well, he's not that big in London,' thing shoved back at me. Dele Oniya, who produced that week's show, had relented, but instead of having Steve as a proper sit-down guest, he had him dressed up as Father Christmas doing a few impressions and handing out presents. I was really annoyed about it, while Dele thought he'd made the greatest, most earth shattering creative decision ever.

Our other guests on the show were Jimmy and Sinbad from *Brookside* and Janice Long. With three Scousers I thought I'd have a bit of Mancunian versus Scouse banter with them, but it didn't really work and at one point – God knows where it came from – I turned to the camera and said, 'There you go, Scousers: thieves and liars the lot of 'em.' It was meant to be totally tongue-in-cheek, but perhaps it didn't come across that way. After the show Stephen Garrett was seriously annoyed and would hardly speak to me, he hadn't been pleased with my performance the week before when we were live from Universal Studios, either, and I got the impression that he was at the end of his tether as far as I was concerned.

If I had to choose one incident where I think Stephen Garret really went off me, it was as a result of an ill-advised *Q* article. Each month their leading journalist Tom Hibbert would create a semi-literary and very entertaining piece of writing with the headline, WHAT THE HELL DOES X THINK HE/SHE/IT IS? It was a very popular column, amusing and well written, but it was a hatchet job, and while Tom was an imaginative writer, in the case of the four or five pages he wrote on Amanda, myself and *The Word*, WHAT THE HELL DOES THE WORD THINK IT IS? was a work of pure fiction. We'd just come back to do the first *Word* show after Christmas and Amanda had finally married John Taylor on Boxing Day

Firstly Mr Hibbert wanted to meet up for lunch in a restaurant in London. He gave us a choice of venues and Amanda and myself chose an Indian restaurant. When I arrived and was introduced to Tom, I got the limpest, sweatiest handshake ever. I turned away and walked over to the bar with our press bloke Neil Redding and said, 'Listen, there's no point in me talking to this twat, he's going to take the piss out of us.' I was reassured that Mr Hibbert was a fine journalist and that this would put *The Word* on the front page of *Q*.

When Amanda arrived we sat at a table to eat and do the interview. Amanda had just got married and this was the first time I'd seen her since, so I said congratulations and she asked why I hadn't bought her a wedding present. I light-heartedly batted it aside by replying that as I didn't know the date of her wedding and wasn't

Looking tremendously well turned out – I've never looked so smart since (F.J. Luty, Moss Side)

Below left Me, patrolling the streets (with gun) in 1967. A shape of things to come. Our Mary and our Kevin are also in the shot.

Below right Brookes Bar, 1966; Kevin, myself (aged 4) and our Mary, with our Tony (far left) and cousins Colin and Chris

Devil's Advocate, 1981. (Above) Discussing the burning issues of the day: mass unemployment and whether it's cool to wear white socks. Host Gus MacDonald looks disturbingly like Ned Flanders

Left A callow youth (revolutionary?), in the tv studio in between selling jumpers, September 1981

OPPOSITE PAGE

Main picture My Radio Derby publicity shot, February 1982

Inset Bad tank top, bad t-shirt. An interview with Subway Sect (later JoBoxers) at BBC Radio Derby, January 1982

Prince Naseem, former world champion and former MBE, showing off his southpaw lead (Joe Bangay)

The Word Christmas show – like the 1914 match in no man's land, an ultimately doomed attempt at seasonal goodwill, 1993 (Joe Bangay)

Young love. Me and Tim Burgess of The Charlatans, Northwich, July 1990 (Matt Squire)

Me and Caroline Ahern (consistently looked over by *The Word*), May 1992
(Granada Television)

Big hair, big lips, big ego . . . Amanda de Cadanet is also in the picture (Idols)

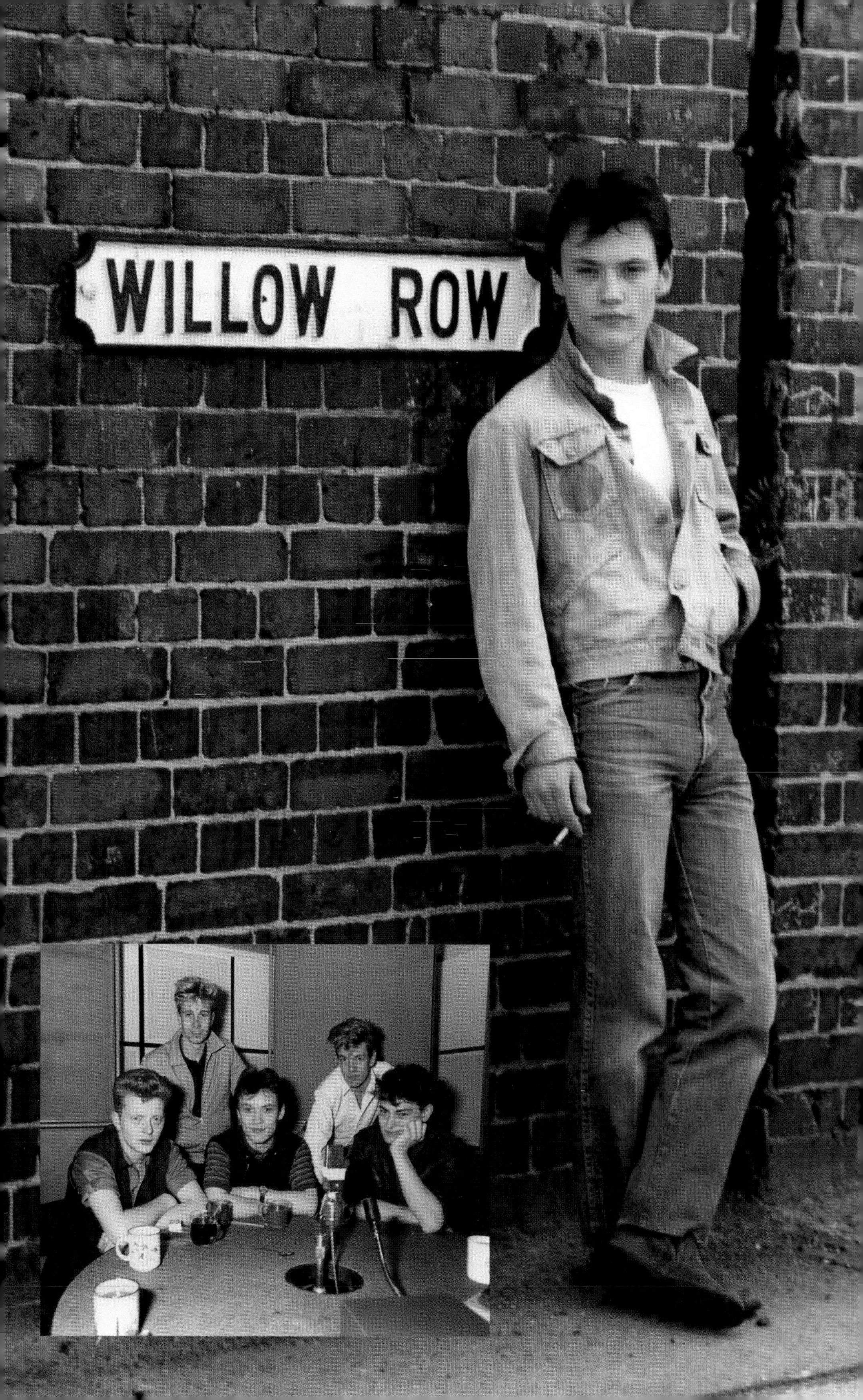
WILLOW ROW

Clockwise from top left On the sofa with Traci Lords; glamour model Kathy Lloyd; Did you pack him in or did he pack you in?, Veronica Webb; Only 16, Anna Friel, never mind

So, Ian, what do you think about being stuck out on the wing for England?

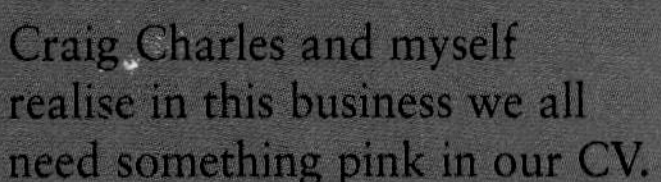

Craig Charles and myself realise in this business we all need something pink in our CV.

Sepultura fulfilling the wishes of quite a few of the show's critics, turning the thumb pressure up to 11, 1995

invited, it would be a bit odd if I had bought her anything. We just indulged in the usual light banter, but when the *Q* article appeared, I'll confess it was well written, very amusing and clever, but it bore no resemblance to what went on over lunch.

On the first page of the article, bearing in mind that the interview was conducted in an Indian restaurant, the first quotation from me had Mr Hibbert writing, 'Terry said as he nonchalantly speared at his chicken korma.'

CHICKEN KORMA?! – Me? A guy who likes hot and spicy? But it was clever, you see, because of what it was suggesting: Terry – northern, parochial, thick, inarticulate – likes his pie and chips and meat and two veg, but stick him in an Indian restaurant and the only thing he'll try is something bland. Then he had the exchange between myself and Amanda De Cadenet, concerning my failure to buy her a wedding gift.

Amanda: 'Why didn't you buy me a wedding present?'

Terry (defensively): 'What do you mean? I didn't know nothing about no wedding; I didn't even get no invite to no wedding.'

Now I'm not Oscar Wilde in the eloquence stakes, but the double negatives aren't even Mancunian vernacular, it's more Arthur Daley and Terry out of *Minder*. I was from Old Trafford in Manchester, not Bow or East Ham. The article then went on to make me sound as rambling and thick as possible, saying things like the show was a complete load of shit, everyone who worked on it was shit and the audience were all absolute scum.

Needless to say, I was summoned to Stephen Garrett's inner sanctum after he'd read the offending article and warned that I'd be sacked, especially for the crime of describing our audience as scum. I tried desperately to make Stephen see that Tom of the limp-lettuce handshake had made it all up, but again it seemed that if you speak with my accent and are from my background, posh people automatically assume you're a dishonest liar. Yes, I was naïve about the press and imprudent in terms of saying what I thought, but the whole *Q* magazine article was a complete work of fiction.

In the new year, when magazines were printing their end-of-year polls, I was most distressed to see my name mentioned in several of them. Both Andi Peters and Dominik Diamond – experts in children's television and computer games respectively – both nominated me for prat of the year in some teen mag like *Just 17*. Very hurtful, not so much for the nomination rather than the nominees; they obviously didn't get out much at the time. Despite the fact that I'd held fire when it came to other TV presenters, they all seemed to have an axe to grind with me. I don't know why? They had successful careers, so why should they be jealous of me presenting a TV show featuring some of the coolest bands around, flying to LA and New York, interviewing top Hollywood stars and having people constantly talk about the show I presented, whether it was Ned Sherrin on Radio 4 or Simon Bates and Steve Wright on radio 1? Perhaps they'd heard the whispers in the night saying, 'It should have been you.' Perhaps Andi Peters wanted to come out of the broom cupboard, drop a few Es and go on tour with the Happy Mondays, or Dominik Diamond wanted to lend his balding, incisive, intellectual heavyweight gravitas, which he later revealed in his regular column for the *Daily Star*, to *The Word* sofa. Later I read an interview with Dominik in a magazine like *Smash Hits!* where his intellectual Scottishness mentioned that when he'd auditioned for *The Word* presenter's job, somebody on the team had told him he should have got it.

I asked Charlie whether this was the case. 'Ergh, God no,' he replied.

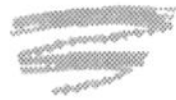

The decision to extend the first series of *The Word* from eighteen to twenty-seven weeks meant I could renegotiate my contract with Waheed Alli. The contract offered covered the whole year. I was contracted to 24 Hour Productions and they had first call, which meant I wasn't allowed to do any other work, even a guest appearance on any other TV or radio show, without 24 Hour productions giving written permission. They also stipulated that any other show I appear on always mention *The Word* when introducing me or speaking to me. I would never be just Terry Christian, but always Terry Christian from *The Word*. It certainly worked from their point of view, but from my point of view it was an albatross around my neck which I've never managed to shake off. In return, my money for the last nine shows of the series would increase from £600 per show to £850 per show. In between series one and any possible series two, I would receive £400 a week, then once we were in pre-production this would increase to £750 per week and I would receive £1,300 per show for series two, increasing to £1,500 per show for a possible series three.

To be frank, I was fairly clueless about how much I was worth. I was facing Waheed, a self-made millionaire by the time he was twenty-four, and this was his territory. I did point out that if I had the money he had then, I'd probably retire and write slim volumes of bad poetry while sunning myself on a tropical beach. If he ever found himself flat broke, I had no doubt that within in a few years' time he'd have found a way to make an even bigger pile of money.

'Probably,' Waheed replied.

'So I think the best thing you can do, Waheed, is give me more of your money, that way you'll be spurred on to increase your empire.'

Waheed didn't agree with this, but he did offer to personally manage me, probably thinking I needed all the help I could get. In fact, he once subtly suggested I have therapy. Having Waheed as a manager was extremely tempting, as I knew he would do a really good job, but he was also my boss and Charlie's partner. I was still finding Charlie's controlling personality suffocating and my head was in bits at the time. I'd struggled to adapt to being 'famous', and found the constant recognition embarrassing. I felt under a lot of pressure, and the ravages of my sore arse weren't helping. In my mind I acknowledged that I'd never felt as unhappy or cut off from my family and loved ones, but, financially at least, the next year or so looked good, so I decided I'd better buy a house in Manchester before it all went pear-shaped.

One day in the office Charlie gleefully handed me a cutting from the previous day's London *Evening Standard*. It was a report on a convention held by the BBC at the Hacienda in Manchester about youth television. The main speaker, of course, was Janet Street-Porter and she was quoted as making a thinly disguised attack on myself and *The Word* in her speech: 'Young people are interested in x, y and z, what they're not interested in are boring northern presenters.'

That week in my *Manchester Evening News* page, I made reference to the fact that, despite all the kerfuffle about access and youth TV at the BBC, if you were northern with an accent, you had no chance of getting a gig working at the BBC in your home town while Janet Street-Porter was there. In reply, Janet fired a letter off to the *Evening News* denying that she'd said any such thing, while I suggested to the *Evening News* editor, Mike Unger, 'You should do a proper investigation, Mike, into how many people working on Janet's programmes come from outside the Thames Valley corridor, then confront her about it. Also, find out how many of them actually stay in Manchester from Friday to Monday.'

No wonder Charlie was smiling, he'd defeated Janet and, from what I heard later, *The Word* was constantly thrown in her face by her bosses: 'Janet, why can't we make a show like *The Word*?'

For the rest of series one I felt like I was walking on a razor blade and as though I didn't have a friend in the world. Trish Kinane had gone off to have a baby and was replaced as the executive producer by Dubliner Tony Boland, who had worked at RTE for years on their big shows like Gay Byrne's *Late Late Show*. Tony was great at giving me guidance on TV presenting, telling me to simplify everything: 'There's no need to cue every item in, just say 'Let's have a look at this film.'

My performances improved, but the flak from the press came thicker and faster. Our first show after the Christmas break had Keith Allen and glamour model Kathy Lloyd booked in as guests. I didn't know much about Keith Allen, other than he was a maverick, talented all rounder who liked to cause a bit of bother. 'Honestly, Terry, he's a Rottweiler.'

I quite enjoyed it when guests had a go at me, and would almost encourage it to get some banter going. As soon as Keith came on we showed a clip of him performing as Reginald Arkwright, the industrial northern gay. In the clip, Keith is dressed in a studded leather vest, hot pants and 1950s Marlon Brando *Wild Ones* leather biker's cap.

'My name's Reginald Arkwright and I'm an industrial northern gay, but when I say gay, I don't mean I find Frankie Howerd funny and I'm not talking about nightclubs. No, what I mean is I like plenty of good northern beetroot.'

Straight from that clip to me with Keith Allen and I fire in my first question.

'So, Keith, what is northern beetroot?'

'I'm sure you've had plenty in your time.'

'Don't you slur my character.'

'Oh I see, suggesting you're gay is a slur on your character, is it.'

I'd been torpedoed by the son of a submarine commander (if what he told me was true).

It got worse as the show went on. Kathy Lloyd and myself were having a bit of banter about her topless modelling and I was implying that it was a bit low rent for a nice girl like her, who read books and had A levels – it was all light-hearted and, as we're both from the Northwest, we both knew it was just a bit of fun. Kathy then said, 'Actually, Terry, if I had a body like yours, then I probably wouldn't bother showing it off either.'

In reply I said, 'If I was meant to be a topless model I wouldn't have been born a sensitive, deep-thinking individual – I'd have been a woman instead.' OK, poor taste, but a joke nonetheless.

The nasty press came thick and fast after that. Garret was onto it. Is Terry homophobic? He's really sexist as well.

Next there was a semi-positive piece in *The Face* about *The Word*, which said, 'Terry Christian is improving and isn't too bad, except for an incipiently nasty streak of homophobia.'

Several weeks later I was asked to do an interview with *The Face*. I knew the girl who would be interviewing me, as she was living in

Manchester and involved in the music scene there when I was doing my radio show, so I presumed that at least the article would be balanced in terms of 'Well, he might not be much cop on the telly, but he's very knowledgable about music.'

We did the interview in Manchester and she asked me about the accusations of homophobia. I just laughed it off as ridiculous. She then brought up the Keith Allen moment and I explained that I was mucking about and obviously acting the outraged old colonel when I said, 'Don't you slur my character.' She then asks if it could be interpreted as homophobic, and I rather flippantly replied that a phobia is a fear of something, 'What I said wouldn't make you think I was scared of homosexuals, it would make you think I didn't like them, so it wasn't homophobic.'

Try reading that one in the press as a cold piece of copy, and she'd also put in the old lines about me being thick and inarticulate. I saw her several months later in Manchester and pulled her up about it, but she explained that it was editorial policy at the *The Face* to not like Terry Christian, so she had to put it in. I then said that I would never have allowed someone to change my copy to that degree if I had written the article. I put it all down to her being southern middle class and highly ambitious.

On the next show we had Lemmy from Motorhead as a guest. We'd been told on pain of death that there was to be 'no smoking on air', for either the presenters or guests, but Lemmy, of course, immediately lit up a fag after referring to the whole show, quite poignantly, as 'Bread and Circuses'.

All the Channel 4 bosses were in, watching like hawks, and Charlie screamed down my earpiece, 'Terry, tell him to put that cigarette out!'

Lemmy broke off halfway through a comment to ask, 'Have you got an ashtray?'

'Well, you're not supposed to smoke, Lemmy, it's a bad influence on the kids.'

'It's an even worse influence if I'm flicking my fucking ash on the floor like a dirty cunt,' he replied.

Garrett had had enough. Charlie was hard at work fighting like a lion for me behind the scenes, but he liked to let me know about it by saying things like, 'Stephen Garrett was going to sack you at Christmas, Terry'

In the pipeline to join me on the show and give it a less laddish feel was actress Michelle Collins, who'd just finished a long stint on *EastEnders*. We'd met briefly, many years before when she was singing with Mari Wilson and the Imaginations at the Blue Note Club in Derby and we'd had her on as a guest on show eight of *The Word* as well as being the guest on the unaired pilot. Michelle was a great girl, but I was in the throes of semi-depression at the time. I think employing her was meant to bring some confidence and experience to the team, as she was a level-headed, fun-loving girl-next-door type.

For Michelle's first show we had Vic Reeves and Bob Mortimer, who I'd be interviewing, and Chris Isaak, the star of New Country, as it was being hailed. We also had Amanda De Cadenet coming live from Bristol at a big reggae sound clash featuring Daddy Freddy and Asher Senator amongst others. The plan was to go over for four visits, culminating in a full live song from there, while the live music in the studio would come from under-rated ex-Soul II Soul singer Caron Wheeler, who was singing a track from her début solo album *UK Blak*, and ex-Undertones, That Petrol Emotion. It was a good show on paper, and although Vic and Bob could be a bit all over the place, I had high hopes.

In the dress rehearsal before the show started, Charlie was in full effect. Firstly, he didn't like what Michelle was wearing: 'It makes her bum look too big,' he said over the talkback, which Michelle could hear. She went away and got changed and Charlie started again, saying she didn't look right, she looked old. Michelle was twenty-seven and didn't look old at all, but Charlie started banging on about crow's feet around her eyes, which he wanted covered with make-up. I couldn't believe that I was hearing all this in my earpiece, along with everyone else. It was Michelle's first show – an absolutely terrifying experience – and with less than an hour to go before we went live, Charlie had behaved in a way that would stop most girls nipping out for a loaf at the corner shop, never mind appearing on national television. Welcome to the team, I thought resignedly.

The show itself was going nicely, with Vic and Bob messing about with food, as ever. I'd noticed in the research notes that Chris Isaak is from a place called Stockton in Virginia, and I thought this was quite amusing as Bob's from Darlington and Vic's from Middlesbrough. After Chris Isaak had serenaded Michelle on the couch with an acoustic version of his hit 'Wicked Game', I then introduced him to Vic and Bob and said how strange it was that they were all neighbours from the north east, informing Vic and Bob that Chris was from Stockton. Bob then said, 'It's got the widest high street in Great Britain,' while Chris Isaak looked a bit confused. Then I went over to Amanda in Bristol. As the camera came back to me, I had picked up a banana to pretend it was a microphone in answer to Vic Reeves fannying about with the fruit bowl. Almost immediately Charlie shouted an ominous warning down my earpiece: 'Terry, Stephen's saying that that is incredibly racist.' I didn't understand, so I carried on pretending to use the banana as a microphone for a few more seconds.

At the end of the show I was again told I'd been racist.

'In what way?'

'Waving that banana around when we came out of the piece at the reggae sound clash.'

It took me a moment to twig what they were trying to say, and I was really annoyed because I'd had nothing but false assumptions pushed on me since the show had started. Every journalist asked me if I was gay because I wasn't spotted out and about in the West End with a bevvy of young chicks on my arm and because I wore loud flowery shirts on the show, then in the next breath I'm called homophobic because I say I'm not gay. Then my boss inferred I was misogynistic, and now I was a racist. With my temper just about kept in check, I confronted Stephen Garrett. Explain to me, Stephen, what a banana has got to do with black people?

I knew it was some football hooligan thing, but I hadn't seen bananas being thrown at black players or heard monkey chants at Old Trafford since a Luther Blissett hat trick for Watford in 1978. Neither of Manchester's teams' fans had tolerated any BNP or far-right leafleting, and many of the United and City hooligans had been involved in the SWP squads who had literally kicked the National Front out of Manchester. Nowhere in my upbringing, which was far from politically correct, had I ever seen any association between black people and bananas, except for an old Harry Belafonte song. I turned it back on Mr Garrett, suggesting that if he thought bananas related to black people in any way, then he was the one who had a problem, not me. Stephen was in agreement with my point.

I often felt a victim of an innate upper-middle-class snobbery where there's an assumption that all white working-class people are ignorant racist, homophobic, sexist hooligan trash. After all, we are the demographic group who grow up alongside, go to school with, play with and have daily contact with immigrants of all races. As for homophobia, which demographic group you belong to doesn't determine your sexuality or your attitude towards people who are gay. All adolescent boys joke about homosexuals and being a puff just to reassure themselves that they're heterosexual, simply because of an innate fear of being different. In fact, if you grow up on a council estate it's more difficult to hide what you are, as everybody more or less knows your business. The area I grew up in was tough, staunchly Irish Catholic and West Indian – not staunchly ignorant and bullying.

The last show of series one was something of a damp squib, guest wise. I'd invited my long-suffering girlfriend Sue along to prove I wasn't gay, and my younger brother Kevin and come down and put five of his mates, who were all living off Brick Lane in London's East End, on the guest list for free drinks. Our Kevin turned up at LWT studios at about 9 p.m. with his friends and they were all absolutely steaming, having been out on a bender since lunch time. One of his mates even puked up in the lift. They didn't want to go and watch the show in the studio with the audience as they wanted to hang around in the green room and watch it there while having free drinks.

'Look, behave yourself, all right, because all my bosses are in there,' I warned them.

The show flew by, with guests Sinitta and Hale and Pace, while Amanda came live from Tennessee with the late Hollywood actor River Phoenix and his band Aleka's Attic.

Afterwards, we had a series wrap party backstage. I heard the horror stories from my girlfriend, who was crying as she tried to stifle her laughter all the way through the show. Not because of the witty content of the show itself, but because of the loudly voiced, sarcastic comments our Kevin made as he watched along side Charlie Parsons, Stephen Garrett and the rest of Channel 4's entertainment politburo.

'Fuckin' hell, Sinitta! They're really scraping the bottom of the barrel now.'

Afterwards Stephen Garrett seemed in a happier mood than usual, perhaps because he had the weight of a series he hated off his shoulders for another five months.

'Oh, Stephen, by the way, this is my girlfriend, Sue, and this is my brother Kevin.'

On meeting my younger brother, Stephen recognized him immediately.

'Oh yes, you were watching the show with us. You'd probably be better at this game than him.'

Then astoundingly, Stephen turned to my girlfriend and, indicating towards me, said, 'This show has two million viewers, and it's all because of him.'

I was astounded, but confused, too. Maybe it was an olive branch for a new start between us.

chapter nine

'You have plumbed the depths of degradation, and made me feel very ill. To show a person inhaling a condom through his nostril, then pulling it out through his mouth, while some overweight homosexual with feathers in his arse looks on approvingly and claps his hands...well. Don't ever, ever show this filth again. I withdraw all my support from your channel. My personal phone hasn't stopped ringing, so I can't imagine what yours must be like.' Channel 4 duty log

By the time I'd moved back to Manchester and given up the flat in Colindale, I was more famous than I wanted to be. Recognition dogged my dirty days and just going to the shop or the chippy became a bit of an ordeal. Everyone seemed to look at or say something to me, most of it embarrassingly positive.

I remember my first Tuesday back in Manchester, feeling quite flush and waiting for the 256 bus – I hadn't yet bought a car – into Manchester town centre to do a bit of shopping and mooching around. It was ten o'clock in the morning when I got on the emptyish bus at Trafford Bar and went upstairs to enjoy the ten-minute journey. As the bus pulled up at the stop on City Road, opposite St Brendan's Irish Club, where Old Trafford joined onto Hulme, hundreds of green-and-white clad semi-drunken Scotsmen piled out of the club and surged onto the bus. The bus must have been at the stop for over twenty minutes until it was standing room only, as these

Celtic fans, cans of beer in hand, clambered on.

'Hey, look, there's that radge off *The Word*. What are ye daeing oan the bus, where's your fucking Maserati.' The Celtic fans who'd come down to Manchester were there for an all-day drinking session before watching their side play Manchester United that evening for Bryan Robson's testimonial match.

'Are ye going tae the game?' they asked, then proceeded to explain how the local priest had opened up St Brendan's Club for the itinerant Celtic hoards at eight o'clock that morning, providing both a full fried breakfast and a bar.

As soon as the bus set off, Republic of Ireland tri-colour flags were hung out of the windows and the Celtic fans were treated me to a chorus of Irish rebel songs, such as 'The Merry Ploughboy', 'The Manchester Martyrs' and a rather risqué song about the chap who stalked his way into Buckingham Palace and met the Queen in her bedroom. 'Michael Fagan fucked the Queen, when he did she didn't scream,' – so much for my quiet shopping trip, but they were all top lads and incredibly chuffed as *The Word* was one of their favourite shows. I knew my demographic.

I had bought a three-bed semi-detached house a couple of months earlier in the posher Firswood part of Old Trafford for £63,000. The house desperately needed decorating and I knew that my old colleague from KFM radio, Craig Cash, who'd presented a regular show with Caroline Ahern, had been a painter and decorator. A few months earlier KFM had been taken over by Signal Radio, who immediately fired Craig, Caroline and Jon Ronson. Within four years, Craig and Caroline would be in receipt of two Baftas and Jon Ronson would be on network television having won the prestigious 'Journalist of the Year' award.

I offered to pay Craig to decorate my place, so when I wasn't working and my girlfriend was out running her record promotions business, I'd hang around and watch Craig work. I'd inherited my dad's inability to do any kind of DIY – although he did at least know how to hang wallpaper – so I was fascinated. I was often reduced to tears of laughter because Craig is naturally one of the funniest people you'll ever meet, as anyone who ever watched *Mrs Merton* and *The Royle Family* will agree. We used to say that Craig and his best friend from school, Phil Mealey, were a double act waiting to happen, although it would take another twelve years before the BBC2 comedy series *Early Doors* would illustrate the point to the rest of Britain.

Craig was fascinated by TV, comedy in particular. He'd been writing a live stand-up routine with Caroline Ahern, which she would perform at pubs and clubs. Caroline was another person with a razor-like wit, but she lacked the confidence to do stand-up. The way she overcame those inhibitions was to adopt a series of different characters, like Harry Enfield and the late Dick Emery, which she hid behind. She would dress as an Irish nun, Sister Mary Immaculate, who would come on and tell jokes like, 'How many protestants does it take to change a light bulb?' 'Why bother, they live in eternal darkness.' She also had a band and would do gigs as the Mitzi Goldberg Experience, pretending to be a Jewish Country and Western singer, and numerous other characters, one of which, Gail Tuesday Super Glamour Model, she gave to comedienne Brenda Gilhooley, who did quite well out of it.

In between stripping paper and plastering, Craig would talk to me about TV, and we both had similar feelings about what did and didn't work. So much television was contrived and set up to be funny when it wasn't and often, rather than working as a team to make something good, everybody wanted to have their say and ended up ruining a good idea.

In the meantime, I'd been offered two days a week working on MTV Europe by the boss Brent Hanson, he even gave me a free satellite dish and box. His only stipulation was, as I was still under contract to 24 Hour Productions, they wouldn't send me off filming in the States between April and September. In an industry fuelled by gossip, I've yet to hear or meet a single person with a bad word to say about Brent, who's unassuming but passionate about both music and people. I'd also never heard a boss speak with so much praise and appreciation for his employees or who, in turn, was so respected by them. Brent could see how low my confidence and self-belief was, and made me feel welcome, looked after and valued, which after my first year at 24 Hour Productions, I appreciated profoundly.

There was still my very painful fissure to get sorted out, though, so I went to my GP, who told me it would be another five or six months on the waiting list, so I decided to go private. I went to see a consultant in Manchester and explained that I wanted the operation on a Monday as I had to work in London for MTV on the Thursday and Friday. The consultant was rather snotty about all this, explaining that the private operations happened on a Thursday or Friday so I couldn't have one on a Monday. I replied quite logically that as I was paying for the bloody operation, I wanted it to suit me. He then petulantly said I could get it done on the NHS at North Manchester Hospital in Crumpsall in a fortnight's time on a Monday. I couldn't understand what had gone on, but it seemed that by paying a consultant £120 I'd bumped myself up the waiting list and could finally get the operation done.

The operation itself is basically some surgeon giving you a fisting while you're sedated. After an hour of having various junior doctors sticking their rubber-gloved digits up my bum-hole, I went to the smoking room to have a cigarette and noticed they had MTV on the television all day for the patients to watch. I walked in and a woman in her mid-thirties said she'd seen me on *The Word* and also on MTV. She then asked me what I was in for. I was about to reply by saying a minor operation, when this rather burly middle-aged bloke in a dressing gown drily growled, 'He's in here to get his arse sorted out. That's what happens if you get a job on Channel 4.'

I had to laugh. There must have been a good grapevine in that hospital as I'd only been admitted an hour or so earlier. The next day, as I gingerly walked past the smoking room on my way home, trying to avoid my buttocks rubbing against my arse, which felt like a chewed orange, all the other patients, who were no longer in any doubt as to the nature of my operation, wished me well.

'Stick plenty of Vaseline on it next time, Tez.'

It was that fu****g burly bloke again with his lacerating one-liners.

I was really beginning to enjoy my stints on camera at MTV and had been offered additional money and the kudos of filling in for Ray Cokes on MTV's *Most Wanted* while he was off on his holidays. *Most Wanted* was the station's flagship show and went out live across Europe, where Ray was a huge star, especially in northern Europe and France. Then suddenly 24 Hour Productions informed MTV and myself that I was needed for *The Word*, breaking their promise to MTV and leaving them pissed off at me.

I was informed over the phone that I'd be off to the States, flying first to LA with new producers Danielle Lux, who had been working on Def II, and one-time *Network 7* presenter Jaswinder Bancil. I was also informed that Charlie was no longer the show's editor but had moved up to become executive producer – not that I ever found out what they did – and that the new editor would be another old face from *Network 7*, Janet Street-Porter's number one in Manchester, Sebastian Scott. I have to admit that the idea of working with more ex-*Network 7* public-school types made me groan inwardly.

That very day Sebastian phoned me at home for a chat and arranged to meet me in London the day before I flew out to the States. Sebastian was actually a decent bloke, but I hadn't really liked *Network 7* or *Reportage* and the overwhelming southern poshness of either show. While we were chatting, Sebastian talked about *Network 7*, saying how ground-breaking it was and that it was real journalism. I quite cruelly added 'with lots of designer gear', I scoffed at *Network 7*'s pretensions to journalism and said how public school and upper middle class 90 per cent of its presenters were.

'Good journalism! Listen, Sebastian, I remember seeing one show where some faceless public school no-mark was interviewing British black Rastafarian film-maker, DJ and musician Don Letts about his work. At one point this numpty asks Don Letts, 'Erm, Don, how big an influence on you was Martin Garvey.'

I then explained to Sebastian that had the reporter come from a working-class inner-city area, he would have grown up around kids adopting the Rastafarian look and discussing it's lifestyle and would have known exactly who black nationalist leader Marcus Garvey was.

Sebastian sort of accepted my point of view, but I knew I hadn't changed his mind about anything. As far as I was concerned, the jury was out on Sebastian.

Dreading the flight as usual, I met up with both Danielle and Jaswinder at the airport. Jaswinder was quite pretty but had a taciturn bordering on hostile expression on her face. Danielle was a lovely, friendly Home Counties girl; she'd just been working at *Reportage* and *Dance Energy* at the BBC in Manchester, and had been asked to come on board the new *Word* team by Sebastian. I asked her what he was like, and she was fairly glowing about him, but as he'd given her the job, I took it with a pinch of salt.

The plan was to fly to LA, where we would be interviewing Will Smith, Laura Dern, Sherilyn Fenn, Sandra Bernhard and Tim Roth. then filming two pieces I wasn't so keen on: shark cage diving and an all-day surfing competition in San Clemente.

We landed in LA at 10 p.m., and by 4 a.m. the following morning I had to be dressed and outside, ready to take a taxi to Long Beach, where I'd then take a two-hour ferry journey to Catalina Island, where I'd be having a scuba-diving lesson in their underwater park with a guy called Steve, who went under the moniker of 'Mr Shark'. This would have been fine if I hadn't been suffering from a sore throat, slight temperature and blocked nose – either a heavy cold or early-stage flu.

Having had only two hours sleep, I nodded off as the cab drove for sixty minutes to Long Beach, then I bought a ticket and got on the uncomfortable 6 a.m. ferry for the two-hour journey to Catalina, where Steve would meet me off the boat. He was a tall, muscular, well-built, tanned American around thirty years of age. He'd worked in LA as a stockbroker, made a pile of cash and invested it in what he loved best: a boat and a shark-cage diving business. For $1,500 you could hire Steve's services and go out onto the ocean to take part in the new yuppie danger sport, shark cage diving.

Steve briefed me about the equipment, air tanks, mask, applicator, flippers, watch, life belt (called a buoyancy conveyor) and weight belts, then he ran me through the things we'd be doing.

During the lesson itself I nearly drowned 45 feet down. My ear felt like someone was driving a knitting needle through it, my mask wouldn't clear and kept filling with water and I was choking because I'd accidentally inhaled some seawater through my nose. I then tried to swim to the surface, but Steve grabbed my ankles and hauled me back, worried that if I rose faster than my bubbles I'd get a bends-style headache. For fuck's sake I felt like I was drowning. I then found out from Steve that I shouldn't have been having a lesson so close to flying, and just to cheer me up further he bought me a beer and told me lots of horror stories about sharks and surfers with limbs missing.

The Sandra Bernhard interview was at least on dry land, in her agent's office, with me standing about 12 feet away from her with the camera man shooting over my shoulder while she stood, a good five inches taller than me, up against a large window with a view of the Hollywood Hills behind her. I wasn't impressed with the set-up as neither myself nor Ms Bernhard felt particularly relaxed or comfortable. Again I'd been given a list of questions, including the one about her affair with Madonna, but the way the interviews were constructed and conducted weren't really me.

Throughout my radio career I'd always been complimented on my interviewing technique – I liked to approach things from the angle of, what's it like to be the person you are now, making it more of an exploration than an inquisition. I liked to listen and wait, watch and be aware, seeing how far I dared probe, but mostly just making sure my subject was as comfortable as possible. I'm not a fan of writing questions down as it's not what you'd do when you're having a conversation. However, my style of interviewing didn't suit the cut-and-thrust sound-bite style of a live TV show or make for easy editing.

It was trying to make this leap from my usual style of conducting interviews to a new live-TV-friendly style that made me seem aggressive, abrupt and rude. The problem in television is that there are so many technical things going on that the ability to listen, wait, watch and be aware are seriously hampered, plus a second of silence on a TV show feels like an eternity, whereas on radio it can often add something. There's also the unnatural intrusiveness of cameras and soundmen, which make it a more 'armoured' experience.

Danielle, God bless her, was trying desperately to deliver Charlie something 'different'. We interviewed Will Smith, who was very funny, and I reminded him that before his acting career, he'd a fair bit of credibility for the hip hop tune he'd recorded with Jazzy Jeff as the Fresh Prince called 'A Touch of Jazz'.

We also made our way down to English actor Tim Roth's favourite bar on Melrose, the original idea being to interview him there. He'd just finished filming *Reservoir Dogs* and was a really decent bloke. We talked about football and I seem to remember he was a Chelsea fan, he certainly knew about Mickey Droy, David Speedie and Kerry Dixon. We talked about British films and writers and how the lifestyle in LA was very different, then Danielle decided that it looked too boring and could we do the interview walking up and down Melrose. I explained to Danielle that it would be a nightmare technically, with the camera man and sound man walking backwards in front of us, filming while heavy trucks and cars rumbled past, not to mention dodging the people on the sidewalk.

By the twelfth take, Tim Roth had had enough. He'd tried answering the same questions umpteen times but it was getting flatter and flatter. Danielle's experiment had well and truly failed. 'I told you it wouldn't work, Danielle,' I said – I never could resist the endearing habit of saying 'told you so'.

It was an unnaturally cloudy and cool day when I set off on the shark boat from Catalina Island for the Pacific ocean. We cruised around, 22 miles off the Californian coast, churning minced-up raw fish into the ocean behind us. The idea was that the sharks would be attracted both by the rhythm of the boat's engines and the smell of fish blood in the water, then they'd come along and explore. In the meantime my sniffle had blown up into what felt like full-blown influenza again, and I shivered snottily in my wet suit, waiting endlessly for the sharks to appear.

Jaswinder was directing this shoot, and it wasn't long before we became heavy company for each other. She was saying how great *Network 7* was, and I was disagreeing, saying that the *The Word* was better and would be better still if we got out of this south east upper-middle-class way of seeing things. For instance, why were we filming a piece on shark cage diving and another on a surfing competition when Catalina Island was hosting the first official rave in California that day, featuring Manchester's 808 State, A Guy Called Gerald, The Beloved and Adamski all on the bill, plus big name DJs from the UK.

Jaswinder just shrugged the point off, said all that rave stuff was boring, and besides, she liked Guns 'n' Roses. She couldn't see the point I was making that something that had been so huge in the UK was about to happen in the US, and how interesting it would be to see what the American kids made of the whole scene. She started on about how she'd produced *7 Sports* and covered surfing on that, and also reiterated that *Network 7* was ground-breaking and good journalism. I scoffed in disbelief and gave her the example of the posh public school-type interviewing Don Letts and thinking Martin Garvey was Marcus Garvey.

'Oh, that was just Sebastian.'

My blood froze. It was the only example of bad journalism I could remember from *Network 7*. Shit! I'd told Sebastian, my new editor, the same anecdote, using lots of expressions like 'faceless public-school no-mark', not realizing that it was him who'd done the interview. I had no doubt, though, that Sebastian would have thought I knew he'd done that interview; he just didn't rise to the bait. Me and my big gob; I felt awful.

We then talked about football and she was full of scorn for Manchester United, herself being a West Ham fan, and bragged that she even used to go to some of the games. Blimey, what a fanatic! With Jaswinder, any conversational difference of opinion was considered a debate to the death, rather than just some light-hearted two-way banter. She took everything extremely seriously.

I then rather cruelly got on to Jaswinder herself and why on earth she'd chosen to go on holiday for a week on her own to LA of all places. She asked me where I'd been away on holiday that summer and I confessed that my girlfriend and I had gone to Turkey for a fortnight. Jaswinder then said that she would never go to Turkey. I interpreted this as snobbery against package-holidays, but she then told me rather portentously that her best friend had gone on honeymoon to Turkey several years earlier and had returned with a viral infection in her brain – three weeks later she was dead.

I laughed so much I thought I was going to die. It wasn't *what* she said, it was the *way* she said it. I had to lie on the deck of the boat, holding my sides as tears streamed down my face. I knew I shouldn't, but I couldn't stop. I knew it was terrible, her best friend dying like that, but the more I tried to stop, the more I cracked up. All this while, Jaswinder just stood there, lasering hatred in my direction.

Jaswinder then sprang into action. 'Enough idle chit-chat, Terry. We can't wait for these sharks all day, so get ready and climb off the boat and I'll film you getting out of the water.'

I knew it was wholly unnecessary, but I felt bad about laughing, so I reluctantly agreed. I put on my wet suit, then the forty pounds of lead weights, the air tanks and life jacket, all the while talking to camera. I filmed a couple of opening pieces, referring to the new dangerous yuppy sport of shark cage diving then got into the water off the back of the boat and hauled myself in and out about a dozen times. I was fairly fit, but absolutely exhausted by the end of it, and my wet suit had little pieces of minced-up raw mackerel stuck all over it. I was freezing and my temperature and shivering were uncontrollable. I was slightly nervous but still praying for the sharks to turn up just so the day would be over. After five hours of bobbing on the ocean, Mr Sharkman Steve let out a loud, 'Oh no.'

'What is it, Steve.'

'We've got a sea lion following the boat. We won't get any sharks now as they're afraid of sea lions.'

Sharks afraid of sea lions! We stopped churning minced fish into the water, and an hour or so later the sea lion left, though it was two more long hours before the sharks finally arrived – nine of them in various sizes.

We had two specialist underwater cameramen – one would be in the cage with me, while the other would be swimming around outside, filming me in the cage with the sharks surrounding me. Unlike in *Jaws*, where the man is lowered into the water inside the cage, this cage was lowered to a depth of twenty feet and I had to swim past the sharks to get into it. I didn't even think about feeling afraid. Inside the cage, the sharks, the biggest of which was over five and a half feet in length, swam around. It was an amazing primordial sight as they attacked the full mackerel we threw out. I even fed one, gingerly holding on to the tail of a whole mackerel as it bit. Eventually I swam back out of the cage, did a quick piece to camera as I dripped on the boat, then got out of the cold, fishy wetsuit I'd been wearing for the past nine hours.

We then returned to Catalina Island, got the ferry back to Long Beach and faced a 150-mile taxi ride to a motor lodge somewhere on the freeway near San Clemente in northern California. Of course, nobody told me or the taxi driver which exact motor lodge it was, or what name it had been booked in. It was gone midnight by the time we found the right one, and I'd been up since 3 a.m., on a shark boat from 7 a.m. and hadn't eaten a morsel all day, plus I had a raging thirst. There was no food available in the hotel and all the local pizza delivery places were shut, though they did have a soda machine, but no change. I paid the cab driver $220 – they'd assumed back at the office that the fare would be about $100 – leaving me with five dollars. Feeling sick, fed-up and exhausted, I plonked my body on the bed after drinking copiously from the tap in the bathroom.

The following day it was more fun and games. I felt so ill I could hardly stand. The waves were all wrong, the weather was bad and the surfing competition wasn't well attended. I interviewed the then world surfing champion Kelly Slater, who did all the stunts for the film *Point Break*, but he was monosyllabic and as dull as ditchwater. Kelly just wasn't animated or articulate enough to provide the pseudo *Zen and the Art of Surfing* piece I suspect Jaswinder had in mind, although he had been to Britain.

'Where abouts?'

'Cornwall, a place called Newquay.'

'Oh right. What were you doing there?'

'Surfing.'

We vox-popped a few surf groupies and then, with nothing much happening, Jaswinder turned round and said in front of the surf groupies, Jo Owen and the American Crew, 'Right, strip off, Terry, you're getting in the water.'

I was sick as a dog, with a raging temperature, blocked-up nose and sore throat. It was only 11 a.m. in the morning, we didn't even have a towel on us and other than the shorts I was wearing, I had no other clothes. San Clemente is northern California and the weather there is more temperate than LA, with a very cool breeze, and I was already shivering. She repeated her demand and I explained that I'd do it later, but that as I had a temperature, rather than do it now and be hanging around wet and freezing for the next seven hours – the competition finished at 6 p.m. – if it was really necessary for the piece we could do it at the end of the day.

We carried on filming, with Jaswinder making constant references to the fact that I would be getting in the water soon. It's fair to say it riled me. Eventually I took Jaswinder to one side, away from the crew and interviewees, and said, 'Listen, Jaswinder, I've told you I'm not well, but if you want me to and it's necessary, I'll get in the water for you later. In the meantime, it's just not going to happen, so can you leave it out now.'

Two minutes later: 'Terry can't, because he's getting in the water to do his opening piece now.'

What can I say, no food, no sleep, sick as a dog and at the end of my tether, I just blew.

'Are you fuckin' deaf as well as stupid. I've told you several times, it's not happening, so that's it. I don't know who the fuck you think you're talking too. Let's just get this shitty non-event that will never be used filmed and then you can get back to enjoying your holiday in LA'.

Jo Owen looked on horrified, while the American crew, who'd been on the shark boat the previous day, looking askance at

Jasmine's peculiar working methods, stifled giggles. At least I'd found some allies, but it's a big no-no to argue in front of a hired crew, and that's why I'd taken Jas to one side, so as to leave her in no doubt about the consequences. She still worked my ass into the ground for the rest of the day on her non-story, though.

At the end of the day, as the crew packed away, the main underwater cameraman from the previous day's shoot approached me: 'Hey, Terry boy, she's a genuine pain in the ass. Listen, man, do you wanna smoke this with me before we head back to Long Beach.' He then produced a joint of pure grass and, hiding from Jaswinder like two naughty schoolboys, we proceeded to get very stoned and giggly.

The crew took us back to Long Beach, where we had to wait for taxis to take us to Santa Monica to drop Jaswinder off, then take Jo Owen and myself back to our hotel in Beverly Hills. The cameraman said we could call a cab from his houseboat in Long Beach harbour and have a sandwich and some refreshments with him and his girlfriend if we wanted. Soon after, we were all sitting comfortably drinking beer and enjoying the hospitality of his cosy living room when he invited me to come and see his friend's boat. We walked onto his friend's empty boat and he took out a huge spliff, which was even stronger than the one we'd smoked several hours before. By the time we returned to his boat I was stoned out of my mind and slightly giggly.

I sat in his living room, thinking what a hellish two days of filming it had been, but grateful that it was now over. I looked at Jaswinder and felt a wave of empathy come over me. After all, I had disagreed with most of her opinions, and in television that's often interpreted as the equivalent of calling someone's mother a whore. I thought about her losing her best friend to a freak virus; she seemed like a young attractive woman who'd had a tough life in some respects, and here she was alone on holiday, trying to mask her vulnerability, undermined and insulted. I decided to act like a man and apologize for giving her a hard time.

'Listen, Jas, I'm sorry about us getting off on the wrong foot, and particularly for laughing about your. . .' and then, just as I was saying, 'friend who died of a brain virus' I collapsed into hysterics again. Everyone in the room was laughing as I rolled about on the floor, trying to breathe and drag myself back from the midst of uncontrollable mirth. But the marijuana and the fact that the whole room was now in hysterics, except for Jaswinder, just made it worse.

To be fair, she maintained her dignity well, merely saying, 'I'm not accepting your apology.'

But do you know what? Behind the howling gale of laughter, I was truly sorry; it's what we Catholics call a perfect contrition.

The taxi was heavy with an oppressive atmosphere. The silence between Jaswinder, Jo and myself spoke volumes. When the taxi pulled up outside the hotel where Jas was staying, she got out. She gave Jo a showbiz farewell kiss and totally blanked me. Oh well, I was never much cop at networking luviness anyway.

A few days later I had to get the red eye from LA to New York. It's a five-hour overnight flight, arriving in New York at five in the morning. The following day I'd be meeting Sebastian Scott while we filmed a junket of a new movie called *Mobsters*, starring Patrick Dempsey and Christian Slater. I got to the Paramount Hotel off Times Square at just after six in the morning, feeling exhausted, and the desk clerk asked me for a credit card. I didn't have one, either on me or in real life. It's hard to imagine, but that was the way it was. Without a credit card, he wouldn't allow me to go to my room.

Look, I explained, there will be a guy called Sebastian Scott arriving from London at midday, he will have a credit card to cover my room – in fact, with a posh name like Sebastian he'll have hundreds of credit cards and buy your fucking hotel and sack you – in the meantime, it's already paid for. You can have my luggage, $300 and £2 of English money.

An hour later I get into my room and sleep until Sebastian calls and asks if I'd like to meet him in the bar.

I have to say that after the previous days of filming I felt happy to see Sebastian, and his credit card while we're at it.

Sebastian accompanied Jo Owen and myself to the onset junket for *Mobsters*. The moment we arrived I caught Christian Slater's eye and semi-nodded in his direction. I knew what was coming next. We were informed some twenty minutes later by the film's PR people that Christian Slater refused to be interviewed by *The Word*. I knew exactly why, of course, but decided to act as mystified and outraged as Sebastian and Jo. 'Fancy that, and we got on great when I interviewed him last time; we had a good laugh. Weird bloke.'

Sebastian was very posh and also from a severely privileged background, but he was sharp, witty company and I felt really comfortable around him. I saw this as a challenge to my inverted snobbery, though, so decided to be a bit sour with him and give him a good ribbing.

Meanwhile the show needed another female presenter. Michelle Collins had gone off in a huff after giving Charlie a piece of her mind, and Amanda was pregnant and would soon need replacing. Sadly, my suggestion that they consider Caroline Ahern fell on deaf ears, and the decision was made to do '*Wordsearch*', which was basically a process like *Pop Idol* or *X Factor*It was the chance for anyone who fancied being a presenter on *The Word* to audition, and we announced it in the press and on Radio 1.

Over 5,000 videotaped auditions were sent in and the best 500 attended auditions in London, Birmingham and Edinburgh. These in turn were narrowed down to a final eighteen, who attended a day of auditions at The Channel 4 studios on Charlotte Street in London, with all the auditions being filmed for broadcast. The final auditionees consisted of Davina McCall (again), Canadian Justine Priestley, sister of *Beverly Hills 90210*'s Jason, DJ Jez Nelson, *Teenage Health Freak* actor and Britain's youngest stand-up comedian, fourteen-year-old Alex Langdon.

What I was really pleased about was how super-enthusiastic and passionate about the programme Sebastian was. Everything about *The Word* was supposed to be accessible, making the glass on the TV screen between the show and its audience as thin as possible. This was the fundamental idea Charlie and I had built the show around, and it was great to see that Sebastian was going to carry it on. As he said, '*Wordsearch* is a vast exercise in accessibility.' I'd mentioned that screening auditions was a good idea to Charlie after he'd lent me a video of the original *Word* presenter auditions to see if I thought any of the girls might be worth trying out again. The tape was hilarious viewing and I said it would make a good show in itself.

In the meantime, Sebastian Scott was ultra-keen to employ the American woman who hosted Channel 4's *Manhattan Cable*, Laurie Pike, as our new presenter. I'd seen the show but thought Laurie was a bit pseudo, and completely wrong for *The Word*, especially as Sebastian liked her and I was determined to be diametrically opposed to him. As far as I was concerned, it was another case of the London media mafia's fascination with New York, and I thought most people I knew would see Laurie as some annoying Yank and would prefer a more earthy presenter.

Wordsearch was a programme made about the audition process. At the end, the final eighteen auditionees had to come in and do a mocked-up outside broadcast with up-and-coming Mancunian boy band Take That, after which they'd have to interview the ex-leader of Liverpool's infamous Labour Militant city council, Derek Hatton, and myself. A few of them were OK, but most were much of a muchness and came from fairly privileged backgrounds.

By lunch time I'd had enough and, rather than head to the Channel 4 canteen with everyone else, Derek Hatton, Take That and myself dodged out to a pub round the corner. The lads from Take That were great and I knew about Jason and Howard's reputation as part of a Manchester dance/footwork crew who had beaten the best dance crew from London in a big showdown at the Hacienda. Also, the girls who helped make the first Take That video, Ro Barret (née Newton) and Angie Smith, worked on *The Hitman and Her*, where

Jason and Howard had been regular dancers, too. They were fantastic lads, by no means squeaky clean, and I reckoned they'd do well, especially after the rather grand behaviour of bands like New Kids on the Block after they'd made it big. If you stay fairly down to earth and be yourself, you'll go far, as long as you can do your job and don't cause any trouble. There they were, soon to be the biggest band in Britain for the next five years, stuck in a pub with two blokes who would start an argument in an empty room, Derek Hatton and myself.

I hadn't done anything all morning, as it was the afternoon session where I was due to be interviewed by the people auditioning. I'd eaten nothing, had three pints of Guinness and was feeling unbearably cocky, as everyone would discover during the course of the afternoon – my belated apologies to all of you.

I remember one American girl at the auditions who was so confident and composed that she slightly unnerved me. What also stood out was that, like Laurie Pike, she had red hair, and if you closed your eyes she had a very similar voice and presentation style, too. It was no mystery to me who Sebastian would pick as the new presenter, although to be fair, she was the most memorable and also asked the most *Word*-type questions during her interviews. Welcome, Katie Puckrick.

Katie reminded me a bit of Lene Lovitch and seemed very arty with pretentions to intellectualism. It was our Kevin who came up with the killer angle: 'She's basically a homosexual's idea of what a woman should be like.' I sort of knew what he meant, but worried slightly that Katie might take herself too seriously. . . the very thought!

The team had changed somewhat from series one, as Sebastian had brought in his own people – yet another parade of Home Counties types – but I was comforted by what an absolutely fantastic show *Wordsearch* had been; really well put together and edited. Fair dues to Sebastian, with the odd exception, all the people he brought in were very good at their jobs, but it was still much too Londoncentric, and there were no black people or people from state school.

The only exception was Jo Whiley, who came in as the music booker. I'd worked with Jo when she was the researcher on a Radio 4 show I'd presented, which she had subsequently gone on to present herself a few years earlier. She was a nice girl, very ambitious, but massively fearful of getting something wrong. All I remembered about her taste in music at the time was that it was Goth rock and, being a Northampton girl, like many people from small towns and the suburbs, her musical tastes were dictated from a young age by 'pub rock'.

Jo was better than Tim Byrne in that she would never want to miss out on something big or a band there was a buzz about in the music press, and she really tried to keep on top of a music scene that was shifting more than ever. Although the Madchester thing was still big, the music-press backlash was beginning to take effect, but Jo would still go with something if she really liked the record or if someone explained to her why it was good. However, if she really hated it, or the press thought it was totally uncool, you were onto a loser. Having said that, I did feel she allowed herself to be led too much by what bands were being championed by the *NME* and *Melody Maker*, both of which were starting to lose their reputations as bibles of new music in the 1990s.

Amanda's nose was put out of joint a bit when Katie came on board, but Amanda was pregnant and insistent she couldn't keep flying to the States in her condition. She'd always wanted to be in the studio with me anyway, and now for the first couple of shows of series two she'd have her chance.

Sebastian showed his metal, and the first thing he did was get us a much bigger studio in which to film *The Word*, Limehouse Studios in Wembley. Then, as we'd suggested all the way through series one, he decided that we'd have three bands on each show rather than two; he also increased the audience size from up to 100 people to a whopping 300–350. In many ways, the whole look of *The Word* and the show it became was down to Sebastian. Under his editorship the show got a real atmosphere. No longer would the studio be full of disinterested dancers and a couple of mates of the bands, instead it was full of people who loved *The Word* and fans of the groups we had on, leaving the dancers to take a much more peripheral role.

Another new team member in series two was Producer Murray Boland, son of Tony Boland, another ex-*Network 7* presenter and, unfortunately for him, scarred by being the main presenter of the second series of *Club X* for Charlie, a trauma he related to me most gleefully. Murray's main job would be to produce the outside broadcasts with Katie Puckrick, along with probably the best director on the first two series of *The Word*, a wild-looking Scot called Hamish Barbour, who was married to ex-*Tube* presenter and media mogul Muriel Gray.

Murray was a good-looking, friendly, charming bloke in every way, and extremely diligent about work, which is very un-Irish in my experience. When I mentioned this to him, he admitted he'd had his moments, but light-heartedly explained that he'd been brought up Protestant. Murray's close working relationship with Katie eventually blossomed into a romance, which lasted for at least three years, but which I suspect eventually cost Katie her job on the show, as I'll explain later.

Despite my initial reservations, most of the people Sebastian employed were really nice, one of my favourites being Tammy Summers, a tall, stunningly attractive woman with a great sense of humour who was a bit of a party animal. Having said that, though, there was one guy, a new producer who was from my neck of the woods and was being hailed as some kind of genius, though as far as I could make out he was pretty useless at everything except welding his lips to Charlie Parsons' ring piece. He was an object of some fascination in the office, as he dressed like a sixth-former, in jeans, sports jacket, shirt and tie, and on his desk was a large photograph album containing nude Polaroids of all his sexual conquests.

He used to take some eighteen- or nineteen-year-old out for a meal, then back to his place, and once the relationship was, er, cemented so to speak, he'd get the old Polaroid camera out. Amazingly, he was more than happy for anyone to flick through this catalogue of exploits – and I have to confess he had standards – but what was even stranger was that he'd also had a fling with one of the secretaries who worked within six feet of him, and she too appeared in the book!

Behind the scenes everything was much more professional and there was more of a team atmosphere, but again my lack of confidence began to emerge. On the whole, what we did, we did well, but I still worried that we were too Londoncentric. This wasn't an anti-London thing it was simply to try and avoid an obvious weakness in other youth and light entertainment shows which often weren't accessible to everyone around the country because all the references were too London-related. It's a testament to how well we succeeded that over the years many viewers I met were surprised when they heard that we filmed all the shows in London. In that way, it was very un-Channel 4.

If Charlie Parsons was all frenetic energy and sudden mood and mind changes when it came to his vision for the show, Sebastian had the self-confidence and man-management skills to deliver. The whole atmosphere in the office changed under Sebastian's guidance, but I still had a paranoid hangover from series one, and felt as agitated as ever about my own imprint on the show.

The first show in series two was truly terrifying. Sebastian had decided we should scrap the autocue all together, so all the presenters had to either learn their lines or busk it. I howled in protest and called Sebastian all the names under the sun, even setting Amanda on him. When I looked out, the audience was a seething mass and it was like being on the terraces at Old Trafford before a United match. The cheering at the top of the show was deafening. There was part of me that thought Sebastian was trying to stitch me up just as I was getting into my stride, by throwing in more complications, like a bigger, rowdier audience, while taking away our autocue and notes, but in retrospect it was exactly what the show needed to move forward.

On that first show our guests were Bo Derek and Shaun Ryder and Bez from the Happy Mondays, who were also performing their new single 'Judge Fudge'. The studio football crowd were totally intimidating, and Bo Derek walked on in a daze. I had the buttock-clenching task of presenting her with the golden raspberry award for being the worst actress in a film that year. She'd been really pleasant and, though I'm cheeky and direct, I'm not nasty, so I wasn't looking forward to it, even though I knew the show demanded it. I think she was spaced out enough to hardly notice, although most Americans, it seems, are consummate professionals in situations like that and tend to save up their grievances for their agents to pass on after the show is over.

Having done the dreaded deed, I then had to interview Shaun and Bez, both of whom looked rather worse for wear. The story was that Shaun Ryder had been interviewed on MTV and jokingly said that he used to be a £40-a-night rent boy to make money when he was younger. The *News of the World* then went and printed it as a story, quoting Shaun in cold print. Having Shaun and Bez on the show created an awed hush in the seething crowd as everyone pushed forward and strained to hear what they had to say.

I went straight in with the edge-of-seat question everyone wanted an answer to: 'Shaun, what are these allegations that you used to be a forty-pound-a-night rent boy?'

There was a groan of 'Oh nooooo' from the audience.

'What can I say, Terry? I said something on the telly as a joke and that **** put it in the *News of the World* as if it was true.'

'So, what are you going to do now?'

'We're going to sue.'

'Well, you won't be the first people to sue the *News of the World*, will you,' I replied.

'Will we fuck.'

It was a TV moment to savour. Two very naughty lads from Little Hulton, sitting monged out on *The Word* sofa, smoking cigarettes as the smoke curled up into the face of a visibly uncomfortable Bo Derek, Hollywood actress, body beautiful and symbol of Californian health consciousness. It was a moment that summed up the uniqueness of the programme. No show before then would have dared to have the Happy Mondays on live, but we had a punky attitude and didn't think twice about it.

My worries that our new girl Katie might take herself too seriously were unfounded, as was proved when she found herself on her first outside broadcast with a fat male strip group called the Blobendales and threw herself into the who-gives-a-fuck spirit of the programme.

The rehearsal seemed to take for ever and I was twitching about on the couch. One of the cameramen chatted to me as usual: 'We're doing well at the moment, aint we,' he said.

'What? The show?'

'No, Man United.'

'What do you mean, doing well? We just got beat by Sheffield Wednesday 3–2 on the back of draws at home to Liverpool and Arsenal! Anyway, I thought you were a Crystal Palace fan?'

'That's right, I am. I mean the Man United shares, haven't you got any.'

I never understood the whole shares thing with United, but I shudder to think how much money our cameramen made out of them. None of my United-supporter mates had bought any shares, firstly because they didn't understand what it was all about, and secondly because most of them were broke, having followed United on away legs to France and Poland, then forking out for tickets for the European Cup Winner's Cup final in Rotterdam against Barcelona. These cameramen, however, were money mad – I wish I'd bought some of those United shares, though.

On the second show we had the marvellous Margi Clarke on as guest, one of Britain's best ever actresses if anybody could find her the right part. Margi was a one-time punk rocker from Kirkby in Liverpool who had a volcanic personality and used to proudly boast that she'd once waggled her naked breasts in Joy Division singer Ian Curtis's face. She was loud, direct and guaranteed to push the boundaries of taste, but she had so much charm it was impossible not to like her.

She walked on to the show and immediately addressed the audience in her broad scouse accent, 'Hey, girls, how can you tell if a fellers got a small dick? If he goes straight down onto your muff.'

And to think that Margi's mum was the Mayoress of Kirkby at the time. Also on the show, by way of a contrast, was eighteen-year-old black English actress Thandie Newton. Thandie was very posh, having been at an all-girls boarding school in Devon before taking the Oxbridge route, and she seemed quite overwhelmed by the show. She'd just starred alongside Nicole Kidman in an Australian movie called *Flirting*, which was set in a girl's boarding school, and she related how she and Nicole had become good friends, a friendship which endured and resulted in Thandie starring opposite Tom Cruise in *Mission Impossible II*.

At the end of the show, the Manic Street Preachers came on. We'd had a terrible time trying to get Tim Byrne to put them on with Motown Junk in series one, so had kind of missed the boat with them, which was a shame, but it was great to have them on and I was pleased to have Manchester hip hop artist MC BuzzB on the show, with Manchester underground classic, 'Never Change', a song that sampled Bruce Hornsby and the Range's 'That's Just The Way It Is' seven years before Tupac Shakur did the same.

MC BuzzB was described as the Morrissey of rap because of the sensitivity and literary nature of his lyrics. He had an immense talent, but no desire to be a star, so *The Word* was his only national television appearance ever, another testament to our uniqueness.

The ambience of the show had become brighter and much more self-assured. I still half-heartedly tried to give Sebastian a hard time, but I could feel how great the show was. We'd blagged and stumbled our way through the first series, but the tweaks and changes Sebastian had implemented had given the show some 'soul' and made it really unmissable.

Show three of the second series was a true watershed moment in terms of musical recognition for us. For the third week running I'd managed to get Jo Whiley to include a Manchester band, Intastella, which was fronted by Moston girl Stella Grundy. They were a phenomenal live band and Stella had a great voice, but unfortunately they still hadn't quite come up with the right song to showcase themselves, and by the time they managed it some two years later, they'd missed the boat. I walked over to Jo's desk in the office and asked which bands she had booked for that particular week. Because we were heavy with guests, we only had two – she'd already booked Intastella, and told me about the other band as if I'd know all about them: 'Nirvana,' she said, 'they're fantastic, aren't they.'

I didn't want Jo to think I didn't have my finger on the pulse music wise, so I pulled a face and said, 'Erm, all right.' That's TV land ego, subtle and stealthy, sneaking up on you when you're least expecting it.

The guests on the show that night were the fashion designer Jean Paul Gaultier and, under much duress, Rob Newman and David Baddiel of comedy sensation *The Mary Whitehouse Experience*. I'd watched the programme and found it one of the least amusing comedy series of all time, lacking anything but clumsy varsity-style humour. Rob Newman had done some of the first TV skits of *The Word* and used to start by making out that absolutely nobody watched the show and doing an impersonation of me saying strange un-Mancunian things like 'stuff and nonsense', then passing over to Amanda, who was played by an inflatable blow-up doll. The previous Christmas I'd blown up an inflatable doll that had been handed to me by Steve Coogan dressed as Santa Clause and said, in very poor taste and judgement, 'Just what I need, another female co-presenter,' so the wit wasn't exactly original.

What was galling was that Newman and Baddiel had only agreed to come on the show if I was 'nice to them', so I'd been told not to refer to the fact that Rob Newman had auditioned with me for the job as presenter of *The Word*, not to take the mickey out of them, say their humour was a bit studenty or comment on the fact that they'd both been to private schools. Consequently, I had to sit through their lame and unfunny attempts at taking the piss out of me, all the while dying to just burst out, 'You pair of southern middle-class wankers are about as funny as anal surgery.' Alas I had to take it on the chin – not fair rules, lads, and they were the only people who ever came on the show in five series who made that kind of pre-condition.

Jean Paul Gaultier, meanwhile, recognized me from my brief stint on MTV Europe and said he used to watch me all the time.

I commented, 'I bet you couldn't understand my accent, though, could you?'

'Yes, you're right, I couldn't.'

On the night, Nirvana and Intastella had had something of a tiff. I'd discovered from talking to Jo Whiley that the buzz about Nirvana was all focused on their brilliant new single 'Smells Like Teen Spirit', and they were being well looked after by their record company, who were making them a big priority.

When Manchester's Intastella arrived looking bedraggled the researcher assigned to look after the bands walked up to the drummer, Spencer, and said, 'Are you Nirvana?'

'Yeah, that's right,' they lied.

Intastella were then lead through the corridors of the Limehouse studios to a big dressing room full of beer, champagne, Jack Daniels, crisps, sandwiches and even sushi. They proceeded to polish half of it off before being overwhelmed with guilt and confessing that they were in fact Intastella.

When Nirvana arrived they were non too pleased with the state of their dressing room and Kurt Cobain elected instead to hang out for most the afternoon and early evening before the show in the coffee bar with what I assumed was his manager or record company representative. I remember sitting with Intastella's manager, a Manchester-based Chorley girl called Caroline Elleray, who was later the person to discover and sign Coldplay and Keane to BMG, looking over at Kurt and commenting on how completely out of it he looked: 'Fuck me, it's Shaun Ryder with longer hair, a goatee and clothing coupons for Millets.'

Even in rehearsal, though, and bearing in mind that I'd seen what must have been a thousand gigs in my life, Nirvana were awesome, full of passion and rawness. After the dress rehearsal I bumped into Kurt, in conversation once again with his manager/record rep, in the corridor near the make-up room. 'Hi, Kurt, I'm Terry the show's presenter, just thought I'd say you were brilliant. I like your Captain

America T-Shirt. Is that the band or the Marvel comic character?' in reply he grunted and groaned a semi thanks, though it didn't reach his eyes.

That night the show was top heavy with guests, a VT interview with Laura Dern, which I'd recorded in the USA, a live outside broadcast with Katie and Italian Porn star turned MP La Cicciolina and comedians Newman and Baddiel. By the time we got to Nirvana there were just over two minutes of the live show left, and as soon as they were introduced, Kurt Cobain got on the microphone and said, 'Courtney Love out the band Hole is the best fuck in the world.'

There were no sharp intakes of breath over that, not on *The Word*, but I do remember thinking, Get on with it, mate, you've only got a minute and a half left for a song that's over four minutes long. To be frank, I'd used up my small reservoir of patience with Newman and Baddiel and couldn't really be bothered with some desperate American rocker who thought he was going to give us all a big shock.

Later, at the after show party, I was chatting to David Baddiel and Rob Newman about football, amongst other things. I told them about John Sheridan, the then Sheffield Wednesday and Republic of Ireland midfielder, and his brother Darren, who was playing for Barnsley. I mentioned how they'd gone to the same school as Morrissey and played in the same school team as several of my mates, and how my dad's best friend who he drank with every Sunday in the Platford pub was Tommy Cody, the Sheridan's Grandad.

Rob Newman replied by saying, 'So you have got some credibility?' Honestly, there are times when one despairs at the fickleness and fakery of media land, so I shan't soil this passage with my reply.

Around this time Harry Enfield was filming his new series at Limehouse Studios and used to pop in occasionally incognito to watch the bands and have a drink. I was quite taken aback once when Harry came over at an after-show drinks do and said how horrible he thought Newman and Baddiel had been to me, despite the fact that I was being very nice to them. It was after that I decided I was no longer going to just sit there and allow the upper-middle-class flotsam and jetsam to come on the show and take the piss out of me without getting a good mauling in return, no matter what might have been agreed beforehand.

By now, the show was a visual reflection of what it was, a seething bear-pit of anarchy. The following week our commissioning editor Stephen Garrett came down, full of praise for how everything was going. I thought he must have been on the happy pills or something, but was glad he was now off my back and that I no longer had the 'Stephen wants you out; he thinks you're crap' stuff in my ear week after week from Charlie. I was really pleased to see that Stephen was accompanied by my old friend Henry Normal.

I'd first met Henry back in 1986, when he'd been a guest on my Radio Derby show. Henry was a stand-up performance poet, but as with that all-time great John Cooper Clarke, he straddled the middle ground between comedian and poet with integrity, which I thought meant he'd never receive the recognition, financial rewards or the accolades he deserved. Henry had almost single-handedly built up the alternative comedy scene in Manchester, from the moment he moved there in 1988.

He had an amazing ability to encourage people and bond them together, and he was also a worker with unbelievable drive, whether it was writing his own poems, puns and jokes or helping others write theirs or get published, organizing gigs or encouraging promoters on Manchester's alternative cabaret scene. Steve Coogan, John Bramwell – the singer/songwriter behind I Am Kloot – John Thompson, Bob Dillinger, Dave Spikey, Caroline Ahern, Craig Cash – Henry helped them all out at one time or another and was the person most responsible for creating the Manchester comedy scene that produced characters like Peter Kaye and Johnny Vegas, and TV sit coms like *Phoenix Nights*, *The Royle Family* and *Early Doors*.

Henry was a living, breathing catalyst.

Henry had just written a comedy series based on *The Muppet Show* and set backstage at a theatre-type venue called Packet of Three, and it introduced to television for the first time Frank Skinner and Jenny Eclair. Henry had created the show and written it, but he was slightly miffed that Stephen Garrett had over-ruled the original plan for it to be Frank Skinner, Henry and the late Sheffield-based comedienne Linda Smith. As far as Garrett was concerned, Linda didn't look right on TV, which was media speak for overweight or not attractive enough. Henry explained that there was a natural repartee between Frank and Linda, whilst Jenny was more of a performer rather than someone who bounced off other people, so he was afraid the show might not be as good as it could be.

Stephen Garrett was keen that we get Frank Skinner on *The Word* as a guest. I'd already suggested him to Sebastian, as Craig Cash had raved about Frank and more or less performed his whole set for me at home while I watched him paint the kitchen wall.

Frank Skinner was the first guest we ever had on the show who seemed completely at ease. As he sat on the couch near me during the break, he looked at all the attractive girls in the audience and said, 'I bet you don't go short, mate.' I explained that you're much more likely to be fancied if you are an attractive, high-achieving male, so I was sorry to disappoint him, but he made me laugh.

On the show we had Amanda doing an outside broadcast with singing dogs – you couldn't make it up, could you – and coming out of the item Frank said,

'I used to have a dog, you know. Behind my house there was a back alley that used to be used by courting couples, and my dog used to eat the used condoms. The thing is, you could smell it on his breath' – pause – 'and I used to wonder, what if the neighbours could smell it on his breath? What would they think of me?'

On the same show we had Hollywood actor Michael Biehn, whose movie *K2* was hitting the big screens. He was accompanied backstage by his wife, who was in a very terse mood, especially with Michael as there had been allegations in the press that day that he'd been caught dallying with Patsy Kensit. It was a good show and I was pleased that both Craig Cash and my girlfriend Sue had come down to see it and were staying over at my OAP flat in St John's Wood.

Afterwards Frank said something that really touched me. 'You're too real for all this, mate, too real.' Frank may just have been being nice and saying, I thought you were a complete wanker before I met you, but really you're not so bad, but to me it was an affirmation about *The Word*, a show that was different and wasn't afraid to cut through the bullshit and take risks.

Of course there was plenty of gossip surrounding the show. Amanda had interviewed Denzel Washington on Hampstead Heath and her opening question was along the lines of 'Denzil, here you are, a huge star, and yet two years ago nobody had heard of you.'

To which Denzil replied good-humouredly, 'Two years ago I won the Oscar for best supporting actor in the film *Glory*.'

In fairness to her, Amanda's pregnancy received very little understanding or sensitivity from any of us, and as her hormones raged, so did she. She was away one week and was replaced by her sixteen-year-old brother, a pupil at Harrow public school known as Bruiser, but whose real name was Alexander. Like Amanda he was a posh scally, but his Harrovian accent was so posh it made him difficult to understand. I rather cruelly introduced him at the top of the show by saying, 'He said he had half a mind to present on television, and I told him then he'd be overqualified, please welcome, from Harrow public school, Bruiser De Cadenet – oh, and Bruiser, don't bite the biscuit.' This was a reference to a legendary public school game involving masturbation and a digestive.

The arrival of Amanda's baby, Atlanta – conceived in Atlanta years before Posh and Becks used that theme – was approaching and the search was on for her replacement. One night a few hours before the show, two girls showed up – one twenty-year-old posh brunette London-type and one seventeen-year-old blonde London-type. I sat with them as they auditioned and was asked what I thought by Sebastian.

'Stereotypical,' I replied.

In the end the presenting gig went to the blonde seventeen-year–old, who was called Dani Behr. She was ex-theatre school and had been in a band called Faith, Hope and Charity when she was fifteen. Dani was confident in a way that I could never imagine being at just seventeen. In fact, when I was that age and studying for my A levels, I couldn't even land a Saturday job due to our M16 postcode and had to rely on the few quid I'd saved from summer jobs for money, plus £1 a week from my dad if he was feeling generous. We were from different worlds.

As soon as Dani got the job, there was some friction stirred up between her and Amanda by the team and it was all leaked very quickly – and accidentally on purpose – to the press. Amanda was quoted as saying that Dani was trying to be like her, while Dani was quoted as saying Amanda was a bimbo. When asked for my view by one publication, I rather mischievously said that I thought they were both right.

Although Dani was quite posh, she wasn't in the same league as Amanda, and I suspect that at the time she wanted to be. They both had this peculiar way of semi-Americanizing their consonants when they spoke, saying affected things like 'pardy' instead of 'party' and appreciaded instead of appreciated. They also both liked to use this awful American teen speak, sticking the word 'not' on the end of a sentence in a half-cocked attempt at sarcasm.

Whereas Amanda was very flirty and definitely a bloke's girl, Dani, despite her youth and good looks, was very much a girl's girl and always had plenty of her theatre-school and Mill-Hill girlfriends down at the show. Unlike Amanda, Dani had had a very stable upbringing and didn't seem as old-headed as Amanda, which, though I'm sure Dani didn't think so at the time, made her more like a typical teenager. However, given my shall we say rather twisted cynicism, it meant I struggled to have any kind of real conversation with Dani, so I just left her alone. I was practically middle-aged compared to her and, like a typical teenager, especially one with a few bob, she was into clothes and shopping, which, as anyone could spot by my sartorially challenged dress sense, I wasn't. But although we didn't have much to talk about, I never felt unrelaxed or awkward around her, and I don't think she did around me either.

By this stage of series two I felt I was becoming a bit too cosy, sinking into a Des O'Connor-type comfort zone. Dani seemed to be taking everything in her stride and was very professionally focused, like-wise Katie, so there wasn't the *frisson* that had existed between Amanda and myself, which in some ways I missed.

However, I still came across as too aggressive and abrasive when I wanted to wind guests up on the show, so I decided the way to do it was to niggle them slightly if they were known for having a temper, before they even set foot in the studio. I'd often go and have a quick chat with guests before the show, sometimes catching them mid make-up and cheekily saying things like, 'You can't polish a turd.' This backfired slightly the week we had Sandra Bernhard in. I'd read her autobiography, which was extremely well written, and interviewed her before in LA, though that had never been broadcast. I'd got on with her fairly well, yet because of that she was dull, and we couldn't have Sandra being dull on the show, so I went to meet her in make-up to light the fuse.

She was sitting in the make-up chair as I walked in, and I said how great it was to see her and told her a bit about the show. 'Have a laugh and don't be too serious or boring, like you were in LA,' I said.

She was having lipstick applied at the time, but I could see a glare come into her eyes, 'I can't speak now, I'm having my lips done,' she replied.

'Pretty big job as well,' I jibed and dodged out the door.

Unfortunately for me, I'd done too good a job of winding her up, and throughout the show she gave me a really tough time, at one point threatening violence as she glowered at me and said, 'You are wearing my ass paper-thin,' to which I replied that if it was true we could market it as an alternative Christmas fitness video. 'Then you can suck my dick,' she countered. Honestly, some girls shouldn't be allowed out.

It was one of the weirdest shows I ever did as our other guest was Spanish actor and star of some big Spanish movies by Pedro

Almodóvar, Antonio Banderas, who at the time could only speak Spanish waiter-style broken English, so had to be interviewed via the rather gorgeous interpreter sitting beside him on the couch. The idea of putting him beside Sandra Bernhard was that in the Madonna documentary *In Bed With Madonna* there's a scene where Madge is drooling over Antonio – as were all the girls on our production team – at a dinner party and is gutted to find out he's there with his wife. Sandra Bernhard, meanwhile, is accompanying Madonna at the dinner.

After the show, when we were having drinks, I looked over to see Sandra leaning against the wall, all alone and glumly looking over at me. I half wanted to go over and apologize for setting her up. She looked so vulnerable and shy and I remembered what she'd said in her autobiography about feeling alienated, growing up the geeky kid, the outsider. Once again I'd sacrificed sensitivity to get a firework display, and not only that, I'd let various members of the production staff know what I'd done. I would be made to suffer for it in the future, but at the time I couldn't be arsed to go over and chat to her, after all, we'd only had her on because Charlie was obsessed with Madonna.

The press still hadn't let up on the show and I was regularly given a good going over in the tabloids and music magazines. Think of a paragraph and include all these adjectives alongside the name Terry Christian: inane, banal, boring, dull, inarticulate, thick, moronic, irritating, inept, unprofessional, stumbling, bumbling, stuttering. Strangely enough, not one article bothered to back up any of these adjectives with an example from the show, and the press's attitude towards me seemed completely out of kilter with that of the viewers.

The Word had already become a fixture on *Spitting Image* and each week they'd have my puppet using the catchphrase 'Shag you later' after interviewing various people, from LA riots victim Rodney Franklin to Boy George even the Queen. They were very funny and I loved the opening statement of my puppet when interviewing the Queen, 'Er, so, forty years on the throne, you must have a sore bum,' and 'So how do you feel being named after a glam-rock band.'

Alistair McGowan did a brilliant job of mimicking my voice and captured the horrible nervous cackle I sometimes emitted. After *Spitting Image*, every time I went out I'd be greeted by choruses of 'Shag you later'. This always mystified me, I mean, how was I supposed to respond? I'm walking down the road minding my own business and some blokes shout, 'Shag you later.' Am I meant to go over and say, 'Hi, lads, do you want to go for a pint? Let's be friends for life, or we could all go on holiday together to Ibiza or something.'

Charlie was most pleased with our notoriety: 'Isn't it great that *The Word* is on *Spitting Image*, Terry?' To wind him up I'd simply say, 'What do you mean, *The Word*, it's me they're ripping off.'

Despite Amanda's huge tabloid presence and the fact that Katie had joined the show, the public still saw *The Word* as my show and I suspect that this wasn't what Charlie wanted. Matthew had already told me that the one thing Charlie had taken on board from his time with Janet Street-Porter was her advice never to let the presenters take over the show and to keep them in their place. I noticed this when we first arrived at Limehouse Studios to film series two. My dressing room was like a police holding cell, and you could touch the white walls on either side by stretching out your arms. There wasn't even a sink or a window – believe me, minimalism wasn't the word for it. I was a bit put out, but presumed that all the dressing rooms were of a similar borstal-like grimness, only to discover that all the guests and Amanda's dressing rooms were massive, with leather three-piece suites, separate shower cubicles and everything. Not only that, there were two that were unoccupied, so I made sure I got moved straight away and left everyone in no doubt as to my feelings about the other dressing room: 'I felt like I was waiting for the warders to come back and give me a kicking.' I wasn't being precious, but as we spent an average of ten hours at the studios on the day of the show, a bit of comfort was important.

Meanwhile Amanda was looking more and more pregnant and unleashing her hormones on Sebastian Scott, who hated it. She'd even started to do strange things, like time the minutes she was on air and compare them to how many minutes Katie and myself got.

There was always an element of playground competitiveness at *The Word*, with plenty of big kick-offs, especially on location shoots, where the arguments were always about who was in charge, the producer or the director. *The Word* wasn't just about discovering and nurturing presenter talent, it was supposed to be about bringing on new directing and producing talent, too.

I remember when Andy got his first directing shot on *The Word* and was due to accompany producer Matthew Bowes and myself to Tenerife in the Canary Islands for a long weekend to interview controversial comedian Roy Chubby Brown. Chubby, as he's known, told childish poor-taste jokes about body parts and sex, of the 'My mother-in-law has a fanny like a clown's pocket and piss flaps like a two-part canoe' variety. The shoot was simple, we were to follow Chubby on one of his annual holidays to Tenerife, where he pays for his whole entourage to stay at a five-star hotel for the week, and interview him before his forthcoming sold-out run at London's Dominion Theatre. It was hard to dislike Chubby and very amusing to watch the crowds mob him for autographs – even the Spanish waiters and bar staff had seen his videos in their bars. Andy was astonished.

'I've never heard of him,' he said.

'Erm, why am I not surprised?'

I was looking forward to the trip as it was a chance to get reacquainted with Matthew. Matthew was head and shoulders above most of the other producers on the show in terms of experience, and was often Charlie's unappreciated right-hand man. In comparison, Andy was a first-time director, and as with most inexperienced directors, he liked to work your backside into the ground, taking twelve hours to shoot something that should have taken four.

The piece was a straight-forward interview with Chubby Brown, his Geordie manager George and some of his mates, but I must have recorded and scripted over eighteen pieces to camera. We shot that much film and so many repeated questions that it felt like we'd been filming *Ben Hur*; we ended up with exactly three hours of free time before we had to fly back from a two-day shoot.

On our last night, I ended up staying out a bit too late, having gone to a nightclub with a young lad from Salford. He'd introduced me to some seriously moody lads who were all ex-ICF West Ham hooligans, now based in Tenerife selling time-shares for a major villain. In a drunken haze I realized the time was 6.30 a.m. and our flight back to London was at 8 a.m., and after a lot of panicking, I managed to find a taxi and got back to our hotel just as Matthew and Andy were about to leave for the airport. When we landed in Britain, we heard the news that newspaper magnate Robert Maxwell had fallen overboard on a yacht and drowned off the coast of Tenerife. It wasn't anything to do with *The Word* or Chubby Brown, honest.

The following Tuesday we vox-popped people as they were going to see Chubby at the Dominion theatre on Tottenham Court Road in London. Most of them were very smartly dressed middle-aged blokes and their wives who looked like they used to hang out with the Kray twins. We needed some younger faces and eventually found a bunch of rather posh young lads who worked in the City, and a lone black lad, who again was very smartly dressed, waiting for his mates. 'Why have you come to see Roy Chubby Brown? I mean, not only is he really sexist, his material's pretty racist too.'

With a straight face and a mere hint of a smile the black lad said, 'Roy Chubby Brown? I thought it was James Brown.'

Brilliant, I thought, there's Andy's pay-off line for the whole piece. But when I watched the final edited version, at the end there was no black lad saying, 'I thought it was James Brown.'

'Bloody hell, Andy, that was a great pay-off line, like manna from heaven, why did you cut it out?'

'Well, he'd made a mistake and gone to the wrong gig.'

My jaw was on the floor. 'Andy, watch my lips, he was taking the piss, obviously.'

'Well, I didn't understand it; it wasn't clear and it just sounded like he went to the wrong gig.'

I despaired. The lack of humorous banter was clear from the off. They say Americans lack irony, but among the Home County set there was a complete inability to grasp throwaway humour. 'I don't get it, why is it funny?' This invariably meant that it mustn't be funny or a joke, because they weren't attuned to it. Maybe when you work in a mundane, low-paid job which doesn't value you, you develop a sense of humour about everything and look for something to make you laugh in every situation, just to keep you amused and fend off the boredom – it's the old line of if you didn't laugh you'd cry. I felt that the more privileged people were, the more seriously they took themselves, so they failed to pick up on this style of self-deprecating humour. Invariably, what they saw as jokes were so painfully and obviously telegraphed and of a sneering, bullying nature that they weren't funny at all. It's like watching Johnny Vaughan on the TV, he'll tell a joke, but with all the mugging at the camera and laying it on so thick, you can see the punchline a mile off. A telegraphed joke, like a telegraphed punch in boxing, will only ever hit the stupidest of targets.

At last we were starting to get guests who enjoyed the spirit of the show. Lisa Stansfield came on and talked amusingly about how she was getting fed up of reading the lines 'Down-to-earth northern-, eeh bah gum, black pudding,' every time an article about her came out. I asked her if, because she'd been famous around Manchester since she was fourteen, it frightened the lads off chatting her up, and whether she used to have to chat them up, and she admitted to doing all the legwork herself.

On the same show we had gay icon, singer, comedian and drag artist Alan Pillay. He was doing his 'only gay in the village' act and got a bit carried away, at one point pulling a condom out of it's packet and waving it in the air in front of the audience, shrieking, 'I want to penetrate Charlie Parsons. Woo-hoo, Charlie.' All this, of course, was going out live into people's living rooms, while Lisa and myself were doubled up with laughter and Charlie was freaking out in the gallery, because his parents had come down to watch the show.

There was a lot of excitement when Sinead O'Connor agreed to appear on the show. At the time she was constantly in the headlines, a female artist of world renown who was all attitude, and as far as the British press were concerned, the wrong sort. She used her celebrity to get Jah Wobble, one-time bass player with Public Image Limited, onto the show with his band. Jah Wobble had a new album out called *Rising Above Bedlam*, and Sinead was the guest vocalist on one track called 'Visions Of You'. Sinead had agreed that she would be interviewed on *The Word* couch on condition that Jah Wobble came on, too, and that the band played live in the studio. I didn't have any real thoughts or opinions about Sinead, though I thought it was very cutesy crying in the video for 'Nothing Compares 2 U', and I liked the way she got everyone's back up, but I became her biggest fan for making *The Word* get Jah Wobble on.

I'd first met Jah Wobble when his band had played at the Blue Note club in Derby ten years earlier. I'd spent most of the night getting drunk with them in their dressing room after the gig and he was hilarious company, a real East End boy who was mad on West Ham. Sometimes you meet people and instantly warm to them, and Jah Wobble was one of those people for me.

With all the strange press Sinead had had, I couldn't quite get a handle on her obvious friendship with Jah Wobble, but then I thought, the more down-to-earth people are, the more the press seem to dislike them. When I met Sinead she seemed very shy and quiet, but not unfriendly, and she had an aura of a fantastic sense of humour simmering beneath the surface. I was a bit lame and introduced myself by saying, 'My mum and dad are from Dublin.' As soon as I said it I felt stupid, but Sinead was very nice about it and, probably taking the piss a bit, said, 'Yes, you sort of look Irish.' Of course, at the time I felt that this meant we'd bonded in some mysterious Celtic way. Two kindred souls connected by centuries of mutual oppression, steeped in that Gaelic counter culture, although the only Irish culture my dad ever expressed was Mass on Sunday, Guinness down the pub or club, the bookies and the insistence that Tony Cascarino was outstanding at leading the line for Jack Charlton's Republic of Ireland team.

Sinead was fairly chatty and was pleasant to everyone who came over and didn't hide in her dressing room. I imagine that most of Sinead's real problems came in Ireland itself, where I'm afraid Samuel Johnson's description of them as a race who haven't got a good word to say about anybody is as accurate a description as I've ever read. The Irish media wanted some doe-eyed dark-haired *cailin* – like that girl from The Corrs, a kind of female Daniel O'Donnell, and instead they got a rebellious pot-smoking teenager who, until she got her hair cut, looked just the part.

After performing with Jah Wobble's Invaders of the Heart, Sinead and Jah Wobble joined myself and Boy George on the couch. There had been a bit of nonsense in the press between Sinead and Boy George and I couldn't help laughing to myself. Here we were, Jah Wobble, Boy George, Sinead and myself, all prime examples of what an interestingly fucked-up diaspora that country at the Western edge of Europe had produced.

Boy George always made me smile. It seemed that every time he came on the show we had some big-name star alongside him and he used to feel slightly put out, like he was the support act. This was odd really considering that Boy George is probably one of the most recognizable pop stars of all time. It wasn't as if you ever had to explain to an audience who he was. Unfortunately for Boy George, more than all the Sinead O'Connors and Whitney Houstons, he was condemned for life to be a star, subjected to the stares and whispers of curiosity.

Sinead was fairly reticent during the interview, and was obviously only there to make sure Jah Wobble got the publicity he deserved for his excellent new album. There was a story going around that Hollywood was remaking the story of Joan of Arc and wanted Sinead to play St Joan, and Sinead admitted she was considering it, depending on several different options. At the end of the show I thanked everyone and said to her, 'Thanks, Sinead, and maybe we'll have you on next time with your own band?' She looked at me as if there was no chance of her ever appearing on a show like this again and semi-sarcastically said, 'Maybe.' In an embarrassed tizzy I quickly shot back, 'Or maybe we'll just show a clip of you being burned at the stake.' I felt awful about how cuttingly it came out, but God bless her she did laugh – not as much as Boy George, though, I seem to remember!

The guests and bands on series two were probably the best we ever had. We had a bevy of beautiful young actresses come on, including Halle Berry, who was so pretty, petite and vulnerable that all the hetero lads, from the cameramen to the runners, fell in love with her. We also had Tara Fitzgerald on the show, and there was something so intangibly sexy and energetic about her that I felt like the biggest, ugliest oaf on the planet. I was also very excited, though not necessarily in a sexual way, when Natasha Richardson, daughter of Oscar-winning actress Vanessa Redgrave and legendary British director Tony Richardson, came on. Natasha arrived with her younger sister Joely, who was very beautiful but also incredibly shy. Natasha was very friendly, and as I spoke to her in the dressing room I told her how I'd once been a member of her mother's Workers Revolutionary Party. Natasha smiled and probably thought, there's one born every minute.

It's odd that I can act so cocky, and yet in front of somebody as attractive, well-spoken, successful and talented as Natasha Richardson, I went back to being that scruffy little kid showing his hands to the librarian to prove they were clean, speaking in a whisper so the thickness of my accent didn't mark me out as another kid from the estate, where they'd nick anything that wasn't nailed down. Natasha and myself were the same age, but how different our journeys and expectations had been.

Everything at the 24 Hour Productions office had gone a bit mad. Tony Boland and Bob Geldof's company, Planet Pictures, had merged with 24 Hour Productions to form a new company, Planet 24. Tony Boland had used his twenty-odd years of television experience to put together a proposal for a daily breakfast-time show for Channel 4 called *The Big Breakfast*, but how would things go? There was Waheed the businessman, Sir Bob Geldof the big public figurehead and spokesman, Charlie Parsons the TV expert and Tony Boland – an even bigger TV expert than Charlie. Mysteriously, as *The Big Breakfast* was announced, Tony Boland was shoved out of the picture and Planet 24 became Waheed Alli, Charlie Parsons and Sir Bob Geldof. What happened to Tony Boland? Well, it just wasn't mentioned, despite the fact that his son Murray still worked at Planet 24.

As far as I was concerned, as a show, we were annoying all the right people, which was basically just about everyone – how could something be so right. I felt as if the media had been suffering a huge sense-of-humour failure when it came to *The Word*, and that the best thing we could do would be to publish a book full of backstage shenanigans, funny stories and a glimpse into how extraordinarily ordinary it was behind the scenes.

I put the idea to Charlie, who was keen, but worried that we didn't have any photos. I'd already looked into this by discussing it with one of our cameramen, Phil Piotrowski, who seemed to think you could easily freeze-frame stuff from video and, provided you published in black and white, it would disguise the lack of quality. I ran this past Charlie and then spent most of the following weekend writing up a detailed synopsis of the book. The following week, when I went into Charlie's office, there on his desk was a freeze-framed photograph of excellent quality, and in colour too, of Katie Puckrick the instant she was struck in the eye by a flying piece of jelly in the previous week's studio event 'Grudge Match', which had descended into a mass riot of jelly-flinging.

'There you go, Charlie, told you it'd work. So what about this book?'

Charlie seemed a bit miffed that I'd noticed the picture and acted like he'd been caught out about something.

'Erm, I'll have to think about it and talk to Channel 4,' he said shiftily.

During the Summer I was sitting at home one day, bored and

restless, when the phone went. I picked it up.

'Hello, Terry, I'm Martin Cunning, I'm going to be working on the next series of *The Word*, but I've got to write this *Word* book and I need to interview you for it.'

I was fuming. I'd gone to Charlie with yet another idea, even finding out how to get the photos we might need, and he'd gone and passed on the project to someone else. It was called *The Word Quiz Book*, was absolutely cack, and it taught me that whatever Charlie had in mind, I was never going to get on under his stewardship.

chapter ten

'Those hooligans and tarts aren't presenters... they, er, they're just gits' Channel 4 duty log

It was a shoot I was really looking forward to. I'd always been a huge reggae fan and all the black kids I'd grown up with in Manchester used to dream of one day going to Jamaica, though it was a dream that, for most of them, seemed an impossibility. Musically I thought of it as my home country, and now here I was, excited about seeing the places I'd heard mentioned in all those reggae songs – Trench Town, Spanish Town, Tivoli Gardens and Negril – it seemed that every place with any kind of population in Jamaica has a song about it. We were in Jamaica to interview nineteen-year-old Buju Banton about his record 'Boom Bye Bye', which advocated shooting homosexuals on sight. It was already a huge world-wide reggae hit, and was indicative of some worryingly violent attitudes to homosexuals on the dance-hall scene.

At Kingston airport at 3 a.m. after a harrowing twenty-three-hour journey, all the locals rushed to the customs desks, leaving me the last in the queue, with just one suitcase and one piece of hand luggage. The Jamaican passengers who jumped in front of me seemed to have the equivalent of a large corner shop for their luggage and the customs officers diligently searched every one of them. The worst items were the huge tubular barrels filled with shoes, curtains, sheets, dresses, trousers, shirts, perfume, hairspray, toothpaste, cakes, biscuits and booze. At Christmas in Old Trafford the West Indian families would all send barrels over to their relatives in Jamaica, if they could afford it, and it would be filled with all sorts, just like the ones being opened in front of me.

It took me two and a half hours to clear customs, and only then because I almost started a fight with a man who rolled three barrels in front of me as if I was some kind of traffic bollard. I uttered a whispered threat, but as I'd now been awake, stressed out and hung-over from my flights, he took one look at my psychotic blood-shot eyes and the scowl on my face, sucked his teeth and waited behind me. 'Oi, I'm next,' I shouted with venom, as the man with the barrel tried a last-minute manoeuvre to grab my place at customs.

It took me exactly two minutes to get my passport stamped, then it was out into the warm, humid Caribbean air. I sat in a minibus and told the driver I was staying at the Pegasus Hotel in Kingston. He asked me where I was from, chatted to me, but didn't start the minibus. 'Well, are we going or what?' I asked.

'It's a minibus, man, I have to wait for more passengers.'

'Listen, mate, there were only about four people behind me in the queue and they won't be out for ages, here you are,' I waved a twenty-dollar note under his nose and he immediately started the bus. As we pulled out past the terminal the man with the barrels was rapping at the window, sweating, surrounded by his luggage and two women who were also dragging heavy baggage.

'Can I stop for the people, man?' the driver asked.

I wasn't in the mood, especially as the guy had tried to jump the queue in front of me.

'Fuck the people and let's get to the Pegasus, I'm knackered.'

I didn't get to bed until 7 a.m. in the morning, almost ten minutes before my phone rang with my early morning call from a far-too-awake-sounding Martin Cunning. I explained about my flight delays to him, so he said he'd call me at midday and arrange for me to be picked up and taken to Buju Banton's manager Donovan Germaine's office, as he'd be looking out for Buju, who would be recording his first-ever interview for the international market when we filmed him for *The Word*.

I met up with Chris and Martin. It was going to be a very long day for all of us. They introduced me to our Jamaican fixer, Carl Bradshaw, a tall, gangly Rastafarian whose face looked incredibly familiar. Also accompanying us were two muscle-bound ex-university students who, along with Carl, would help watch both us and the equipment, our Jamaican camera crew and two plain-clothes armed police dressed in T-shirts and jeans who didn't speak all day. The familiarity of Carl Bradshaw kept bugging me. 'Were you in a band?' I asked 'A drummer or musician maybe?'

'No, man,' he replied.

'What about any of those Jamaican films like *Rockers* or *The Harder They Come*?'

'No, man.' Carl was very taciturn, not a smile crossing his lips. A lot of Jamaicans act this way when you first meet, stroking their chin and sucking their teeth.

I persisted all day: 'I've seen your face before definitely.' Then I'd regale him with questions about what had happened to various reggae greats of the past. 'I heard Junior Byles was begging for a living on the streets, is that true?'

'Yes, I heard it also.'

'What happened to Delroy Wilson? What happened to Garnet Silk?' But all I could extract was one-word answers from Mr Bradshaw. Hundreds of youths crowded around outside producer Donovan Germaine's studio, both within it's barbed-wire compound and outside. As we walked through with our security, they were all begging for money. I knew that this was what happened in Jamaica as there had been stories of London-based white reggae DJ David Rodigan wandering through the ghetto handing out dollars left, right and centre, but it was hard not to be moved by the abject poverty of the surrounding neighbourhood. There were small children roaming the streets barefoot, and unemployed youths surrounded us, telling us they hadn't eaten since the previous morning. I handed out any single US dollar bills I had on me, making a crush around us. It was different, I felt sharp and aware; it was a bit like being back in Manchester.

We interviewed Donovan Germaine about Buju and the state of

reggae music. After Bob Marley, there were no Jamaican artists with good enough backing to step into that gap. Marley had been a one-off, a project for Island Records boss Chris Blackwell, who spent the same amount of money marketing him as most majors spent on their priority rock acts. This was unusual, and it had meant that Marley reached a far bigger audience and left an impression that other Jamaican artists were never able to match.

Reggae had also suffered from not really catching on with black Americans. In fact, when Bob Marley's greatest hits album, *Legend*, was first released in the USA, it only sold 100,000 copies. Now, however, there were big Jamaican communities in Toronto, Miami, New York and Philadelphia, and all the Californian white surfer kids had adopted reggae as their soundtrack, so the music was starting to penetrate the American market.

Donovan told us how Buju had a one-and-half-million-dollar-deal on the table from one of the major labels in the USA. He was fine about us interviewing Buju, but if we had any questions about the content of his record 'Boom Bye Bye', the interview would be stopped immediately. Chris and Martin agreed to this, but they were lying their heads off. We'd been vox-popping the local youths about the record, and they all thought it was great and very funny. When we asked them why they thought the idea of shooting homosexuals in the arse was worthy of such mirth, they all quoted the Old Testament Leviticus 18, which states that the sentence for a man laying with a man is death.

We drove to the ghetto where Buju had been raised and was still living. It was a collection of shabby wooden structures with earth floors and corrugated-tin rooves, a veritable shanty town alongside the 'government yards' – Jamaica's equivalent of council houses – enclosed rows of semi-detached and terraced single-room buildings. The sun was blazing down and Buju was incredibly articulate and well-educated, able to talk maturely about the politics of Jamaica, reggae and the difference between an uptown and downtown sound. Downtown was dance hall, pure vibes, slack lyrics full of sexual innuendo and different dance crazes and novelty songs on various themes, whilst uptown was the roots and culture, going back to Africa and consciousness-raising stuff favoured by the middle and upper classes who lived uptown. Buju intended to mix both styles, as we'd see when we went to watch him perform at a big posh fashion show in uptown Kingston that night.

I spent ages talking to Buju while the cameras rolled. Both Martin and Chris struggled with his patois, but after all the time I'd spent round mates' houses listening to reggae and touring Britain's Afro-Caribbean centres, I found it completely understandable. I was using my old radio-interview technique of listening and waiting, watching and being aware, it wasn't an inquisition but an exploration.

Buju told me about his mother and how, please God, he hoped his music would mean a better life for her and his siblings. He talked about the struggle for the youth on the streets and the political parties who promised much but delivered nothing to the people in the ghettoes except guns and more violence. He spoke about how excited he was that he'd be touring all over the States and South America, and how he wanted to ape that other great reggae artist Freddie McGregor, who learned many of his songs in Spanish and Portuguese when he played in South America and even sang a song in Japanese when playing a big Sun Splash event in Japan. Most of all, Buju was hoping to see and play in Africa. All his hopes, dreams and feelings were poured out during the interview and we spent almost two hours filming.

All the time, in the back of my mind, was the niggling question I had to ask him. What would the repercussions of Buju's answer be? I looked around at the surrounding shanties, a world too forlorn to be flexible and generous to social climbers who were just passing through, and realized that we were there to keep him there, snatch his dreams away over some dance-hall lyrics that were nothing more than a horrifically bad joke, which, in turn, reflected the fundamentalist, ingrained religious views on the island.

Those were always the most stressful times for me. Martin Cunning and Chris Fouracre were under pressure to deliver the story, and I knew there was no going back until we had it. I didn't think

Buju deserved the crucifixion he was about to get. He'd been brought up on the bible and as a naïve nineteen-year-old he was prepared to give a point of view based on a holy book written some 3,000 years ago. In the end I sneaked the poison chalice question in by disguising it, saying how amusing the song was and praising him for its commercial success. The ruse worked and he started to talk about it, quoting Leviticus like the boys on the street had done. I pointed out that in the same text where it says that homosexuals should be sentenced to death, it also said that fornicators and adulterers should be put to death, in fact, having sexual relations with your wife when she had her period meant banishment from the tribe. Buju laughed at this, but went on to explain how a man and woman was natural and that God created Adam and Eve and not Adam and Steve – the usual tripe. Then again, give or take the odd religious reference, it's a view that I should imagine isn't that unusual amongst many adolescent males, even in the industrialized, developed world, never mind the gruelling poverty of the area where Buju was raised.

Buju talked about the record and why it was so popular, how people hated homosexuals and though he'd never met one, he considered what they did an abomination in the eyes of God, although 'Boom Bye Bye' was supposed to be a novelty record to make you laugh. I looked at the rusting corrugated iron lids on the ramshackle clapboard buildings around me and wondered if maybe the idea of shooting a stranger up the arse just because they have a different sexuality from you is funny to adolescent males. I then asked Buju if he really would shoot someone and again he couldn't get to grips with the question, as if it was a situation that would never arise in his life.

I felt bad about what we'd done to Buju. I had no sympathy for the sentiments of the song, but seeing the desolation Buju and his friends called home, I couldn't help but ponder what the real issue was. What was it like to be a person who'd grown up with that level of poverty and now to be nineteen and carrying your whole neighbourhood's hopes and dreams? Because Buju Banton was the neighbourhood hero, open-handed and generous, and certainly not a strutting Yardie. I felt as if I'd brought a seed of destruction into a world already full of turmoil. I somehow knew that this insignificant interview about a record few people outside the reggae fraternity would have heard of was a crucial digit affecting an enormously complicated calculation, and it made me feel like a traitor to everything I believed in. The horrific treatment meted out to homosexuals in Jamaica was written into the Statute books. It was the govenment of the island that deserved the full glare of the West's media admonishment, not some teenage reggae star.

That night we filmed Buju performing for the well-dressed, snobby Uptown Kingston folk. I noticed how, although the audience was black, almost none of them were dark-skinned. It was a parade of WhitneyHouston/Lionel Ritchies, dancing in the night to the sounds made by the ghetto youth.

To contrast this, at 3 a.m. we headed for Spanish Town in the heart of the ghetto. There was a huge dance taking place there in a football stadium, but the police wouldn't allow us to film inside so, along with thousands of others, we set up on the street outside to listen to the music. I heard Junior Byles old standard 'Fade Away': 'The man who thinks of only wealth and not of his physical health will fade away.' It was apt after filming all day that it was Junior Byles I heard, I wondered if he were among the street people gathered on the sides of the road, as if waiting for some pageant to pass.

A group of six barefoot children aged between five and nine surrounded me. 'Why you chewin' so 'ard?' they asked.

I had a bumper pack of chewing gum that I'd bought on my five-hour stopover in Miami.

'I'm tired,' I replied. 'Why aren't you kids in bed?'

'Y'ave a dollar?'

One of the kids started trying to impersonate my accent, much to the amusement of the other kids. In my pocket I had my last remaining twenty-dollar bill. I handed the pack of chewing gum to the eldest kid, who immediately started sharing them out, then I folded the twenty-dollar bill small and tight in my pocket, looked around to check that no one was watching me and swiftly put it in the oldest kid's hand.

'Share it out,' I whispered.

They all turned and ran away from the crowd.

By the time we finished filming it was 4.30 a.m. We had most of the day free the following day, apart from a meeting with Jamaican female star Patra. Today was our first and last day with Carl Bradshaw. I'd been speaking at him all day, but he'd refused to engage with me and had been very sparing with his answers. Pervert that I am, though, it just made me ask him even cheekier questions. We got into the minibus with our security guys and plain clothes policemen and Carl drove us towards the hotel.

Our security guys were twenty-one-year-old graduates of the Jamaican University, and I remember chatting to them about what they had studied there. Two had studied engineering and one had a degree in physics, but it was the same story: there was no work in Jamaica without great connections and no chance of going to the USA or Canada for a while. What struck me most about the three lads was how frighteningly bright, informed and well read they were. I mentioned to Neil, the body-building physicist, that I'd bought a hardback copy of Stephen Hawking's book *A Brief History of Time* and told him that although I'd done A level physics I couldn't make head nor tail of it. I told him I'd hated physics at school, and one of the other lads looked at me like I must be mad.

'You didn't like physics?' He was unable to comprehend how anybody, given the opportunity to learn something so wonderful, wouldn't grasp it with both hands and be grateful.

Neil then said, 'I read about that book in the newspaper and seen the guy on TV, but it will be a long time before they get it in the library and you'll have to wait a year before your turn comes up, nobody will have a copy to sell in Jamaica.'

Here I was with three brilliantly educated and obviously hard-working lads who, despite their degrees, weren't able to find regular work apart from security for Carl Bradshaw.

Suddenly Carl passed a huge spliff back down the minibus and began chatting away to me like he was my best friend. 'I been watching and listening to you all day, man, you just keep rapping and rapping, you're a good presenter, man.' Then he opened up. He had indeed been in both the films I'd mentioned, *The Harder They Come*, and the starring role in *Rockers*, and he'd played on a variety of records with The Roots Radics and other groups under the name Leroy Horsemouth Wallace. Chris Fouracre, Martin Cunning and myself had watched in amazement all day as crowds had parted for Carl, it was as if he was 'the Man' in Jamaica, and he seemed to know everyone. He told me of his visits to England and his friendship with Chris Blackwell, how he'd spent time in Cheshire and had been to Manchester a lot, too.

I suddenly felt so privileged to be in Jamaica, there was something special about the place, a kind of magic in the air that seemed to penetrate your soul. It made me think of seeing Bob Marley and The Wailers in concert at Bingley Hall in Stafford when he opened with the song 'Natural Mystic'. That's what Jamaica had, a natural mystic, an intangible vibration I've never felt anywhere else in the world. The people we'd met had overwhelmed me and it had been a long tiring day full of laughter, despite the guilt I felt towards Buju Banton.

Carl, the security guards and our plain-clothes coppers came back to the Pegasus, and at 5 a.m. we ordered sandwiches and Red Stripe beer and sat up drinking and chatting. I went up to my room to get my copy of *A Brief History of Time* and gave it to Neil.

'Are you sure?' he said. 'I know how much this book costs, are you sure?' I felt humbled by his obvious gratitude. It had cost me about eighteen quid and I was now earning £2,000 a week, which would go up to £2,500 when the show started, so it was a veritable drop in the ocean to me.

'I'll treasure it, man. I can't tell you how much this means.' The other graduate security guards gathered round Neil and began bargaining about who would borrow it next. I had to smile, as I couldn't imagine any British security guards being over-eager about sitting down and wading through it.

We bade our sad goodbyes, and Chris, Martin and I discussed how frighteningly bright and on the ball Neil and the other lads were.

Chris, who was in charge of the budget for the shoot, said, 'I felt a bit guilty because they worked a twenty-one hour day and the agreed fee was about £14 each, so I chucked them £20 each instead and they responded as if they'd won the pools.'

A couple of days later we arrived in Negril and checked into Hedonism, the anything-goes Jamaican holiday resort where everything is about sex, sex and more sex, according to the advertising. The only problem was that blokes outnumbered girls by about five to one and most of the women were in their thirties or forties and looked like Jerry Springer's audience in a bikini.

'Hey man all the action takes place in the Jacuzzi at midnight.'

Urgh pubic-hair soup, I thought.

Chris panicked when he saw how old the Hedonism crowd were: we needed some young people to film, otherwise it would never make it to air. With this in mind, Chris and Martin headed off into Negril town, while I availed myself of the all-inclusive facilities by drinking various cocktails and Red Stripe at the resort's beach bar.

Chris and Martin returned having found three young attractive British girls, real EastEnder types from the Gascoigne Estate in Barking, Essex. There were two sisters, twenty-one-year-old Tracey and seventeen-year-old Lorraine, and their mate Jody, who was twenty. All three girls were five foot nothing, slim and petite and right characters. They were spending the year back-packing around the world together and had been all over Jamaica, travelling on the local minibuses.

'Ere, those buses are mad, ain't they, Trace, one bloke was touching my arse – a big geezer, too – so I turned round and I told him, "You do that again and I'll knock you out."'

The girls were unbelievable, dumping their bags in their room the moment they arrived and heading straight to the pool where they made good use of the free bar.

'Wassat you're drinking, Jody?'

'I dunno, it ain't half strong though.'

'Get me one then.'

I'd bought a huge amount of grass from one of the locals and couldn't believe how much you got for ten dollars. As soon as the girls found out, there was a constant chorus of, 'Skin one up, Tel.'

Chris had to pay for the three girls to stay at Hedonism out of our budget, and I can say, hand on my heart, that it was the greatest bit of casting ever. In between interviewing the Hedonism management and vox-popping the Americans who were willing to appear on camera – some complained to the hotel management about the filming – I spent many delightful hours getting completely wasted with the girls. Lorraine was complaining, though, as just before the girls were approached by Chris and Martin about coming to Hedonism, she'd been asked out on a date by an up-and-coming American actor she'd met at Rick's Café in Negril.

'Oh, he was lovely, and you spoilt it for me, Trace, by making me come here.'

'He looked a bit gay to me, go and have another drink and get Tel to give you a smoke.'

The up-and-coming American actor in question turned out to be none other than Brad Pitt, and Lorraine was truly gutted. However, the girls came down to *The Word* studio a year later, once they'd returned from their worldwide travels, and Tracey told me that when they were in Los Angeles some random British bloke was driving them around and at one point said, 'See that house? Brad Pitt lives there.'

Tracey and the girls immediately shouted, 'Stop the car!' piled out, went straight up to the gate and rang the buzzer. As it happened, Brad Pitt was in and was quite delighted to find himself in the company of three pretty British girls. They proceeded, in their inimitable fashion, to drink all his beer, smoke all his grass and play him at pool all day. Then Brad suggested all three might want to stay the night, but was informed that they were off now, so he called them a cab to take them back to where they were staying.

The girls certainly made a splash at Hedonism. One particular day, when I had a three-hour wait in between filming, they suggested, after first encouraging me to drink copious amounts of cocktails and dip into the seemingly everlasting bag of marijuana, that I should go

To Rick's Café in Negril with them to sample the magic-mushroom tea. In my state of mind it all seemed like a fine idea – not so several hours later when I was so wrecked I could hardly speak while filming some pieces to camera. It's the only shoot I've ever been on where I kept my sunglasses on, and I'm sure you'll understand why. It makes me look at Magenta Devine on telly with a new understanding – only kidding, Magenta.

The girls were hilarious to be around, especially when various desperate American guys came to chat them up: 'We're all with Tel here, ain't we, darling,' they'd say.

'Oh I see, lucky guy. Hey, if you'd like to swap?'

'Tel's got no time for swapping, we're jealous.'

The only other slightly attractive women around were half a dozen or so fake-breasted American glamour models on a calendar shoot. At the weekly underwear party, one of the American glamour models was chatting to me at the bar, and as she was talking to me the girls were all pulling faces at her, so she asked me if I was with them. 'No, we're just using them on the shoot,' I replied, 'as we needed some young lively people that our show's audience could to relate to.'

Soon all three girls came up and dragged me off. 'Tel, you're with us, don't be running around with all those other girls.' The American model shot off and the girls all collapsed into giggles.

What was fantastic about that first shoot with Martin and Chris was that they seemed to really get what the show was about and had a great ability to take the piss and have a laugh while using a lot of initiative. Chris was moody but not precious, although I did try and wind him up all the time about being ex-public school and half German. Martin was from a lower-middle-class background in Glasgow and his parents were school teachers. He was Catholic like myself and a huge Celtic fan, as well as being very well read and able to make some really funny observations about people and places.

In the end I was sad to leave Negril and Hedonism, but considering how exhausted and tetchy I was after all the drinking and drug-taking, it had to be done. However, I almost exploded with fear and anger when Martin and Chris casually explained over breakfast that instead of travelling overland across the Blue Mountains and Jamaica's lush interior in the van with our Jamaican film crew, they'd booked us on the mail plane from Negril to Kingston, a ninety-minute journey with a stop to drop off the post at Montego Bay.

'Why? We can't be insured. What's the hurry? We don't fly to Miami until tomorrow and this is a once-in-a-lifetime chance to see the countryside.' Like I gave a shit about the views.

I heatedly accused them of being quislings, traitors and creeps to Charlie and Channel 4, as well as every name under the sun. I'd say any and everything to get out of flying in a tiny plane, but it had already been decided.

I absolutely cacked my pants when I saw the miniscule aeroplane with a single propeller at the front – it looked like the three of us and the pilot would only just squeeze in. While the plane wobbled, shook, bumped and lurched through every stiff breeze, I said dozens of Hail Marys and Our Fathers in my head. Under normal circumstances I'm extremely talkative, to the irritating extreme where I don't shut up, but throughout that hellish journey I didn't utter a word.

'Wow! I've never known Terry be quiet for so long, that was fantastic,' Chris said while I looked daggers at him.

'No, Chris, the word you were looking for was traumatic.'

Bidding farewell to Jamaica, we flew to Florida for our final assignment on the trip. We arrived at our very nice art deco hotel on Miami's South Beach, feeling exhausted but excited. It felt like we were on holiday. We had two nights there, then it was off to Tampa to interview seventeen-year-old supermodel Niki Taylor, but first we had a very early start the following day.

At 4 a.m. the next day we stepped into a hotel room in downtown Miami to interview a policeman from Arizona who was about to undergo a penis extension – an operation we were there to film. His wife, who was actually born in Scotland, confessed she didn't really know whether his penis was small as she'd been a virgin when she married him and therefore didn't know any different. He would be getting *The Word* treatment in full, but for a payment of $2,000 towards the operation. We were given carte blanche, although I'm not sure whether he would appreciate being referred to as 'the copper with a little chopper'.

It was the usual questions, why are you having the operation? How small is it? When did you first notice it was tidgy? What results are you hoping for? While all the time trying to keep as straight a face as possible, after all, this was a serious piece about a medical condition – or at least that was the impression the copper with the tiny chopper had been given.

We then told him to get ready and we'd follow him to the clinic where he was to have his operation. I noticed a huge bum bag on the dresser of the hotel room, 'Blimey is that your luggage?' I asked.

He unzipped the bum bag and removed a Glock pistol the size of a small cannon: 'It's my gun, I never go anywhere without it.'

At the hospital, the gruesome details of the operation were explained. It involved cutting a tendon that joins the scrotum to the skin on the shaft of the penis, then taking fat from the pubis and injecting it into the penis to increase it's girth. The doctor explained that the length would be increased by an inch to an inch and a half, but it was in the girth that the most difference would be noticeable. However, the new girth would disappear with time as the fat broke down.

It was hard to keep a straight face as the surgeon described the problems people came to him with.

'We have people with very small penises that taper to a point at the end – what you might refer to as a needle dick or pencil dick – I've met people whose penises are so small they can't even lift it out of their fly to urinate when they go to the bathroom.'

I fought back a smirk with some difficulty, then asked the killer question, 'What's the smallest one you've ever seen?'

'The smallest was one inch in length when erect.'

Phew! That was tough. Chris wanted a reverse shot of my reaction to hearing that the smallest penis size was only an inch long. I tried to portray that fuckin' hell, thank God it's not me look and Chris said great, but when I watched it back, it reminded me of the face I used to pull when trying to take a dump while I had my anal fissure.

While Chris hung around to film the operation, Martin and myself went for some breakfast at a diner round the corner – although I skipped the sausages. So far everything about the shoot, though tiring, had been worthwhile. We had loads of good material, but the Buju story was still causing me angst.

That night, after a three-hour drive, we checked into a motel outside Tampa. The next day we'd be interviewing Niki Taylor in her local park. Niki was a seventeen-year-old Cindy Crawford lookalike, but so thin it was frightening. This was in contrast to her mother, who was big enough to have given birth to another three full-grown Nikis. Our only problem was that we'd all run out of clean clothes; the only item that was clean and unworn was Martin Cunning's Celtic football shirt, and when I put it on I noticed I had the start of a paunch, which I blamed on the free food and alcohol I'd enjoyed at Hedonism.

Trying to suck my stomach in, we waited in the park whilst being eaten alive by clouds of mosquitoes as the cameras set up and irritation began to set in. We wandered around, looking for another location to take some more shots of Niki and myself enjoying a quiet stroll in the sunshine and I lit a cigarette. Immediately Niki asked for one and then hid smoking it, peeping round the corner to check her mum wasn't watching. She may have been a millionaire supermodel at seventeen, but there was no way she was trying to be Miss Sophisticated, she was just a typical teenager. Her mother looked most unimpressed with us, and I could see her point of view: lack of sleep, too much boozing, too many long days and too much travelling had taken it's toll and we looked like a bunch of scruffy students at the end of a boozy freshers' week. This new series of *The Word* could be the best yet.

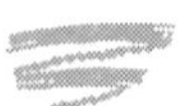

'Fuck me, Keith Richards.' I was astonished. Keith Richards had his first ever solo album, *Main Offender*, coming out on Virgin US and had agreed to record only one interview for TV – and it was going to be with me at Café Tabac in New York. This was all down to the head of Virgin America, formerly head of Circa Records in the UK, a guy called Ray Cooper who was an affable old-school A&R man who'd signed groundbreaking acts like Neneh Cherry and Massive Attack and who was also big mates with my girlfriend. I'd ventured out for the odd drink or three with him in London as well as seeing him around in Manchester, and he had granted *The Word* a world exclusive with Keith.

He'd agreed to fly me out to New York first class on Virgin airlines, pay for two economy seats for a director and producer, finance a film crew for two days, put us up at the Paramount hotel off Times Square and grant us at least 90 minutes with the legend himself. However, Ray insisted that the interview we recorded had to be aired on the one particular Friday show and that we had to agree not to use the camera crew for any other shoots. This was going to be interesting.

Spike Lee had a big movie coming out called *Malcolm X*, starring Denzel Washington. Mark Lamarr had already interviewed Spike and Planet 24 were planning to do some filming with the crew paid for by Virgin after our slot with Keith Richards, as well as getting Dani Behr to knock off a quick interview with Betty Shabazz, Malcolm X's widow, the following day. As everything was being paid for by Virgin records, Planet 24's only outlay would be for an economy seat on Virgin and two nights in a hotel for Dani.

I quite enjoyed being the only member of *The Word* team luxuriating in first class on the plane, sitting next to a charming young lady from Virgin records called Alison. We both got steadily drunk on the flight and watched the Steve Martin, Goldie Hawn film *House Sitter*. When we landed we were met at the airport by a stretch limo, again provided by the record company, which took us to the hotel.

Dani was quite miffed that she hadn't been flown first class, too, and I enjoyed winding her up over things like that. After leaving our bags in our rooms we met up in the hotel bar and I began the wind-up ritual I used on all my fellow presenters whenever we stayed in the same hotel: 'I can't believe this hotel, there's all what looks like crisp crumbs on the carpet in the lounge bit of my suite, the movie channel on the TV in the bathroom has a fuzzy picture and the Jacuzzi only jets out water on one side.'

It usually takes about ten seconds for the green-eyed monster to get a grip.

'What? You've got a suite with a Jacuzzi?'

If they insisted on seeing it you had to confess that it was really just a bog–standard room, otherwise you keep stum and conspiratorially informed your colleague that it's all in the contract your agent negotiated with the TV company. That usually resulted in them charging over to the hotel reception desk and demanding a room upgrade, ringing their agent or the Planet 24 offices.

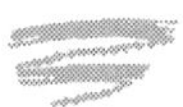

Chris Fouracre and the film crew were busy filming around New York with Dani. Meanwhile, I was sitting in Café Tabac, looking at my watch and worrying that they wouldn't have time to set up for the interview with the soon-to-be-arriving Keith Richards.

Café Tabac was owned by two rather groovy pony-tailed Italian-American brothers who were renowned for being unimpressed with celebrity. Indeed, according to our New York-based producer Jane Buchanan, they once turned away Madonna when she arrived without a reservation. However, the guitar legend Keith Richards was different, and they were so excited that they were giving us all the five-star treatment.

In the end, Keith arrived twenty minutes before Chris and the crew. The owner and record company reps, who were getting quite annoyed, introduced me to Keith and we sat at a table drinking and chatting. Oddly, I felt instantly relaxed in Keith's company and didn't struggle for things to say. I've always been a big blues fan, so we talked about all the old blues musicians, guitarists like BB King, Robert Johnson, J.B. Lenoir, the harmonica greats like Sonny Boy Williamson, Sonny Terry, Little Walter Jacobs, Jimmy Reed and

British blues greats like John Mayall who, though not the greatest singer/songwriter/musician, had a fantastic knack for bringing great talents together in his band line-ups, including big names like Jeff Beck, Jimmy Page, Peter Green, Eric Clapton and Mick Fleetwood.

Keith was great company, and it was obvious that if you stripped away the multi-million-dollar material success of playing with the Rolling Stones, he'd be cranking out blues numbers down the Dog and Duck on a Sunday night for a couple of free pints and a packet of pork scratchings. He was just interested in playing music.

I told Keith how, a couple of years earlier, I'd met up with legendary blues pianist Champion Jack Dupree and stayed up drinking with the seventy-nine-year-old blues legend in a small hotel in Derby until 4 a.m. with my then girlfriend. Jack managed to pull the middle-aged barmaid before heading off to his room with her following discretely behind.

What struck me most about Mr Richards was that he wasn't a fake. He sat across from me drinking screwdrivers, listening and even asking about Paul Gascoigne and England's chances of qualification in the World Cup. It was like going down the pub with one of my uncles. When we started filming, the conversation continued to flow easily and good-humouredly as he gently took the mickey out of Mick Jagger, saying he hadn't let him hear his album in case he moaned that certain songs should have been saved for the next Stones album. He also talked about the Stones on the road, Bill Wyman's women and how he was desperate for Bill to come back to the band. The anecdotes flowed and his musical knowledge and simple philosophy came across. He asked me about Manchester, and spoke fondly about the time he'd spent up there with the Stones doing *Top of the Pops*. He surprised me by saying with some vigour that the worst thing that ever happened was moving the show down to London, because of the special vibe the audience up there had.

We carried on drinking, then the crew filmed him slaughtering me at pool. Keith confessed to playing regularly on tour with Ronnie Wood, who was big mates with Ronnie O'Sullivan the snooker player, and apparently a mean pool player himself. I felt elated, and the two hours that I spent with Keith sort of restored my faith in human nature. The owners and waiters at Café Tabac kept bringing drinks over, and Keith must have necked six or seven huge screwdrivers in those two hours. He was genuinely courteous and polite and seemed almost embarrassed by his star status; Keith's a blues man first and foremost, and to be that, you have to be a genuine human being.

I first met Mark Lamarr at a photo shoot with Katie and Dani for the forthcoming third series of *The Word*. Everyone was really pleasant to him, as we understood what he was letting himself in for. During the previous series I'd requested that we get Mark in as an interview guest on the show, since my mate Craig Cash told me he was quite funny and off-the-cuff in his stand-up act. I remember pestering everyone to get him on for weeks, until finally Sebastian relented and sent our researcher/celebrity booker Fiona to go and see his act. Fiona returned saying he was awful, unfunny and aggressive, but I wouldn't take it on board and told her she must have seen him on a bad night as I'd heard he was good. Despite my continuing to pester, that was it, no Mark Lamarr as a guest.

The next thing I heard was that, under our new commissioning editor, the show was to have a new male presenter. Max Beesley had been a success when he'd co-hosted a Sunday lunchtime Planet 24 show called *Surf Potatoes* with Dani Behr, which was quite *Word*-ish, so it seemed more or less a done deal, even to the extent that we filmed a new opening credits sequence with Max in it for the forthcoming series. Max was very excited and I thought it would be a good laugh, but I did wonder whether anyone at Channel 4 had noticed that Max was also from Manchester. I knew this would be an issue with Channel 4 who, more than any other channel was heavily London biased.

You may be thinking, you would say that, Terry, but it wasn't me who first pointed it out, it was Charlie Parsons, who warned me not to wind up the media about its obsession with London, as many of the Politburo at Channel 4 were just as Londoncentric, and felt that my sniping comments were aimed at them personally. In many ways they may have been right.

The choice of Max made me laugh. Max is a nice lad who comes from the same part of Manchester – Burnage – as the Gallagher Brothers of Oasis, but unlike the Gallaghers, who came from a council estate, Max lived in a nice house and had professional musicians and showbusiness people in the family. While other local kids were scallying around, Max went to the famous Chetham's school of music and was in the Manchester Boys Choir. I used to rib him for being as middle class as all the London luvvies, but being a Mancunian, Max understood that it was just a bit of banter rather than a personal attack.

The initial photo session with Mark, Dani and Katie came to a premature end as I refused to get undressed and lie under a big blanket in my undies with them, since I thought it sent out the wrong message to our audience, as if we were saying we were cooler and more attractive than them. Afterwards, Mark and I went to a pub near Euston Station and sat there chatting for about two hours. I was aware of the fact that I needed an ally on the show, someone I could bond with and who in turn would deflect some of the flak aimed at me. Mark was pleased that I'd stood up to the photographer and I explained that it was no big deal, we were just TV presenters not glamour models, and they'd have us doing all sorts if we didn't put our foot down from time to time.

I think I was a surprise to Mark and not at all what he was expecting; perhaps that was the reason he ended up disliking me so much. As soon as it was announced that Mark would be our new presenter, he was in the papers talking about how he would put me in my place and how he'd never wanted to work on telly. However, he had been doing Camden community cable television for free for six months – you get an even bigger anorak for that than you do for hospital radio. He also did audience warm-up for Jonathan Ross's *Saturday Zoo*. I suppose it showed a certain amount of passion and conviction, which is no bad thing, but it's not exactly cool, which is probably why he was at such pains to keep it quiet.

Also, according to Mark's interviews in the press, Channel 4 *forced* him to play third fiddle on *The Big Breakfast* to Chris Evans and Gabi Roslin and then *made* him do *The Word*. All Mark's talk in the papers about not really wanting to be on telly, even though, here he was on Channel 4, led him to give off the desperate, sweaty air of the man in a brothel who insists he doesn't really need to pay for it.

For series three *The Word* was branching out. We had a spin-off show called *Access All Areas*, which was recorded on the day of the show for transmission at 6 p.m. the following Thursday. *Access All Areas* was exactly that, plus we had a slot each week for an unsigned band, who were looked after by Gary, the first and only black production person we ever had working on the show. I was really keen on the unsigned-bands idea, and as my girlfriend was a regional radio plugger, I obtained a list from her of all the new music/indie shows on the BBC and ILR stations across the country who might showcase local bands. I then presented this list to Gary with a letter and suggested he find the groups that way. After all, if the artists were deemed good enough for local airplay, it was a better and easier way to find good groups than a free-for-all hunt through demo tapes and videos, 90 per cent of which would be shit. Also, it would have the added bonus of all the radio shows and stations plugging *The Word* and publicizing the fact that one of their local unsigned acts was to appear on it.

As I've explained, though, there's a certain dimness of thinking in TV land. Gary never did take me up on my offer, instead, with the odd exception, we showcased some of the worst unsignable bands in the country. However, what we did get was loads of Gary's London contacts getting a slot on the show, plus a couple of artists doing cover versions, which wasn't what you needed on a show that was trying to discover new talent. It all boiled down to lack of organization, patch-protection and stupidity, and it meant that what could have been an excellent ground-breaking slot ended up being thrown together in an inexcusably slap-dash manner.

As presenters we were supposed to rotate so we all got a chance to present *Access All Areas* and *The Word*. For the first five weeks, though, it was business as usual, with me presenting the live *Word* show and Mark presenting the pre-recorded *Access All Areas*.

Mark had a scriptwriter, or gag writer, who'd accompany him on the day of filming. I remember asking Charlie during series one whether, given the low standard of writing from the show's producers, he shouldn't employ a decent scriptwriter. Charlie responded as if I'd asked him to film the show in black and white, and whenever I suggested that I should receive a writing credit on the show, he refused. However, under pressure from Mark's manager and Channel 4, who were grooming Mark for bigger things, Charlie allowed Mark to have his own scriptwriter and agreed that he wouldn't be made to introduce any of the ultra-tacky pieces, like condom flossing.

Mark's friendliness towards me decreased steadily as the weeks went by and I remained presenting the live show while he fronted the pre-recorded one. This was no reflection on Mark, it was just that Charlie didn't want to throw him in at the deep end, like they'd done with me, preferring to give Mark the chance to get used to working in front of a camera on a pre-recorded show first.

The first shows were tough, as the guests we had on weren't great and we often had to slot people in on the Thursday night before the show. On the very first show of the series I struggled with Vanessa Paradis, now Johnny Depp's wife, who didn't speak fantastic English and had a tendency to get distracted by the audience and dry up on me. During the ad break, as I tried to collect my thoughts before Neneh Cherry joined me on the sofa, Mark Lamarr and the *Access All Areas* camera crew jumped up on the couch and Mark started asking Vanessa Paradis what she thought of me and my interviewing technique. Vanessa just looked embarrassed, so he turned to me and said, 'That was a stupid question, Terry, when you said, "Acting, er, acting," why did you say it twice?'

If you've never worked on live TV, this might not strike you as odd, but if you're twelve minutes into presenting your first live TV show for over six months and you're having difficulty gelling with your guest in front of an audience of 300 people you don't need some Brylcreamed 'comedian' butting in and putting you off your stride. I was really annoyed, not so much at Mark as at the *Access all Areas* producer and director Andy Margetson.

'Look, fuck off, Mark,' I replied. 'You'll understand why when you're up here.' He obstinately stood there, though, and started giving me aggressive verbals a quarter of the way through a live show. After that the programme passed by in a blur for me. I received a half-hearted apology from Andy Margetson, but none from Swindon's Shakin' Stevens.

Afterwards, at the usual after-show drinks party, I spotted Bob Geldof, who was now one of the bosses. I'd been a big fan of the Boomtown Rats when I was younger. It was that strange Irish descent thing in Old Trafford, where nearly every lad around my age, even if they weren't into the whole punk/new wave thing, seemed to have a copy of the Boomtown Rats album *Tonic For the Troops* in their collection and those of us who thought we were hard-core fans had the first album with the epic 'Joey's On The Street Again'.

I thought I'd go over and introduce myself to Sir Bob – after all, he was just a Dubliner like my dad, albeit higher up the socio-economic scale.

'Hiya, Bob, nice to meet you. I'm Terry.'

'Yes, I know, we've met before.'

'Er, well, actually we haven't.'

'I've met you before.'

'Honest, we haven't.'

'We have.'

This was all quite perturbing for me. Here was Bob Geldof, Boomtown Rats frontman, part of my youth and Mr Live Aid – I'd even got our Mary to buy me a copy of his autobiography for Christmas five years earlier. Not only had I never met Sir Bob before, but he was giving me the 'Yes, we've already met,' line as a not very well-disguised, 'Yes, we've already met and I thought you were a twat and didn't like you at all.' Fair enough, but we *hadn't* met before.

I always found *The Word* difficult and demanding, I wasn't a trained sea lion or natural showman, but I deserved some respect for fronting a successful and popular show, and I felt Mark had overstepped the line with the personal comments he'd made to me in front of Neneh Cherry and Vanessa Paradis, to say nothing of the studio audience. Whether or not Mark rated me as a television presenter wasn't the issue, he was confusing his opinion of the way I came across on TV with a real person, and I found that very odd.

In the end I decided to call him at home the following Monday to clear the air: 'Mark, it's Terry.'

'Urgh, what d'you want?'

'I can't live with the way you talked to me on Friday.'

'Well, wotcha gonna do about it.'

'Are you some kind of prick or something? What am I going to do about it? I'll kick your fake wannabe arse from one side of London to the other if you talk to me like that again.'

'Yeah, you can try.'

It was a mistake. I'd lost my rag and come down to his level.

I arranged for a showdown meeting with Mark, the editor Paul Ross and Charlie Parsons to clear the air. Charlie didn't show up, and when I asked Mark why he'd suddenly become so aggressive around me, despite the fact that I'd been nothing but friendly, helpful and generous with him, he just growled, 'I hate you,' like something out of *The Exorcist*.

I was shocked. If you feel that strongly about someone, it's usually because they've done something harmful to you, so I asked what it was that I'd done.

'You get on my nerves.'

The conversation was going nowhere and I felt an aggressive anger rising up that I hadn't experienced since school, which, if I'm honest, is where what went on between Mark and myself belonged. His hard-man act and lack of respect was really starting to wind me up.

'I'll tell you what I'll do, you speak to me like that again, you prick, and I'll kick the shit out of you, you jumped-up fake wanker. Where I grew up, they wouldn't waste their time on a twat like you, somebody would just stick a knife in you.'

The whole conversation had got out of hand and Paul Ross looked on in quiet astonishment. As Mark walked out the door, he pointed his finger at me and growled that he was going to kill me.

As far as meetings went, it was certainly different to any of the other little get-togethers we'd had in the Planet 24 office and I wondered whether Charlie's absence had been pre-planned. I was particularly shocked at the level of anger and violence I felt personally, but it was bad enough that I'd had to bare the brunt of the criticism and flak the show had received over the past two years. It made me wonder what it would have been like to front an unpopular and unsuccessful show!

The guests on the shows so far that series had been a bit on the lame side and were often intimidated by the size of the audience standing within five feet of them. Then suddenly we had a coup, with top American comedian, the late, great Bill Hicks, and legendary British actor Oliver Reed booked to appear on the same show.

I was excited about both guests. Bill Hicks was the new Lenny Bruce and even used the old Lenny Bruce line about Christians wearing crucifixes and what would Jesus think of that on his return. 'Hey, it would be like wearing a small sniper rifle on a chain for John F. Kennedy – "Jackie, look, just thinking about John."' Bill was booked onto *The Word* because he was doing a special for Channel 4, but he wasn't at all pleased about appearing on a show like ours. He did his best, as I fed him questions, which meant he could just do part of his comedy routine.

Oliver Reed was a really exciting guest with a whole history of British film-making, Hollywood and hell-raising with the likes of Richard Harris and Richard Burton, but in my opinion he was being completely wasted. The idea was to lock him in his dressing room with two bottles of 100 per cent proof vodka, then get him roaring drunk and riled before bringing him on to do his out-of-control drunk act, before joining rock band Neds Atomic Dustbin on stage for an impromptu version of The Troggs huge sixties anthem 'Wild Thing'.

I argued endlessly with Paul Ross about wasting this great guest, saying it was an insult to Ollie Reed, annoying to large sections of our audience and a rather contrived attempt to create controversy. I may as well have been talking to the wall, though. I liked Paul, but he was too wrapped up in contriving magical moments for the tabloids, which I felt would arise organically if we were as honest and earthy as we'd always been. Once you start getting bogged down with gimmicks and contrivances you become predictable and dull, and it went against the grain of what I felt *The Word* was about.

In the end Bill Hicks sleepwalked through his interview, reciting highlights of his stand-up routine in answer to my pre-planned and pre-agreed questions. Bill just didn't want to be there and I could tell.

Oliver Reed was filmed secretly and supposedly unawares in his dressing room with his vodka. We sent in an overly camp actor wearing a cravat, who pretended to be the show's director or producer – believe me a real one would have done just as well – who tried to wind him up and call him darling – as if Ollie would have had a problem with a camp homosexual luvvy after all his decades in film and theatre – then we sent in some dwarves, which again Ollie hardly responded to. It was obvious he knew that we were filming him and didn't give a rat's behind.

There was a big spin on this particular show, but from a viewers point of view it wasn't worth the effort. Ollie came on pretending to be far drunker and more aggressive than he actually was. I held my hand out to shake his when he finally staggered onto the set in a really staged drunken manner and he was polite enough, but rambled on a bit about his dad being a conscientious objector in the war. When Katie revealed that we'd been secretly filming him, he sarcastically said, 'Gosh, that was a surprise.' Katie then asked if he'd known, to which he replied, 'Would I know anything, madam?'

I tried to move him on and he just glared at me: 'You'll get your chance in a minute, although I hear you're heterosexual.'

He then got up and sung 'Wild Thing' with Ned's Atomic Dustbin, and afterwards I thanked him and held out my hand to shake his.

'Don't raise your hand to me, boy,' he growled in a semi-whisper that briefly frightened the life out of me. I could tell he was just acting drunk, though, and enjoying the mad atmosphere with all the youngsters in the audience chanting his name, so I stood there with my hand out until eventually he muttered something about me being very brave and finally shook my hand.

His attempts at semi-incoherence were a bit too exaggerated, but he obviously preferred that to answering lots of namby-pamby questions about his acting career that he'd heard a hundred times before in previous interviews. He just wanted a laugh and a chance to sing, which he did in a really comic way, semi-out of time and very out of tune – no wonder his song as Bill Sykes in the musical *Oliver* was dropped from the final cut.

As the show finished, I introduced the final band, an all-female American grunge act called L7. They were pretty ropey musically and sounded like plodding student rock to me. As they twanged and banged about on stage, their lead singer and guitarist, Donita, dropped her jeans, showing off her flabby bare arse, then lifted her guitar up to reveal a rather hairy vagina. Straight away a cameraman zoomed in for the beaver shot and I had no doubt that the director in the gallery would ensure the whole nation saw the 'chuff shot' on national TV.

Afterwards, Donita talked to me in the green room. She was feeling really pleased with herself for flashing her badge and came up with a load of Californian artistic mumbo jumbo as to why she'd done it, as if I gave a shit. I was quite amused by her comments in the music press, where she said that flashing her minge had raised the level of the show; in my eyes it put her on a level with some kid from Stoke eating a worm butty – at least the kid eating worms was doing it for love, rather than prostituting himself to sell more records and get in the papers.

Of course, the show made the headlines, but it was the usual lazy tabloid take: 'Ollie Reed drunk on *The Word*,' and 'They got him drunk' bollocks that was fed to the press by our PR. There were the usual shock-horror headlines, too, but thanks to Olly, Donita showing her chuff on live TV almost went unmentioned.

A lot of the younger audience were only aware of Oliver Reed through his drunken antics and not because of the fact that, along with Richard Burton, Albert Finney, Michael Caine and Sean Connery, he was one of the most charismatic and powerful actors Britain has ever produced. To me that was the travesty of it all, and I was beginning to lose my appetite and enthusiasm for the show as a whole. I wanted us to be truthful and entertaining, not to jump on the whole media pigeonholing bandwagon. I'd been told that Oliver Reed was more of a social drinker and would have been in a very relaxed and entertaining mood had he enjoyed a few pints in the bar and plenty of company before the show. Paul Ross admits now that he was brought in to give *The Word* a complete tabloid makeover, and that Charlie and the bosses at Channel 4 were desperate to pander to the red tops. Unfortunately for me, it was my life and future work that suffered.

Under Paul's editorship *The Word* was becoming a caricature of itself, degenerating into the sort of shit show everyone had already written us off as. We ran a piece on one show about plastic surgery for pets, which Katie had filmed in the USA. I had nothing to do with the piece, but joked about what you could do if you thought your pet Dalmatian was too spotty or your Collie dog had too big a nose. The next thing I knew our PR bloke Neil Reading had put a story out to the tabloids saying that as a result of this piece I'd had death threats and had gone into hiding. The story appeared the following morning, without them bothering to check out the facts first, of course, and as I went to get on the train back up to Manchester, I had various people shouting out, 'Terry, I thought you were in hiding.' That Sunday afternoon I was sitting in my front room watching the United game on Sky TV with five or six of my mates when the phone went.

'Hi, Terry, it's Piers Morgan, I've heard you're in hiding.'

'So that's why I'm sitting at home watching the football with my mates. Listen Piers, write what you want. See you.'

I hung up the phone and it immediately rang again. It was Piers: 'Terry, I'm warning you, don't you dare hang up on me again.'

'Fuck off, Piers,' I said and hung up.

I was really looking forward to seeing the results of my Keith Richards interview, with all his great stories about Jagger, Bill Wyman, groupies, legendary bluesmen and of course the infamous Mars bar incident. For some odd reason, the footage had been given to a new producer, another public-school-rebel type, to edit. He came in raving about what a great job he'd done on it, so I sat down and watched it with mounting fury.

He'd basically spent hours editing Keith Richards', ers and ums together, interspersing this with two eggs being fried in a pan. Like all of them he was obsessed with being trendy, and as per usual it meant you couldn't see the wood for the trees.

'Well, I mean, the Rolling Stones are finished. Look at Keith, his brain's fried, and everyone will love us for doing this. The new big thing is Carter the Unstoppable Sex Machine.'

I exploded.

'So instead of all those great stories and anecdotes, you think watching four minutes of ers and ums and eggs being broken into a frying pan are more entertaining, as if you're making a big statement about the state of rock music. You useless public-school muppet. And you think Carter the Unstoppable Sex machine are going to be bigger than the Stones! I mean, they've got some good tunes, but they're basically a band for students and posh hippies. Who the fuck are you?'

I knew the lad talked a lot of shit, but up until then I'd thought he was OK. I went storming off to Paul Ross and did my nut. Paul hadn't seen the piece and when he did his reaction was similar to mine, but as there was no time for a re-edit before we broadcast, the whole piece wasn't aired.

In the meantime, Ray Cooper at Virgin had somehow found out what had gone on in New York and sent an invoice to Planet 24 for the first class return air fares, hotel rooms, limousines and two days' worth of film crew. This really hit where it hurt them – in the budget

– and Planet 24 sacked the offending Carter fan. Had their employment policies been based on what people knew rather than their backgrounds, though, they wouldn't have employed the sad numpty in the first place.

Mark Lamarr's first bash at the live *Word* show came in week five or six of the series. The guests that night were Marky Mark Wahlberg, now a successful Hollywood actor, but then better known as the brother of Donnie from New Kids on the Block and as an up-and-coming hip-hop artist; Dannii Minogue and reggae star Shabba Ranks, who had performed live for the first time on British TV on *The Word* two years previously. Also scheduled on the show was the video piece I'd recorded in Jamaica with Buju Banton about the record 'Boom Bye Bye'.

For the first time that series we actually had all the guests booked a good week in advance and there were no changes to the line-up. I also had a vast knowledge of, and interest in, reggae and Jamaican culture, having managed a reggae band, promoted reggae gigs and written numerous articles and radio pieces about Rastafarianism, the Twelve Tribes organization and the history of British reggae.

I was excited to at last have a show I could get my teeth into, so I wrote a script, got it over to the office on the Monday, went down to London on the Thursday, had a meeting about that week's show late that afternoon, went off to voice the video items late that Thursday night, then waited in my flat from 10 p.m. for a final version of the script and running order to be biked round to me. At 11 p.m. there was still no script, so I rang the office. 'It's on it's way, Terry,' I was told, but by midnight I was feeling agitated as it still hadn't arrived. I was again told it was on its way, but by 1.30 a.m. I was getting frantic. I had a show to do the following day and still no script to find out what the hell I was going to be doing. I was absolutely furious at how slow and amateurish they were being, so I rang the office again. 'What's the f***ing hold up? We know what's on the show, it's now a ridiculous hour. Where's the script and running order?' I gave them my address again to make sure there were no mistakes and waited, but by then I was so agitated I couldn't sleep.

Finally, at 3.30 a.m., the script arrived. I opened it wondering if the whole line-up had been changed and found that there were two scripts, one for *The Word*, which apparently Mark Lamarr was presenting and one for *Access All Areas*, which I was presenting.

All week I'd had phone calls about the guests, I'd been asked to write links and get them in, I'd even had a meeting about that Friday's show, and yet nobody had once said, 'Well actually, Terry, this week Mark is presenting the show and you're presenting *Access All Areas*, so write a nice script for that. I was absolutely fuming. Yes I was annoyed that he was presenting the one show in the series so far with decent guests and subject matter, as well as time to prepare for it, but most of all I was angry that nobody had bothered to tell me. And not only hadn't they bothered to tell me, they had tried to cause me as much inconvenience and annoyance as possible. I couldn't understand it, after all, it wasn't a decision they had made that evening, so why on earth hadn't they told me?

According to Paul Ross, the decision was made partly because he didn't want Mark to be seen merely as the presenter of *Access All Areas*, but also because Mark's agent had pushed very hard for Mark to be allowed to do that particular show. From my point of view it seemed that Mark was able to pick and choose shows at his leisure so he could build a credible profile because they were grooming him for bigger and better things. As you can imagine, to me that was intensely irritating but understandable, but what really infuriated me was the fact that nobody at Planet 24 had had the guts to let me know.

I was still feeling resentful the following day, but also slightly relieved that I didn't have the pressure of presenting a live show. I could see that Mark looked nervous. He'd talked the talk, now he had to walk the walk, and on a live show like *The Word* that's never easy. I realized that he was also absolutely knackered as he'd continued to get up at some ungodly hour every morning to present the 'Where are you, Mark' strand for *The Big Breakfast* as well as doing cameo appearances on Jonathan Ross's *Saturday Zoo* and warm-ups for the audience. He was effectively only getting Sunday off in what must have been a hellish schedule, and I could see that that kind of lifestyle wouldn't necessarily make you sweetness and light to be around.

I wandered over to Mark in the bar before the show and gave him some very basic tips on the sticky points in the show. I told him to take it at his own pace, not to finish too abruptly, wrap things up and make a spare ten seconds or so, even if the gallery were screaming in his ear to move on, to try and enjoy it. Most of all I advised him to take control and not dance on the invisible strings of the talkback. I also advised him not to wait for the applause after each item to die down before speaking, as to an audience watching at home that wait seems like a huge pregnant pause, and although the studio audience wouldn't hear what he was saying the TV audience at home would be able to.

All of this wasn't me being saintly as such, it's just that when you grow up a nice Catholic boy from an area like mine, it's hard not to feel empathy towards people struggling to fulfil their dreams. It was the same clawing frustration I'd lived with and seen around me as I was growing up. No matter how much I may have enjoyed seeing Mark fall flat on his face on a live show, I didn't want any of my actions to be complicit with those feelings – then I'd be just like the rest of the overly competitive crabs-in-a-bucket media wannabes. So in a way I did it for myself, not for Mark.

On the show itself, Mark was a bit twitchy and kept blinking at the cameras in a very weird fashion, but he wasn't phased by the live audience because of his experience as a stand-up comic. On a show like *The Word*, though, you're never in control as you never have the audience's undivided attention because there's so much going on around them. His interview with Dannii Minogue descended into a water fight, he tried and failed to bait Mark Wahlberg and just generally tried too hard, peppering his presentation with four-letter words – something I never did in five years of presenting the show.

Finally he interviewed Shabba Ranks, and during the interview an edited piece of the item I'd filmed with Buju Banton was played. It was very unfair to me, as I'd been desperately trying to get Buju to open up about the record 'Boom Bye Bye', and it almost made it look like I was agreeing with Buju's homophobic sentiments. After the clip, Mark asked Shabba what he thought of Buju's record and beliefs with regard to the random shooting of homosexuals. Shabba Ranks then went into the fact that it was in Leviticus 18 in the Bible, which said the sentence for homosexuality was crucifixion – in fact it says death, but there's no mention of crucifixion. Mark then had his moment: 'I've never heard anyone talk so much shit in my life.'

Personally I'd prepared for that week's show and could predict Shabba's reply as I'd heard the Leviticus quotation so many times in Jamaica. I had intended to point out to Shabba, who claimed to have slept with over 400 women, that the sentence for fornication and adultery was also death, according to Leviticus, so he, in fact, was as big a sinner, according to the Bible, as any homosexual. Jesus also suggests in the Bible that if you even look upon a woman with lust you are as guilty as if you'd fornicated with her and that it's better to tear your eye out rather than be lead into sin. This would of course mean that millions of so-called Christians should be walking around with at least an eye patch and many with white sticks, accompanied by endless articles in the press decrying the Christian habit of self-mutilation and the resulting costs to the NHS. I thought my way would have made a better, stronger point.

Channel 4 were overjoyed by Mark's performance, which seemed strange to me. Here was a show I'd basically devised the format and tone of and now it was as if they couldn't wait to show me the door. To make things worse, the press, while praising Mark, once again turned their guns on me.

My reaction was just to carry on, knowing that for the time being Mark and I would rotate presenting *The Word* and *Access All Areas*. On the next show my guests were American musician, poet and actor, the rather intense and muscular Henry Rollins from the band Black Flag and Mrs Bob Geldof, the enigmatically kooky Paula Yates. The bands on the show included an all-female group called Huggy Bear, who were basically four middle-class student types from Brighton. Two of the band members sharing a rented house with

Everett True, the assistant editor of *Melody Maker*, and despite not having released a single, the band had – surprise surprise – already been on the front cover of *Melody Maker*. They were apparently 'riot girls', which was an early take on the Spice Girls' 'girl power'. Jo Whiley had booked them, knowing that they were getting a bit of air play for their forthcoming single and aware that there was a good chance they'd have a lot more press coverage, at least in *Melody Maker*.

The show was going along nicely, with Paula being her usual coquettish, sometimes fiery but always entertaining self. We ran a video item that had been filmed in the USA by Katie Puckrick on identical twin blonde female models who were surgically enhanced and had dubbed themselves the real-life Barbie twins. The piece was fairly undemanding, with them making a few air-headed statements and lots of shots of them in bikinis dwelling over their amply enhanced bosoms. It was no big deal, but as soon as we came out of the item, all hell broke loose in the studio.

The members of Huggy Bear and their entourage were kicking off, throwing things at the couch area while some sickly looking bald bloke and a member of the band shouted, 'Terry, you fucking woman-hater.' This would have been news to my girlfriend, sisters and mother back home, but the fact that I had all these self-publicizing middle-class student wankers pretending to be radical just to sell some of their shitty records gave me the raging hump. I smilingly brushed it to one side and said, 'After the break, more from Paula Yates and Henry Rollins, plus music from X, then thinking we were off air, I turned on the gobby bloke and said, 'Come up here and say that.'

Needless to say he didn't, and the members of Huggy Bear, those radical riot girls, were hustled out of the studio after punching Georgia, our five-foot-two female floor manager, and Ruth, a nice Irish girl who was looking after the audience that day. The trouble is the cameras were still rolling and my 'Come up here and say that' moment was broadcast to the nation, making me look a right yob. In the meantime, Paula was busy ransacking our set decoration of

Barbie dolls, outfits, swings and cars to take home for Peaches, Fifi Trixibelle et al – looting amidst the rioting. Emily Pankhurst eat your heart out.

Normally I love a bit of trouble, but this was too pre-planned and contrived – although Paula nicking the Barbie dolls for her kids was spot on – so it just looked sad, desperate and naff. It wasn't exactly The Sex Pistols on Bill Grundy or the Stone Roses kicking off on BBC2's *The Late Show*. In the annals of rock 'n' roll radical females Huggy Bear will finish somewhere behind the girls from Shampoo and Wendy James from Transvision Vamp. The following week in *Melody Maker*, Huggy Bear were again on the front page. Sales of their single, 'Her Jazz', as performed to a huge 2.78 million audience on *The Word* that Friday night were a staggering 1,600 copies. It was less a testament to the band's musical ability, as to their two front covers on a national magazine, a national TV appearance and reams of tabloid press.

What narked me most was all the made-up quotes *Melody Maker* had attributed to me. All I'd said with regards to Huggy Bear was that it was like a student rag week stunt, that they were crap and passionless live and that the song was rather lifeless, plodding and ropey. However, according to *Melody Maker*, I had said, 'How dare they come on my show and do that, this is my show and they were a disgrace and spoilt *my* show.' Even less likely, was a reference to me saying about Huggy Bear, 'I've just witnessed the most socially significant worldwide music phenomenon since Bob Marley and the Wailers.'

Chrissy Illey, a freelance journalist who wrote for the *Daily Mail*, was a regular at *The Word* every week. She had always been reasonably fair to me – i.e., she didn't consistently say I was shit – and was writing a huge article for the *Mail on Saturday* magazine. It was an article that haunted me for years, and it was a pack of lies, but before I get to that, and with reference to our marvellous press and the diligence of British journalism, here's a great quote from Mariah Carey, 'When I watch TV and see those poor starving kids all over the world, I can't help but cry. I mean, I'd love to be skinny like that, but not with all those flies and death and stuff.'

It was quoted in *VOX* magazine and the *Independent* – it's funny, fantastically insensitive and stupid, and it leaves Ms Carey looking like a self-indulgent, uncaring half-wit. Like I say, great quote, except of course that it's all bollocks and she never said it. It was originally made up in a satirical magazine and then picked up by lazy journalists.

And so we come to my very own urban legend, only what aggrieved me about this was that it didn't originate from someone trying to take the piss, no, the little anecdote that gave me my very own 'Mariah moment' was made up by *The Word*'s own commissioning editor, Stephen Garrett.

It was in a 2,000-word article written by showbusiness journalist Chrissy Illey in the *Daily Mail*'s Saturday magazine and was part of piece about *The Word*, a bête noire at the time to the *Mail*, who had described Channel 4 supremo Michael Grade, as 'the king of porn', and was entitled 'What's Wrong With the Word'.

Part of the article was an interview with my beloved commissioning editor, who had originally commissioned the programme, Stephen Garrett. He had just stepped down as commissioning editor at the end of series two, and our intrepid reporter was after his overview of the show, which at that time was the most successful youth programme Channel 4 had ever made. And I quote:

'So, Stephen, what's wrong with *The Word*?'

'Basically, Terry Christian.'

'What would you replace him with ?'

'I don't know. . . a cactus.'

'What makes you say that?'

'I remember one of the first shows, when Terry had Whitney Houston as a guest live in the studio. She told Terry that she kept a gun in the glove compartment of her car, and Terry's next question was, "So when's your album coming out?"'

'I knew from that moment on I was finished with him.'

I remember reading that article and nearly choking on my cornflakes, something that became a bit of a habit during my time as a presenter of *The Word*.

Moron, cerebrally challenged, a disgrace, unprofessional, professional northerner, famously inarticulate, loudmouthed, chip on shoulder, clueless. I'd received every insult going, and now here was my old boss slagging me off in the national press. I ignored it, even though I knew it wasn't true. What's the point, I had a show to do and a life to live and I'd already been told by Charlie and others that Stephen Garrett couldn't stand me, even though I hadn't completely believed them at the time.

I didn't get a chance to confront him until 1999, four years after *The Word* had finished. I was asked to take part in a panel on youth TV for Mentorn television as part of the Birmingham film and television festival. The panel included Stephen Garrett; Duncan Gray, ex-*Word* editor of series five – more about that later – who had just been made head of light entertainment at Granada; Magenta Devine, ex-*Network 7* and *Rough Guide* presenter, and an assortment of producers from the BBC and Channel 5, as well as an audience of about 400 media students. After I'd said my piece, Stephen Garrett came to the front and again repeated this mythological story about Whitney Houston and my irrelevant question. I listened thinking – this is the polite version – 'You cheeky thing,' but waited until afterwards to pull him up about it. He insisted in front of witnesses that it was true, but I was 100 per cent certain it wasn't.

A few years ago I was putting together a show reel and thought I'd include a quick montage of some of the big-name stars I'd interviewed on *The Word*. I watched a video of the live show with Whitney Houston and on the same show was the taped interview I'd recorded with Cybill Shepherd in Toronto. I asked her what it was like being Elvis Presley's girlfriend back in Memphis when she was starting out, and she laughed and said it was great, then went on to say how he was such a normal down-to-earth and homely kind of guy, yet slightly haunted, and how she couldn't imagine any human being ever being able to live with that level of fame. She also added that ever since John Lennon had been assassinated, she had carried a .38 Smith & Wesson hand gun in the glove compartment of her car. After this taped item had been shown, the programme returned to

Whitney Houston and myself live in the studio, and this was the conversation that followed:

> *Me:* 'So, Whitney, have you got a gun?'
> *Whitney:* [deadly serious] 'No I have not. None of my family or anyone around me has a gun, I wouldn't allow it.' [then smiling] 'I'm protected by the light of God' [cheers from the audience as she laughs] 'Hallelujah.'

To be kind to Mr Garrett, in my career in national TV, he wasn't the only one. I can admit it, but I can't fully explain my propensity to kick the institutions and enterprises I've served in the teeth, not to mention the individuals who run them. This may have been interpreted as deliberate treachery, but if that's the case, I never did it consciously.

The false Whitney Houston story became legendary in television circles, and even more confusing is the fact that Rory Bremner included Stephen Garrett's false anecdote in his live act for over three years. Yes Rory Bremner, another self-important TV personality who should be in receipt of a solicitor's letter for slander.

Just as some added food for thought, imagine if Chrissy Illey had been interviewing me and I'd said something similarly defamatory about Stephen Garrett, I'd bet every penny I've ever earned that she would have checked it out first before putting it in her article. Obviously with my rather ordinary background and accent, I might have been lying, where Stephen Garrett the posh-sounding commissioning editor had to be taken at his word. Several years later I brought this up with Chrissy Illey. She apologised.

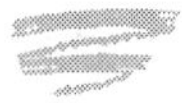

The Word was beginning to struggle for guests. *The Big Breakfast* had siphoned off a lot of our money and we didn't have the cash to pay for big-name guests unless we doubled up with *The Big Breakfast*. The worst time was one Friday when up til five o'clock that evening we had no guests. At around six o'clock they drafted in Wendy James of Transvision Vamp, who had just released a solo album, much of which had been written by Elvis Costello after she'd written him a pleading letter. There was still no sign of another guest until literally fifteen minutes before our 11.05 p.m. transmission, when I was informed we had the Marquis of Blandford as a guest on the show.

'What are you going to ask him, Terry?' Charlie asked, looking keen.

'I'll ask him about scoring class A drugs in Ladbroke Grove where he was caught the other night.'

'No that's sub-judice we can't discuss that.'

'OK, I'll ask him what a marquee is exactly.'

'It's not pronounced marquee, it's marquis. Listen, haven't got time. . . erm, ask him about music. Apparently he likes Pink Floyd.'

Fuck me! We were a live show and we had a drug-addict aristocrat coming on who couldn't talk about his drug problem – that and his posh title was all there was to him really.

On the couch I posed the question, 'In royalty you've got like your emperor, your king, your queen . . . your, er, Jack – this was meant as a joke – where does a marquis come in the pecking order.'

'Underneath a duke.'

'Anyway, I've heard you like Pink Floyd, is that before or after Syd Barrett.'

To say I was drowning would be the understatement of the decade.

To get me out of the studio and give Katie a go at *Access All Areas*, they sent me to LA to present a live outside broadcast from a gay club in Los Angeles off Sunset Strip, where they held a 'Big Hair' pageant. It was just a load of gay drag artists in big wigs so it was about as interesting visually as it is to read about here. It was my idea of a sneak preview of hell, and just to make things worse, they asked me to compere part of the pageant for them. I walked on stage in front of 400 screaming trannies and queens and thought, what do I say? I don't even understand the point of all this. I decided to start with a joke and tried a Julian Clary line.

I walked on stage to shrieking and applause and said, 'Thank you very much, I do like a warm hand on my entrance.' There wasn't a smile, not even a glimmer of one, more a lynch-mob murmer throughout the crowd. It must be the way Julian tells it.

The Big Hair pageant wasn't the main reason I was in LA. The kind people at Motown UK had flown us over first class to interview Eddie Murphy about his solo album. I was excited about meeting Eddie as I'd been a fan ever since getting hold of his first album of stand-up material back in the early eighties before he appeared with Nick Nolte in the film *48 Hours*. Rather than a new Richard Prior, I saw Eddie as more of a streetwise black Robin Williams, liable to go off at tangents and be very raw and funny. However, his album gave me a very different view. It was written, produced, mixed and sung by Eddie Murphy, with help from Stevie Wonder, Paul McCartney, Shabba Ranks and a host of other big names, and it was absolute aural purgatory. Not only was it badly mixed and produced, his voice was a thin, tuneless, reedy falsetto.

In the hotel bar the night before the interview I was having a frank discussion with the black lad from London who was Motown's A&R man looking after Eddie in Britain. I asked him if he honestly thought the album would sell more than 500 copies and who on earth would play something as piss poor and badly produced on radio.

'Well, it's Eddie Murphy and he's one of the biggest if not *the* biggest movie star in the world, so I would imagine it will sell at least 150,000 copies worldwide.'

I raised a quizzical eyebrow and retorted that Prince sells albums by the bucket load and is one of the biggest music stars in the world, but I doubted many people would fork out for an album of stand-up comedy by him.

We had a full hour to film our interview with Eddie Murphy in a suite at the Mondrain hotel where, three years earlier, I'd spent a happy afternoon on the roof with Johnny Marr and Bernard Sumner.

We arrived at the Mondrian with a list of Mr Murphy's demands, which were as follows:

1. Every flat surface in the rooms to be covered with a particular scented uncut potpourri
2. Dozens of incense sticks of a particular kind were to be lit in the rooms
3. Dozens of a particular brand of scented candle must be lit in the room
4. All curtains in the room had to be drawn and certain lighting specifications met, with Eddie's chair facing away from the doorway with the window to his front right.

The shoot director, a ginger-haired public school kid who was cool as a cucumber, directed the setting up of the potpourri, candles and incense, sorted out the room positions and lighting, then we waited for the arrival of Eddie Murphy superstar.

Eddie arrived with his battalion of minders and hangers-on forty-five minutes late. As he walked into the room, the director lit a Marlboro cigarette and was immediately surrounded by body-armoured Fifty Cent lookalikes in puffa jackets and baseball caps while the offending cigarette was disposed of and Eddie was asked if it was OK to proceed.

I walked over to Eddie, proffered my hand and said, 'Hi, Eddie, nice to meet you, I'm Terry from Channel 4 and I'll be conducting the interview.'

Eddie ignored me completely and turned his back on me, so I retreated in a rather embarrassed semi crouch and waited for his royal highness to be seated.

Eventually we were positioned and the interview commenced.

The interview itself was fine, with Eddie Murphy in full flow, quite funny, very engaging and performing for both myself and the cameras, just as Robin Williams had done all those years earlier. There was just one difference, Robin Williams was personable and sensitive, while Eddie Murphy with his shit vanity album, huge entourage and uncut fuckin' potpourri, was without a doubt a man with his head all the way up his own arse. After the interview I thanked him and again proffered my hand, but he immediately turned away from me. Weird guy and not at all the way he'd been throughout the interview, but I realized that with all his unreasonable demands beforehand, he'd ensured the interview was totally in his control.

I still couldn't work out the best way to interview actors. It seems to me that they're the most difficult people of all to interview as the whole point of an interview is to find out what the person in front of you is like. And the problem with actors is that they're invariably different people according to which role they're involved with at the time. They seem to find it uncomfortable being themselves, since that's the person they're effectively erasing when they take on a role.

My own bad press didn't let up once during series three, and with just three shows left to run, Mark Lamarr decided to jump on the anti-Terry bandwagon, sticking the boot in in the press, delivering the cultural cosh.

I'd been interviewed by Manchester University magazine about *The Word*, and the student I talked to asked me how Mark and I got on and did we ever have a drink together after the show. I rather flippantly replied that I rarely saw him after the show because he was always too busy trying to get off with the girls out of the bands we'd had on. This was actually said off the record as a casual piss-take, based on what I'd been told, namely that when Huggy Bear were thrown out of the studio for disrupting the show, Mark had moaned about it at length because he'd thought he was well in there with one of the girls. Now this might not have been a piece of gospel truth, but Mark was a bit groupyish around musicians, so I thought it would be a nice little story to expose how uncool and affected he was and give him a taste, albeit on a small local level, of what he'd been giving me nationally.

The student journalist put this story in the student paper and Mark's girlfriend's brother's mate happened to be at Manchester University, and as neither of her siblings particularly liked Mark, they showed it to her. The fact that she finished with him over something so minor is something I would have felt really bad about had I known, but Mark had been spoiling for a fight for weeks, so this was the just the chance he'd been waiting for to bring simmering hostilities out into the open.

It was Mark's turn to present *The Word* from the studio couch, and I had the rather cushier option of being behind the scenes on *Access All Areas*. The guests on the night were Blair Underwood from the American TV series *LA Law* and Ruby Wax. I chilled out in the bar with nothing to do from 10.30 p.m. until almost midnight when the show had finished and I could grab a few minutes with Ruby Wax. I was chatting with our props man Dean, about to take my first sip of a pint of Guinness, when Mark came over looking extremely flustered and sweaty. It was only fifteen minutes or so before he was due to go live on air, so I was surprised to see him lurching towards me.

'I'm fucking sick of you slagging me off. Come on, outside now.'

I could see he wasn't kidding, but I thought it was a bit comic given the circumstances: stepping off for a dust-up just before a hundred grand's worth of live telly was about to get under way.

'Let's talk about it later, Mark,' I said.

We'd had our big threatening bust-up months earlier and had more or less agreed to hate each other from a distance, so after weeks of studiously ignoring each other, this seemed to come out of the blue.

Once he realized I wasn't going to start a major punch-up there and then, he came up close and grabbed my right shoulder. Inside, I could feel a familiar coldness and shakiness welling up. I pushed his hand away thinking, he needs counselling, and he agitatedly pretended he was about to launch into me shouting, 'Don't fucking touch me.'

I later found out that this verbal assault in front of about seventy people was because I'd caused his girlfriend to split up with him. It was all highly embarrassing, more for him than me. As I wasn't exactly Channel 4's blue-eyed boy, chinning him just before the show would undoubtedly have cost me my job and, by my reckoning, about £200,000 in the next year alone, so I didn't find it hard to restrain myself, even though I was boiling inside.

As I waited for Ruby Wax at the back of the studio as the show finished, Mark wandered past, turned to me and made this strange animal growl in my direction. By then I'd had enough, so I stepped forward, gave him a two-handed push, went to step forward again and the crane carrying the overhead camera rolled straight over my right foot. There I was, trying to look controlled and angry, but desperately trying to fight back the urge to scream with pain due to my newly crushed foot.

Afterwards, as I nursed my badly bruised bare foot in my dressing room, Charlie Parson popped his head round the door.

'Any repeat of that behaviour Terry and I'll sack you,' he threatened.

Fuck me! What had I done? 'Sack me, then,' I replied.

When I explained that Mark was the one who'd actually flipped his lid and tried to provoke a fight, Charlie said, 'Well you shouldn't keep winding him up.'

Winding Mark up wasn't the most difficult thing to do:

'Oh, Mark, I was on *That's Showbusiness* with Mike Smith this weekend on BBC1, so I put a good word in for you with the producers if you fancy doing it.'

Mark was from Swindon but spoke with a Cockney accent, even though he'd only lived in London for five years. His conduct so annoyed several of my friends back in Manchester that they were determined to go down to London and give Mark a good kicking.

Mark was in the habit of going to every launch party and record-company function in London. Several years later he went to one for the Manchester band The Dust Junkies, whose manager Johnny Jay was one of my best friends. Johnny was rather annoyed at Mark turning up uninvited, and as Mark walked past, Johnny muttered something insulting under his breath. Mark immediately started acting aggressive towards Johnny who, in reply, leaned towards Mark and told him if he didn't vacate the premises that very second he would kill him. Mark immediately did exactly as he was requested.

All kinds of made-up crap kept appearing in various publications with regards to Mark and myself. There was loads of shit about how we both wanted to be number one on the show and that we hated each other on sight, all supposedly fed to the press by a *Word* insider. I only ever saw Mark on the Friday of the show, and from Saturday to Thursday I lived in Manchester, so I don't know why he just didn't ignore me.

One of our guests was Zsa Zsa Gabor, the infamous Hollywood siren who had married a succession of rich and powerful men, including the hotel owner Conrad Hilton. She was a game old girl for seventy-four, quite bossy, funny and very outspoken. I interviewed her and she suggested fixing me up with her unmarried daughter as she thought, with my facial bone structure, we'd have attractive children. She was a great *Word* guest and exuded that fading Hollywood glamour.

When Mark spoke to her, though, he accused her of being a slag and shagging all and sundry, using exactly those crude phrases to her face. It made me feel really uncomfortable, as the bottom line was that she was seventy-four and you shouldn't even use that type of language in front of a woman that age, let alone to her. Imagine my fury when I was later shown an article from the *Birmingham Evening Post* accusing me of using crude and unacceptable language on TV to a seventy-four-year-old woman. The female journalist concerned had got me mixed up with Mark. I called the journalist immediately and went ballistic. She apologized and said she'd put it right next time around, but I felt the damage had been done and no matter what happened we would always be tarred with the same brush just because we were on the same show.

In contrast, the week I had Jonathan Ross on the show, Mark told the *Access All Areas* crew what great mates he and Jonathan were. I was chuffed to meet Jonathan, who was far more cuddly than his brother Paul, but still seemed to be interested in everything. Jonathan was quite relaxed on the show and took the gentle ribbing I gave him in good humour, even when I made him introduce the band, who were making their live debut on British TV, Jamiriquoi. Given his slight speech impediment, it was quite amusing.

As we were coming off, we were told that there were loads of armed police around the studios as some lad had rung in to say that his mate had got a gun and was coming down to shoot Terry Christian. I didn't take it seriously, but Jonathan turned round and said, 'It's bound to happen here one day, it has in the States.' I told him that was one scoop he was welcome to, but his words came back to haunt me years later when Jill Dando was tragically murdered on her front doorstep.

Things came to a head between Mark and myself on the final show of series three, when we had Margi Clarke on as a guest again, along with American/Jamaican reggae star Shaggy and Shaun Ryder. It had just been announced that the Happy Mondays had split up after their disastrous fourth album *Sunshine and Love*. The Mondays had spent nearly all of Factory Records' money recording the album in Eddie Grant's studio in Barbados, where they'd been sent because the island's supposedly free of heroin and Shaun had developed a bad smack habit. It seemed a good idea to send him and his heroin substitute over there in the hope that he'd be able to focus on writing the album.

The story is that at the airport on the way over, Shaun's bag containing a month's supply of Methodrine fell and smashed. Once in Barbados, the hunt for drugs started, and the only thing available on the Island was crack cocaine. Shaun and the other band members started using it, ran out of money to pay and subsequently started selling off the studio furniture to the local dealers, much to the horror of Chris Frantz and Tina Weymouth of Talking Heads fame, who were out there to produce the album. Shaun was desperate for cash now that he'd returned, and with no band but plans for another, I knew he would be happy to come on as a guest for the right fee, so I suggested it to Paul Ross.

Shaun is great value for money and always gets any radio or TV show he appears on talked about, so if we offered him a couple of grand cash in an envelope, he would do it. Obviously Mark was keen to interview Shaun as Shaun had an aura of cool street cred, whatever that is. When Shaun heard Mark was going to interview him, his response to the producer was, 'If that twat says anything I don't like, I'm gonna smack him one.' Shaun arrived accompanied by his new girlfriend, the very pretty Oriole Leitch, daughter of sixties pop star Donovan. As soon as he got his money, he must have had a bag man ready with his fix. Both Craig and myself went for a pee before the show and found Oriole standing outside a locked cubicle where a cameraman was having a dump, while Shaun lay on the floor in front of the cubicle, trying to stick his head through the gap between the floor and the door while shouting, 'Oi, lively in there.'

The cameraman was obviously taking his time, and as Craig and myself relieved ourselves at the urinal, Shaun joined us for a synchronized piss. 'Eh, Shaun, that lot are nothing without you,' Craig said in humorous but honest fashion. Shaun gazed at him, gave him a sagacious nod and grimace, zipped up his fly and returned to the floor in front of the cubicle.

'Oi, fuckin' lively in there.'

Half of Manchester had come down for the show. Besides Craig Cash, there was my younger Brother Kevin and some of his mates, my girlfriend and her best mate from Preston. As northerners have a tendency to congregate like wildebeest, Margi Clarke chose to sit and have a drink with us in the bar before the show. Within ten minutes of Margi leaving, a researcher came in and told me Margi wanted to go through a couple of things with me in her dressing room. When I got there, Margi rather unconvincingly came on to me and I immediately smelled a rat, as I'd just been joking with her in the bar ten minutes earlier.

'Show us your plums, Terry.'

I took two kiwi fruit out of the fruit bowl and held them over my groin. 'Wow, Terry, they're massive.'

Because the camera was behind me, on telly it looked like I'd unzipped my knackers for my scouse chum. I could sense it was a secret filming job, but just thought, fuck it! Let the kids play. By the time the show went out, Margi, who was mortified by the whole experience of sitting with my loved ones, had informed my girlfriend and everyone else about the secret filming, much to the producer's annoyance, even to the extent that he threatened not to pay her fee.

Margi had also invited Mark into her dressing room and done the same cod-seduction trick on him. Mark responded by hurrying out of Margi's dressing room and telling every producer and researcher how 'that Scouse tart' had just offered him casual sex in her dressing room, even, according to Duncan Gray, saying that he might nip back later and slip her one. However, when Mark found out that it had all been secretly filmed he went psychotic, threatening death and destruction all round. He even came crashing into my dressing room, demanding to know if I knew about the secret filming and cursing Charlie Parsons and Waheed to high heaven. I just thought, join the club and welcome to *The Word*.

We did the whole show with Mark skulking around the studio. Then came his moment with Shaun Ryder. Mark's classic opening question came without a hint of irony and contained the line, 'Well, Shaun, you're off the heroin now.' Honestly, I nearly wet myself with laughter. Shaun's eyes were in orbit, the morphine nod in evidence and totally incoherent. At the end of the show the last band on were Eurobop, with two blokes dressed as Zippy and Bungle doing a techno/house version of the *Rainbow* kiddies TV programme theme. Without any prompting, Shaun rushed the stage and, to everyone's delight, started playing the bongos while squeezed between Zippy and Bungle. It was sheer, unadulterated drug-fuelled madness of the kind that could only happen on *The Word*.

Afterwards, at the after-show party, Mark was sweating and raving like a lunatic with his hands around Charlie's throat, threatening him with hospitalization over the secret filming with Margi Clarke. Dani Behr came over to where I was chatting with our editor Paul Ross and said, 'Paul, what's up with Mark?'

'Oh, he's got a major problem with Charlie.'

'Just like everyone else on this fucking circus of a show,' I interjected.

Charlie told me later that Mark tried to strangle both Waheed and himself.

'Well, Charlie,' I replied, 'you shouldn't keep winding him up.'

The relief I felt when the series ended was immense. I had a number of meetings with other TV channels, set up by my agent Michael Cohen, and I was determined to move on. My contract with *The Word* was finished, and as far as I was concerned I'd lasted three years longer on national telly than I'd expected to. Mark was Channel 4's choice. What irritated me most was that *The Word* had been a show I'd influenced in every way, with a format based on my radio shows, a tone that shifted guests out of their comfort zones and an eclectic range of music. Even the mad guests we had on, like Shaun Ryder, and the show's name were down to me, yet no one at Channel 4 had once said, 'Well done', despite how successful we had been. It would have been easier to turn my back on it all if it hadn't been for all the aggravation between Mark and myself. As it was, walking away felt like surrendering, so when Planet 24 suddenly offered me another two-year contract, I decided to play a hunch.

As presenters on *The Word*, we were rarely if ever informed about the viewing figures for each show. However, lingering around the office, I got talking to Paul Ross's personal assistant, a really nice Dutch girl. I asked her if I could see a list of the show's viewing figures and she handed them over to me, instructing me not to tell anybody.

I pored over them, examining the week-by-week breakdowns and bingo! There it was in black and white. Not only had the overall figures for the show gone up each year, but examining the weekly figures, it seemed that when Mark fronted the show, the viewing figures were between 500,000 and 700,000 less than when I fronted the show. I faxed the figures through to my agent Michael Cohen and instructed him to chase up a list of demands, including a writing credit, associate producer credit, a lot more money, more notice before flying off to film and an agreement that I would no longer have to conduct any more interviews with the press.

'Terry, you're going to be rich,' he promised.

Not only did Michael almost double my money, giving me a contract worth over £140,000, rising to £160,000 for a possible series five, he also got them to agree to work on other TV projects at Channel 4. I wasn't quite as pleased as I should have been, though, because Planet 24 still refused to give me any formal recognition for my part in creating the structure of the show.

The stress I'd felt over the year had turned me into a physical and mental wreck, to the extent that the very thought of working on a television show made me feel sick to my stomach. The self-consciousness, sneering and sniping, the made-up press stories and the way I was becoming so self-obsessed. Although socially I was always very chatty, friendly and gregarious, I began to notice that I was much more guarded on nights out with friends. Old schoolfriends got really fed up of random strangers imposing themselves upon us, and any friends of mine who were six foot or over, especially if they were black, got really pissed off with people asking them if they were my minders.

I got so used to being recognized and people coming over to speak to me, that I often used to stand in the same spot all night and expect anyone who I knew to come over and speak to me. Understandably, this made a lot of my old acquaintances think I was being stuck up and stand-offish, which in a way I was, and in return I thought they were being a bit off with me.

Strangers used to think I was acting like I was some big telly star, expecting everyone to queue up to met and greet me. I remember one skin-headed Scottish bloke coming up and saying, 'Terry, why are you a cunt on that shit show *The Word*?'

'Listen, I don't know you, so why don't you just fuck off.'

'Hey, there's no need to be so offensive.'

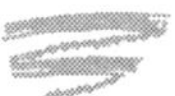

I wanted to go on holiday somewhere posh, but I didn't know where to go. I was nouveau riche in every way and a bit clueless. I remembered that Dani Behr had been on holiday to the Dominican Republic over Christmas, and as Dani was posh as far as I was concerned, I decided to take my girlfriend there. We stayed in a four-star all-inclusive hotel complex and suffered from constant diarrhoea for two weeks. At least I relaxed, though, surrounded by third-world poverty and casinos where we'd play black jack until the early hours while washing down diarrhoea tablets with the free cocktails.

As soon as I returned to Manchester I noticed that my hair was falling out at the back of my head on the left hand side. It wasn't long before I had a perfect round bald patch the size of a fifty-pence piece. It looked weird and was really noticeable, so I went to the doctor's. He said it was alopecia and was caused either by stress or the malaria tablets I'd taken on holiday; he told me to take it easy and it would grow back eventually.

'When?' I asked him.

'It could be a few months or even a few years, or it could get worse.'

To say I was pissed off would have been the understatement of the century. I was self-conscious enough with all this fame lark, and though I'm not excessively vain or narcissistic – except, according to my girlfriend, when we argued – it really got me down. Like my anal fissure, my alopecia became another dark secret I hid from everyone. A friend of mine from primary school called Anthony was a top hairstylist and he devised a way of cutting my hair that left it a bit long all over, especially at the back to cover up my bald spot. I looked a right goon without my usual semi-mod short cut.

Next I noticed that I was beginning to go white in patches all over my head, so I decided to dye my hair. I picked one of those wash-in wash-out colours and ended up a blondey ginger colour. I felt like becoming a hermit. Now I had a crap haircut, alopecia and, as one of my mates put it, I looked like the blond Elvis from *Kissing Cousins*. I decided to wear a baseball cap for a while before dying my hair again to cover the gingery blond colour, especially as Anthony the hairdresser had said using dyes might exacerbate my alopecia.

Then I get a phone call from my agent. I've been offered a two-week stint filling in as the presenter of *The Big Breakfast* while Chris Evans is on holiday. Just the thought of doing it exhausts me. Not only that, before the two-week stint they want me to do a pilot with Gaby Roslin in the *Big Breakfast* house to check that I can cope with it.

My agent talks me into it, but I don't feel like it at all. I'm so self-conscious about my hair and I feel totally unhealthy. I'm chain smoking, drinking too much and feeling really depressed. I can hardly drag myself out of bed at noon, never mind at 3.30a.m. in the morning to present *The Big Breakfast*. In the end, though, I relent and agree to do the pilot with Gaby.

On *The Big Breakfast* audition I insist on keeping my crap baseball cap on all the way through. Everyone keeps telling me to take it off, and though I can see where they're coming from, I feel so self-conscious and uncomfortable that I'm almost in tears. Gaby is absolutely lovely to me, really encouraging and friendly. I'm not used to anyone treating me like that in TV, and that almost has me in tears, too. Throughout the pilot I feel like a six-year-old who's been taken to the big boy's playground in the park by his big sister.

A few days later I'm informed via my agent that Channel 4 are keen to let me do the *The Big Breakfast*. However, as Chris Evans is only paid £400 per show, the most they can offer me is £3,000 a week or £600 a show. £600 for getting up at 3.30 a.m. and presenting a three-hour show on live TV doesn't strike me as worthwhile, especially as I've been offered a personal appearance in Belfast for a couple of hours that will net me £3,000, plus hotel and flights.

'Listen I'll do it, but can I have two days off to go to Belfast?'

Channel 4 and Planet 24's reply is a resounding no.

'Well, what if I do just one week instead of two?'

The answer is no again.

I knew I should have presented *The Big Breakfast*, it was a great opportunity, but I felt shot to pieces and drained, and my confidence was really low because of my alopecia. All I could think about was the stress, attention and the mither of working on yet more television, so I turned it down.

Looking back, although I should have done it to prove I could blossom outside the confines of *The Word*, I have no regrets. I think you only have regrets when you have choices, and at the time, given the fragile state of my physical and mental health, I had no choice but to say no. After all, series four was around the corner, and I wasn't looking forward to it one bit.

This may sound strange for those of you who harbour ambitions, secret or otherwise, to present on television, be famous for fifteen minutes or be a full-blown celebrity, but for me it was all too much. Three years earlier I'd been working on radio, going to see bands, writing my column in the *Manchester Evening News* and laughing with my friends. My ambitions were modest and attainable. To be well known and famous wasn't me, I needed to be sociable, to mix freely and on equal terms with people, not have to face a load of preconceptions and spend my whole time trying to justify myself.

Nobody told me that *The Word* would be huge and that even more people would read about the show than watch it, and that this would affect how they acted towards me. I could accept the insults and mistruths from tabloid journalists – they were just doing their jobs after all, even if they were doing it in an unimaginative way – but it was starting to seriously get me down. I never went to launch parties and press parties, I didn't thrust myself into the limelight, or do any of the other things hacks use as an excuse to denigrate so-called celebrities. That hackneyed line, 'They use the press to get famous, and don't like it when we slag them off,' just wasn't true in my case. I'd never put myself above anyone or tried to be a role model or aspirational figure. I didn't brag about the money I was paid or the lifestyle I led; I didn't claim to be a special or uniquely talented individual and was very anti the whole idea, so much so that journalists like Rick Sky at the *Mirror* and my new commissioning editor Bill Hilary were astonished by how disinterested I was in the idea of being a star. But despite all this, I was hounded and castigated in a most pernicious fashion by the press and slandered constantly by other TV presenters, as if I was some kind of criminal instead of one of four presenters on a successful and fun show. And what did a fair few of these critics of mine invariably have in common? Well, let's just say they'd never in their lives relied on the state for their education, housing or welfare.

'For God's sake stop being so dim and downmarket, get more good bands and do some cookery or something'

As series four began I decided to care a bit less about the show. I was, after all, just one of several presenters by then. My job as a presenter rather than *the* presenter paid well, and it wasn't rocket science. I'd started to get quite a bit of advertising voice-over work, too, which paid a pretty penny or two on top. What amused me was that all the products that seemed to want to be advertised with a northern accent were food or drink: crisps, chocolates, burgers, yoghurts, cakes, pickles, ice-cream bars and lollies, bitter and lager. Maybe that's what everyone down south thought northerners did? Talked funny, ate junk food and drank alcohol. Maybe I was promoting an unhealthy lifestyle? Eat crap and be like Terry Christian. The voice of reason – 'Eat food: it's good for you', 'Drink beer: it often makes you feel better'.

I remember going along to read several scripts for a huge burger company, and as I sat in the little booth with my script in front of me, in came a woman from the agency to sit in on the session. After a couple of read-throughs this woman, who was German, said, 'Vot iss zis accent?', and when informed that it was a northern accent, old Brunhilda threw a teutonic tantrum and told me straight that I wasn't wanted on this particular advert. I walked off muttering to myself that the Germans had basically ruined the whole twentieth century for the human race, and not just because of the wars and genocide either. Fuck me, the East Germans used to cheat like mad in the Olympics.

Bloody hell, three whole years in the public eye and I'm still being bugged about my accent. It was enough to give someone a complex.

The months in between series dragged endlessly and I just wasted them. There were no fantastic radio work offers and few TV shows clamouring for me, and if they did they were turned down flat in writing by Planet 24. I spent long days just hanging around the house in Manchester, not in the mood to go out, toying with the idea of writing something, but feeling bored and unmotivated.

Katie Puckrick hadn't had her contract renewed and I couldn't work out why. Was it the politics of Planet 24? It was strange with Katie. It was only when she got the heave ho that I realised how much I liked her. It felt to me as if none of us presenters were allowed to get on, and yet the show would have been so much better if we'd been allowed and encouraged to bond more.

Why had Katie not had her contract renewed? She wasn't unpopular with the audience, she was a colourful character and quite ambitious but not ruthlessly so. Was it that Paul Ross saw her as Sebastian's girl? Or did our new commissioning editor, Bill Hilary, think she wasn't up to being on the couch in the studio? Katie had escaped much of the criticism aimed at the rest of *The Word*'s presenters and was often praised, yet they had unceremoniously elbowed her in favour of a new presenter and the chance to continue with Dani Behr. If anything, Katie was the *only* popular *Word* presenter, as she had the least polarizing personality.

By the time filming in the USA commenced for series four, I was eager to get back on board. After all, I was now a grizzled veteran of Los Angeles and the Hollywood scene. There was a holiday atmosphere on that shoot, thanks to the fact that we were put up at the Loews hotel on Santa Monica beach and most of the stuff we were filming was fairly straight forward. Dani came over to interview the sixteen-year-old up-and-coming actor Leonardo DiCaprio, while I had Tia Carrere, the babe from *Wayne's World*, and the brooding, moody bad boy of Hollywood, Mickey Rourke.

Santa Monica was like a little England, with loads of rave clubs and the like, all run by assorted scallies from London, Manchester and Liverpool. The stories we heard about the assorted illegal Brits in LA were both scary and funny. We met guys who'd done the plumbing in Sylvester Stallone's house, mowed David Coverdale's lawn in Palm Springs and sold an old motorbike to Bruce Willis. There were stories of British gangsters in LA and their dealings and minor turf wars with local Angelino gangs; there were even stories of the odd lad who'd come out and just disappeared completely.

We spent an afternoon with Eddie Murphy's brother Charlie, who was entering the world of acting in one of those straight-to-video gangsta-rap type comedies, as part of a whole piece we did about siblings of the stars.

To interview Tia Carrere in a very posh and exclusive Beverly Hills Restaurant, I got dressed up in a white granddad shirt and black Armani lightweight three-piece Beatles-style suit. I thought I looked very elegant in a Jeremy Irons/Rupert Everett sort of way. While we were waiting for Tia to arrive, I strolled outside to smoke a cigarette, looking cool and detached, yet sharply dressed. A very flash-looking black convertible pulled up and the man driving it beckoned me over.

'Is this a new restaurant?' he asked.

'Yes, it is actually.'

'Could I have a menu to go.'

Fuck me! I was in my best trendy get-up to look good for Tia Carrere and he thought I was a waiter or valet parking attendant.

The interview I was most excited about doing was with Mickey Rourke. He'd just finished filming a stylistically violent western set just after the American civil war for HBO. The film wasn't very good and a bit clichéd as westerns go, but Mickey Rourke was an interviewer's dream. We drove to his office above a boxing gym, where his various acting awards adorned the walls alongside various framed press cuttings and certificates. He had a huge Wurlitzer jukebox in the corner with some fantastic records on it, including a lot of rare early Sixties soul and R&B, like Chuck Jackson, Little

Milton, Jackie Lee and all sorts. A man of good taste, I thought.

He came in dressed in his boxing gear but with a woollen Celtic scarf draped around his neck, which he fiddled with throughout the interview. This was Mickey Rourke, once hailed as the new Marlon Brando, the brat packer most likely to be brooding, mean and moody, outspoken, and a true Hollywood rebel. He'd said that actors were a bunch of wimps and self-obsessed moaners and that Hollywood made too many shit, meaningless films. He'd supposedly supported the IRA and tried to make a living as a professional boxer, and his drunken brawls and arrests had made the headlines all around the world. However, *The Word*'s angle on Mickey in the pre-shoot script was that he'd upset the Hollywood establishment so much he couldn't make a living as an actor, so he'd tried to make it as a boxer and failed at that, too. Now he was trying to make a living as a poet, as he'd apparently written several poems for a charity book.

Firstly, let me say what a fantastically refreshing bloke he was to spend an hour or more with. During the interview we talked about our common Irish ancestry, with Rourke opening up about the accusations in the British press of him being a terrorist sympathizer:'I did this movie called *Francesco* and gave a small amount of money to education and community programmes sponsored by Sinn Fein. As far as I knew they were just an active political party in Northern Ireland and the money I donated was for charitable causes, not to pay for some crazy shootouts with the British army or terrorist bombings.' All the time Mickey looked me up and down, trying to suss me out and obviously wondering if I was there to stitch him up.

Eventually, we got onto the subject of his film career. I liked all his early films, like *Rumble Fish* and *The Pope of Greenwich Village*, and I've always been a fan of Michael Cimino, even his massive flops like *Heaven's Gate* which Mickey had a part in, as well as *Year of the Dragon*, which was a Seventies-style cop thriller. I asked Mickey how he'd become a big-name star and he brushed the question aside.

'It's the formulaic movies that studios make money on, and when that happens, well, the actors in them are automatically "movie stars".' I mean, nothing I did ever really made money, and films like *Rumble Fish* were probably only seen by about four people in the USA.

'Actors annoy me. They live in a bubble, suddenly or accidentally end up in a big movie and then whine and complain about their lack of privacy, while at the same time employing an army of PR flunkies to get them on the covers of magazines and keep them on that Jay Leno/Conan O'Brien/Letterman talk show circuit. I can't stand actors. When I did the movie *Angel Heart* with De Niro, he was the biggest cry baby I'd ever worked with in my life and I've felt more "heat" with other actors I've worked with, who aren't any where near as well known as De Niro.'

I asked Mickey if that's why he got into boxing.

'Sports have always appealed to me. I've boxed since I was a kid, and I just thought it's now or never. I mean, I had eleven fights, drew one and won the rest. I got beat up, though: a broken nose, broken and compressed cheekbone. It was tough. The trouble is I took five years out doing that, and when I came back to acting, none of the studios wanted to know. I never had a problem with producers or directors wanting to work with me, it was always the studios, the money men. Now I'm trying to make my own movies and start again from the bottom up, but it's hard when you think your talent is bigger than the things you say and do outside of work.'

On his wall is a large framed poem of his. It's a stupid question all sorted out in the pre-shoot script back in London.

'So Mickey, what's this poem? Where's that come from?'

'Oh, a friend of mine was running a fund-raising charity and asked a lot of well-known people to contribute poems. I was filming this piece of shit at the time called *Harley Davidson and the Marlboro Man* with Don Johnson, and Don Johnson was trying to co-direct it, so I had a lot of time hanging around on set and wrote a few poems and hooked the guy up with some other people for this charity. So by way of a thank you, he framed this poem for me.

'So are you trying to make a living as a poet now?'

Mickey smiles a resigned smile and replies good-humouredly.

'Nooo… fuck that.'

I ask him about stories that say he blew forty million dollars and query where did the money went?

'Hard to say, travelling, drugs, drinking and humping.'

I ask him about his travels and he mentions that he was living in London for quite a while.

'What were you doing there?'

'Drinking and humping.'

He then talks of his time living in Dublin. What were you up to in Dublin?

'Drinking and humping.'

He's still fiddling about with the Celtic scarf around his neck, so I ask him about 'soccer' and whether he's a fan. He tells me that the manager of his film company is from Glasgow and is a big Celtic fan, and that he bought him the scarf. I ask him if he's ever been to a football match.

'Yes, I was living in London and stupidly I answered an advert for an old Volkswagen Beetle. I thought I'd buy it to drive around for the couple of months I was over there. The address was this garage under a railway arch in north London, and when I got there the car was nothing but a rusting heap, so I was like, no way am I buying this. The guys in the garage got kind of mad and I told them to stick it. Then they picked up crow bars and pick axes and started after me. I ran and they chased me, and the next thing I came across thousands of people heading for this football stadium, which seemed like the safest place to go and hide, so I mingled with the crowd and went inside. It was cool, that team saved my life.

'Which team's ground was it?'

'Tottenham Hotspur.'

At the end of the shoot I was indulging in some chit-chat with Mickey about his jukebox and what a great selection of records he had on it – it was an Aladdin's cave for collectors. There was some early Drifters, Del Shannon, Kathy Kirby, Doris Troy, a bit of Jan & Dean and a comprehensive section of soul and Vegas-type Ratpack stuff. I mentioned the Chuck Jackson single in particular, and he immediately called somebody from the office upstairs who came down with some keys and open up the jukebox, then he handed me the precious vinyl. I felt totally embarrassed until I thought it was the kind of thing I'd do myself. The contrast between Mickey and the level at which he engaged with you as a human being was in stark contrast to a lot of the younger Hollywood stars, and I have to say that he was probably the most interesting and genuine person in all the hundreds of actors – big, small, young, old or up-and-coming – that I've ever met. His talent, passion, conviction and sensitivity shone through.

One of the most unusual pieces we did on that trip involved a flight up to Portland, Oregon to interview MCA records' white rap sensation 'Chilli T'. What was sensational was that twenty-year-old Chilli T's dad was Phillip Knight, the guy who effectively owned Nike. His son had managed to get a recording deal, yet hip hop, forever urban and street, wasn't quite what you'd expect to come from timber country like Portland. We were invited out to Chilli T's house, which was Phillip Knight's house, as he still lived at home with his mum and dad, and who could blame him. It wasn't quite South Fork, but it was set in acres of grounds, cloaked by pine trees which hid it from the road completely. The house was a large two-storey affair with a swimming pool on an upper deck and a clear view across the dense pine forest that stretched seemingly forever to the volcano, Mount Hood.

The angle for the piece on Chilli T was to be that he was the antithesis of hip hop, with mega millions behind him, living in a huge house with a separate building containing a full-sized indoor basketball court. He was effectively 'the homeboy without a posse', recording in his bedroom and knocking about the house all day. In reality, though, the house was fairly moderate and tasteful considering how rich his father was. There were loads of fascinating native American exhibits from various Indian tribes, such as lances, bone armour and head dresses, all with museum-type labels on them saying, 'Spokane Indian war lance, 9th century'. I didn't twig until later that all the artefacts his mother collected must have been priceless.

Having spent the day with Chilli T, Chris, Carl and myself all felt quite sorry for him. He was fairly unassuming and very laid back, but he seemed morose. Here he was, a rich kid overloaded with material possessions, and yet his days appeared somehow empty, rattling around the big house with his friends using the state-of-the-art home cinema as a drop-in centre and the local neighbours' younger kids coming round to use their swimming pool. His only brother was a bit of a black sheep and was off living in New York, so life seemed pretty lonely. As for his music, well, let's just say it was pretty shit, but the piece gave us a glimpse of another life, another existence and a feeling that maybe the grass on the other side isn't necessarily greener.

As you'll be aware through reading this book, from day one of it's existence, *The Word* consistently attracted brickbats from the media. Personally, I couldn't understand why they were so bothered about what was basically a fairly lightweight entertainment show with some good bands. I recall being chosen as one of the faces of Channel 4's autumn launch in 1993, alongside Clive Anderson and Jonathan Ross. Apparently I had agreed to be interviewed and photographed by the *Mail*, *Express*, *Mirror*, *Star*, *Evening Standard* and a couple of other publications, and also to take part in a long 1,500-word double-page interview with the *Sun*'s Matthew Wright, who was, at the time, Piers Morgan's right-hand creep on the gossip column.

I'd had a problem with the *Sun* over their attitude towards Hillsborough and football fans in general, and their politics – letter pages baying for immigrants' blood and complaining about scrounging single mothers etc. – so I was quite forceful with Mark Borkowski, who was doing the shows PR, that I should have complete copy approval or I wouldn't do the article. Of course I was told that this was agreed . . . I confess to getting rather drunk with several of the actors from *Brookside* at the launch event and then staggering around sitting on a garden bench being photographed with Clive and Jonathan, who were both very funny and affable. I then returned to the hotel bar and was approached by half a dozen journalists rather snottily demanding their interviews as agreed.

Most eager amongst them was Matthew Wright and I have to say that the minute I met him I thought he was your typical public schoolboy type, although I'm sure in real life he's a great guy! I was then badgered by two female journalists from the *Daily Mail* and the *Daily Express*, plus assorted others, so I announced, 'Listen, I'm feeling a bit done in, so why not all do the interview together here and now, because I haven't really got time to do all of you today, unless you club together, and let's face it you'll all ask the same questions and write the same things anyway.'

There were murmurs of discontent, but eventually, with deadlines looming and seeing that I really couldn't give a toss either way, they agreed.

'Right, you've got fifteen minutes.' I made a point of looking impatiently at my watch.

As you can imagine, none of them was too pleased about this. We were in a rather noisy hotel bar, Matthew Wright thought he had me to himself for at least an hour and I suppose the other journalists had been offered what they no doubt would have seen as individual quality time in my company. The truth was I couldn't give a monkeys what they wrote about me, so whether I was charm personified or obnoxiousness on legs for the next twenty minutes, they were never going to write anything glowing or factual about me, so I decided to have some fun with them.

Unfortunately for the journalists, there was only one free chair in the bar, and as I was feeling a bit wobbly after several glasses of champagne, a few red wines a couple of pints of Guinness, plus a couple of whiskey chasers, I thought I should occupy it and stay put.

'Can we go somewhere quieter?' they asked.

'It's all right here, I'm comfortable and I talk quite loud anyway.'

I could tell Matthew Wright had the hump. Eventually, I sat on my throne with Matthew Wright and the other journalists crouching around my feet.

I can't remember what I said, but it was probably along the lines of, you are all just a bunch of public-school twats and that's a bit of a daft question, etc. Don't get me wrong, when I want to be horrible

I can be worse than anybody, especially when I've had a drink.

Needless to say, I didn't get copy approval from the *Sun*, and when the article appeared I remember it opening with the line: 'Terry Christian is even more arrogant and obnoxious in real life than he is on *The Word*.' The rest of the double-page spread went on to say what a complete waste of space I was and how terrible *The Word* was. It was quite spiteful, but if I'd exercised copy approval, I wouldn't have changed a word. As our editor at the time, Paul Ross, used to say, 'Don't read it, Terry, just weigh it.' It struck me that in terms of numbers and length of articles, you were always guaranteed bigger write-ups when the journalist had the chance to slag you off.

For the first show of Series four in the studio, they used both Mark and myself again. He was seriously fed up and he wasn't hiding it, so the usual negative gloom descended. When our guest, the young black American comedian Dave Chappelle started describing Mark as looking like Tin Tin, Mark just glowered, looking pissed off as the studio rippled with laughter. It wasn't Mark's style back then to be the butt of the guests' lighthearted on-air jokes, although in many ways that was exactly what the show was about. We weren't the clever ones, we were just trying to entertain, and as our guests were, in theory at least, more entertaining than us, we had to facilitate that by not pulling Kevin the teenager-type faces. Vic and Bob were guests again on the show, and their best line came when we introduced new *Word* presenter Hufty, a shaven-headed Geordie lesbian, to gasps from the audience. Mark turned to Bob Mortimer.

'Bob, what do you think of Hufty?'

'I believe her to be Satan.'

Hufty wasn't Satan, just a nice Catholic girl from Southshields who happened to be a lesbian. She was great fun down the pub, into football to the extent that she understood positions and tactics properly and that was it. Hufty wasn't some flag-waver for lesbianism and I suspect that's why some people at channel 4 were a bit disappointed by her performance.

The whole politically correct thing was getting way out of hand at Channel 4, and was beginning to smack of McCarthy-type witch-hunts. I remember once being involved in a conversation with a couple of gay blokes who worked in the offices who told me that all men have sexual fantasies about other men. I disagreed and said I hadn't, not even subconsciously in a dream. Perhaps I would if I was locked away in Strangeways prison for twenty-five years, but so far all my sexual fantasies involved the female gender. This bald, bold statement had them accusing me of being homophobic, and they weren't just doing it as a wind-up either. Poor Hufty, it seemed, was never allowed to just be a woman who was sexually attracted to other women and liked a pint and the strike partnership of Beardsley and Cole up front for the Magpies.

As a TV presenter I was feeling more relaxed. I still made mistakes, but what consoled me was knowing that other people who thought they knew what they were doing cocked up too.

All the time I'd been presenting *The Word* I'd continued with my *Manchester Evening News* column of the same name, filing 2,000 words each week on the latest up-and-coming bands, club nights, and gigs in the Greater Manchester area. I began to feel like a fraud, though, as my interest was waning and I was getting fed up of bands not only mithering me to put them in the paper, but pestering for plays on my radio show on Rock FM in Lancashire, and pressuring me to get them on *The Word*. I used to tell them that that just because they were from Manchester and had a record out didn't qualify them for a slot on *The Word* – sometimes Mancunians needed reminding that The Dooleys were a Manchester band, too! However, the music that was around, and what made it on to the show, had me up in arms. I was tired of being the conduit for their ambitions and a large part of me was heartily sick of the limelight

The music industry is a strange beast, but ever since that heady period between 1976 and 1978 when punk came to the fore, whenever there's been little around, the London-based music press always try to revive the corpse of that scene, the last time London had a music scene as far as I'm concerned. The King's Road, Wardour Street, Carnaby Street, basically anything that harped back to London as the centre of British music culture.

By series four of *The Word* we were stuck with a cack-handed scene called New Wave of New Wave, which was just a clumsy attempt by the music press to recreate a punk scene to replace the Madchester one they'd all lashed out against. It was pub rock versus urban rock with crappy groups like These Animal Men, Smashed, Compulsion, and plain old pub rock-type bands like Kinky Machine.

It was all fairly ploddy and ordinary, much like the other so-called music scene in London, Acid Jazz. All that involved was 1970s classic funk, a bit of Stevie Wonder, a bit of Charles Wright, some James Brown and Bobby Byrd, then get white guys with goatee beards and Frank Spencer berets to play it, with maybe a black girl singing. To me it boiled down to the funk equivalent of pub rock, and as I'd often explain in articles and interviews, 300 people on a night out in Manchester in a club dancing to old funk records is called a good night out; 300 people dancing to rehashed funk in a club in London is known as a scene – it's all down to the media, who seem to turn into a pillar of salt if they move outside the M25. It's all so fake and made up it could give you a rash.

Yet here I was, listening to our new music producer and Paul Ross planning to fill the music slots on *The Word* with all sorts of horrendous nonsense like Corduroy, Mother Earth, and other four-week music-press wonders.

Compulsion appeared on the show one night and were fairly shoddy. I felt aggrieved that the music booker had put them on, so I pulled him up and he said he couldn't think of anyone else for that week and mentioned a gig he saw them at in London. I reminded him that only around thirty people had attended that gig and yet he'd felt they deserved airing on a network TV show.

'Well, they're not from London, Terry, they're Irish?'

'Do you think I'm arsed about a band's geographical origins?' I replied. 'What's up with you? Bowie was from London, wasn't he. the Stones, The Kinks, The Small Faces, The Who, The Pistols, The Clash. And weren't, The Jam one of the greatest bands of all time, from the Home Counties. My beef is with all this retro pub rock bollocks and the Emperor's new clothes way of jumping on sterile bandwagons. If there aren't better bands than Kinky Machine and Salad out there, I'll be very surprised.'

Honestly, these lads were ultra sensitive and precious, and despite working with me, some of them for two or more years, they still didn't get me at all. However, when it came to having a strange sniffy attitude, some of the bands were the worst. I made a point of leaving most of them to the job of feeling all trendy and hip and kissing the music press's arses. The only times I bothered speaking to the bands who appeared on the show was if I was especially chuffed that they'd made it big, if they let on to me first or I knew them.

I was really pleased that Pulp made it after their 'overnight success' that took the best part of twelve years. I remember talking to Jarvis Cocker in the make-up room about a great single they'd recorded back in 1986 or '87 , called 'They Suffocate At Night', which I'd featured heavily on my radio show at the time. Jarvis and Pulp had a fantastic integrity about them, just like bands like The Fall. In some ways their success ruined things for them, but at least they got some kind of financial rewards for all their great tunes. They were a band that understood that great music isn't about dressing up and trying to be cool, it's about passion, honesty, conviction and sensitivity. Sheffield musically has always reminded me of a mini Manchester in some respects, and with bands like the Arctic Monkeys, Milburn and Little Man Tate coming through now, that wit, honesty and anti-fashion pop-kids thing is still, I'm happy to say, alive and well.

Channel 4 had a chat show with Clive Anderson called *Clive Anderson Talks Back*, and one night his main guest was Rory Bremner. I expected them to discuss Footlights, punting on the river, refectories and wearing purple trousers with W H Auden and other Oxbridge nonsense. Instead I watch open-mouthed as Rory Bremner, who did a very poor impression of me on his TV show, launched into an unprovoked tirade about how thick and moronic I was. Now this wasn't a thirty-second tirade, it went on for a full three minutes, at the end of which Clive Anderson, who had met me only a few weeks earlier at the Channel 4 press launch, was trying to get Rory to move on to something else, as the comedy value of what he was saying had disappeared two minutes and fifty-five seconds earlier.

Rory Bremner and I had never met, but he was working at the time with my old commissioning editor Stephen Garrett, who had obviously described me to Rory in glowing terms! Blimey I'm one of four other presenters on a show and Rory, who no doubt chokes over his cornflakes every morning at the fact that Jordan's tits get more column inches than the situation in the Middle East, spends three whole minutes of a television show laying into me.

A few days later my home phone in Manchester rings. I answer it and it's Piers Morgan.

'Hi, Terry, how are you?'

Piers sounded strangely cheerful. 'Awright, Piers,' I replied, thinking, What's he after?

'Erm, Terry, what do you think of Rory Bremner slagging you off on *Clive Anderson* and saying you're thick.'

'Never met him, Piers. Anyway, you're the one always calling me a moron and cerebrally challenged.'

'Ah yes, but that's just in fun. I mean, you're not thick, are you?'

'Well, no one except your good self and Mr Bremner have ever said it, but who knows?'

'I mean, you've got some qualifications, haven't you?.

'Well, yeah,'

'How many O levels and A levels have you got?'

'I've got eight O levels and three A levels.'

'So you're not thick, are you?'

'Well I wouldn't say academic qualifications make you bright, but how thick I am isn't normally the first thing people comment on.'

'Well Rory Bremner is always slagging you off and he impersonates you in his set as somebody who's a moron. What do you think of Rory Bremner?'

'Look at it this way, Piers, if I was a plumber and as adept with my pipe benders as Rory Bremner is at doing a Mancunian accent, I'd be on the dole and not fronting my own show on Channel 4.'

'Thanks, Terry, that's great.'

The next day in the *Sun* Piers had got his little story on the battle between me and Rory Bremner.

'"How dare he say I'm thick,' said Terry, 'I've got eight O levels and four A levels. I'll challenge him to a general knowledge quiz any day."'

Piers Morgan, the whole truth and nothing but the truth.

While filming in LA I'd gone to see Manchester band James play a sell-out gig at the Roxy on Sunset Boulevard and then nipped next door to see Stereolab playing at The Whiskey A Go-Go. I thought Stereolab were quite different, with that Sixties psychedelic garage thing going on, so I suggested we get them on *The Word* for show three of series four. As the show finished I approached them and told them how much I'd enjoyed their gig at The Whiskey in LA, and they looked at me as if I'd come over and spat in their faces, then blanked me. I'd never met them, but they were obviously pseudo enough to believe any old toss they read. Weird. It often makes me wonder who these arseholes thought was responsible for *The Word* going after cutting-edge bands, then again, nobody was going to read that in any of the articles about me. On the same show as Stereolab we had young *EastEnder* actor-cum-pop star called Sean Maguire. Sean was a really nice young lad and a talented mimic and he did an impression of me on the show that was pretty good.

'Hey, Sean, that's really good, have you ever thought of being an impressionist,' I asked.

'No, not really.'

'It's not hard, I mean, you don't have to be funny, just look at Rory Bremner.'

Within two minutes of me uttering this, Rory Bremner was on the phone to Channel 4 complaining. Then a few months later I was on *Loose Ends* with Ned Sherrin when Rowland Rivron made some reference to Rory Bremner looking a bit fat and Rory was on the phone immediately whinging about it. Talk about people in glass houses.

Now let's move on to the music press, that cutting-edge tool that pioneered the way for successive youth movements in music. There was one young lad who covered Manchester for the *NME* called John Harris. Yes Manchester, which along with Liverpool was responsible for the British Beat explosion in the Sixties, and had produced all the interesting bands in Britain since the late Seventies: the Buzzcocks, The Fall, Joy Division, The Smiths, The Stone Roses, the Happy Mondays and, of course, soon to be featured on *The Word*, Oasis. A City with numerous venues for live music, a well-supported local music scene and a population of six million, and we get one stringer for a national music paper who's an Oxbridge graduate from the posh leafy suburb of Wilmslow twelve miles out of town. You couldn't make it up.

John Harris, twenty-one years of age and full of idealistic zeal, went to see the debut gig of a band called The Sugar Merchants, who were mostly from the Hulme/Moss Side/Salford area. The lead singer, Martin Merchant, is black and a superb singer, the only person from outside London to sing as part of Lewisham's famous Saxon Sound System, which gave us artists like Papa Levi, Smiley Culture, Tippa Irie, Peter Hunnigale and Maxi Priest. Martin is a massive fan of Sixties beat groups like The Small faces and Manfred Man, loves The Stone Roses and, of course, The Smiths, and his band The Sugar Merchants were an unusual mixture of rootsy reggae rhythms with an overlay of glittering Sixties psychedelic hard–edged pop. The buzz about them on the strength of some demos aired on various radio shows around Manchester was incredible and they played their debut gig at PJ Bells on Oldham street, with over 400 people crammed into the corridor of a club with a long bar, while 100 people, many with tickets, were locked outside. The audience was a mixture of indie kids and reggae fans who just loved hearing Martin sing. Nowhere other than Manchester or Bristol would you experience such a racially mixed crowd for an indie music gig. The Sugar Merchants were electrifying, and four encores later they came off stage.

The following week in the *NME*, John Harris wrote, 'Over four hundred people crammed into PJ Bells on Oldham street to witness the debut gig of Manchester band Severe.'

Mr Harris had decided to review the gig as if the support act, two thirty-year-old blokes from Wilmslow who sounded like a third-rate New Order circa 1981 were the headliners and had pulled the crowd. No mention of The Sugar Merchants (who later became Audioweb). I saw Mr Harris on *The Word* set the following week.

'How come you didn't review The Sugar Merchants?' I asked. 'They were fantastic and I've never seen a band pull a crowd like that on their debut?'

'They weren't my cup of tea and I didn't think they were an *NME* band.'

They weren't an NME band! What on earth did that mean? A bunch of talented twentysomethings who tore the roof off and pulled that crowd don't get a mention, and what's worse he said that his mates had pulled the crowd and headlined the gig.

'That's what the *NME* said about The Stone Roses in 1985, 86, 87 and 88' I replied.

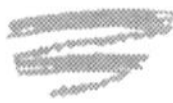

I felt suffocated by all the fakery surrounding me. Was it me or was it them? Luckily I had Craig Cash, who though writing with Caroline Ahern, was eager to learn about TV, and he noticed the same mistakes being made on *The Word* as I did. We were a live show, with 350 people in the audience, yet I'd be on the couch interviewing some nervous guest, and during the interview some dork of a producer would start setting up the contestants for the 'Male Rear of the Year' contest, causing the audience to turn round, look and murmur, which put the guest off as nobody appeared to be listening. I'd told them not to set things like that up during a live section of the show, and to do it when a video taped item was running, but evidently that would involve some common sense, and there was always a distinct lack of that amongst *The Word* team.

Our last show of 1993 came a week before Christmas and the guests were Gabrielle and Alexis Arquette. Alexis Arquette was horrendous really and told this dreadful joke about incest and menstruation that was so tasteless I didn't know where to look.

There were dozens of complaints about it, and I have to say it was an all-time low for the show, especially as I didn't have a clue who or what Alexis Arquette was supposed to be.

Our first Christmas show had the whole office buzzing. Mark Lamarr was going to be presenting a quiz show as his outside broadcast called 'Win or Weep'. The idea was that members of the public would gamble a treasured item hoping to win the big prize, but if they lost said item would be destroyed before their eyes. Paul Ross was particularly excited about a woman who had put her dog forward, volunteering that if she lost we could shoot the dog! Another contestant that excited Paul was a woman who wanted to gamble her dad's ashes, which she kept in an urn on the shelf behind the bar of the pub she owned. As her dad had been a big gambler, she felt he would understand.

'Shoot a dog? No way is anybody going to agree to that,' I commented.

'But it's fantastic, Terry, can you imagine it. Great television.'

I wasn't arsed about 'Weep or Win': it smacked of being funny for the first ten seconds as an idea and then less and less interesting as the minutes ticked by. This was very much a Planet 24 scenario: dragging out a split-second funny idea ad infinitum, especially on *The Big Breakfast*, which specialized in that kind of television.

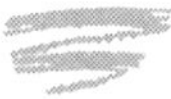

I suspect the effects of Colombian marching powder were proving too much for some of the other members of the team. In fact, the old nose ningle was pretty rife in the Planet 24 office, and the more enthusiastic and hyperbolic team members became, the more obvious it was that they'd put something up their hooters.

Despite all this, I was excited about the fact that our live guests were the footballer with the highest scorer in the football league at the time, Ian Wright, and Danish Hollywood star and the ex-Mrs Stallone Brigitte Nielsen.

On the night, Brigitte was acting like she had been in the toilets to powder her nose with a few of the Planet 24 staff prior to the show. It was odd that she acted so weirdly on *The Word* and yet the press never mentioned it, but when she was all over the shop on *Fantasy Football* and later *The Frank Skinner Show*, it was reported as some kind of revelation.

Ian Wright was part of Graham Taylor's England team, but he wasn't being used in the right way. He'd scored something like thirty-eight goals the previous season for Arsenal and was seen by football fans as the natural successor to Gary Lineker as England's main striker, but England were struggling, and when I asked Ian Wright about it he bemoaned the fact that he wasn't able to play along side Peter Beardsley, whose unselfish play and great vision had resulted in Andy Cole scoring around forty goals the previous season for Newcastle United. Ian also complained that another reason he wasn't banging them in for England was Graham Taylor's instruction for him to carry the ball into the wide areas and try to cross it for David Platt, who would run into the box from deep positions to score. Absolutely crazy, but revelatory stuff. I expected the papers to be full of it over the next couple of days, but I forgot that very few people who worked on *The Word* were into football and that our PR people didn't understand the game at all.

The following day was the third round of The FA cup, and I was travelling on the train back up to Manchester in the morning, along with a fair few Queens Park Rangers fans, whose team had been drawn against Stockport County. I got talking to a young sports journalist from the *Independent* or *Observer* called Henry Winter, who was covering the game, and he was fascinated by what Ian Wright had said on the previous night's show. He told me that he was covering the Stockport versus QPR game.

'I quite fancy Stockport to get a result. They're well organized with Kevin Francis and Andy Preece up front, a dodgy pitch, decent goalie and some good young midfielders.'

'Really, I can't see QPR having any problems.'

'Stockport have been doing well and they're no mugs in that division; they won promotion on merit and QPR, although doing well, seem a bit fair-weather to me.'

I smiled as I read Henry Winter's report the following day in the paper. Stockport County 2, QPR 1. He didn't mention my prediction, but I should have gone down the bookies.

There was more controversy missed by the press on the following week's show. The guests were East 17 and two young actresses who had just shared an infamous lesbian kiss on *Brookside*, sixteen-year-old Anna Friel and Nicola Stephenson. Both Anna and Nicola were lovely young northern girls with a good sense of humour. Anna was fantastic as she seemed like a real sixteen-year-old, whereas in the media I seemed to be constantly meeting girls of seventeen who were trying to act like they were thirty-year-old sophisticates.

There had been a story in one of the tabloid supplements that they'd both been out in Manchester and that United's Roy Keane had tried to get off with Nicola. When I put this to the girls, Anna immediately interjected.

'It wasn't Nicola he was trying to get off with, it was me.'

Oh, I thought he was trying to get off with Nicola, so did you not fancy him, Anna?'

'God he was so absolutely drunk I just wanted to get away.'

I wonder if Fergie was watching. I have to say I felt quite guilty. After all, Keane was part of a United team that were beginning to look awesome.

After the show, we had some drinks in the bar and then all the members of East 17, together with Anna, Nicola and her actor boyfriend Kieran, headed back to my hotel to carry on drinking until the early hours. Brian Harvey, Tony Mortimer and the other lads in the band were flirting with Anna, who like a true teenager was totally oblivious, while I mischievously kept saying, 'For God's sake lads, at least wait until she's done her GCSEs.'

For the second time in eight shows, Mark was presenting from the studio couch with guest Julian Clary, who for some reason really makes me laugh with his gentle dry humour, even though a lot of his lines aren't that great. He's a born comedian, like Les Dawson or Eric Morecambe. I was being sent off to the furthest western edge of

Europe, the small village of Belmullet in County Mayo in Ireland, to do an outside broadcast where we introduced three of Britain's best club nights to the so-called yokels of that cut-off corner of Europe.

I was very keen to go as I hadn't been anywhere in Ireland apart from Dublin and Belfast. However, most of my friends in Manchester were of Irish descent and had relatives in those western cut-off areas of Ireland, and they assured me that they were as likely to be listening to the latest hip hop, house or indie rock tunes as anybody else, and that they had fantastic night clubs out there, in fact better than any town of the equivalent size in Britain. The idea was that these poor Irish were still listening to The Chieftains and Daniel O'Donnell, then we'd arrive and give them three different sets of DJs and dancers from Britain's trendiest club nights, the award-winning gay night 'Flesh' from Manchester's Hacienda, the bad taste disco known as 'Misery' from Edinburgh, and the trancy, trendy new-age hippy chic of 'Whirligig' from London.

I flew out from Manchester with the girls and lads from Flesh in a small propeller plane, which touched down at Knock airport. Knock had bad associations for me, as my abiding memory was getting very drunk at Christmas as a teenager, waking up with a raging thirst, finding a bottle of lemonade in the cupboard and swigging half of it down me only to find it tasted like dirty, dusty old water. I spent the whole of the next day vomiting and defecating, and was informed by my mother that the bottle contained Holy water from Knock that my auntie Mag had brought over with her from Ireland in a lemonade bottle so we could bless ourselves from the little Infant of Prague holy water receptacle that was tastefully screwed into the wall in our hallway.

We arrived at Knock airport at 3.30p.m. in the afternoon and the show wasn't on until 11p.m., so we boarded a minibus with the lads from the Edinburgh club. The driver told me it was about a two-hour drive from Knock across the undulating bog roads out to Belmullet, so if we needed the toilet he'd stop off in the main county town of Ballina. It was obvious from the way the driver talked that he thought I was in charge, so I decided the best thing to do was to take the lead, look after my charges and give them a taste of the old country.

'Listen, it's a two-hour drive or longer out to Belmullet, so rather than be there for ages hanging around, I think we should stop off for a few jars and maybe some food in Ballina for an hour or so.' Everybody was most agreeable, but then again, regardless of sexual preferences, I was in a minibus full of Scots and Mancunians.

'Just drive around for another half hour or find somewhere to park and join us, we've got plenty of time,' I told the driver.

We'd been in the Broken Jug pub in Ballina for about four hours, but I still had plenty of entertainment float money for the drinks as nobody seemed that bothered about eating. Well, not after the first three pints and whiskey chasers had gone down.

'Well, Anne from your office has been on the phone asking after you. She's wondering where you are.'

'Just tell her we're on our way and we've had to stop for petrol.'

'Ah, that's what I said an hour ago.'

'Er, well, tell her we've stopped again as everyone was hungry and insisted we stopped.'

'Well whatever you say, I can't say as I blame you.'

My eyes were blurry, my speech was slurred, but here I was in County Mayo and I was in charge of a dozen people and not a man or woman amongst them was unappreciative of my leadership qualities.

When I eventually rounded up the troops it was almost 8.30p.m. I shouted our farewells to the amused locals and hostelry workers and then they sent over a free round of drinks. 'Er, have you got any twiglets?'

We sat down again, and finally, just gone nine, we staggered onto the minibus, which stopped twice to let a couple of us be sick – those bog roads are very wavy and make you feel almost sea sick. At fifteen minutes to eleven, and about twenty minutes before my first satellite link, we slumped past a panic-stricken Anna Lavelle, the producer for the shoot, and into the Anchor Pub/club. The Anchor was owned by The Mcteague family, and their oldest son Connor who was a huge fan of *The Word*, had just returned to Belmullet from working in Germany. The pub/club complex attracted locals from a sixty-mile radius and stayed open all night Friday and Saturday. The front part was a traditional Irish pub with traditional live Irish music, while at the back there was a night club that could hold in excess of 1,000 people and which had all the latest Technics decks, integrated sound system and lights.

Everybody was absolutely hammered. I tried to speak when the red light came on the camera but my mouth felt as if Richard Burton and Oliver Reed had both died on my tongue. Nevertheless, I shouted a lot, the crowd are good and lively and it all seemed to go swimmingly. In fact, it shouldn't be *The Word*'s audience that was half drunk every week, it should be the presenters.

Except for the pot-smoking anal retentives from Whirligig, everybody was totally blitzed, and when the crowd voted for their favourite club night, Flesh came first, Misery second and Whirligig got only a half-hearted cheer – they took themselves far too seriously with their daft didgeridoos. There was a huge black guy in a kilt who was one of the dancers from Flesh and he laughed his head off as some old farmers in the front bar encouraged him to get some of the local girls up the duff to put a bit of colour into the local population. By three in the morning the whole complex resembled Hogarth's Gin Alley and the atmosphere was fantastic; it was just a shame we had a little thing like a TV show in the way. The next day, however, I somehow ended up back in Manchester – after a hair of the dog at Knock airport, of course.

I was relaxed about the whole TV lark now and was really enjoying it. The show was entertaining enough and I was fed up of worrying about a long-term TV career. It seemed to me that no matter how well you present or how many people watch the shows you make, it wouldn't have any bearing on what jobs you were offered. Shows seemed to be handed out to presenters in a fairly willy-nilly fashion and the northern thing was still an issue.

My blood boiled over the following week, though, when I watched the final edited version of my Mickey Rourke piece. It had been butchered and married up with some footage of Mickey Rourke being arrested outside his nightclub in Miami, so that all the interesting stuff about him doing this 'piece of shit called *Harley Davidson and the MarlboroMan* and his observation that 'De Niro is the biggest cry baby I ever worked with' had ended up on the cutting-room floor. Not only that, the voiceover script I had to record onto the package had me saying the lines, 'Mickey tried to make it as an actor in Hollywood and failed, he then tried to make it as a boxer, and failed, so now he's trying to make it as a poet,' then I had to read out his corny poem. I was blazing about it. The whole piece bore no resemblance to the actual interview or the person I'd met. They'd stitched him up in the most tabloid fashion. All my respect for Paul Ross and his TV philosophy went out the window, and if he wasn't such a likeable bloke down the pub, I'd have hated him. What was worse was that they shifted the running order of the show around so I wasn't even able to comment on the Mickey Rourke piece after it had been shown.

When it came to our American guests we suffered from the age-old problem of two nations separated by a common language. Whether talking about Fags, fannies or anything else, the interpretations is always different. We say pavement, they say sidewalk; we say autumn, they say Fall; we say futile, they say United Nations – you know the type of thing. One week I had black American model and actress and one-time girlfriend of Spike Lee and Robert De Niro, Veronica Webb, on the show. During the interview, I asked her if she had packed Spike Lee in or Spike Lee had packed her in. She looked shocked and asked me to repeat myself, so I asked her again.

'Did you pack Spike in or did he pack you in.'

'Erm, I don't understand.'

'Who packed who in? Who finished with who?'

The relief on her face as she went on about it being mutual was obvious. I then said, what about Robert De Niro? Did you pack him in or did he pack you in? Afterwards, she leaned over and said, 'I can't believe you asked me that. It's funny, but it's shocking.'

After the show I was informed that the phrase 'to pack someone in' over in the USA, means to shag them up the arse. I suppose a lot gets lost in translation. Still, the answer to that question would perhaps have been even more interesting.

It would be true to say that outside of doing a holiday show, no other TV programme gave its presenters as much opportunity to travel the world. We were covering our own made-up Mr University International in Hawaii at the University of Honolulu. For me the journey was a nightmare, ten hours and thirty minutes out to LA, then six hours from LA to Hawaii. A few people from *The Word* team were already in Hawaii to set things up, and as we arrived at the airport they put Polynesian flower garlands around our necks. We were staying at the Hilton Hotel in Honolulu, close to Waikiki beach, and I would be there for a total of three days, with Dani Behr flying out with our British Mr University winner, Alex, the following day.

All I knew of Hawaii, other than that Captain Cook was killed by the Islanders, was what I'd seen in a couple of dodgy Elvis films, and that according to Manchester folklore it had the best grass in the world, grown on the slopes of volcanoes.

With not much action going on, I decided to hit the streets of Honolulu and find some of this mystical powerful substance. So at eight o'clock on my first evening I was wandering past the usual hookers and junkies in a place that looked like any other regular US city, looking for some Hawaiian grass.

I spotted four huge Jonah Lomu lookalikes in tracksuits loitering next to a phone box. They towered over me, but I decided they were a likely place to start my hunt and began chatting to them. I found out that they were Samoan, and then asked them if they knew where I could get some Hawaiian grass.

'Right here, dude.'

'Let's see.'

He showed me his wares. It looks just like California sticky bud to me, I tell them, and two of them laugh at my cheek while one looks slightly sour. Eventually, after being extremely and probably unwisely cheeky, they tell me I'm on the wrong island to get the proper Hawaiian stuff and sell me some over-priced sticky bud. It's a decent smoke, but I'm disappointed that I've come all this way, probably for the only time in my life, and not been able to sample this black truffle of the cannabis world. Nevertheless I take my wares back to the hotel and share it with my fellow workers, telling them it's Hawaiian grass – bunch of southerners wouldn't know the difference anyway.

We have a great time in Hawaii, where the whole of Honolulu is readying itself for St Patrick's day. The few full-blooded Polynesians I meet confess to having a great grandparent who was Irish, normally off the many whaling ships that called in during the last century. I'm a bit disappointed, though, as everywhere looks just like the USA: same highways, same burger joints and pizza places.

If you were looking for a semi-religious icon on Hawaii, don't think of the statues of Easter Islands, think early Sixties Elvis Presley. Our researcher Andrew Newman has tracked down a six-year-old Elvis impersonator; it's quite funny, but all kids love Elvis and Michael Jackson, it must be something genetic, like enjoying cartoons. We buy very bad-taste Hawaiian shirts – are there any other type – and walk around wearing them. Hawaii is full of Japanese people wearing bad golfing gear, so we look almost chic in comparison.

It's obvious to me that there has been some kind of underspend on *The Word*'s budget as there are six of us in total enjoying the sunshine to film Mr University International. The British winner is a tall, handsome ex-public school boy called Alex, with blond hair, blue eyes and an aristocratic bearing. He's a right laugh and is really enjoying himself. He flew over with Dani Behr, seventeen hours at 33,000 feet, plus stopovers in LA while changing planes, and complains to me that Dani hardly spoke a word to him all the way over. Dani is going through a slightly grand phase, but I would have thought Alex, who's posh and good looking, might be her type. I ask him over a drink if his family's rich and he says they're fairly comfortable but not stinking rich. 'Well that, Alex my boy, is where you've gone wrong. I'll turn the tables for you with Dani, just watch and play along with me later.'

Every evening we were in Hawaii, at about 5.30p.m. we'd gathered in my room for a quick spliff before hitting the night spots of Honolulu. Dani never indulged in marijuana, so she sat there patiently as we all got high, trying to make sensible conversation in between piss-taking and guffaws. It's then that I start on Alex.

'So, Alex, is it true that your family are stinking rich landed gentry?'

'Well, I suppose we're rich... yes.' Alex is playing along like an absolute star and the tension in the room is palpable, as they all think I'm in full piss-take mode.

'So have you got a castle?'

'Er, no, we haven't got a castle.'

'Well, what houses have you got?'

'We've got a large stately home in Dorset, a farm in Devon, a lodge up in Scotland and an apartment in Monaco.'

'And what cars have you got?'

'A Bentley, a Rolls, a Porsche etc...' Alex is really convincing.

'And what about boats? Got any of them?'

'Erm, well, we have a 100-foot yacht in Monaco and a powerboat.'

'Have you got a helicopter then?'

'Er, no, we haven't got a helicopter.'

'There you go, you're not rich, more nouveau riche.' I cackle mockingly while Alex smiles.

Then suddenly Dani pipes up, 'Leave him alone, Terry, stop picking on him.'

Alex and myself fold up with laughter while the rest of the team, including Dani, look on bemused. That night we visit a few bars and Dani chats away to her new best mate Alex, in fact you'd need a crow bar to remove her. I feel quite jealous really as Alex is my Hawaiian buddy. 'Just imagine if you'd said you had a helicopter,' I tease him later.

The Mr University contest is a non-event. After all, there isn't really a Mr University International contest taking place in Hawaii. What we've done is set one up with American students from the local university pretending to be Mr France, Mr Germany and Mr Italy, depending on their ancestry. We line them up on the beach in their swimming trunks, make them race each other in the swimming pool and drink some beer. Alex wins that event like a true Brit. I have the old Michael Aspel chinwag to see what their personalities are like and introduce them as they do their catwalk thing. 'First up is Mr USA, his name is Rob and his hobbies include scuba diving and grid iron, etc. I come to Mr Germany give his hobbies and then at the end say, 'But let's hope he doesn't win, as nobody likes the Germans anyway.'

I forget all about this, get on my flight back to LA and am not displeased to discover that instead of flying to Heathrow, my Virgin flight has been re-routed to Manchester airport because of an IRA mortar attack. I leave for my flight while Dani does her nut at the check-in desk because her flight has been re-routed via Birmingham, as if they're going to change it just because she complains, God bless her. Thankfully, this strange phase of Dani's was short-lived.

I get back to England and then hear that some wags in the Channel 4 politburo are complaining that I'm not politically correct or a good role model for British youngsters – blimey has it taken them four years to work that out – because I made a 'racist' joke about the Germans. I'm a bit fed up with all the sniping, so my response is that they accuse me of not being a good role model when half of the Politburo snort cocaine, as do several of the presenters on other Channel 4 shows. In fact, one presenter has done time in prison for conspiracy to deal cocaine. It seems odd that I'm damned as a bad role model to young people for making a statement like 'Let's face it, no one likes the Germans anyway,' when in the area of Manchester I grew up in teenagers are shooting each other to compete for the right to sell cocaine to my so-called colleagues. All this political correctness smacks of fascism to me. On the outside these people portray themselves as socialist/liberal, free-thinking caring and sensitive, but inside what they represent is a fascistic narcissism. I suggest, all good naturedly you understand, that rather than apologizing for my so-called racism they get drug-tested first. I've no doubt that this went down like the proverbial rat sandwich, but in truth I have no respect for what they think or feel any more.

In *The Word* office there has been one of those stupid disagreements going on for weeks. The bands this series haven't been that great, and I've been pushing for a new band from Manchester to be on the last show of series one. I've seen them a few times and gave them their first proper write-up in my evening news page some eighteen months earlier. The band are called Oasis. There are several problems with getting them on, according to our music booker Ed Fosdyke, the one who loved New Wave of New Wave, ha ha ha. Firstly, on the last show he has booked an all-Asian rap band from Manchester called The Kaliphz and, as Ed puts it, 'We can't have two bands from Manchester on the same show.'

This is an easy argument to counter. 'So, Ed, you wouldn't have two bands from London or New York on the same show?' Ed then changes his argument to the fact that the single the band have coming out won't be in the shops for at least three weeks after the show has aired.'

'But, Ed, are we an entertainment show or an extension of some record company's marketing department. Oasis are good, they might be huge and they can play live, unlike Whiteout and Compulsion, who weren't quite ready, and various other so-called hip bands we've had on this series.'

In fact, I'd been under pressure to get Oasis on the show for months, both from the band and my girlfriend Sue, whose company were plugging them regionally. My girlfriend's record promotion's company worked The Inspiral Carpets and she had known Noel Gallagher since he was their roadie and instrument technician. Also, Noel's then girlfriend of six years, Louise Jones, who Noel shared a flat with in Manchester, worked for my girlfriend, as did Noel's fellow roadie and friend from his Inspiral Carpet days, Liam Walsh. To help Oasis get booked on *The Word*, I'd suggested that Noel and Liam Gallagher come down to the show one night when they were in

London and pester Ed Fosdyke as, along with the quality of their demo single 'Columbia' and the good write-ups they were beginning to get in the music press, this might swing it. In fact, when Noel and Liam walked into the studio as the show finished they virtually bumped into Ed and I made the introductions.

'Yeah, Oasis, I went to see you at the Water Rats the other week,' Ed said.

Noel asked him what he thought and he replied, 'Actually I couldn't get in, it was too full.'

'There you go, Ed, they are popular, that's why you should get them on, there's a buzz about them.'

I left Noel and Liam to peck Ed's head, but made sure I kept him thinking about them by pestering him for the next four or five weeks. Fortunately for Oasis, for our final show of series four one of the bands had to pull out and they were slotted in. Blimey, two bands from Manchester on the same show, whatever next?

We had a decent line-up for the final show. Our studio guests were up-and-coming American actor Stephen Dorff, who had just played original Beatle bassist and friend of John Lennon, Stuart Sutcliffe, in the film *Backbeat*; American comedienne and actress Kathy Najimy, who'd been in the films *Sister Act* and *Sister Act 2*; and plugging his new album, our boss and one-time Irish punk Sir Bob Geldof.

There was a real feel-good factor around the studio and a few old faces from Manchester. Indeed, in the case of The Kaliphz, I'd given them a rave write-up some six months earlier and even hammered their fantastic demo 'Pakiz In The Hood' on my radio show.

The only thing I was annoyed about was the so-called outside broadcast. It was the usual unfunny stunt where we caused untold misery to the show's fans and I was absolutely furious about it. The idea involved laying on a coach to bring fifty young people from Manchester down for the final show. The twist was that instead of the coach arriving at eight in the evening, it would be delayed, get raided, break down and arrive at midnight after an eight-and-a-half-hour journey. I couldn't see what was funny about it. People would have taken a half day or day off work, some would have arranged to meet people and the stunts the show intended to get up to on the coach weren't even funny. As usual, though, I was a powerless lone voice – I just couldn't understand the second-rate thinking that thought ruining people's day was funny. 'Oh it's just because it's a coach load of Mancunians, Terry,' was the sort of dim reply I received. What arseholes some of the people were. They go to all that expense and trouble in order to treat people like shit.

I was invited into Sir Bob Geldof's dressing room before the show for a chat and he was extremely warm and friendly, perhaps to make up for the fact that he'd hardly nodded in my direction before. The American actor Stephen Dorff was a decent lad, too. I'd interviewed him on the first series of *The Word* when he was only eighteen and had done a boxing movie set in apartheid South Africa called *The Power Of One*. I decided to play a trick on Stephen, though. For an American he'd managed a quite passable scouse accent for his part as Stuart Sutcliffe and had spent a good deal of time filming in Liverpool. I had a brand-new Manchester United shirt which I intended to give him as a gift on the show and encourage him to wear it by saying it would be very popular with football-mad Liverpudlians.

The only nerves I felt on the day were about Oasis. I'd really stuck my neck out to get them on the show, but had only seen them live twice. At one gig at The Boardwalk back in 1991 they were third on the bill and ended up in a punch-up with another band, The Cherries, and at another gig at the Hop and Grape bar at Manchester University, Liam had been so shy he'd sung the whole set with his back to the audience. However, I'd heard great things since then, plus the demo they'd recorded was fantastic and my girlfriend and her mates were constantly harping on about what a good-looking lad Liam was.

As Oasis prepared to rehearse I watched Liam Gallagher mucking about on the stage. He seemed in his element, cheekily chatting up the female dancers. When they ran through their number 'Supersonic', I was very impressed not only with the performance, but with the song.

Everybody was whispering about American country rock band Soul Asylum, whose lead singer was going out with Wynona Ryder. Wynona was actually down at *The Word* that night, but would remain hidden away in the band's dressing room. I rather cheekily suggested to Paul Ross, 'Instead of torturing a coach party of *Word* fans, why don't you get a pretend psycho stalker to kick the dressing room door in, that'll get you big laughs and a byline in the *Daily Star*.'

Bob Geldof was good fun on the show, but he got the hump when I asked him whether he was a wealthy man – somebody had told me he'd made loads of money from dealing antiques, so any money from his music or TV was just a bonus on top. He said he was broke and didn't have any money, so cheekily I took a ten pound note out of my pocket and offered it to him live on air.

'Here y'are, Bob, take it, I get paid plenty.'

'No, put it away.'

'No, come on take it.'

'No thanks.'

'No, I insist, take it.'

'Now fuck off and put it away, will you.'

I did overdo it a bit, but it was an old trick as my friends and I back in Manchester always say, it's only people who are loaded that constantly go on about having no money. Oasis did their song and Sir Bob was knocked out by them, as indeed he should have been, and I explained to him how they were Irish lads from Manchester.

Next Stephen Dorff came on and talked about Stuart Sutcliffe, The Beatles and learning how to speak scouse properly. I flirted for an instant with informing Stephen that Sutcliffe didn't really speak with a scouse accent, it was more of a Lancashire accent, or at least that's what the late Mr Sutcliffe's sister had told me when I had her on my radio show a couple of months earlier. At the end of the interview I offered the Manchester United shirt to Stephen, explaining how much Liverpudlians loved football and that this was the shirt of the team that made them feel really emotional. He thanked me profusely and I then cajoled him into wearing it proudly for the rest of the show, even getting him to turn the collar up on it à la Cantona.

'There you go, Stephen, everyone in Liverpool will be going mad now.'

Backstage after the show, all the lads from Oasis wanted to meet Dani Behr, but she was reluctant to hang out with them for too long as she seemed more interested in Stephen Dorff. Paula Yates came over and bit my face after saying how excited she was at hearing all these Manchester accents and how much we all sounded like Jason Orange out of Take That.

'No, Paula, Jason Orange sounds like us,' I said. I tried my best to enjoy the company that night, but found myself assailed by the late arrival of the Mancunians after their eight-and-a-half-hour coach trip that had been attacked en route by four fat raiders. None of them, as I'd guessed, could see the funny side, and several of the girls were genuinely traumatized and close to tears. 'Why did you do it, Terry?'

I explained that I'd known nothing about it until that very day and that I'd thought it was a shit idea, but despite what people thought I had no say whatsoever on the show's content. I pointed out the real culprits to a couple of the lads and suggested they go and punch their smarmy faces in, 'Honestly, lads, it would be no loss to the wonderful world of light entertainment, in fact, it would be no loss to humanity.'

Over the summer we did the usual cut-and-paste best of *The Word*, a euphemism for more repeats on the box. We featured all the big guests and two thirds of the bands from the previous series, though they didn't use Oasis performing 'Supersonic'. Within six months, by the time Oasis were on their way to becoming the biggest band in Britain, our one-time music booker Ed Fosdyke was claiming he had always intended to book Oasis and had been their biggest fan, while all the show's producers said how great *The Word* was for having Oasis on before anyone else. Strange then that Oasis weren't even in the best 66 per cent of the bands we'd had on that series, and that when I'd asked why Oasis weren't on the repeats, I was told they weren't big enough. As the old saying goes, 'Success has many fathers, but failure is an orphan.'

Another series of *The Word* was over. We knew the next series would be the last one, but would anyone have the guts to change it around and shake things up, or would we carry on trundling down that spiralling road of laughing at the peasants?

'Terry Christian, the most hated man on television'
Daily Mirror 1994

By the end of series four of *The Word*, I'd landed myself a regular little afternoon pop show on Sky One called *The Hitmix*. It was a one-hour music magazine show featuring different charts, a live band and live guests. Also, as our competition strand, we had the comic genius of Caroline Ahern doing a series called 'Whose Mother?', where every week she would dress up and act like a famous pop star's mother, giving some very funny clues as to who she might be. I had also been offered a Sunday night show starting in January of 1995 on the UK's first commercial talk station Talk Radio, now Talksport, and was keen for Craig Cash to co-present it with me, or at least contribute, which he did for the full eight months I lasted on air.

I felt as if the pressure was off concerning *The Word*. Paul Ross had gone off to do more presenting and Charlie had promoted a producer, Duncan Gray, who'd been a humble researcher only eighteen months earlier, to the rank of editor. Duncan's promotion upset a few people who were much better qualified for the job, and I have to admit I was surprised when Tammy Summers didn't get it. I liked Duncan as a bloke, but he was stereotypical TV executive material: he acted about twenty years older than he was, had very little programme experience, no real empathy or sensitivity for the audience and, most importantly, went to a good public school and Oxbridge. Within two years he would be made head of Light Entertainment at Granada Television. Previously, he had managed to annoy Vanessa Feltz so much on *The Big Breakfast* that she poured a plate of beans over his head as well as managing to annoy Richard and Judy within weeks of being made executive producer on their show.

Before the series commenced, there would be the usual trip Stateside to film new stories. This time around I was teamed up with a brand-new associate producer on the show, a young Scotsman called Phil Edgar-Jones, and a Cumbrian director called Michael Cummings, who had just been working on *Rough Guide* and *Lonely Planet*. The schedule for our forthcoming American jaunt was ridiculous, with eleven flights in nine days and back-to-back filming. We started in New York, where we'd been booked into the grottiest hotel ever with one lift the size of a dumb waiter. We were in New York to do a story about a transvestite finishing school that was being run by an ex-prostitute. The idea was that this was a place where men who wanted to be women were shown how to be ladies. Of course the ex-hooker, who operated out of her apartment, charged her clients a fortune.

I'm not sure why we were even covering the story, as it seemed to have limited appeal to any audience of any age, but as one of the producers back in the office was a transvestite, it was pushed through. What was worse, before the ex-hooker would allow us to film her clients, we had to assure them all that we were gay – in writing no less. Rather sour-faced, I turned up at the hooker's apartment with our camera crew director and producer and was introduced to the madam, no doubt a popular choice for men with a fetish for larger ladies, and two transvestites, one a bald six-foot-four Irish-American truck driver in his late thirties, the other a forty-year-old five-foot-six lisping queen, who looked like Bette Davis in *What Ever Happened to Baby Jane?*

We spent all morning hearing how our hooker taught them to depilate, put make-up on and even take them out shopping to co-ordinate their outfits with their shoes. The Irish-American truck driver was never going to look like a woman, not even with major surgery and hormone treatment, and the Bette Davies lookalike was frankly scary and kept staring at us as his penis grew erect while it was strapped and trussed up under his frock. I gave the afternoon shopping trip a miss, which was a small mercy.

That evening we joined the hooker, her maid and her two students at a restaurant. The rather attractive young waitress whispered to me, 'What are you guys doing here with those?'

'We're from Channel 4 in Britain and we're filming a piece about a transvestite finishing school.'

She looked dubiously at the trucker and Baby Jane, saying, 'Those guys are finished?', then shook her head and walked off.

We were also saddled with filming a piece about fat liberation. In the office, this was sold as a chance to film lots of grossly fat wobbly Americans moaning about how they were treated, all the time going, nudge, nudge, wink wink, who ate all the pies.

We met up with one of the main women for Equal Rights for Fatties, or whatever it was called, and in the interview she sounded so reasonable. American corporations and the food processing business spend billions advertising to people. Fast food, TV dinners, sugary drinks, sugar in the bread, sugar in the milk, then when people are overweight they are embarrassed on airlines, sometimes charged double for a seat and basically had less rights than people who weren't obese. We meet the American senator who was fighting their cause. He wasn't really overweight, but there were millions of voters out there who were concerned about the issue, which made it a powerful political lobbying platform.

Their arguments are so reasonable it makes us feel slightly ashamed, as really we're just there to laugh at American fatties. In truth, it was a serious subject worthy of being addressed seriously, but it was that old bullying public-school thing again. We left the Fat Liberation woman and the US senator, promising to meet up at their convention and party in Grand Rapids Michigan in eight days' time. In the interim, we had some serious business to attend to before getting over to Grand Rapids to watch lots of wobbly bottoms getting down on the dance floor to Chic's 'Le Freak' at their after-convention party. The over-sized bottom line was that that was all we were after, and I had a feeling that it was only a matter of time before these rather bright people rumbled us.

We had to change planes three times in Atlanta and Nashville before arriving in Chattanooga, Tennessee. We were there to film the queen of the pre-teen pageant scene, Blair Pancake. The pre-teen pageant scene is big amongst the moneyed classes in the deep south and basically involves dressing up six- to twelve-year-olds as Scarlett O'Hara from *Gone With the Wind* and getting them to demonstrate their musical and dancing talents. Blair Pancake was the undisputed queen of the scene, having won hundreds of competitions. Now she was twelve and was the biggest ever pre-teen pageant queen in American history.

I was looking forward to spending a few days in Chattanooga. Unfortunately, though, to save money, our production people in London had booked us into a Holiday Inn that had neither restaurant or bar and was 14 miles outside of town.

As the planned pre-teen pageant had been cancelled for some reason, we had to stage a pretend one in a huge old theatre in Chattanooga, which was, funnily enough, just opposite a Holiday Inn in the centre of town. This meant that we ended up with a day off in Chattanooga while a mock pageant was being organized, though there was, of course, absolutely nothing going on in town.

In the end, we decided to visit the local attraction known as Lookout Mountain, a mountain containing a series of deep tunnels and caverns that were used as a base in both the American War of Independence against the British, and by the Confederates during the American Civil War. It was fantastically dull, so we ended up in a bar in Chattanooga. Suddenly it began to fill up, as if it was a Saturday night at eight o'clock, and we asked one of the waitresses what was going on. She told us that Tuesday night everyone goes to church and then pops out for a quick beer and a burger. The excitement levels were just too much to cope with.

We decide that pre-teen pageants are appealing to the same dubious audience as the TV show *Mini Pops*, so we leave Chattanooga for more Bible-belt fun in South Bend, Indiana, home of Notre Dame college football. We get to the airport to find that the office hasn't sorted out our tickets. We just about make the flight, which takes us via Cincinnati before plonking us down almost four hours later. Then we have another fun-filled day of filming ahead of us, this time with a very scary twelve-year-old preacher.

Michael Shaun Walters is a macabre pasty-faced kid with curly white-blonde hair and a complexion so pale he looks like he's been sharing a cell with the Count of Monte Cristo for the past ten years. His father and younger brother accompany him as he preaches to the faithful in revival shows on the evangelical Christian circuit. Ten minutes in the company of Michael Shaun Walters' father, who looks a bit like Lloyd Bridges, and you can hear those duelling banjos ringing out loud and clear. Then just when we think it can't get any worse, we meet cousin Leroy – think Boo Radley out of *To Kill a Mocking Bird* or that big bloke out of Steinbeck's *Of Mice And Men*, then imagine somebody who's about six foot five, weighs 22 stone, has a head the size of a widescreen TV and a brain. . . well.

Twelve-year-old Michael Shaun Walters was one of a long line of snake charmers and speakers in tongues from pure Texas hillbilly stock and he was about as Christian Fundamentalist as you can get. The reason they had agreed to let us interview young Michael is that our show is called *The Word* and we are aimed at young people. The Walters clan think it's some kind of semi-religious show and that we're there to let the young people of Britain hear the word of the Lord. Michael Cummings sets up the camera for our first interview with Michael in the swimming pool of the cheap hotel we're staying at. I've only met him for twenty minutes or so, but already my heart goes out to him. This kid is so young and tired-looking; he's just a gimmick to bring in the greenbacks.

Michael preaches to me about Jesus, explaining how Jesus came to him and how, at the age of four, he was preaching to a group of Hell's Angels outside McDonald's. I then think in *Word* mode: fundamentalist Christians are at their most rivetingly entertaining when talking about the Devil and his disciples, so I ask young Michael who the Devil's disciples are.

'The Devil's disciples are everywhere, witches, warlocks, murderers, thieves, fornicators and gnomes.'

'What gnomes? The little blokes with the beards and pointy hats,' I query.

'Yes, sir,' he replies.

'Gnomes are the devil's disciples?'

'Yes.'

'Does it say that in the bible?'

'Yes, sir.'

All those years of synoptic gospels and catechism at Catholic school and here I am, finding out for the first time that gnomes are described in the Bible as the devil's disciples. It's a great line for our piece, but as usual, by the time it's edited and put out, the best bit has been omitted.

The following day we film young Michael eating and playing video games at his favourite hang-out. It's a pizza place called Chuck E. Cheese's and it's basically one of those children's play places with slides and ball ponds, the kind of place that stinks like a primary-school classroom bin but is great fun for a six-year-old.

I feel awful for young Michael as he looks so ill. Just before getting to South Bend, Indiana, he'd been preaching outside Miami, Sarasota and Tallahassee, then he'd been driven the 1,200-mile journey to South Bend, Indiana. The poor kid had a hacking cough and looked the picture of bad health, but as far as we could see, all his family were concerned about was preaching the word of the Lord and passing round the collection plate.

That night we were due to film the kid in full flow, preaching to the locals at a dingy church and doing some hands-on healing and slaying (where he would touch the person on the forehead and they'd fall to the ground twitching, blinded by the Holy Spirit or whatever). We were asked by Shaun's dad if we'd give cousin Leroy a lift to the church, so there we were, Phil Edgar-Jones, Michael Cummings and myself, with cousin Leroy discussing the big wide world. Cousin Leroy has shucked off his dungarees and is dressed in a yellow tie and a jacket that looks like it's made out of carpet underlay; he's not the brightest spark you'll ever meet, but he's fascinated by us coming from Britain.

'Y'all come from England?'

'Er, Phil's Scottish.'

'Is it October in England, too?'

'Erm, yes.'

'So y'all have the same calendar as us in England.'

'Er, yeah, course we do, same everywhere, isn't it.'

Leroy then states in an ominous tone of voice, 'The Jews have a different calendar.'

I'm half tempted to say, 'Yes they do, the twentieth century and Nineteen Ninety Four, but I've got visions of Boo Radley getting hold of us and screaming, 'Soooooeee, squeal like a pig.' So instead I just say, 'Oh, right.'

At the revival meeting in the church it all goes semi-pear shaped. Young Michael is feeling the strain – big congregations in Florida, thousands of miles travelling in a beat-up Cadillac and two days filming with a British TV crew and now he's got to preach again. He's only twelve, his cough is terrible, he's got laryngitis and he's about to be filmed again. He locks himself in the loo at the back of the full church and refuses to come out for over an hour. His father knocks on the door, no reply. Cousin Leroy knocks on the door, no reply. Then they send me.

I've kind of bonded with him, but then I'm from a big family with lots of nieces, nephews, cousins, second cousins and younger brothers, and I'm good with kids. Perhaps it's one hillbilly to another, but young Michael comes out. I'm at the back of the church and he starts preaching, or should that be screeching, to the assembled faithful. His voice is so hoarse that his shouting is completely indecipherable and he's in obvious pain and distress.

He gets the audience to sing 'Jesus On The Mainline', but it's all too much for me. My head is banging with the worse migraine I've had for years and I have to get out of this weird place. I sneak out the back door. Thirty minutes later the congregation flood out. A lot of them – mainly old and middle-aged semi-menopausal women –

stop to greet me on the way out. 'Why did you step out?' they ask, 'You missed him giving us his blessing.'

'I've got a bit of a headache.'

'Well you should have asked that young boy to give you a blessing, that would have sure healed you.'

I thank them and agree, when really it was that young boy's screeching and the bizarreness of the past couple of days that have given me the headache in the first place.

We decided to drive to Grand Rapids, Michigan for the Fat Liberation convention and party. It should be an easy three days before we head off to Fort Lauderdale in Florida to interview John Wayne Bobbitt, the only man alive to have his todger chopped off and sewn back on again so that it all works properly. John's just made a porn film and is doing a series of personal appearances where he flashes his penis scar to the masses and we'll be filming his next one at a gay club in Fort Lauderdale.

Like South Bend, Grand Rapids is another Bible-belt midwestern shithole, not too far from Lake Michigan. The hotel is big and gloomy, dirty and smelly, and we see lots of very obese people wandering around. Tomorrow is the start of the convention and the day after is our money shot: lots of fat people jiggling about at the after-convention disco.

A call comes through for Phil and Michael. We need to go to Florida a day earlier or we'll miss John Wayne Bobbitt's personal appearance in the gay club – *quelle dommage*. Could we get the Fat Liberation people to bring their party forward by a day? It will mean we'll have to buy some balloons and sort everything out with the organizers. Phil and Michael relay the message to me and I laugh them out of the room.

'Phil, do you think the Fat Liberation people we've met are stupid?' Do you believe they'll agree to moving their party forward a day, just so some British TV company can film them wobbling about to "I Will Survive" without sussing out that that's the only reason we're here.'

Phil and Michael agree with me – at least I think they do – but it's their job, so they go and buy the balloons anyway and approach the woman organizing the event. They basically tell her they aren't interested in what is going to be said at tomorrow's convention, but they are interested in filming everyone drinking and jigging about for the cameras. As predicted, they are told exactly where to go, meaning we've wasted the whole trip and the piece, thankfully, won't be used on the show.

The next day we drive to Chicago to catch our flight to Fort Lauderdale. It's all been a surreal and ridiculous trip and we've laughed ourselves sick. Having said that, for Michael, Phil and myself, apart from Michael's superb John Peel impressions, it's been a series of fat jokes, paedophile jokes, incest and *Deliverance*-style humour all the way.

Fort Lauderdale looks beautiful. There are blue skies, the beach and a great hotel. First, though, we have an interview with John Wayne Bobbitt, his porn-star girlfriend and his manager, who was once married to La Toyah Jackson.

John Wayne Bobbitt is an ex-Marine and he's very friendly, he's also fairly inarticulate and profoundly thick. I listen in fascination as he tells me what happened the night his wife Lorena cut his penis off with a carving knife.

'Well, I'd been out drinking with an old buddy of mine and we got back to the house and he was sleeping on the couch. I got into bed very drunk and Lorena started playing with me, and when I was semi-erect, she just cut it off and ran out of the house with it in her hand.'

'So what did you do?' I asked.

'There was a lot of blood, and I guess my Marine training came in. I just got a towel to staunch the blood flow and tried to wake my buddy up to drive me to hospital. I found it difficult to wake him, and at first he kept saying he couldn't do it as he'd had too much to drink. I was in shock, as you can imagine, but insisted he drive me to the hospital as quickly as possible. He then said, "Wait a minute," and then went into the bathroom to brush his teeth first!

'When I got to the hospital I was lying on a trolley and they asked me where my penis was. I told them Lorena had it and they said if they could recover it within the next few hours they might be able to sew it back on. I tell you, that was a scary time. The cops got Lorena and at first she wouldn't tell them what she'd done with it. Finally she relented and told them she'd thrown it out of the window of the car when she drove away. Luckily for me, the cops found it lying in the bushes by the side of the road and managed to get it to the hospital just forty-five minutes before it would have been useless to me.'

It was hard not to laugh about his mate brushing his teeth first.

John kept repeating all the way through the interview that he'd never hit Lorena or beat her up. What was strange, though, was that no matter what I asked him, even if it was about what he was up to at the time, he kept on repeating this fact.

'What's your favourite part of Florida, John?'

'Well, I love the Keys, but I never beat Lorena up like she said.'

I felt truly sorry for John. He was surrounded by people who were all making money out of him, including the glamour model porn star posing as his girlfriend. It was all too sad for words, but I suppose he was at least fortunate that his dick was still working.

'Sometimes it's a bit half-cocked,' he explained. His scriptwriter worked on that type of material, it's just a pity he couldn't work on John's delivery.

That night we went along to interview him further and film him on stage at the club, but as we went in a crowd of surfer/redneck types shouted threats at us. We surmised that Fort Lauderdale wasn't exactly gay-friendly.

The following day, the orders came through from London that before we fly to LA to interview international porn star Veronica Brazil, who played John's wife Lorena in the porn film, *John Wayne Bobbitt Uncut*, we must film an opening piece to camera in front of a butcher's shop with sausages hanging up in the window. I find this information rather interesting, and even Michael has twigged the obvious. Firstly, where do we find a butcher's shop open on a Sunday in Florida – remember, we're in the Bible belt and it's the Sabbath. Secondly, where would you find a butcher's shop with sausages hanging in the window in a tropical climate where it's virtually 100 degrees in the shade and the humidity is akin to that of your average tropical rain forest. All you'd find is a pool of grease.

'Well, there's no chance of that, nowhere will be open, and even if we found a butcher's shop around here, it would look like your local branch of Iceland, not like some olde high street in the Cotswolds.

'Don't be so negative, Terry,' I was told.

Mark Lamarr has gone; he's either left or his contract wasn't renewed, but either way I'm not arsed. We have two new presenters joining Dani and myself: a very pretty, friendly young girl of Indian descent from Southall called Jasmine Dottiwala and a twenty-two-year-old Cambridge University graduate called Alex Connor, who has a PHD in theology and is having a year out. While he's on *The Word*, though, he'll be known as Alex Hamilton. They're both nice young people and are already being lined up as the latest cannon fodder for the unimaginative.

'Duncan, you're an arsehole,' I shout.

Our new editor Duncan Gray has just informed me that although he's a huge Oasis fan – now that their debut album *Definitely Maybe* is at number one in the charts – we can only have them on *The Word* performing 'Whatever' if it's an exclusive. This is ridiculous. Oasis have been offered *Later. . . with Jools Holland*, and on that show they'll be allowed to perform two or three numbers. That's great for Oasis, but I don't see how it matters to us, after all, if I'm a fan of a particular band, I don't give a monkeys how many TV shows they appear on, in fact, the more the merrier. Since our last series finished, Oasis have had three hit singles, two of which have been in the top ten, and the biggest-selling number-one album in Britain; they are massive and they want to do *The Word*, but understandably they want the slot on *Later* as well.

Duncan is on his high horse. Eighteen months earlier he'd been a researcher on the show. The audience at home just want good entertaining stuff and most of them wouldn't have been aware that we'd had Oasis on as an exclusive the first time around. Now that they're the number one band in Britain, this is our chance to put them on and crow about that first early appearance, but Duncan still wants the exclusive. He's banging on about how *The Word* did them a favour early on and that we should get some respect for that.

Meanwhile, I'm open-mouthed with shock, as the bosses didn't even want them on first time round.

'Duncan, we make TV shows for the viewing audience, not to impress our London media mates.' In the end, Oasis don't come on the show, instead we get an exclusive from Dog Eat Dog. Funny how nobody ever noticed that fantastic exclusive.

To be honest, the fifth and final series of *The Word* was a load of old wank. We were short of ideas, and what we did was contrived. The guests peaked after the first show where we had on Naseem Hamed and Ricki Lake (again), followed by Kathy Lloyd (again) and Timmy Mallett. The bands were also piss poor, with only Dodgy and Goldie featuring Mancunian singer Diane Charlemagne standing out. Otherwise we had Michelle Gayle, Lisa Moorish and The Cult on. The show has gone so downmarket and cheap, it's hard to dredge up any enthusiasm.

Duncan's media career began as a production assistant at BBC Radio London as one of Chris Evans's cronies, then he did a stint as researcher and producer on *The Word*, then editor. I complained about the poor quality of guests and, as a tester, asked Duncan who his ideal *Word* female guest would be that week. He mentions Liz Hurley and I reply that Liz Hurley is only famous for being Hugh Grant's girlfriend and for wearing a dress stuck together with safety pins. In effect, she's built a career around one tabloid photo, and most people outside of London at that time who took no notice of the Londoncentric gossip pages, wouldn't have a clue who she was. Duncan still insists she'd be ideal.

A week later Liz Hurley was mugged in London by a group of sixteen- to eighteen-year-old girls; when they were arrested they all admitted they had never heard of Liz Hurley.

'There you go, Duncan, those muggers are our audience and they even live in London and still don't know who Liz Hurley is.'

I'd managed to make Duncan an enemy for life. Although I didn't dislike him as a bloke, I could tell he hated being disagreed with.

Charlie Parsons was effectively the editor of this last series of *The Word*, but as he was also executive producer and effectively editor of *The Big Breakfast*, he didn't have a chance to look at *The Word* line-up until Thursday afternoon. This basically meant it was pointless going all the way over to the Planet 24 office on a Thursday, as I'd just have to hang about for hours twiddling my thumbs and getting annoyed about the cocaine-fuelled lack of creativity around me. I decided to go straight to a hotel late Thursday afternoon, and when they'd sorted the show out by seven or eight o'clock that night, they could send an associate producer or researcher round to the hotel and brief me about the show in the bar.

Duncan didn't like this, as it stopped him feeling like the boss. I explained the reasons why, how it saved me time and stress and that going into the office to hang around for four hours was futile. Duncan then phoned my agent and threatened that if I didn't go into the office on a Thursday afternoon for the pre-show meeting – which never used to happen anyway – he'd sack me, 'But don't tell Terry that bit,' he added. Of course Duncan knew my agent would panic about his commission and tell me, but I just replied, 'Let him sack me.' I really didn't give two hoots, and the likelihood of Duncan Gray, or anyone in their first job as editor, putting their neck on the line halfway through a successful run of a final series with good audience figures was as likely as bumping into Elvis Presley cleaning the toilets at Thames TV studios.

Even funnier was the time Duncan bumped into Channel 4's head of entertainment, Dawn Airey, at our after-show drinks. Fishing for a compliment, he said, 'Well, Dawn, I hope you think I'm spending our £90,000-a-week budget wisely.' Dawn looked aghast: 'Your budget is £120,000 a week,' she replied. Independent production companies, doncha luv em.

As usual, we chased the tabloid headlines furiously. When Lynne Perrie from *Coronation Street* came on, alerted by our in-house PR, the national press reported that she was drunk and incapable, but the truth was Lynne was charm personified and didn't have a drink all night, though she was on really strong anti-depressants because her only son had been diagnosed with Aids that week. Ah, so sensitive and caring. Mickey Rourke's ex Carré Otis came on, too, and was absolutely off her face on something. Our other guest on that week's show was Dale Winton. Dale was being his usual friendly self, but everytime he said anything, Carré doubled over with laughter. Carré could hardly speak and Dale was wilting with embarrassment at this crazy woman going into spasms of hysterical laughter every time he opened his mouth. I suspected, after being with Mickey Rourke, that anyone would seem a bit camp, so I gallantly came to Dale's rescue.

'Carré, you can't keep laughing at Dale, he's a national institution. It's like laughing at the Queen.'

This was met by gales of laughter from Carré and the audience. Oh well.

Everyone on the show was desperate that we should go out with a bang, so the content became more and more extreme and contrived. One of our producers was a scouse lad from Warrington called Gary Moynihan. He had been Chris Evans's right-hand man, and as such, he was hailed by Duncan Gray as some kind of genius. If contrived tasteless bollocks that involves hours of setting up for a slight grin that lasts a second is genius then I'll second that. As an example, we did an outside broadcast with Alex Hamilton where he went to a council house in Wythenshawe that belonged to some lad's grandparents. The lad was minding his grandparents' house and had decided to have a party there, which *The Word* were going to film. However, Alex was supposed to turn up and play games, which just involved drenching the grandparents' house in paint. It got thrown all over the furniture, carpets and walls, and then the lad's parents and uncles turned up. Very funny – for about one second.

The repercussions, which weren't filmed of course, were that the place wasn't redecorated properly or in time for his elderly parents to move back in, their fitted carpets were ruined and the whole house almost destroyed, causing untold upset to the family.

By now I was thinking about other options. In a month's time I was due to start a new radio show on Talk Radio UK. It was ironic that despite my long association with new bands and music, I'd never even been offered so much as a bank holiday Monday filling-in slot on Radio One. I was obviously tarred by *The Word*, the irony being that everything the press hated about the show, apart from myself of course, I hated too. In fact, by this series, I had no say in the show's content whatsoever, as you may have gathered.

In the meantime, David Stephenson, our new commissioning editor at Channel 4, seemed, to everyone in the office, determined to make getting rid of *The Word* someone else's idea. After each show we ran a phone number for people to complain about the show, which seemed really odd to me. We had an official complaint on it about a piece on 'The Hopefuls' where somebody slipped their feet into a pair of sandals filled with dog pooh. The same night on *Eurotrash*, which followed *The Word*, there was a piece about a copraphiliac orgy in France, which showed people rolling around naked in human faeces and stuffing it in their mouths. Oddly enough, there were no complaints about that from the public. Of course, *Eurotrash* was a David Stephenson show, while *The Word* wasn't.

My routine for *The Word* was the same every week. I'd head down to London on a Thursday, stay there to present *The Word* on Friday and *Hitmix* on Sky on the Sunday Afternoon, then head back to

Manchester for the week. Every week my girlfriend's mother, Pat, would travel over from Preston on the train and I'd pick her up at the station in Manchester and drop her off at our house, where she'd stay with my girlfriend from Thursday to Sunday.

In the final week of January 1995 I was asked to travel down to Birmingham on the Wednesday night to appear on Anne Diamond and Nick Owen's mid-morning programme to publicize my forthcoming Talk Radio show. My girlfriend didn't like being in the house on her own while I was away, so her mum was going to come over on the Wednesday. I would hang around, pick her mum up around midday, then head down to Birmingham. All morning I waited for the my girlfriend's mother to phone so I could go and pick her up, and finally at around 1 p.m. the phone went.

I picked it up and a strange voice on the other end said, 'Pat's dead.' I didn't twig for a few seconds that Pat was my girlfriend's mother's name, and when I did it was like being struck by lightning. The phone call had come from my girlfriend's sister's best mate. My girlfriend's sister was a single mum who had just moved back into her mum's council flat with her three-year-old kid to escape an abusive relationship. I was absolutely stunned. Pat was only forty-nine years old, and she wasn't overweight or unhealthy, to look at her you'd think she was at least ten years younger. Now I had to drive into town and tell my girlfriend her mother was dead and had been found by her three-year-old nephew.

It was the worst day in my life so far. I drove my girlfriend in the rain and the sleet over to her mother's council flat in Preston, and the following day I went down to London to present that week's edition of *The Word*, though I would take the following Friday off to attend the funeral. I left my girlfriend the car and got a taxi back. The radio was on with commentary on that night's big match, Manchester United versus Crystal Palace. During the match, unprotected by the referee, Eric Cantona kicked out at Palace defender Richard Shaw and was sent off, and as he headed for the touch line he was abused by some racist thug and launched a Kung Fu-style kick at the mindless terrace terror. I'm numb to everything, even Cantona.

For that week's show my head was in bits. I asked Duncan to let Dani Behr do the interviews, and though he lets her interview American rap star Coolio, he insists that I interview Jeremy Clarkson. I've seen Jeremy on the telly and think he's quite funny, but I'm the least car-obsessed person on the planet. To me, they're just a method of going from A to B. If anyone asked me what car I drove, I normally answered honestly, without a hint of irony, 'A blue one.'

Jeremy is a northerner and is being really friendly and looking for some jokey banter. I forgive him for liking rugby, being xenophobic and being a public school boy, but I don't think I've never been as unintentionally rude to a guest in my whole career. My mind just wasn't there. It was a mistake to even try to do a show with my head in such a state, I couldn't even go through the motions. I remember trying to ask Jeremy something and completely freezing, my mouth gaping for what seemed like an eternity. I hadn't slept since the Tuesday night and all I could think of was having to clear out her mother's flat the following week, so the council could give it to someone else; they'd flatly refused to allow my girlfriend's sister and her little boy to carry on living there.

Very reluctantly, everyone at Planet 24 agreed to give me the following Friday off for the funeral. They would either get Dani to present the show with Alex and Jasmine or bring in a special-guest presenter. The following Friday morning, outside the requiem mass in Preston, my girlfriend's mobile rang.

'Terry, if we send a car for you and then drive you back there after the show, can you come and present it?' I tried to explain to the producer, who, God bless her, felt terrible for asking, that it was impossible. I wasn't there for me, but for my girlfriend and her family, who were all in absolute shock, and the worst bit – the cemetery – was still to come.

I heard later that Shane Ritchie was drafted in to do the show. I've never seen the episode or heard much about it, but I'd bet a million quid that he made them cough up about £10,000 to present that night. No wonder they were so keen to get me back.

One night soon after, at the after-show party, I was approached by

John Prescott's son. He had heard I was a Labour supporter and wanted to see if I would get behind the campaign for Tony Blair. I told him, in a nice and humorous way, thanks but no thanks, and that I thought Tony Blair made Jim Callaghan look like a member of the loony left. It might as well be David Owen and the SDLP, or whatever they were called then. There ended my links with cool Britannia. Funnily enough, I saw him chatting to Chris Evans later, who for most of series five, turned *The Word* into his Friday night homework. He'd arrive with his jotter and take notes, getting ready to copy certain elements on his forthcoming *TFI Friday* show.

TV didn't matter to me any more. A few weeks earlier, on *Hitmix*, my live interview guests were Liverpool band The Farm and those lovable Geordie's Ant and Dec. I'd bumped into Ant and Dec a few times late at night in my hotel in London, and spent several hours drinking with them at the bar, talking football and bullshit into the early hours. They were fantastic lads with a great sense of humour, not least about their dodgy records, which still sold by the bucketload. They were big fans of *The Word* and said they'd love to come on the show. I suggested it and got the usual negative waves about them not being cool enough and being too kids' telly, but I persisted and eventually we had them on *The Word* couch.

The irony is that the person who put up the most resistance to having Ant and Dec as guests on the show was our one-time music booker turned producer, Ed Fosdyke, who is now the editor of *Ant & Dec's Takeaway*. He's also the bloke who said Oasis couldn't come on the show because they were from Manchester, and we couldn't have two bands from there on the same show! Ant and Dec were on with gay American comedian Scott Capurro, who was very funny. After the show, Scott told me how incensed he was at the show's producers: 'They kept telling me to give you a hard time, Terry, and not to answer your questions properly and be uncooperative. I mean fuck them, I'll decide what I do on a show.'

To me, that said it all. I'd heard similar stories from other guests who I'd met socially after they'd been on the show. It was bad enough that I had to work with a bunch of people, 80 per cent of whom I thought were complete plums, but then they try to get guests to put me off on a live show in front of 350 noisy, semi-drunken people, and they slag me off in the press. I hated the business and everyone who worked in it and seriously looked down on all of them. Yes I was arrogant, but it wasn't because of the aphrodisiac of fame.

The following week, my guests were Rob Morrow, who had starred in the movie *Quiz Show* with Ralph Fiennes and a pair of American lesbian models cum pop stars called Fem2Fem, the predecessors of t.A.T.u. eight years later. During my interview with the girls, Rob jokingly invited some of the audience to come up and sit with us. One girl came up to the couch area, strode over to where I was sitting, stood in front of me, froze for a second or two and then walloped me as hard as she could across the head. It was really scary and I was furious. I managed to keep my cool and go calmly into the break while security carried her off back stage. It was a clear case of assault, but I decided not to press charges.

The following day the press was full of it, saying that she'd done what everyone else had been wanting to do. They even had the girl quoted as saying, 'I thought he was being so inane and banal.' I met this girl afterwards, and she wouldn't have been able to spell banal or inane, let alone understand them. She was interviewed on BBC Radio London the following morning and could hardly speak. I suffered the usual witch hunt in the press about how I'd deserved it because of all the times I'd humiliated people. Yet again, it was a case of them getting the contents of a show mixed up with me as a person, and it was all rather unnecessary and nasty.

Not only did I have to put up with that crap, on Saturday night Channel 4 ran a late-night series of repeats, including a repeat of *The Word* at around 2 or 3 a.m. To present this strand they'd have a couple of so-called comedians, who without fail would pour their scorn not only on the show, but on me in particular. I remember once seeing Johnny Vaughan and Mark Thomas having a right go. There was Mark Thomas, a posh socialist. . ., and Johnny Vaughan, who's not exactly been a stranger to problems with big-budget ratings.

I had been threatened with the sack by Stephen Garrett some years earlier for criticizing my work colleagues and Channel 4, but they seemed quite happy to hire two Channel 4 ratings failures to slag off the most watched entertainment show for sixteen to thirty-four-year-olds the channel had ever seen. The hypocrisy was unbelievable. I pulled up our commissioning editor David Stephenson about it, and he seemed to think it was really funny. 'Put me on it and I'll comment on *Eurotrash*, *The Mark Thomas Product* and all that other bollocks you're responsible for, David,' I suggested. 'I guarantee it will be funnier.' Needless to say, he refused my kind offer.

The Mrs Merton Show launched on TV on a Friday night on BBC2 at 11.15 p.m., directly up against *The Word*, and initially it suffered for it. But Craig Cash, Henry Normal and Caroline Ahern knew how to make TV shows and stay in control. When the very first *Mrs Merton Show* was recorded and in the can, the editor proudly showed it to Caroline, Craig and Henry. They then informed him that he'd cut out all the funny bits, to which he replied. 'Well, I wasn't sure people would understand that,' and, 'What does this mean?' There were deep sighs all round, and from then on they sat through every edit with him, until the show won it's BAFTA, which the editor gladly accepted.

When it was getting fantastic write-ups and critical praise, plus a huge audience, the BBC wanted it to be filmed down in London. The comedy triumvirate of Craig, Caroline and Henry refused, resisting the pressure to share their limelight with a bunch of careerists behind desks. Craig maintains that all the years he spent coming down to see *The Word* being made had taught him how *not* to make a TV show.

One night, after another episode of *The Word*, I was in a hotel suite in London with a fairly well known northern band. I know them quite well and they're famous for their excesses. Young girls wearing nothing but their knickers were wandering around, while fat lines of cocaine were chopped up on every surface. A roadie from the band proffered me a Pringles tube full of Doves, an ecstacy trip and a half. In the toilets, the band's lead singer, off his box on a cocktail of drugs, is attempting to have sex with a girl while four or five members of the band and road crew joke that he's having sloppy sixths as they've all just 'rinsed her'. One of the band, who invited me over, tells me to help myself to a bottle of Grolsch from the minibar. I turn round to help myself, and when I turn back, he's roughly fucking one of the girls from behind on the bed, her knickers round her knees, whilst cajoling one of her friends to crawl underneath and lick her clitoris.

The whole thing is surreal, but then it's the ultimate expression of their fame, and the reason so many people want and crave the aphrodisiac of celebrity. It's the power to realize all your imaginings, and this, it seems, is the limit of most people's imagination: a free-for-all, drunken, drugged-up orgy in a series of posh hotel suites. It wasn't a new sight to me as I sat there, drunk and detached, swigging my beer, which is warm because the door to the fridge-sized minibar has been open for hours. Here was the ultimate Friday-night experience: sex, drugs, beer and hedonism in the company of true rock'n'rollers, while MTV blasted out on the TV. Where are the cameras when you need them?

In the weeks leading up to the final episode of *The Word*, there were plans for a huge, corny send-off. I thought it was all too forced. There was a lot of excitement around the office, especially among the producers and researchers who'd managed to get jobs with the BBC and Granada, as it meant escaping from Planet 24 drudgery. I started to feel a bit odd. I was pleased that at last this programme that had been the centre of my existence and owned my soul for five years was about to finish. It was a feeling similar to when you walk into school on the last day of your GCSEs or A levels, or the last day of your package holiday when you're hanging around the hotel, waiting to leave for your flight home. I didn't care who the guests were or what daft items they had on, I was just happy it was over. During the rehearsals in the day I had a laugh with the camera crew in the studio, fiddled about in my dressing room, watching the telly and going through the motions. Our guests were Mary J. Blige, Nick Rhodes and Simon Le Bon of Duran Duran and Jimmy Hill. Towards the end I had them all sitting on the couch with me, so I reintroduced them in the final break and commented that it was possibly the worst panel ever for the World Cup. As Duran Duran played us out at the end, I couldn't believe I'd done five years of national TV, over 100 shows and was still there, the last man standing from the first show back in August 1990.

That was *The Word*. Planet 24 made its name from that show, but delivered nothing really original after it, unless you disagree with the idea that *The Big Breakfast* was just crackerjack for students. I felt the full brunt of the backlash against 'pioneering television' for five years afterwards, while many of the show's producers and editors went on to run channels and departments. Turn your TV on now and Channel 4 still looks like a refuge for fourth-rate southern public-school educated comedians. Originality doesn't exist. Nowadays, the public are flogged and humiliated on TV for our entertainment.

Talent spotters didn't exist at Channel 4 in my day, someone like Steve Toon, a guy with no formal education to speak of and who's now on the dole, but who employed Craig Cash, Caroline Ahern, Jon Ronson and myself for KFM radio station.

We knew series five was going to be the last series of *The Word* whatever happened. Our figures had gone up with each series, but with new commissioning editor David Stephenson eager to use the show's budget to find his own talked-about shows, it was inevitable. The problem was that in terms of figures and sponsorship, *The Word* had been very successful. David Stephenson's big problem was that if he replaced it with a show that had fewer viewers, his big boss Michael Grade would want to know why he'd made that decision, so throughout series five of it's run, *The Word* was the subject of a series of 'viewer's complaints' to the ITC, which in turn were relayed to Channel 4's board of governors.

The irony is that the shows David Stephenson commissioned were all based on aspects of *The Word*, just usually the rubbish, gimmicky, contrived parts. First there was *Eurotrash*, then there was *Naked City*, and when *The Word* finished there was *The Girly Show*, then *Something for the Weekend*, which was incredibly rude, crude and fiercely unfunny. Yet none of these shows, or their presenters, ever received the weight of criticism *The Word* did. Why?

Here's the recipe. In order to get good publicity, or at least avoid the bad, you pay a PR company. You basically pay one bunch of semi-toffs from the south-east to stop another bunch of semi-toffs from the south-east slagging you off. Hey presto! Bad ratings become 'critical successes'. It's a Danny Kaye moment again. 'The king is in the altogether now.'

I thought I'd feel an overwhelming sadness when *The Word* finished, but it kind of ended as it started, with a whimper rather than a bang. The fact that all these years later people still talk about it as part of their youth makes me smile. It was a show that hit the heights and plumbed the depths, often in the same five minutes. As for me, well, in the space of five years I managed, via articles, TV shows, radio shows, panels and every other which way, to slag off the tabloids, the broadsheets, the glossy style mags, the music mags, other TV shows and presenters – only in revenge, of course – alternative comedians, political correctness, public-school kids, Oxbridge graduates, students, new punks, the middle classes, the Tories, the south-eastern media hegemony and Tony Blair (long before he was Prime Minister). Not bad going really for someone who thinks they're reasonable.

The Word was over. After the last show I talked to Simon Le Bon about Man United, had a few drinks, said some cursory goodbyes, packed up and fucked off. Terry Christian disappeared and was never heard of again.

epilogue

yes i am a twat, but not the sort of twat you say i am

My dad used to take two hours to read the *Daily Mirror* and never read a book, but he understood power and fakers, shysters and exploiters when he came across them. Blokes of my dad's generation could smell a fake a mile off, whether it was Tony Blair, Jim Callaghan or even Harold Wilson. They didn't need some Oxbridge satirist to point the way, to them the jokes were all too well worn. Scandal is only interesting when it's shocking, and there's nothing shocking or unfamiliar about what governments do to the powerless. Perhaps that's the real reason why middle-brow Victorian liberals posing as socialists don't have many working-class viewers for their TV shows: it's not that the audience are too thick to understand the weak jokes and satirical observations, it's that they don't offer anything new. Jokes about something that ties your life to economics aren't that funny when you're at the sharp end.

When I think back to my five years presenting *The Word*, I never understood why it drew so many brickbats from every direction, except the general public. Nowadays you don't read a magazine and see Jimmy Carr slagging off Dermot O'Leary or June Sarpong sticking the cultural cosh into Cat Deeley while Tess Daly stabs a stiletto into Russell Brand. Yet every young presenter on TV seemed to think it was fine to slag off Amanda, Dani, myself and *The Word* from episode one. I've spent the last few months watching the whole of series five back, and all I can think is, what an entertaining, fun and unpretentious little show it was, a bit gimmicky and contrived towards the end, but still fun to watch and, most importantly, popular with it's target audience. It was a ratings success, so why did that annoy so many people?

Once *The Word* was finished I was consigned to the TV dustbin, along with *Ready, Steady, Go!* and *Muffin the Mule.* I was just another in a long line of TV presenters who seemingly disappear – it's a bit like asking where flies go in winter. A semi-recognizable face in the half light of *Countdown*'s 'Dictionary Corner', it wasn't long after *The Word* finished that a member of the public approached me and innocently enquired 'Didn't you used to be Terry Christian?' I couldn't help but laugh.

I remember once talking to Andrew Newman, who worked on *The Word* and went on to be a producer at BBC2 – he's now some bigwig at Channel 4. . . such talent! He was making a documentary about the history of youth TV, chronicling its beginnings from the days of the *Oxford Road Show* and *Something Else* through to *Network 7* and *The Word.* The premise of the documentary was to compare all these shows and their influences. Andrew wanted me to be the whinging mouthpiece, banging on about how public school the majority of the programme makers were, just as he was himself, and how most of the programmes reflected the views of that small sub-section of society, as if this would be news to the majority of people in this country.

I couldn't be arsed to do it now that I was out of the firing line. Everyone knew or suspected that the media was a Home Counties public school zone, and as I pointed out to Andrew, all that was going to happen was that they'd make this documentary and the conclusion at the end would be that the best youth programme of all time was *Network 7,* because that's the show the documentary's editor had started out working on, way back in the eighties. That's telly, at least the factual entertainment side. As for Andrew, name any new, gimmicky freakshow on Channel 4, presented by someone who's trying far too hard, and it'll be one of Andrew's, God bless him.

In just five years of national telly I'd been accused of being homophobic, racist, misogynistic, thick, banal, loudmouthed, whinging and inane. At times it got me down, but overall I just let it wash over me, because what I loved back then more than money, fame, celebrity and all that over-rated toss was the occasional opportunity to get up and say my piece, and the more annoyed people got about it, the more I knew I was pushing the right buttons.

Of course, all the critics and my work colleagues were right. Looking back at the person I was fifteen years ago, I can see I was arrogant, obnoxious and even thick at times. That's the very reason why everything on *The Word* worked and was different: I genuinely was an outsider in that world in every way imaginable.

When *The Word* was finally axed, I got a lot of sympathy from members of the public. 'Never mind, Tez, you'll be all right.' Here were blokes who worked for a minimum wage feeling sorry for me earning pots of money and spending £400 a week renting a two-bedroom flat in Maida Vale, with a huge sundeck and a key to some private gardens around the back. What's worse, I sometimes accepted their condolences as my due and let them feel sorry for me.

Radio One controller Johnny Beerling once astutely described me as, 'a crusader'. I wanted to make a difference and I was uncompromising when it came to fighting my corner. After all, the Terry Christian people saw on *The Word* wasn't really me, I wasn't that cheeky, seemingly insensitive, bumbling, naïve, annoying cardboard cut-out northern scally that appeared on the telly every Friday night. I can imagine an aged Eva Braun and Adolph Hitler sitting in their front room somewhere in South America watching the documentary series *The Nazis: A Warning from History*, and Adolph turns to Eva and says, 'But Eva, they don't know the real me.'

Nowadays the media swarms with wannabes more than ever before. I can't help but wonder what it is they want from life. Even as I signed one TV contract after another with Planet 24, I could see that there was no solace in the applause, the stares of curiosity from strangers, the figures in my bank statement, memories of sex or articles in praise of clever things you might have said or done. One commentator described it as 'mere diversions, the pranks and scribbles of immaturity'. All there is really is a battle for truth, and those of us in privileged positions in the media who don't pursue that truth deserve to be exposed. I thought a lot of what went on in the media was extremely snobby and anti-working class, and I said so. Big deal. I wasn't the only one who felt that way. There were other people from my background with a passion for truth, but perhaps they were wise enough to just murmur about 'jobs for the boys' under their breath.

I didn't need alcohol or drugs to mess me up. It was all there in my choice of profession. It's not the job I hated, but the passionless, dishonest manipulators that worked in the industry. The amusing part is – as Samuel Beckett once said, 'There's nothing quite as funny as human suffering'. I can imagine that I'm used as a warning example to every young TV presenter that you're here today, gone tomorrow.

There are kernels of truth throughout this book, but the ultimate truth is the delusion that we are the heroes of our own stories. For series one and two of *The Word*, I was able to steer the show in a direction I felt comfortable with. By the last two series, I had become just one of four or presenters on the show, yet it was me who seemed to get all the flak from the press. I remember once Rob Bryden's agent, Paul Duddridge, explaining to me how TV works, then looking me squarely in the eye and saying, 'Anyone who presents a high-profile national TV show for four or five years and doesn't end up a millionaire is an arsehole.' Fucking hell! I thought, now he tells me.

As my Mrs will testify, though, it would be pointless me being a millionaire, because I'd never be bothered to go to the shops and spend all that moolah, I'd rather busy myself annoying all those self-important fakes. Maybe it's that kind of fatalistic honesty that truly makes you an arrogant arsehole and a twat.

history of the word

SERIES 1

Show 1: 17 August 1990, 6p.m.
Guests: Bill Dean, Maryam d'Abo
Bands: The Farm, Adamaski

Show 2: 24 August 1990, 6p.m.
Guests: Joanne Whalley Kilmer, Jean-Claude Van Damme, Shanya Schulma
Bands: The Pixies, The Charlatans

Show 3: 31 August 1990, 6p.m.
Guests: LL Cool J, MC Tunes, Deee-lite.
Bands: MC Tunes and 808 State, Movement 98 featuring Carol Thompson

Show 4: 6 September 1990, 6p.m.
Guests: Jason Donovan
Bands: Ocean Colour Scene

Show 5 + 6 + 7
Can't fuckin remember

Show 8: 12 October 1990, 6p.m.
Guests: Amanda Donohoe, Michelle Collins, Stevie V
Bands: Candy Flip, Massive Attack

Show 9: 19 October 1990, 6p.m.
Guests: Monie Love, Julian Clary, James Whale
Bands: EMF, The La's

Show 10: 26 October 1990, 6p.m.
Guests: Jimmy Somerville, Kyle MacLachlan, Margi Clarke
Bands: Jimmy Somerville, Whycliffe

Show 11: 2 November 1990, 6p.m.
Guests: Nell Campbell, Elisa Fiorillo, Pat Cash
Bands: House of Love, Unique 3

Show 12: 9 November 1990 11p.m.
Guests: Boy George, Whitney Houston, Flavor Flav
Bands: Jesus Loves You

Show 13: 16 November 1990
Guests: Holly Johnson, Tairrie B, Paul McKenna
Bands: World of Twist, 808 State

Show 14: 23 November 1990
Guests: Nigel Benn, Trevor and Simon, Whoopi Goldberg
Bands: James, Blue Pearl

Show 15: 30 November 1990
Guests: Thea Vidale, Richard E Grant
Bands: Seal, 10,000 Maniacs

Show 16: 7 December 1990
Guests: Chris Quinten, Kym Mazelle
Bands: Beautiful South, Shabba Ranks

Show 17: 14 December 1990 – Live from Universal Studios in LA
Guests: Ricki Lake, John Lydon, Richard Carpenter
Bands: Dwight Yoakam, Def Jef, Chris Isaak

Show 18: 21 December 1990
Guests: Steve Coogan, Janice Long (Lynda Thornhill), Michael Starke (Sinbad) and Dean Sullivan (Jimmy) from Brookside

Show 19: 4 January 1991
Compilation show

Show 20: 11 January 1991
Guests: Kathy Lloyd, Keith Allen, Sherilyn Fenn
Bands: If, Maria McKee

Show 21: 18 January 1991
Guests: Ellie Lane, Alexander O'Neal
Bands: Jesus Jones, Lindy Layton

Show 22: 25 January 1991
Guests: Lemmy, Carolyn Franklin
Bands: Jellyfish, Tim Simenon (Bomb the Bass)

Show 23: 1 February 1991
Guests: Chris Isaak, Vic reeves, Bob Mortimer
Bands: That Petrol Emotion, Caron Wheeler, Daddy Freddy

Show 24: 8 February 1991
Guests: Frankie Howerd, Edwina Currie
Bands: Definition of Sound, The Mock Turtles

Show 25: 15 February 1991
Guests: Michael McShane, Brigitte Nielsen, Harry Connick Jr.
Bands: Dream Warriors, The Farm

Show 26: 22 February 1991
Guests: Jason Donovan, Darcey Bussell
Bands: MC Kinky, Village People

Show 27: 1 March 1991
Guests: Hale and Pace, Sinitta
Bands: Victoria Wilson-James, Warrant

SERIES 2

Show 1: 25 October 1991
Guests: Bo Derek, Shaun Ryder, Bez, Happy Mondays, The Mission, Salt 'n' Pepper

Show 2: 1 November 1991
Guests: Margi Clarke, Thandie Newton
Bands: Manic Steet Preachers, Bomb the Bass, MC BuzzB

Show 3: 8 November 1991
Guests: Jean Paul Gaultier, David Baddiel, Rob Newman
Bands: Intastella, Nirvana

Show 4: 15 November 1991
Guests: Phil Cornwell, Martika, Nuno Bettencourt from Extreme

Show 5: 22 November 1991
Guests: Cynthia Rothrock, Michael Biehn, Frank Skinner, Donna Summer
Bands: Donna Summer, James, East Side Beat

Show 6: 29 November 1991
Guests: Barbara Windsor, Sandra

Bernhard, Fred and Richard Fairbrass
Bands: Don E., The Farm, Right Said Fred

Show 7: 6 December 1991
Guests: Mr T, Mo Gaffney, Tammy Wynette
Bands: Airhead, Digital Orgasm, Tammy Wynette

Show 8: 13 December 1991
Guests: Alan Pillay, Lisa Stansfield, Cindy Crawford
Bands: Blur, Lisa Stansfield

Show 10: 3 January 1992
MTV compilation special

Show 11: 10 January 1992
Guests: Chris Eubank, Flavor Flav, Nicolas Cage
Bands: Primal Scream, Public Enemy

Show 12: 17 January 1992
Guests: Paul Heaton, Roger Black
Bands: Daisy Chainsaw, Kingmaker

Show 13: 17 January 1992
Guests: Boy George, Jah Wobble, Sinead O'Connor
Bands: Jah Wobble featuring Sinead O'Connor, Ride, Jagdeep

Show 14: 31 January 1992
Guests: Corey Parker, Andrew O'Connor
Bands: Definition of sound, Mega City 4, Teenage Fanclub

Show 15: 7 February 1992
Guests: Candida Royalle, Natasha Richardson
Bands: Brand New Heavies, Opus III, Yothu Yindi

Show 16: 14 February 1992
Guests: John Lydon, Zara Long, Rupert Everett
Bands: PM Dawn, The Jesus and Mary Chain

Show 17: 21 February 1992
Guests: Adeva, Rowland Rivron, Jason Priestley
Bands: Adeva, Charlatans, M People

Show 18: 28February 1992
Guests: David Lawrence, John Lydon
Bands: Natural Life, Public Image Ltd, Hannah Jones

Show 19: 6 March 1992
Guests: Tara Fitzgerald, Brian Regan (Barry) and Paul Usher (Terry) from Brookside
Bands: The Family Stand, Senseless Things, Tyrell Corporation

Show 20
Guests: Antonio Banderas, Sandra Bernhard, Barry McGuigan
Bands: C&C Music Factory, Des'ree, The Frank and Walters

Show 21
Compilation Show

SERIES 3

Show 1
Guests: Neneh Cherry, Vanessa Paradis, Peter Stringfellow
Bands: Suede, Sandals

Show 2
Guests: Dexter Fletcher, Julia Sawalha
Bands: Shonen Knife, Stereo MCs, En Vogue

Show 3
Guests: Marlon Wayans, Lesley Garrett
Bands: Alyus, Faith No More, Heaven 17

Show 4
Guests: Oliver Reed, Bill Hicks
Bands: Ned's Atomic Dustbin, L7

Show 5
Guests: John Thompson, Vanessa Williams
Bands: Lemonheads, Galliano, Aloof

Show 6
Guests: Dannii Minogue, Mark Wahlberg, Shabba Ranks
Bands: Shabba Ranks, Dannii Minogue, Arrested Development

Show 7
Guests: Amanda Donohoe, Tim Roth
Bands: Uncanny Alliance, Disposable Heroes of Hiphoprisy

Show 8
Guests: Milla Jovovich, Nigel Benn, Dolph Lundgren
Bands: Jesus Jones, Nu Colors

Show 9
Guests: Zsa Zsa Gabor, Russell Crowe
Bands: Sunscreem, Sister Sledge

Show 10
Guests: Jean Paul Gaultier, Keith Chegwin
Bands: D:Ream, Belly, Black Girl Rock

Show 11
Guests: Amanda De Cadenet, Nigel Pivaro, Pamela Anderson
Bands: Dinosaur Jr, Gloworm, Trey Lorenz

Show 12
Guests: Wendy James, Marquis of Blandford
Bands: Digable Planets, St Etienne, Eskimos & Egypt

show 13
Guests: Chris Eubank, Rolf Harris
Bands: Oui 3, Rage Against the Machine

Show 14
Guests: Paula Yates, Henry Rollins
Bands: Living Colour, Huggy Bear, Tasmin Archer

Show 15
Guests: Marcella Detroit, Jim Rose
Bands: Kinky Machine, Marxman, Espiritu

Show 16
Guests: Dianne Brill, Stephen Dorff
Bands: Snow, Bang Bang Machine, The Reese Project

Show 17
Guests: Jonathan Ross, Phoebe Legere, Monie Love
Bands: Jamiroquai, Da Lench Mob

Show 18
Guests: Blair Underwood, Ruby Wax, Elvira

Bands: Apache Indian, Stone Temple Pilots, Ariel

Show 19
Guests: Halle Berry, Keith Allen, Bob Holness
Bands: Back to the Planet, Freaky Realistic, East 17

Show 20
Guests: Margi Clarke, Shaggy, Shaun Ryder
Bands: James Taylor Quartet, Eurobop and the Rainbow crew, featuring Shaun Ryder, Hole, Sub Sub

SERIES 4

Show 1: 19 November 1993
Guests: Dave Chappelle, Vic Reeves, Bob Mortimer
Bands: Onyx, Pulp
Hopefuls: Todd Watkins doing snogging a granny

Show 2: 26 November 1993
Guests: – RuPaul, Rhonda Shear
Bands: Salad, The Pharcyde, Stakka Bo
Hopefuls: Andy Lacey eating sheep's testicles

Show 3: 2 December 1993
Guests: Sean Maguire, Lea DeLaria
Bands: Buffalo Tom, K7, Stereolab
Hopefuls: Ruth McArdle having a bath in maggots

Show 4: 10 December 1993
Guests: Jo Brand, Tyra Banks
Bands: St Etienne featuring Tim Burgess, Chaka Demus & Pliers with Jack Radics and the Taxi Gang
Hopefuls: Helen Wimpenny eating sheep's eyeballs

Show 5: 17 December 1993
Guests: Alexis Arquette, Gabrielle, Penn & Teller
Bands: Gabrielle, Thrum
Hopefuls: Matt Bordch and Morgan Lefay licking a fat woman's armpit

Show 6: 7 January 1994
Guests: Brigitte Nielsen, Ian Wright
Bands: Blaggers ITA, Red Kross, Erik
Hopefuls: Jazeena [doing what with] spiders

Show 7 14.01.94
Guests: Anna Friel, Nicola Stephenson, Tom Watkins, East 17
Bands: Inspiral Carpets, Elastica, Carleen Anderson
Hopefuls: Carol Hans in a bath full of horse shit and cow's urine

Show 8: 21 January 1994
Guests: Julian Clary, Barbara Windsor
Bands: Therapy, Déjà Vu, Ultra Naté
Hopefuls: Debra Hands having a slug put on her top lip

Show 9: 28 January 1994
Guests: Oliver Platt, Debbie Gibson
Bands: Whiteout, Me'Shell, Honky

Show 10: 4 February 1994
Guests: Craig Charles, Michelle Burke
Bands: Mother Earth, Reel To Real, Sepultura

Show 11: 11 February 1994
Guests: Snoop Doggy Dog, Charlotte Lewis, Rod Hull and Emu
Bands: Jon Spencer Blues Explosion, Compulsion
Hopefuls: Mark Haines licking false teeth

Show 12: 18 February 1994
Guests: Veronica Webb, Danniella Westbrooke, Richard Whiteley
Bands: Pop Will Eat Itself featuring Fundamental, Cypress Hill, Smashing Pumpkins.

Show 13: 25 February 1994
Guests: Ione Skye, Donovan Leitch, Boy George, Alex Winter
Bands: Blur, Afghan Whigs, EYC

Show 14: 4 March 1994
Guests: MC Hammer, Malcolm-Jamal Warner, Salt 'n' Pepa
Bands: Primal Scream, Senser, Bone featuring Sam Mollison

Show 15: 11 March 1993
Guests: Lionel Blair, Rachel Weisz, Chesney Hawkes
Bands: The Posies, Patra, New Kingdom

Show 16: 18 March 1993
Guests: Kathy Najimy, Bob Geldof, Stephen Dorff
Bands: Oasis, Kaliphz, Soul Asylum
Hopefuls: Simon Dobell snogging a fish

SERIES 5

Show 1: 25 November 1994
Guests: Ricki Lake, Prince Naseem
Bands: Goldie and Metalheads, Prophets Of Da City, Sammy

Show 2: 2 December 1994
Guests: Pauly Shore, Carré Otis, Dale Winton
Bands: Dodgy, Jhelisa Anderson

Show 3: 9 December 1994
Guests: David Alan Grier, Patsy Palmer, Lynne Perrie
Bands: Throwing Muses, The Cult, Two Thirds, Lynne Perrie and band

Show 4: 16 December 1994
Guests: Kathy Lloyd, Timmy Mallett
Bands: Lisa Moorish, The Charlatans, Dog Eat Dog

Show 5: 23 December 1994
Guests: Michelle Gayle, Alex Langdon
Bands: Corrosion of Conformity, The Wombles, Michelle Gayle

Show 6: 6 January 1995
Guests: Frank Bruno, Marc Almond
Bands: Sleeper, Loveland featuring Rachel McFarlane, David McAlmont
Hopefuls: a student drinking his own sick

Show 7: 13 January 1995
Guests: Camilla Power, Harry Hill, Jacqueline Pirie
Bands: Veruca Salt, MN8, Tricky
Hopefuls: sandals filled with dog pooh

Show 8: 20 January 1995

Guests: Keith Allen, Nathalie Simon, Jodeci
Bands: Shampoo, Tyrell Corporation, Hysterix

Show 9: 27 January 1995
Guests: Jeremy Clarkson, Coolio
Bands: Weezer, The Black Crowes, Coolio

Show 10: 3 February 1995
Guest presenter: Shane Ritchie
Guests: Liv Tyler
Bands: Supergrass, Live, Jade
Hopefuls: man licking old man's foot

Show 11: 10 February 1995
Guests: Ant and Dec, Scott Capurro
Bands: Marion, EMF, Jon of the Pleased Wimmin

Show 12: 17 February 1995
Guests: Fem 2 Fem, Rob Morrow
Bands: James Hall, Freak Power, The Boo Radleys

Show 13 (the 100th show): 24 February 1995
Guests: Vic Reeves, Bob Mortimer, Ian Wright, Carol Shaya, Tania Bryer, Alan Titchmarsh
Bands: Judy Cheeks, Reef

Show 14: 3 March 1995
Guests: Bill Gould of Faith No More, Mike Patton, Kennedy Montgomery